PSYCHOTHERAPY AND GROWTH

A Family Systems Perspective

PSYCHOTHERAPY

AND

GROWTH

A Family Systems

Perspective

---

by

W. ROBERT BEAVERS, M.D.

Brunner/Mazel, *Publishers* • **New York**

Library of Congress Cataloging in Publication Data

Beavers, W. Robert, 1929-
    Psychotherapy and growth.

    Includes bibliographical references and index.
    1. Family. 2. System analysis. 3. Psychotherapy. I. Title.
[DNLM: 1. Psychotherapy. 2. Family. WM420 B386i]
RC455.4.F3B4   616.8'914   77-2639
    ISBN 87630-143-X

Copyright © 1977 by W. Robert Beavers
Published by
BRUNNER/MAZEL, INC.
19 Union Square West, New York, N. Y. 10003

MANUFACTURED IN THE UNITED STATES OF AMERICA

This book is dedicated to Jeanette, Bruce, and Bonnie,
my family members, who instructed me
in the development of human competence,
with its limits, strengths, and delights.

Foreword

W. Robert Beavers has written a most exciting and useful book. He has taken a powerful concept, the systems approach, and with incisive brilliance offered it in a clear and viable way towards an understanding of different kinds of families and psychotherapeutic postures. It is a profoundly absorbing book which reaches the heights of intellectual persuasion, like a microscope shifting from low to high power as Dr. Beavers critiques the Freudian psychoanalytic treatment system using family variables.

The book begins in first gear focusing on the limits and restrictions that derive from a closed system point of view toward knowledge and science. The momentum starts as Beavers sharply reinforces the importance of how the self and its development is related to family relationships and communication patterns. What are the factors in family systems that aid and abet differentiation? Clearly the validation in a family of a child's unfolding subjectivity becomes a point of departure in Beavers' description of three types of families.

The pace quickens as Beavers describes the features of severely disturbed, midrange, and healthy families. Family competence is related to psychopathology in terms that are familiar and common. Though I personally have an aversion to classification in general, the manner of categorizing families here is most welcome. The three family types were discriminated by the following variables: 1) systems orientation, 2) boundary issues, 3) contextual issues, 4) power issues, 5) encouragement of autonomy, 6) affective issues, 7) negotiation and task performance, and 8) transcendent values. Most useful was the exposition of these values as was observed in healthy families where conspicuous evidence of reciprocated sharing of individuals' inner experience was part of its ground of being. Healthy families have a participant sense of community and adherence to transcendent values which indicate acceptance of man's paradox re death—while aware of mortality, he lives as if he were immortal. Beavers makes it clear that there can be and are overlapping features in his typology.

Jerry Lewis, with whom W. Robert Beavers collaborated on a distinguished book on healthy family systems, adds a sensitive portrayal of his approach to teaching psychotherapy in Chapter 6. Included is a valuable account of how Beavers' eight variables as expressed in healthy families are used in an active resident course is psychotherapy.

The high point of this book, however, is the critique of the Freudian psychoanalytic treatment system; Beavers, using his eight variables which relate to family competency, describes in measured, effective and brilliant manner the similarities between the Freudian therapeutic system and the closed system properties of dysfunctional families in the midrange. The analogy of the inability to tolerate and accept differences in points of view with resultant need for centrifugal flight of a family member, graphically captures the process of extrusion of Adler and Jung from the original Freudian group of psychoanalysts. Beavers makes it manifestly clear that carbon copy conformity among many contemporary Freudian psychoanalysts is basically antagonistic toward any patient's need to become a self, a process requiring continuous reinforcement in the struggle for differentiation.

An interesting inference evolving from the attitude of the analyst who believes solely in the biological and non-interpersonal determinants in the development of a neurotic patient, for example, is that the analyst is a non-being who functions much like a machine. Beavers' attack on the fixed belief properties of the Freudian psychoanalytic treatment system is specifically related to his wish and hope that a synthetic, pluralistic, scientific psychotherapy can evolve.

I would challenge Beavers' dream, specifically where he cites the desirability of gradual change emerging via "scientific dialogue and treatment results" versus defensive maneuvers of coercion, overt or covert. I don't believe that any synthetic resolution will develop until psychiatry will sanction and commit itself to focus on treatment results. What is necessary is the equivalent of the CPC—clinical pathological conference which is the anchor point in medical education. Consensual recognition of and validation of treatment failure is the first step in mandating learning from experience.

Some years ago I gave a talk with the title, "Helping the Mentally Ill: Failure and Progress." It was published and in my brashness, I neglected to check out the appropriateness of this title with my chief. I was soon called to his office and unmercifully castigated. He ended the barrage with, "There is to be no account of failure published from this hospital." I apologized after by attempting to rationalize my position with "How can you learn anything if there is no failure?"

I am dubious that professionalized narcissism can be replaced by scientific dialogue. Narcissism is too close to the struggle to survive and fear of being replaced.

Beavers admirably makes a strong case for a scientific psychotherapy wherein the therapist can be a humanist. *Psychotherapy and Growth* is a volume which can be read by professional and the interested layman alike. In a stimulating and unique way Beavers has helped immeasurably to clarify how that quantum leap to systems thinking can illuminate a wide array of subjects in the contemporary American psychiatric scene. His book affirmatively answers Bonhoeffer's plea: "We have been silent witnesses of evil deeds; we have been drenched by many storms; we have learnt the arts of equivocation and pretence; experience has made us suspicious of others and kept us from being truthful and open; intolerable conflicts have worn us down and even made us cynical. Are we still of any use? What we shall need is not geniuses, or cynics, or misanthropes, or clever tacticians, but plain, honest, straightforward men. Will our inward power of resistance be strong enough, and our honesty with ourselves remorseless enough for us to find our way back to simplicity and straightforwardness?"*

Psychotherapy and Growth is a beautiful book, which has been waiting to be created. I wish I had written it.

NORMAN PAUL, M.D.
Associate Clinical Professor,
Department of Neurology,
Boston University;
Lecturer in Psychiatry,
Harvard Medical School

Letters and Papers from Prison, 1967 edition, p. 40.

Contents

III. Psychotherapy

Introduction

This is a book about people and how they get to be the way they are, and how helpers can be more effective in furthering the growth of the self. It deals with important variables that influence how it happens that some infants grow to be sane adults, others manifest madness, and still others, though sane, are burdened by painful, neurotic symptoms or self-defeating behavior patterns. It describes qualities common to families and treatment environments that promote competent personhood.

The information comes from many sources. Systems theory, philosophy of science, family interactional data, psychotherapy research, and various treatment systems are all parts of the end product—the description of a scientific psychotherapy.

Though the ideas are sometimes complex and come from technical material, I try to use language that is shared by a large portion of the reading public, and to keep specialized jargon at a minimum. The writing style is personal and often assertive. In this way, I hope to dramatize the pervasive theme that all truth is subjective and incomplete. I believe that no human has or will ever know objective truth. Your subjective experiences—and mine—are unique, essential, and valuable parts of ourselves and our worlds;

any attempt to understand humans must acknowledge this. A science of man that does not respect these subjective perceptions is as destructive to human self-definition and human welfare as are the disturbed families to be described. Clinicians, theorists, and family members, in order to facilitate human growth and competence, must always keep in mind that peas and beans taste different in baby's mouth than in mother's.

In 1973, Leston L. Havens, a distinguished professor of psychiatry at Harvard, wrote a delightful book entitled *Approaches to the Mind*[1] in which he examined several traditions of psychiatric theory and treatment and concluded with a plea for a pluralistic approach to emotional illness that would end the divisiveness of schools or cults of psychotherapy. In 1975, Judd Marmor, then President of the American Psychiatric Association, defined common themes found in different therapeutic systems and asked therapists to abolish schools and embrace the scientific principles found in all successful psychotherapies.[2]

I share the investment of these distinguished psychiatrists in the need for a unifying conceptual framework. I believe in the possibility of a respectable science of effective psychotherapy, one that is as far from cultism as is physics. Such a science can utilize systems concepts, knowledge of behavior patterns seen in families who are competent or incompetent in raising children, research in psychotherapy, and the valued experience of clinicians from many different psychotherapeutic schools. There is no relationship between ideology and treatment effectiveness; however, significant variables are found in the *nature* of the interaction.[3,4]

Psychotherapists, isolated in their disparate schools, jostled passionately but fruitlessly with each other through the early twentieth century, with very little other than rhetoric to defend a particular viewpoint. Eysenck became a gadfly to these cultist psychotherapists, attacking their effectiveness and value with research. He concluded from his data that psychotherapeutic intervention is worthless, that control groups have as much symptom amelioration as treated groups.[5] Since this conclusion differed from the experiences of many clinicians and patients, it was valued primarily by people already hostile to psychotherapy. However,

Eysenck was not debunking all psychotherapy—he had a particular bias for conditioning or behavior therapy as contrasted with relationship-oriented treatment.

Bergin studied the issue from a different point of view. By using Eysenck's own data and adding additional patient groups, he concluded that patients who came into the hands of professional psychotherapists tended to do much better—or much worse—than untreated controls.[6] Variability of patients' personal adequacy after treatment was much greater than that seen in untreated control groups. He concluded that intensive psychotherapy is not worthless, but rather is a potent force which can be constructive or destructive. Bergin's research had a profound effect on me; his conclusion offered a serious challenge to psychotherapists: Who among us hurt people rather than help, and how? Or, whom do we help and whom do we hurt, and how? This research suggests an analogy to radiation therapy in its early days. Primitive machines were developed that sprayed a patient with x-rays. Without full knowledge of the power of such a machine, a therapist was as apt to burn a patient, to make him sicker, as he was to cure. Adequate principles, rules, and safeguards had not evolved. There was no doubt that the therapist was using a potent force, but the question was, could it be harnessed for patients' benefit? A similar phenomenon exists in intensive psychotherapy. It is not fraudulent. There is power involved, but without more precise knowledge of this power and its impact on patients, damage is as likely as improvement.

This warning was a significant factor in the evolution of this book. I believe that lessons from family studies can increase treatment effectiveness and reduce inadvertent damage. They can provide a place to stand in evaluating treatment theory and technique, and a shaft of light that illuminates patterns in various psychotherapeutic systems that limit their effectiveness or promote harm.

Within the family, parents were the original helpers in individual physical, intellectual, and emotional development. Physicians of the body, the mind, and the soul evolved from the family role models as society became more complex and differentiated.

For example, there are some similarities in the coming together of a man and woman who desire to form a family and the coming together of therapist and patient in intensive psychotherapy. Each member of a couple brings to the committed relationship a singular history, an experience within a unique family structure. Each has different cherished assumptions and a host of conscious and unconscious beliefs about what is right and what is wrong. These are challenged as the couple evolves its own particular family rules. Every new family has an opportunity to evolve more adaptive solutions to eternal problems if they question unchallenged assumptions in an atmosphere of trusting negotiation.

Similarly, patient and therapist meet possessing different histories, beliefs and skills; they also attempt to develop a working relationship with shared goals. Of course, the patient is usually expected to change more than is the therapist, who is considered an instrument of change. However, even in this respect, psychotherapy may be similar to a couple's learning from each other. It could be argued that Freud learned as much from Dora as Dora learned from Freud,[7] that Harry Stack Sullivan learned as much from his schizophrenic patients as they from him,[8] that Binswanger[9] learned from his psychotic patients, and that such learning changed his philosophy, self-perception, and treatment concepts irrevocably. This kind of openmindedness on the part of a therapist allows the treatment relationship to match a couple's hope and expectation that each will be enriched by the other.

In addition to the similarity between patient/therapist and a couple, if a psychotherapist is a person who reaches out to another and assists in increasing his skills and autonomous behavior, the relationship has aspects of parent/child interaction. Information about effective and ineffective family systems is presented in the first part of the book, with the expectation that it can assist parents and therapists in developing competent individuals.

While there are similarities between the goals of psychotherapists and the goals of competent parents, there are differences in technique. Not only does a therapist provide the patient with an environment in which to experience a gratifying relationship with another, but he also helps the patient unlearn distorted, maladaptive patterns of behavior and attitudes.

The second portion of this book presents material relating to research on therapists' effectiveness and an evolutionary view of psychotherapy systems. I wish to augment the effectiveness of growth-oriented psychotherapists by showing a way to combine observations and theories from several sources. Such a synthesis requires a world view that is flexible—coherent and organized, but resisting any spurious certainty.

Throughout this book, the term "patient" refers to the person who asks to become involved in a treatment relationship with a therapist. I use this term for two reasons. First, an individual who seeks help from a physician has long been called a patient. This in no way suggests that a patient has less power or fewer rights than any other citizen (or than the therapist). Calling him a client or any other non-patienthood term makes him neither less ill nor more powerful. Second, there is a philosophical reason for using the term: emotional disorders or disease (dis-ease) are no different in principle than physical diseases treated by physicians since antiquity. People are whole, divided into body and mind only with a great disservice to them and to coherent reality. Disease can manifest itself primarily in the body, or in feelings, or in behavior, but it is always an expression of a comprehensive human problem.

My emphasis on systems factors comes from 16 years of research and clinical work with families of widely varying functional abilities. As a psychiatric resident, I conducted a research project centered on a group of hospitalized adolescents diagnosed as schizophrenic. When it became apparent that the "normal" members of these patients' families communicated quite differently from family members of non-psychotic patients,[10] a systems researcher was born! I absorbed communication theory, information theory, cybernetics, and games theory along with the usual psychoanalytic and organic study, and I became fascinated with *family*, the cauldron of individual development.

Following a period of focusing on adolescent problems, both in research and clinically,[11,12] I participated as a research consultant in a large-scale, systems-oriented study of healthy families. This offered an exciting opportunity to explore the hypothesis that all families have common variables, which are altered in definite and predictable ways as the family's competence increases or decreases along a continuum.[13] This book is the result of that succession of personal experiences. If, indeed, both families and growth-oriented psychotherapists have the same goals (to help humans evolve as effective and adaptive individuals), the characteristics of family systems at various levels of competence can be quite important as criteria for evaluating theories of psychotherapy; in addition, the study of optimal families can be instructive to theorists and to psychotherapists in evolving practices that effectively strengthen individual capabilities for relationships.

Chapters 1 and 2 present a view of science and systems concepts especially useful for the study of human behavior. Chapters 3, 4, and 5 are summary statements of system characteristics of families at three levels of functioning, termed "severely dysfunctional," "mid-range," and "healthy."

In Chapters 6, 7, and 8, prominent systems of psychotherapy are evaluated, using the family material and the results of psychotherapy research. In Chapter 6, Jerry M. Lewis summarizes the research on factors found to be correlated with effectiveness of psychotherapy. Chapter 7 discusses Freudian psychoanalytic psychotherapy from the vantage point of the family material, and in Chapter 8 Sullivanian, existential, Rogerian, Gestalt, and behavioral psychotherapies are evaluated in a similar fashion.

Chapter 9 discusses a systems view of aggression; Chapter 10 provides a global comprehension of emotional illness and treatment approaches. Chapters 11 and 12 describe a scientific psychotherapy which invites the patient to be a partner in solving problems and developing an environment similar to the relationships found in optimal families. I will not think the reader less capable than I if he differs with me about beliefs. It is our approach to the patient that indicates whether we are scientists or dogmatists, just as it is the approach, rather than any specific notion, that is correlated with the therapist's effectiveness.

I hope this book will be useful to all psychotherapists who sense that their knowledge is incomplete and who intuit that their usefulness may be dependent on such incompleteness. They may already believe, as I do, that as one becomes an experienced therapist, the progress consists of forging a better method rather than reducing the mysteries found in being human. One can learn an approach to fellow human beings who come in search of emotional health—an approach that offers some hope, shared excitement, a sense of community, and new living skills, but that offers no certainty and no absolutes.

In addition, perhaps some consumers of psychotherapy will find this book useful. The emphasis on shared overt power in a growth experience can be heady stuff to patient and therapist, but I believe they can handle it, survive, and flourish. If this book encourages some patients to question their therapists' previously unchallenged assumptions (remnants of a closed system), I will rejoice. It will not be the first time that a patient has helped his therapist grow.

The discussions of different types of families offer an introduction to family systems concepts and describe the interactional environment necessary for self-development, hence providing guidelines for helpers. Resistance to utilizing systems approaches has been striking on the part of behavior scientists and clinicians alike. I believe this is due to the complexity of theory involving systems concepts which is not encountered in more limited frameworks, such as purely intrapsychic theory, or theories which ignore subjectivity.

Such resistance can be interpreted as parallel to that which Freud encountered when he demanded that thinking people deal with the great complexity of the human unconscious. This resistance was perhaps due not as much to his then shocking sexual concepts as to a human distaste for dealing with the complex. Any gift that complicates our lives, though it opens doors, is hard to accept.

In the last 75 years, most sensitive and competent behavioral scientists have absorbed the lessons of the Freudian revolution. Unconscious motivation is accepted (though different schools give it different names), as is the influence of individual development on the etiology of emotional illnesses. Currently, systems concepts challenge us to integrate and master a view of ourselves not only as people who are irrational as well as rational and influenced by a particular history, but also as actors in a complex series of social systems that affect our self-definition in powerful and potentially understandable ways.

In the community of scientists and of many aware citizens, resistance to systems concepts wanes as the shortcomings of the 19th-century approach become increasingly and painfully evident. As long ago as 1925, Whitehead[14] observed that the intellectual capital of science was dwindling as it remained mechanistic in its foundation and its orientation. As we become increasingly aware of our effects on one another—as the strontium-90 content of the atmosphere in the far north, or the mercury content of fish in the north Atlantic, become as important to a citizen of San Francisco or Des Moines as the amount of his city's air pollution—we require a scientific model which includes the interactional, mutually influencing qualities of parts in relation to each other.

When science is seen as a method to approach the truth, concerned with interrelationships (necessarily tied to meaning), it ceases to be a Procrustean bed, damaging the people it was created to serve. Such a comprehensive definition of science allows one to respect applied and "soft" sciences as much as "hard" sciences such as chemistry and physics. In addition, the integration of systems concepts into psychotherapy allows issues of values to be considered openly. With the first atomic explosion, as J. Robert Oppenheimer succinctly stated, "physicists have known sin."[15] He understood that human values are an integral part of science and must not be "objectified" out of existence. The behavioral scientist's attention to values need not cause him to beg for legitimacy at the back door of the scientific banquet hall. He may, with a systems orientation, become a leading participant in a value-conscious science.

The overall goal of this volume is to provide the mental health clinician with material to illustrate that the scientist can be a humanist and that intensive psychotherapy can be an exercise in the scientific method.

ACKNOWLEDGMENTS

This book has been a fantasy for many years. It became a reality through the continuing interest and hard work of the people of the Timberlawn Psychiatric Research Foundation, Inc. Jerry M. Lewis, M.D., John T. Gossett, Ph.D., Virginia Austin Phillips, and F. David Barnhart, M.A. were towering in their dedication and capabilities in understanding human helping, and in helping me.

I am forever grateful to Virginia Austin Phillips and my wife, Jeanette, for providing their talents in developing the final text. In addition, Deborah Haubrich and Nannette Bruchey have labored long and hard to produce a manuscript.

Finally, I wish to acknowledge the help and trust of many patients and families who opened themselves to provide the data, the basic substance for concepts that can assist in the evolution of competence.

REFERENCES

1. HAVENS, L. L., *Approaches to the Mind*, Boston, Little Brown, 1973.
2. MARMOR, J., "The nature of the psychotherapeutic process revisited," *Canada Psychiatric Association J.*, 20:557-565, Dec., 1975.
3. MATTARAZZO, R. G., *in* Bergin, A. E. and Garfield, S. L., (Eds.), *Handbook of Psychotherapy and Behavior Change*, New York, John Wiley & Sons, 895-920, 1971.
4. FRANK, J. D., *Persuasion and Healing*, Baltimore, Johns Hopkins U. Press, 1973.
5. EYSENCK, H. S., "The effects of psychotherapy" in Eysenck, H. J. (Ed.) *Handbook of Abnormal Psychology*, New York, Basic Books, 697-725, 1961.
6. BERGIN, A. E., "Further comments on psychotherapy research and therapeutic practice," *International J. of Psychiatry*, 3:317-323, 1967.
7. FREUD, S., "Fragment of an analysis of a case of hysteria," *Standard Edition*, Vol. VII, London, Hogarth Press, 1953.
8. SULLIVAN, H. S., *Schizophrenia as a Human Process*, New York, W. W. Norton, 1962.
9. BINSWANGER, L., *Being-in-the-World: Selected Papers of Ludwig Binswanger*, New York, Basic Books, 1963.
10. BEAVERS, W. R., BLUMBERG, S., TIMKEN, K. R., and WEINER, M.D., "Communication patterns of mothers of schizophrenics," *Family Process*, 4:95-104, 1965.
11. BEAVERS, W. R., and BLUMBERG, S., "A follow-up study of adolescents treated in an inpatient setting," *J. Dis. Nerv. System*, 29:606-612, Sept., 1968.
12. BEAVERS, W. R., "Managing adolescent inpatients," *Hospital and Community Psychiatry*, 10-13, Jan., 1968.
13. LEWIS, J. M., BEAVERS, W. R., GOSSETT, J. T., and PHILLIPS, V. A., *No Single Thread: Psychological Health in Family Systems*, New York, Brunner/Mazel, 1976.
14. WHITEHEAD, A. N., *Science in the Modern World*, New York, Macmillan, 1953.
15. SELDES, G. (Ed.), *The Great Quotations*, New York, Lyle Stuart, 1960.

PSYCHOTHERAPY AND GROWTH

A Family Systems Perspective

I

SCIENCE
AND SYSTEMS

_____ **1**

On the nature of knowing: Science and its limitations

All developmentally oriented psychological theory assumes that the human infant must experience the world in relationship and interaction with others in order to develop a coherent self. This self is inextricably intertwined with the subjectively defined world outside, a kind of figure/ground gestalt of the utmost importance to every evolving human. This self will be unique and different from every other who has existed or will exist. As he develops, his view of the world outside will also be unique and different from anyone else's. This process of boundary-making, of separating the known from the knower in some coherent fashion, is every individual's task. It is also the task of theorists who concern themselves with the nature of man and his world. Every culture has a cosmology

3

(for example, how the world began, how thunder is produced, why crops fail, where people come from, the nature of good and evil), cultural answers to the same questions facing individuals in their organization of the self and the world.

Currently, in our Western World, cosmology is largely the business of science. Religious explanations of nature and its works have lost considerable power over the last 200 years, though there is residual power in religious statements concerning *man's* nature. The battles between science and religious authority which have been played out in the 20th century are found primarily in psychology. Psychological concerns with the self, with ego functioning, and with the quality of reality testing are directly related to the issue of the sources of truth. What distinguishes a scientific cosmology from one that is religious? Are they necessarily different? If so, how can one tell the two apart? What is the proper area for science, for religion? Does religion have a place in modern man's life, and if so, is it a sickness or a necessity? To a rather unimaginative chemist, these may seem unnecessary questions, but they are raging controversies at two ends of the scientific continuum, the science of physics and the science of humans, as found in psychology and sociology.

As my research moved from biochemistry and pharmacology to psychiatry, I became aware of knotty and unresolved problems concerning the essential nature of scientific endeavor. It seemed to me that I found more help from physicists than from biological or behavioral scientists as I tried to get a clearer grasp of how humans determine reality.

Physicists are often concerned about the danger in assuming that truth is absolute in scientific pronouncements. Many physical scientists, along with theologians and intelligent laymen, are expressing their fear that a pin-headed, spuriously certain scientism could reproduce the danger to mankind of earlier centuries; they fear a repetition of a theology of certainty that punished heretics with inhumanity in the guise of virtue.

Theodore Roszak has emerged as a leading voice of this educated but anti-science group; he is taken seriously by thoughtful scientists as he challenges the value of a reductionist scientific orientation in providing meaning and purpose for individual members of a society.[1] I find him perceptive and articulate in describing the failure of any human who tries to be both hopeful and rigidly scientific, since classical science is mechanistic and hostile toward purpose or meaning. Modern man often finds himself with the Hobson's choice of either rejecting any presumed needs for transcendence, for centering himself in his universe, or developing a conflict-ridden, split-brain approach to reality, with secular reason allowing him to function presumably in opposition to his irrational fantasies that provide meaning. Roszak's solution advocates a return to the old "gnosis," the primitive religious impulse, which he describes as an advance to a higher sanity that rejects scientific rationalism and replaces it with an aquarian "post-logical consciousness."[2]

It seems to me that Roszak's approach combines an accurate diagnosis of the problem with an unwise solution—it discards too much of value in the laudable effort to give needed hope and purpose. Science is not necessarily anti-humanistic, nor does a scientist necessarily reject religious values. Man has not yet taken its measure and made sure it will be a trustworthy servant of man, rather than a malevolent master. I am deeply sympathetic with Roszak's concern, however. I am reminded of visiting friends in France in the early 1950's and believing with all my heart that I would be a hard-line Communist if I had to live under such insensitive capitalism. If there seems to be no yielding, no increasing sensibleness in the system under which one is suffering, there may appear no other recourse than to break out and find a radically different solution.

We can give up on science and retreat to the flamboyantly irrational, or, preferably, we can make a reappraisal of science, its definition, its limits, its past pomposity and fraudulence, and determine what it can do for us now. Though this question is equally relevant to "hard sciences" as much as it is to psychology and psychiatry, it is in the behavioral sciences that the issues are critical. The attitudes and beliefs that a therapist has concerning knowing directly affect his work and effectiveness with patients.

I will utilize the contributions of three unusually capable men to help state what science is not, and what it is. Though the following is a statement for which I will take responsibility, it is inspired and has been instructed especially by Karl Popper, Alfred Korzibski, and Ludwig Von Bertalanffy. These men were far in advance of their time in understanding the limits of science and in their ability to think critically about man's apprehension of reality. I believe that their insights are just now, after many years, being integrated into the mainstream of Western thought. Their ideas are remarkably similar, though Korzibski was a mathematician and the founder of general semantics, Popper is a philosopher, and Von Bertalanffy began as a biologist.

MISCONCEPTIONS OF SCIENCE

I would like first to attack errors about the nature of science that have given a good field a bad name. It is often believed that science 1) is complete truth; 2) is certain; 3) is objective; 4) is furthered by men who are unusually open-minded, using inductive reasoning; and 5) is a useful belief system.

1) It is not complete because it is simply the historical outgrowth of common-sense knowledge.[3] Its outlines are the formal statements of the puzzles and solutions of practical, pre-scientific men. For example, science replaces the problem of what is a reasonable belief of a sane man by a formal description of the rules for accepting or rejecting scientific theories (Popper). Just as common sense does, science limits its interest to the observable, the pragmatic, and it becomes foolishly pretentious if it claims more. For example, Freud's assumption that religion is evidence of unresolved emotional conflicts[4] or Skinner's belief that internal states are of no significance to the behavioral scientists[5] represents a serious and dangerous progression from elegant common sense to irrational reductionism that is potentially tragic.

2) It is not certain or absolute. The methodology of science allows beliefs to be disproved but never proved. We have the oppor-

tunity to use scientific tools to approach truth ever more closely, but we can never expect to have it in our grasp. Newtonian physics gave way to the Einsteinian era, as a new world opened up and the old one collapsed like a house of cards. Science can never produce a rock of Gibraltar, since uncertainty is built into its necessarily open system. Physicists, with theories of uncertainty and redefinitions of time, space, and matter, have attacked almost every assumption of man and of previous scientists. Now a Cambridge physicist, Stephen Hawking, produces rumbles of another possible revolution with talk of black holes and naked singularity that challenges the foundation principle of causality.[6] Whether this rumble assumes the power of a thunderstorm or ripples off into nothingness, it illustrates that the very heart of science, as contrasted with many other disciplines, is that its truths are tentative. Scientific truth is approximate and incomplete, and those aware of the quality of such truth are forced to be humble, leaving to others the certainty which demands intense loyalty to specific ideas and attacks on dissidents and heretics. Korzibski was empathically aware of this increasingly open system of science when he described a 1930's meeting of physicists as composed of good-natured Einsteinians and strident Newtonians.[7] He knew that genuine scientific wisdom sees the universe as a mystery which never recedes but rather changes with new understanding.

3) It is not objective, since science is a product of men—limited, subjective, biased men—who use their sense organs to develop abstractions that only approximate the nature of the cosmos. With all the mechanical extensions of our sense organs, from giant telescopes to electron microscopes, from radar to sonar, the resulting images are no closer to objectivity. Comprehension and coherence are vulnerable abstractions, devised from raw sensory input. As Korzibski noted, the only objectivity is this incoherent "unspeakable" (pre-verbal) input that is also rawly subjective, dependent on the varying biological characteristics of individual organisms.[7]

To think of or describe the real world, one must develop a subjective abstraction. Words are only a bit more abstract than the subjects about which these words are spoken. Concepts, individual and shared, are only roadmaps of the awesome reality that is always terra incognita. A chasm exists between people and any absolute comprehension; poets and dreamers can jump the chasm fleetingly perhaps, but never scientists.

4) Science is not furthered by unusually open-minded men using inductive reasoning. Scientists are as biased, opinionated, and prejudiced as the general population, and perhaps even more so. A decent scientist is always passionate in the defense of his theories. If he is too obviously "fair-minded" and "objective," he may very likely be unable to sustain the enthusiasm and interest necessary for good research. With all his passion, his methodology does allow him to change opinions when the data forcibly dictate such change. Watson gave a memorable illustration of this quality of scientists in his descriptions of the varied human attributes and motives involved in the discovery of the structure of DNA.[8]

The scientist does not proceed by blindly taking in data from observations and records of individual phenomena which then lead to general statements—hypotheses and theories. This is not the way that any man's mind works. Francis Bacon was responsible, in large part, for this romantic nonsense concerning scientific effort; though not a scientist himself, he was a superb public relations man for scientific endeavor, and his insistence on the virtues of pure, untainted observation and on the evils of speculation have affected research and scientists for centuries.[9] Today, we know more about man and the way he thinks than when Bacon was theorizing about the methodology of science; we no longer assume that any human past the age of six months can observe the world without *a priori* assumptions, either conscious or unconscious. In fact, there is increasing evidence that even the newborn has biological structures which profoundly influence his perceptions. Such assumptions, for example, as causality and concepts of time and space appear to be intrinsic.[10,11]

5) Science is not a useful belief system, for all the foregoing reasons and more. Science can never claim to be the best source of truth and guidance. It can do well as a tool, but quite poorly as a faith. It can provide some power over nature, yet very little to as-

sist in developing purpose and meaning. To give up other sources of meaning, then, such as intuition, visions, dreams, and faith, for some presumed scientific objectivity is to court despair. If a sophisticated secular person elevates science to the level of a faith, he empties his life of much that is the source of joy, delight, optimism, and hope.

In later chapters, I will describe characteristic attitudes and orientations of healthy and disturbed families. The reader will probably observe some similarities between the erroneous views of science listed above and the attitudes found in disturbed families. This should come as no great surprise for at least two reasons. First, there is a relationship between what experts believe and what the average person believes, usually with a lag of many years. (Having long condemned "old wives" as the source of the mischievous notion that masturbation causes insanity, I was intrigued to find masturbation listed as a frequent cause of insanity in an 1865 treatise on the subject by a respectable alienist.) Second, there is a marked similarity between reductionist science and the rigidity and spurious certainty of disturbed family beliefs. Just as 19th-century science broke away from religion, with fear and trembling, and set up a rigid absolutist structure quite like its disavowed parent, most people try to reduce anxiety by absorbing certainty rather than through open attitudes. Ego functioning is tentative and probabilistic; it evolves slowly, just as an appreciation of the uncertain and relative aspects of science has evolved slowly.

I believe the treatment approaches based on concepts of science that include the misconceptions listed above cannot help individuals grow beyond the limits of disturbed families, and interminable analyses and/or treatment failures result from absolutist, closed-system approaches to man's emotional disorders.

Two valuable and original sources of therapeutic insight, Freudian psychoanalysis and experimental psychology, suffer from these erroneous views of science. Both assume objective truth and believe that their respective structures have it. Both tend to be to be at least impatient—and often harsh—with unbelievers. Both have arrogance, or at least complacency, in the place of a valuable uncertainty. Both tend to wreak havoc on the subjective view of reality: experimental psychologists, because of an impatience with so unpredictable a phenomenon as subjectivity, and Freudians by assuming that they understand the subjective and interpret it in a specific predetermined systematic fashion that can brook no serious challenge by the patient or others.

If a scientist deals with non-human material and believes in absolutes, he only contributes to a sterility in that field, the languishing of progress, and resistance to new theory. However, if a scientist is dealing with human material, the Procrustean bed can become bloody. Closed-system pseudo-science then behaves much as old Procrustes, the woodcutter, stretching and cutting humans with an insensitivity to the lost dignity or lost understanding that such fervently held absolutes produce. Examples of this phenomenon are unfortunately frequent: Skinner states (seriously, I am afraid, not in hyperbole) that proper attention to conditioning can lead us "beyond freedom and dignity";[12] orthodox Freudians become pessimistic over the unsolvable problem of man's aggressive/destructive nature and society's unsuccessful fight to control it.

Since these disciplines (not sciences) that concern themselves with the nature of man deal with articles of faith, rather than with theory which may be altered or scrapped, and since they quite violently disagree with one another, how are disagreements between various behavioral schools negotiated? Most of the time they are not, since adherents of the different cults do not often participate in useful dialogues. Freudians, behaviorists, existentialists, and organicists can spend happy years next to each other on the same faculty, never treading on one another's territory. If they do, agreement is quite likely to be reached by political (power) means. This is inevitable if human truth is seen as absolute. One simply cannot negotiate in good faith without a terrible threat to ideological coherence.

I believe that a better appreciation of the nature of the scientific method will allow real dialogue between adherents of different behavioral and psychotherapeutic schools, to the advantage of humanity. In addition, I believe that such an appreciation will lead to the abolition of all schools and cults and a resultant synthesis of the valued contributions of many current theoretical systems.

WHAT SCIENCE IS: SCRUBBING THE LADY AND MAKING HER PRESENTABLE

As the outcome of common-sense knowledge, science: 1) is concerned with increasing man's power in the material world by making sense of things; 2) deals with the refutable and the pragmatic, and is, therefore, limited; 3) is an abstraction, a map of reality; and 4) is essentially a method.

Let's take these one at a time and look at them more closely. First, as science increases man's power in the material world, there is an effort to make sense of things. Such sense has to do with structure and relations.

It is ironic that reductionistic science—the splitting up of complex phenomena into elementary components or units in an attempt to discover the laws governing the parts and to understand the complex from the elementary—was so successful that this methodological short-cut became identified with the whole enterprise. The success of reductionism (Von Bertalanffy calls it Galileanism)[13] obscured an intrinsic quality of science: its dealing with patterns and relations. General systems theory would not have been novel or much of an advance had there not been a long period of mechanistic science reducing the complex to the elemental and leading to the erroneous belief (sometimes stated, often implicit) that the whole is nothing more than the sum of its parts.

Such reductionism has plagued psychology since the beginning of its formal study.[14] In order to gain scientific respect for psychological science, early and contemporary investigators have often felt obligated to follow the Galilean method and study man as an intrapsychic phenomenon, or as a stimulus-response interactional structure, or as a chemical equation. With general acceptance that scientific endeavor deals with structure and relations, the study of sick and well humans as complex, biological beings, enmeshed in a significant social system, can assume its rightful place. Procrustes can return to cutting wood instead of people.

Second, science deals with the refutable and the pragmatic; therefore it is limited. Do not expect a scientist to tell you whether wars should be fought or fiercer weapons developed or whether an atomic power plant should be placed near your town. He can give you the odds of success, but no important social decisions are scientific or technical. They are related to values, consensual subjective reality, and social power. Scientific information is important but not decisive in this arena.

Similarly, do not expect a psychotherapist practicing a scientific discipline to decide whether a patient should get married, get a divorce, have a lover, or rid himself of one. Such decisions, although difficult, are areas of personal choice not to be found in the wisdom of any human other than the one involved, and no amount of therapeutic expertise makes this any less so. Indeed, the professionalism of a helper is in inverse ratio to the frequency with which advice is given. One's Aunt Lucinda usually knows what everyone should do, and a poor therapist gives many directives, but the times a skilled therapist makes decisions for others are few if he is interested in the patient's growth. This is true in acute crises as well as acute psychosis. (I do not consider the management of patients in hospitals to come under the heading of psychotherapy. Patients who have been hospitalized will usually need to have many decisions made for them.)

Third, science is an abstraction, a map of reality. We are in Korzibski's debt for getting us out of the sticky objective/subjective dichotomies of existentialists squaring off against behaviorists and organicists. The only objectivity man has is the raw sensory input before he integrates and abstracts.[7] Objects are lower order abstractions from words, and concepts spiral upward in increasingly abstract symbolizing; for example, *pencil, table, self, motherhood, patriotism, love, God*. Every human has a unique self and a unique world affected by biology and experience. No man has objective truth, scientific or otherwise, and the individual's subjective view of the world is as close to "reality" as anybody's alleged objectivity.

Harry Stack Sullivan's beautiful term, "consensual validation," with which he replaced the Freudian concept of "reality testing," shows a profound understanding of science and of human development.[15]

The process of developing ego strengths or of being scientific (they are quite similar) does not consist of finding objective truths. To believe so can lead individuals and families toward the promotion of illness rather than toward emotional health. Rather, the process consists of negotiating a shared perception of truths in respectful dialogue with others.

Becoming sane may be a somewhat different process, depending on the degree of authoritarianism in the social structure. Consensual validation is the common factor in scientific exploration, and the development of ego strength. In an open society, scientific research may be rewarded, and open discussion of individual differences at least tolerated. Becoming sane, then, can include such ego-promoting dialogue with peers. But in closed, authoritarian societies, sanity may be promoted by being wise enough to concur with the socially powerful, a much different process from respectful negotiation. It is fortunate that, even in totalitarian cultures, there will be smaller groups of friends and families that can have an openness which allows ego development.

A few may have difficulty with this relativistic definition of scientific knowledge and of ego development. Perhaps, for example, a physician specializing in pathology who has wandered into this book by mistake might demur, pointing to a cluster of cells seen through a microscope and saying, "Those cells are not a consensus; they are either cancerous or they are not." I would suggest that unless this expert has shown countless times that he labels his pathological specimens quite like other pathologists, he will not be heard effectively. And if he insists that he is closer to objective truth, he then will engage in a research endeavor. If he is able to develop experiments that support an aberrant opinion, these data are brought into dialogue with his fellows, and the process of consensual validation (or a scientific research) continues.

Since scientific, cognitive knowledge is an abstraction, there can never be wholeness or completeness in such knowledge. A map of a terrain can be of immense help to a traveler, but it is always rather dull in comparison to the real thing. We will always need to rely on dreams, fantasies, poets, artists, and philosophers to help us get a bit closer to the terrain itself. Science will lead us astray if we depend on it for answers rather than guidance, for reality rather than a skeletal structure.

Nonetheless, mechanistic science is far more limited than systems-oriented, uncertainty-ridden, approximate and value conscious, 20th-century science as described and advocated by such innovators as von Bertalanffy, Korzibski, and Popper.

Fourth, science starts with a problem and develops a theory which is vigorously criticized in a dialogue of equals, a necessarily open system. The method of science is a refinement of the effort to learn from one's mistakes. This is essentially all that it tries to do, but it attempts to create rules and discipline that permit the job to be done better and more consistently.

Francis Bacon was quite hostile to speculation and insisted that (despite the human inability to do so) one should approach nature with an open, unbiased mind. He argued that people have a strong tendency to interpret data in the light of their own prejudices. For example, if a man believes that all history is a class struggle, then whatever he observes or reads of human interaction will be interpreted in the light of this belief and will only strengthen it.[9] If one possesses notions that can always be confirmed by his observations, he can learn nothing new. This empty exercise of pseudo-experiments may be not only as a passive observer, as the example above, but also as an active participant. For example, a parent who believes in the innate savagery of humanity will understandably attempt to control his own evil impulses and those of his children by harsh discipline. Such behavior then leads to the very reality— surly hostility lying in wait for an opening—that fits with the theory. On a broader societal level, Michener quoted a Spanish official explaining a harsh government policy, "We Spaniards are so hard to govern, you know." Repression leads to rebellion, which leads to repression: theory unchanged, learning nil. This is the self-fulfilling prophecy to be discussed later in the chapter on aggression. What a predicament! If humans are so enamoured of their theories that all data can fit into them, and the effort to expunge all theory from mind and to learn directly from the book of nature is impossible, things sound rather bleak. Is there a better alternative?

Unlike Bacon, Popper believes there is. He advocates the following:

First, embrace and respect theory; rejoice that man's abstracting and symbolizing capability provides such delightful playthings and tools. Second, insist that all those hoping to have their theories considered scientific, describe observations which, if occurring, would refute them. If all possible events fit the theory, it cannot claim to be a part of scientific dialogue. It may be promoted with enthusiasm, power, threat, or even violence, but certainly not with experimentation and respectful discourse. This understanding is crucial to delineate clearly the difference between theory and dogma. It is important to understand this in order to distinguish between the scientific and the doctrinaire.

For example, if a Freudian theorist cannot describe possible family interaction that would indicate the lack of patricidal wishes in a particular male child, then such theory is out of the realm of science and has become secular dogma. If a learning theorist cannot describe experimental results that would refute a belief in the unimportance of subjective choice or instinctual drive, the belief is dogma. Of course, other areas of Freudian or behaviorist theory held by these adherents may be refutable and, hence, scientific. Please note: stating that a concept is out of the realm of science does not mean that it is false. It simply means that there is no way to determine its correctness.

Third, accept observations as supportive of the theory only if they are severe tests of that theory, and if sincere and capable efforts to disprove it fail to do so.

These simple rules of Popper lay the groundwork for honest scientific dialogue and describe the requirements for scientific progress.[9]

Now, let us see how one can practice the scientific method according to Popper. Remember that this method is simply an elegant outgrowth of common sense, in which men can learn from their mistakes.

First, we start with a problem, either practical or theoretical. We then devise some solution, usually inaccurate.

And then we criticize it.

We test it with experimentation.

We work on the problem; we become thoroughly acquainted, thoroughly immersed, married to it.

Wrestling with this problem makes us an expert on it.

We invite others interested in the problem to criticize our best efforts at solution.

We carry on this critical discussion within the three rules mentioned earlier. The process is productive and endless: Problems, theories, criticisms—problems, theories, criticism—

Now let us look at some of the systems requirements for such problem-solving effort. First, the participants must be relatively free. They must have enough overt personal power to express individual opinions, to share these openly with others, and, if need be, to challenge current socially approved beliefs. (It is ironic that one current behavioral scientist, B. F. Skinner, utilizes these freedoms fully to attack the necessity or even the reality of freedom.) Perhaps this is explainable by virtue of the fact that his theories (at least in Skinner's view) cannot be refuted and, therefore, must be promoted primarily by rhetoric). In addition, participants must be equals. Criticisms of theory can only be potent and effective when carried on in an egalitarian atmosphere. Unequal power squelches such dialogue quickly, as the personal security of the participants becomes more important than the search. Finally, for such a human interactional system to develop, one that includes openness, confidence, and relative personal freedom to think and communicate, there must be a genuine shared respect for the individual person's subjective reality, his creative and productive potential.

This description of the context of effective scientific productivity is also a description of the optimal milieu for ego development, as later family material will indicate. The climate necessary to develop capable people with adaptiveness, ingenuity, and good sense, or capable scientists, seems to be the same.

One can take this description of the scientific method and do a decent job of psychotherapy! Of course, the personal characteristics of the therapist, his training, which includes identification models and information, and his knowledge of some coherent theory are important, but I believe much of the damage described by Bergin that some therapists do to patients will be avoided and the potency of therapists will be augmented by learning scientific methodology and using it.

Let me put these steps in the context of a patient/therapist, and develop the interaction: A person comes to a psychotherapist demoralized and with significant unsolved problems in living. He and the therapist will try to define the most pressing problems as clearly as possible, and in the process the two will become acquainted. The therapist will soon learn what notions the patient has been operating with, and also will have a hypothesis or two of his own. He will offer these to be considered and criticized by his patient. In such a contextual invitation to negotiate, the therapist does everything in his power to develop an atmosphere of equal power, of openness and mutual competence, in order that the process be satisfying and successful. By doing so, an opportunity to experience intimacy is proffered, possibly the first that the patient has ever experienced.

This is a brief summary of the model of psychotherapy offered in this book. Invite the patient to become a colleague in a respectable endeavor; then symptoms abate and ego development occurs. As I try to practice this way, I often feel more the scientist than when I was engaged in pharmacological research. In addition, I have experienced the excitement of two people who respect each other working hard on a problem—the kind of exhilarating interaction I once had in rap sessions with other researchers.

Dealing with human pain, suffering, dreams, goals, and possibilities, the scientist is the humanist, when that scientist is of the type described in this chapter. Of course, when he is the dogmatic authoritarian, he is a danger to himself and others! The difference lies in one's understanding of the nature of knowing. Learning results from mutual exploration rather than indoctrination.

REFERENCES

1. ROSZAK, T., "Science and its critics: must rationality be rationed," *Science*, 186:925-927, Sept. 3, 1974.
2. ROSZAK, T., *Where the Wasteland Ends*, Garden City, N.J., Doubleday & Co., 1972.
3. POPPER, K. R., *The Logic of Scientific Discovery*, New York, Basic Books, 1959.
4. FREUD, S., *The Future of An Illusion*, Garden City, N.J., Anchor Books, Doubleday, 1964.
5. SKINNER, B. F., "Humanism and behaviorism," *Humanist*, 32:18-20, July-August, 1972.
6. HAWKING, S. W., "Symposium on theoretical physics," U. of Chicago, May, 1975.
7. KORZIBSKI, A., *Science and Sanity*, Lancaster, Pa., The International Non-Aristotelian Library Publishing Co., 1933.
8. WATSON, J. D., *The Double Helix*, Patterson, N.J., Atheneum Press, 1968.
9. POPPER, K. R., "Science: problems, aims, responsibilities," *Proceedings of Meeting of the Federation of American Societies for Experimental Biology*, Atlanta City, N.J., April 17, 1963.
10. BURGERS, J. M., "Causality and anticipation," *Science*, 189:194-198, 18 July, 1975.
11. STENT, G., "Limits to the scientific understanding of man," *Science*, 187:1052-1057, 21 March, 1975.
12. SKINNER, B. F., *Beyond Freedom and Dignity*, New York, Alfred A. Knopf, 1971.
13. VON BERTALANFFY, L., "System, symbol and the image of man," in Galdston, I. (Ed.), *The Interface Between Psychiatry and Anthropology*, 88-119, 1971.
14. MORGAN, C. T., *Introduction to Psychology* (2nd edition), New York, McGraw-Hill, p. 8, 1961.
15. SULLIVAN, H. S., *Personal Psychopathology: Early Formulations*, New York, W. W. Norton, 1972.

_____ **2**

Systems theory, family systems, and the self

The ancient Hebrews viewed their deity as so awesome that they would refer to Him only as Yahweh, a name that included only a portion of His real name. They considered it presumptuous to try to express the Whole. Systems theory is similarly awesome; it is filled with possibilities, meaning, and power, and yet is quite hard for one person to wrap his mind around. This chapter will provide a context, some history, and some explanation of systems concepts, with particular reference to their use by behavioral scientists and mental health specialists. For a more extensive and definitive presentation, I recommend von Bertalanffy's *General Systems Theory*,[1] Gray, Duhl, and Rizzo's *General Systems Theory and Psychiatry*,[2] and Buckley's *Modern Systems Research for the Behavioral Scientist*.[3]

The Yahweh analogy cuts a bit deeper. In ancient times, meaning was considered to be a theological issue, and men went to specialists in the supernatural to understand the events in their lives. In the early days of Western world science, there was no competition between scientific and theological explanations; indeed, many early scientists were devout, conventional believers and often priests or ministers. It was not until the late 19th century that science challenged all theology in a dramatic, specific, mechanistic/vitalistic conflict. By that time, science had assumed a messianic verve, and any concern with concepts such as élan vital, organismic purpose, or even teleology placed a person outside the fraternity of scientists.

Nineteenth century science (reductionist, mechanistic, and naive in systems concepts) was viewed as the power of the future, and sciences such as physics and chemistry were the idealized model. Biological and behavioral sciences stumbled along, attempting to ape their betters, trying to force biological and interpersonal reality into neat, mechanistic, Aristotelean boxes.

Without doubt, man's knowledge was increased during this phase of scientific history, and many of nature's secrets were revealed, but there were at least two destructive side effects. First, sheer volume of information has created a stifling logjam. Huge amounts of research data await integration into coherent, useful form. Competent and distinguished researchers report theories and findings in specialized journals. Students learn specialized segments of a whole, with few guidelines provided them to make sense out of their disparate courses. Graduate students in medicine and mental health who attempt to pull it all together are faced with a dilemma: if they try to do what their teachers do not, they are viewed as "mere" clinicians; if they show academic promise, they are encouraged to research and teach, and continue the flow of unintegrated data to a glutted world.

A second problem arose from the belief that nothing was significant or true if it did not fit an objective, mechanistic model. Even Freudian psychoanalytic theory's attempt to plumb the depths of man's subjective experience is entrapped in this falsely scientific concept. One can read of *id* and *superego*, *cathexes* and *libido* described as if these qualities were separable from the person and divorced from the interpersonal milieu surrounding him.

This problem is found not only in the biological and behavioral sciences, of course, though it is here that I address myself. Physicists and chemists are becoming alarmed at the pileup of the wastes of society's uses of a non-integrated, mechanistic science. Radioactive wastes, chemical wastes, and even heat itself[4] threaten us unless some integration and coherence are brought into this science; unless teleology, purpose, and direction are placed in the center of our efforts to know. Theodore Roszak,[5] in his impassioned and yet thoughtful attack on science as it has evolved to the present, makes this point forcefully. He observes that only one science, ecology, has a self-conscious value system at its core. Roszak speaks for a growing number of intelligent but estranged young people as he advocates chucking the whole scientific mess for an intense irrationality.

General systems theory offers an alternative to this either/or dichotomy. One is not forced to embrace either a coldly value-hostile reductionistic science or a flamboyantly mystical anti-rational stance.

GENERAL SYSTEMS THEORY

Gray calls general systems theory a bold new development in human thought which has brought a number of complex fields, previously unapproachable through classic means, into the range of scientific approach.[2] Von Bertalanffy defines it as the study of the relationship of interactional parts in context, classifying systems by the way their components are organized (interrelated) and deriving the "laws"—typical patterns of behavior for the different classes of systems.[6] Miller defines systems theory as "a set of related definitions, assumptions and propositions which deal with reality as an integrated hierarchy of organizations of matter and energy."[7]

The concepts are at once quite new and quite old—new perhaps to a laboratory scientist, but old to a Navajo shaman who intuitively perceives his people's dependence on, and commonality with, the land and its non-human occupants. A systems approach offers science the opportunity to be truly humanistic and to close the gap between man's needs and his technology.

With his first published statement in 1945, Ludwig von Bertalanffy became the founder of general systems theory, but he acknowledges similar and parallel developments by theorists in many sciences from the beginning of the 20th century. In psychiatry and psychology he includes the contributions of Meyer, Goldstein, Menninger, Grinker, Rogers, Arieti, Allport, Karl and Charlotte Buhler, Weiner, Piaget, Maslow, and Bruner. A parallel development occurred in Gestalt psychology, developed by Kohler, Wertheimer, and Kaffka. These writers insisted that wholes are qualitatively different from a group of parts and focused on pattern (structure and relationship) as a vital aspect of human experience. In addition, Gestalt psychology's concept of dynamic regulation is essentially similar to von Bertalanffy's concepts of steady state and equifinality.[8] Alfred Korzibski, the founder of general semantics, also expanded the limitations of mechanistic science by challenging assumptions of absoluteness, objectiveness, and the adequacy of Aristotelean logic; he focused on structure and relations as the foundation of meaning.[9]

In 1954, other capable scientists, including Kenneth E. Boulding, Ralph Gerard, and Anatol Rappoport, joined von Bertalanffy in founding the Society for the Advancement of General Systems Theory, which publishes basic source material for students in this field. Systems theory is not antipathetic to previous scientific work, but places it in a new frame of reference, permitting knowledge already accumulated to be integrated into a new way of viewing the world.

The field is fertile and complex, filled with many words and phrases unfamiliar (and perhaps threatening) to a scientist or clinician trained in a limited field. For example, Gray gives a partial list of key words representing the new concepts: "open systems, steady state, isomorphism, negentropy, anomorphosis, hierarchial organization, equifinality, growth, negative and positive feedback, process, information, matter, information processing, matter-energy processing, transaction, cross-level transaction, regulation, maintenance and change of component elements, goal directedness, steering and trigger causality, multivariable, dynamic interaction, progressive differentiation, progressive centralization, progressive mechanization and progressive deanthropormorphization."[2] To me, such a list is mind-boggling and I will limit this discussion to some of the important systems concepts applicable to living systems, with a particular focus on humans, the family, and the society as three levels of a systems hierarchy.

Qualities of Living Systems

First, the concept of *hierarchy* itself: A system consists of a number of units of a sort characteristic of one level of organization below the system referred to. For example, a family, composed of several individuals, is one level above the individual in a hierarchy of systems. These people relate to each other with greater intensity than they do to individuals outside the family boundary, but they also relate to those people who represent the larger society, a system higher in this hierarchy that includes many family units. If one includes, as von Bertalanffy does, symbolic systems as well as actual physical systems in systems hierarchies, then such hierarchies are as limitless as a man's imagination.

Each system has a *boundary*, a limiting membrane. In a living system this boundary must be both limiting and permeable for the system to remain alive. A tension is necessary. If the boundary is too permeable, the system loses integrity and identity; if the boundary is impermeable, necessary interaction with the larger world is shut off, the system becomes increasingly entropic, and its life is threatened.

The concept of *entropy* is central to an understanding of systems theory, and it has great practical use in family systems work by providing an orienting framework. Though this concept, along with its reciprocal, negentropy, is complex, it does not need to be intimidating. Georgescu-Roegen[10] offers a satisfactory definition: "Entropy is a term which describes the tendency of things to go into disorder. Low entropy (relative negentropy) implies a high degree of orderliness." This is a simple, clear description of a complicated concept—systems can be thought of as having degrees of entropy or negentropy; that is, as being in states of greater or lesser disorder. In addition, closed systems are doomed to increase in entropy—without access to the world outside the limiting boundary, such systems cannot avoid the downhill pull toward increasing disorder. Open systems, however, which are characteristic of living organisms, can interact with the environment and build increasingly ordered (negentropic) structures within their boundaries.

In a living organism, negentropic complexity of structure evolves, which allows adaptiveness, tolerance to change, and differentiation of subsystems far beyond the capabilities of any inanimate system. For example, if one observes a dead cell fixed on a slide, its remarkable organization and structure are immediately apparent. This dead cell is more negentropic than the inert world beyond its boundaries, but it has no flexibility, no adaptiveness. In its rigid complexity, this dead cell is far more entropic than even the simplest living material.

The system grows by *progressive differentiation*, for which it develops a *leading edge*, a decision maker, which *communicates* with other parts and with the world outside the boundary to develop the *power* necessary to accomplish its goals. Such power may be seen as exhibited in control—control over necessary parts of the outside environment, and control over the system itself. In families, power, both within the family and beyond it, is quite important for adequate functioning; further, feedback loops, both positive and negative, are essential to maintain control, the effective use of power.

There is a characteristic size and limitation of life span in living systems, and such limitations conflict with the inherent tendency to progressive differentiation. This is an example of living systems possessing varied goals which inevitably produce *conflict*. For example, an individual may have both thirst and hunger, so conflict resolution is necessary for sequentially defined and expressed goals to be attained; or, a family may wish to save for the future and also go on vacation—the resolution of conflict is needed. Though the overall purpose of the system need not be conflictual, various needs and goals inevitably result in conflict.

All living systems occupy geographical *space*, and there are conflicting demands within the system parts for such space. In human systems, this requirement of individuals for necessary space is both for actual and symbolic, or abstract, space; individual selves occupy abstract space and they can be invaded or, alternatively, respected, related to closely or distantly in a manner parallel to ways that the physical body can be treated.

Time is an integral part of living systems—all time is marked by change, and the biological clock notes time's passage in growth and development, aging, and, finally, death.

Living systems change constantly, as environmental and biological demands impinge and create *stresses* and *strains*. For example, in families there is a succession of stresses—the birth of children, the aging of parents, the loss of members through successful development and through death. In addition, unusual stresses which cannot be anticipated, such as societal economic depressions, job losses, or threatening moves, must be dealt with.

A system always has *hierarchies of values*—its needs and responses are not of equal value, but some are considered to be more important. These values can be determined by observing how the system responds to stresses—its values become clearer to an outside observer as the system functions and makes choices. Choosing, in this sense, is a function of all living material—higher organisms may refine this capacity, but they do not originate it. A one-celled paramecium makes choices just as surely as a prime minister.

Adaptation depends on maintaining enough stability for coherent identity while making necessary accommodations to a changing world. There is no static state in living systems; they progress or regress. The ability to maintain a necessary minimum predictable state (homeostasis or morphostasis) is as important to adaptation as the ability to adapt and evolve new structure (morphogenesis). System sickness consists of rigidity,[6] the temporary or permanent loss of the capacity for progressive differentiation and adaptation.

With a capable leading edge controlling subsystems and making effective decisions that allow for structure and flexible adaptiveness, a living system has relative *autonomy*—that is, power over itself and relative power to choose possibilities presented by the outside world.

The family and individuals may use all of these aspects of systems functioning in an effort to gain greater negentropy, to obtain greater differentiation and autonomy. For a behavioral scientist/clinician to be helpful rather than destructive, he, himself, must possess a negentropic (an open) rather than a closed system of theory and practice. Von Bertalanffy has noted that in a closed system, the entropy law applies, but there is no time limit. As an example, schools of treatment, or families with a closed-system ideology, will reject new concepts. Deterioration is inevitable, but there is no inexorable rate of decay. Clinicians can hold outworn rigid beliefs for many years, clothed in respectability, yet decadent and destructive. Such systems are comparable to "respectable" families who look competent superficially, yet have a rigid, impermeable boundary that prevents new input. In such families, often one child may become the voice for the whole family, crying out for satisfactory, self-defining experiences that are deficient in all family members.

Isomorphism, the presence of similar structure in seemingly dissimilar systems, is a term often used in systems discussions. One may find similar structure at different levels of a hierarchy, such as in individual and group behavior, or in different systems, such as economics and entymology. The frequency of isomorphism encourages the sharing and increased understanding that diminish scientific compartmentalization.

FAMILY SYSTEMS AND THE SELF

Systems concepts are essential in evolving an adequate definition of the human self, the profoundly subjective, personal "I" whose disintegration or impoverishment, when it occurs, is evident to all in the surrounding environment. All psychopathology concerns itself with humans who have defects in this self-system.* Families have always been responsible for assisting the young in evolving a satisfactory identity compatible with the surrounding culture. This is a task equal in significance to that of providing children with the necessities for physical growth and development. A competent identity does not develop in isolation, but in constant relationship to others. Biological factors, the powerful realities of kinship, and the exchange with family members and the larger social system are necessarily integrated by the developing infant. It is a continuing miracle that a unique self emerges relatively "whole." This interpersonal miracle is comparable to, and isomorphic with, the biological miracle of each healthy newborn who has evolved by the confluence of millions of specific embryonic events.

The most dramatic expression of need for self-definition and coherent identity that has been thwarted is found in children and adolescents diagnosed as schizophrenic. This dysfunction was once considered to be purely intrapsychic, but 25 years of family research illustrate that the lack of a coherent self is related to characteristic family relationship and communication patterns. As this correlation became clearer, patterns found in families with nonpsychotic but emotionally ill offspring were studied, and eventually healthy families became the subject of systematic inquiry.

A family exists in systems terms since its members' interactions with one another are relatively intense when compared to their in-

---

*The self, self-system, and ego have been used similarly or interchangeably by many theorists of psychopathology. I prefer, along with such clinicians as Harry Stack Sullivan,[11] Harry Guntrip,[12] and R. D. Laing,[13] the term *self* because it implies the necessary aspect of symbolic subjectivity and essential wholeness which *ego* does not.

teractions with others, creating a family boundary. Even with this definition, the meaning of family varies with the particular culture and context. In some cultures, the modal family group may include at least three generations, with the grandparents being vital to the process of making decisions and raising the children. Such families are usually found in cultures where social change is slow, there is little geographic mobility, experience is valued highly, and individual adaptability depends more on knowledge of custom than on new information.

In contrast, modern American parents in our highly mobile, rapidly changing society are like immigrants in a new land, who must depend on their children for knowledge of behavior and attitudes that are appropriate for new situations.[14] In this culture it is understandable that the modal family unit has come to be relatively young adults with their dependent children.

Most of the family material presented is derived from such nuclear families. Though it bridges a number of disciplines and theoretical frameworks concerned with human development, it is not definitive. There is risk in extrapolating the information to other cultures or to various subcultures. We need more interactional data on, for example, families of different social classes and one-parent families, before a comprehensive picture of family systems can emerge.

A FAMILY SYSTEMS RESEARCH PROJECT

In the following three chapters there is a summary of findings to date important in correlating family systems factors with individual self-definition. Though there are contributions from many sources, many of the family concepts described are derived from a six-year systems oriented research project which studied families ranging in competence from non-clinical volunteers to those with severely disturbed adolescent children.[15,16]

In this research it was found useful to employ the concept of a continuum to order families with respect to effectiveness. At one end of this continuum are the most flexible, adaptable, goal-achieving systems (the most negentropic families) which will raise the most capable offspring. At the other end of this continuum are the most inflexible, undifferentiated and ineffective systems (the most entropic families) in which child-rearing fails miserably. This framework is theoretically satisfying and is supported empirically by available data describing healthy and disturbed families and their offspring. Conceptualizing families along such a structural continuum allows family theorists to avoid the Kraepelinian trap of typology. The process of placing unique, specific people or systems into categories and defining the categories in obsessional detail has often obscured the reality of unitary concepts of emotional health and illness. Levinger remarked on this danger in the early 1970's as he asked about family variables, "Is it a difference of kind or degree? If we are to progress in terms of moving away from discrete typologies and toward variables and continuous formulations, we would want to focus on the degree of difference and dimensions along which these kinds of (family) relationships differ."[17]

Just as schizophrenic states merge almost imperceptibly into depression, neuroses, and behavior disturbances, and these conditions merge gently with the normal, so do characteristics of severely disturbed families blend subtly into those of moderately disturbed (or what shall be termed *midrange* families), which in turn, at their upper end, blend with adequate and healthy families.

Although this uninterrupted progression is characteristic of living material (the Gaussian curve found in biological studies), and human material stubbornly resists fitting well into rigid categories, there is a need for coherent systems of classification. I believe the concept of negentropy provides an excellent basis for such classification. Families can be placed on a continuum reflecting functioning which can also accommodate different family styles that are important but unrelated to specific levels of competence. In addition, family system competence can be related to the qualities of individual offspring.

Diagram 1

Family	Severely disturbed		Borderline		Midrange		Adequate		Optimal	
	10	9	8	7	6	5	4	3	2	1
Children	Process schizo-phrenic, Severe be-havior dis-order, "so-ciopathic"		Border-line patients		Neuroses and behav-ior dis-orders (the sane but limited)		No ob-vious pathology		Unusual individual competence	

Diagram 1 presents a relationship between family competence and individual psychopathology and health. Though schematic, it represents reasonably well the relationship found by our research group between different levels of family system function and the children of the families. There was a statistically significant correlation between raters' determinations of family competence and in-dependent judgments of the degree of individual psychopathology found in adolescent children of the families studied.

This relationship was found though family factors are certainly not the only variables affecting children's competence. In addition, family and individual competence fluctuates, depending on their particular ability to solve problems presented by the internal and external stresses occurring at various developmental periods. This suggests that family and individual competencies have limited ranges of fluctuation which are not sufficient to obscure relation-ships between the two.

Crucial Family Systems Variables

In addition to the interactional study of families, traditional psychological and psychiatric evaluations with individual members were accomplished. Raters were trained to measure a group of sys-tem variables after watching 5, 10, or 50 minutes of videotapes of a family performing various tasks. The variables were defined in a series of 13 subscales which included five areas of family behavior: structure, mythology, goal-directed negotiation, system tolerance for autonomy, and affective or feeling issues.

1. *Structure*

The structure of the family is reflected in three scales—overt power, parental coalition, and family closeness. The first of these—overt power—is concerned with the way in which power is distributed in a family.

During the study of family variables related to the development of a self, the formulation of an accurate measure of interpersonal power was the most difficult. In one sense every member of any group has as much power as any other; a helpless infant can dictate the actions of a household; a schizophrenic adolescent can bankrupt a concerned family; a tyrannical father who seems to control everything in a family may be lonely and hungry for love, not having as much power as his inept and failing son to gain the special attention of his wife.

In early efforts at determining power, raters were asked to decide whether the family was dominated or led by mother or father. Good rater agreement was obtained as to a system's style—whether chaotic, led, or egalitarian—but ascertaining which individual held the power seemed more a matter of the rater's past history than of any particular phenomenon observed. That is, if a rater had grown up in a family dominated, in his mind, by a strong but silent father, he would not see power in verbal output. A rater with a different background would score silence or verbosity quite differently. When rater agreement failed to evolve, it was clear that the difficulty was that the scale was individually rather than system based. It was redesigned to evaluate a family's style of using power. This experience led to the present position presented in these pages: interpersonal power can be either overt or covert; overt power is openly acknowledged by the group and is illustrated by such observable specifics as who speaks to whom and who directs activities. This power can be determined by formal studies of group interaction. Covert power can be most effective, but it is not group-sanctioned. Its nature is illicit, and in families that depend heavily on illicit satisfactions, such covert power is quite important. It is difficult or impossible to measure such power when observing families engaged in tasks unrelated to family-defined goals; raters speak of a feeling that one member is "really" running things, but in this covert power area, rater agreement is difficult to obtain. Covert power can be exerted by individual weakness and helplessness.

A useful way of conceptualizing the beginnings of human development is to consider the mother/infant relationship as the basic experience known to every person who survives. It is characterized by an impotent/omnipotent interaction with another. Both helplessness and great power are possessed by both people in the encounter. Mother has the power of life and death over her infant, yet is forced to forego many other pleasures when the infant cries helplessly. Similarly, the infant is all powerful, yet impotent, in this first relationship.

Human development proceeds by learning more living skills that reduce helplessness and the covert power of such helplessness. This never-ending process develops competence, relative interpersonal power, and effectiveness that always includes vulnerability but does not exploit it in relationships. (I am indebted to R. W. White for his valuable insights into the nature of human competence.)[18] With competence, an individual negotiates from a position of shared overt power, relying neither on intimidation nor helplessness for success.

Symptoms of emotional illness are throwbacks to this infantile impotent/omnipotent relationship style. It is pervasive in schizophrenia. Neurotics and individuals with behavior disorders have areas of functioning that continue the impotent/omnipotent mode—in circumscribed relationship areas there is greater expectation of finding satisfaction and control from a helpless stance or from a position of near absolute power.

Family studies that attempt to obtain rater reliability, a reasonable consensus of subjective views, will be limited to evaluation of overt power differences. All social systems have overt power differences—that is, a hierarchy of social power, a "pecking order." Family systems differ greatly in the ways power is used. Very disturbed families often have such obscure and indirect communication that power is neither clearly claimed nor shared by any family member. The result is a chaotic and extremely inefficient style. The next most entropic style is one of rigid dominance and submission. Here, encounters between family members are coherent, but overt power differentials abound. Interaction proceeds by interpersonal control, with various forms of intimidation. As the family increases in differentiation and functional competence, differences in the amount of overt power lessen, and sharing and negotiation become the rule. Parents in competent families have nearly equal overt power.

The effectiveness of the family is closely tied to the quality of the *parental coalition*. The least healthy is a negative one—one where a parent is relegated to a childlike role, and a child possesses the overt power of a parent. In this way a strong child/parent coalition develops. In the middle range of functioning, a weak coalition is evidenced by unresolved parental conflict, mutual attacks, lack of emotional support, competitiveness, and obvious distancing maneuvers. A strong coalition refers to the parents' ability to work together and to lead effectively. Many competent but pained, or adequate, families possess this kind of strong parental coalition. However, an effective relationship that, in addition, is warm and tender was found only in optimal families.

Closeness includes two apparently separable qualities—the clarity of intrasystem boundaries and the amount of sharing and intimacy evidenced in the family interaction. Previous clinical work dictated this assumption—one cannot be close to another unless they are separate. Without a clear sense of individual boundaries, the murkiness of an amorphous ego mass found in severely disturbed families results; suffocating fusion, rather than closeness, is experienced. In midrange families, some clarity of individual self boundaries develops at the expense of family closeness. In the most negentropic families one finds intimacy and individuality together.

2. *Mythology*

All families have a mythology, an ongoing shared concept of the qualities and capabilities of family members. Families vary, however, in the degree of congruence that their shared view of themselves has with the picture of the family as seen by evaluators. The most entropic systems possess the most incongruent mythology; competent families describe themselves and their interaction in a way that closely approximates the raters' views of them. Such a group perception, able to be easily shared by those outside the family, is a powerful tool for adaptation and change.

3. *Goal-directed Negotiation*

Each family has many problems to solve. In rating the capacity of a given family to solve problems, two aspects are important. The first has to do with the efficiency of the family in arriving at decisions; the second has to do with the degree to which the family encourages negotiation among all its members. Dysfunctional families are quite inefficient at solving problems. Other families with lesser dysfunction deal with problems efficiently, but without true negotiation, and the family response to a problem usually reflects the work of an overtly powerful family member. Optimal families solve problems efficiently, relying on family negotiation to arrive at solutions. Solutions represent the best that the whole family has to bring to problems.

4. *System Encouragement of Autonomy*

In our culture, family competence is closely related to the encouragement of individuals to be autonomous. This is a broadly inclusive aspect of family functioning. In entropic systems, individuals are poorly differentiated, with unclear personal (subsystem) boundaries. Competent families are composed of clearly separate and unique members who cooperate, but are quite able to act separately. To make the concept operational, autonomy was divided into four elements: clarity of communication; the assumption of personal responsibility; the amount of invasiveness found in the system; and the permeability of the boundaries between members.

The first element, communication of self-concept, has to do with the clarity with which members express their individual perceptions and feelings. People in disturbed families are obscure, vague, and often confusing as they attempt to communicate information about their inner selves. The system is intolerant of directness, and individual members are punished if they are clearly unique. Effective families reward such clarity, since it is important in promoting task efficiency and goal achievement.

Taking personal responsibility for expression and behavior is a significant aspect of autonomy. The more entropic families use a variety of mechanisms to avoid such responsibility. These include denial, blame and attack, forgetting, speaking in the second and third person, and objectifying relationships. In competent families the climate encourages individuals to take responsibility for their own feelings and behavior.

To state what another person feels or thinks, that is, to invade the symbolic self, is a most destructive operation. Such mindreading, or invasiveness, if allowed to stand, destroys autonomy. "You don't feel that way; you really love your work." "You're just tired; you're not discouraged." This communicational characteristic is rare in competent and midrange families. When found, it is a powerful indicator of disturbance. It is unusual enough in even modestly capable families, however, that invasiveness is rather poor in discriminating family competence across the whole negentropic continuum.

An important aspect of system tolerance for autonomy is the receptiveness to one another's communications. Such openness, or permeability, encourages personal dignity and self-esteem and is vital for efficient negotiation. An entropic family maintains rigid unchanging patterns by a practiced obliviousness. Effective families welcome input from even the youngest members. This is a powerful way for the system to assert that individuals are valuable.

5. *Family Affect or Feeling*

Like autonomy, affect is a complex and pervasive aspect of family life. A system that functions well, that has structure, flexibility and progressive differentiation toward individual autonomy, presents an enjoyable feeling tone easily assessed by observers. A dysfunctional system, inefficient in tasks and conflict-ridden, has a variety of negative feeling states. For evaluation, affect is separated into four aspects—the expression of feelings, mood and tone (the emotional statement of the group), the degree of irresolvable conflict in the system, and a judgment of the amount of empathy present.

Expressiveness is an important variable in family functioning. Competent families have few proscriptions against expressing feelings. Anger, sadness, and anxiety are as acceptable from members as are tenderness, warmth, and pleasant laughter. Disturbed, more entropic, systems have many rules against expression of feelings since their expression can disrupt tenuous control and threaten rigid structure.

The *mood and feeling tone*, developed into a rating subscale, was most effective in discriminating degrees of health in family systems. Competent families hum with pleasant sounds. As one observes families rated more and more entropic, the feeling tone becomes increasingly negative. Open anger in a group is usually less ominous than pervasive depression or cynicism, because there is some hope for change implicit in such raw expression. Both emotional and cognitive elements are included in this subscale because the expectation (the predictive set) of a family group is quite as important as the feeling state of the moment. Depression, cynicism, optimism, and hope are all powerful words relating to feelings and to expectations. These affective and cognitive qualities are interrelated in a chicken-or-egg fashion; both are cause and effect of the other. For example, a clinician who treats feeling state disorders often finds that the most important thing to change is not the mood, but the predictive set.[19]

Empathy is a concept crystalized and defined relatively recently. The word is not found in dictionaries prior to the 20th century. A modern dictionary defines it as, "the capacity for participating in, or vicariously experiencing, another's feelings, volitions, or ideas and sometimes another's movements to the point of executing body movements resembling his." Determining this variable might seem to require a high degree of subjectivity on the part of a rater, yet it has a high degree of interrater reliability, and is quite effective in discriminating family competence. A necessary function of capable families is the ability of members to sense and respond to nonverbal cues. This is a more demanding task than being responsive to overt verbal input (permeability) but it is a far cry from invasiveness which is destructive of individual self-boundaries. Families have a characteristic level of empathic response and the more disturbed systems cannot respond empathically.

Conflict is ubiquitous in any family, just as is ambivalence in every individual. It is indicative of functioning difficulty only if chronically unresolved. This variable is concerned with the degree of unresolvable conflict in the family and its effect on functioning. In entropic systems which have poor differentiation, poor negotiating ability, and great rigidity, conflict is unresolvable. In competent families, resolution of conflict is accomplished openly and usually quickly.

Individual Choice in Family Systems

There are many significant similarities of structure (isomorphism) between individuals and families. Just as individuals feel ambivalent and have internal conflict, families have conflict which must be resolved by system differentiation and negotiation of differences between members in order that problem solving and goal attainment may proceed effectively. In individuals, the decision-making *I* deals with internal conflict and needs, proceeding with goals and purposes by negotiating with multiple desires from within the self boundary. In families, individual desires compete and produce system conflict. The decision-making leading edge of the family can assist in the resolution of such conflict, or, if insensitive, can promote unresolvable conflict.

Ambivalence has been described as one of the basic symptoms of schizophrenia and as one of the hallmarks of neurosis. It is also characteristic of the healthy human. We humans are plagued with ambivalence because of a remarkable evolutionary quirk; we are possessed of a marvelous frontal cortex which acts in concert with a mid-brain in a way that makes a symbolic life unavoidable and perfection imaginable. Dreams, fantasies, and wishes can remain untainted with ambivalence until we encounter our own finite, grubby fallibility and that of others (our developmental experience probably reverses that sequence). When we contact this real and finite universe, both human and non-human, we experience ambivalence. Nothing is quite as we can imagine. Mothers, fathers, lovers, children, friends, and our own selves let us down, at least as measured by the standards of our dreams.

Individual pathology does not consist of the possession of ambivalence any more than family pathology is due to conflict. Rather, *resolution* of the ambivalence is related to competence, just as, isomorphically, the ability to resolve conflicts between members makes for a healthy, capable family system.

Severely disturbed individuals have chronically unresolved ambivalence that reduces *conation*—the ability to choose goals and to pursue them with energy. Sane but limited individuals characteristically attempt to resolve this ambivalence by repressing or denying the embarrassing or awkward side of their feeling states (such as hostility toward loved ones or tenderness and warmth toward a scapegoated family member).

It requires a capable self to accept these inevitable crosscurrents of feelings consciously and to choose alternatives quickly on the basis of realistic possibilities coupled with personal choice. This progression of self-differentiation has its isomorphic counterpart in family differentiation described in the next three chapters.

In addition to the isomorphic relationship between self-differentiation and family competence, limited family systems hold back developmental possibilities in offspring; fixed and stunted individual character structure is related to fixed and stunted family structure. Unresolved individual ambivalence and unresolved family conflict intertwine.

Personal choice is most significant in relating research and clinical work with individuals and families to concepts of selfhood, subjectivity, science, and systems. The word "choice" emphasizes both self and subjectivity. "I choose" has linguistic reverberations with matters of *taste*, to the essentially gustatory or glandular and sensual aspects inherent in choice of whatever kinds—people, activities, things, ideas, foods. Choice can be objectified: "Seventy-eight percent of adults are for some form of gun-control." "Sixty-five percent of those who try Pepsi like it better than the other leading cola." It can be manipulated, "You don't want to play with that little boy, honey—he's *dirty*." "You don't really want to watch television, you want to study and make good grades so we can all be proud of you." But it cannot be ignored, nor can one person's choice be controlled by another without either irreconcilable conflict between the members of such a system or the breakdown of the integrity of the self so poorly treated.

A clinically useful concept is: *There is no gratification without choice*. The large number of patients who try to find comfort by abdicating their own wishes to others and who try to coerce others in turn is a source of pain and frustration to many psychotherapists. People often struggle for years with unresolved ambivalence, trying to ignore their own feelings and make someone else the deciding force. It is an impossible effort. Even a newborn infant's choice is ignored at some peril. The newborn, with a modest self-definition dependent on biological contributions, knows when he is hungry and when he is satiated. If a caretaker tries to feed him when the caretaker rather than the baby is hungry, various unpleasant phenomena occur, including digestive disturbances, crying, and interpersonal pain. Conversely, proper attention to the baby's choice leads to a contented child and a happier family. Of course, after a while, negotiation is necessary, and the baby has to adapt and learn that mother's choices are important too. Successful interpersonal negotiation can only occur between individuals who choose.

Such a viewpoint, incomprehensible to dysfunctional family members, is demonstrated by negentropic family systems. Individual members develop in an atmosphere of conflict resolution, with decisions arrived at by respectful negotiation rather than by coercive power plays. Such experiences lead to the evolution of individuals with personal dignity, an expectation of competence and social power, and an awareness of their own subjective reality.

If science, hard or soft, does not respect the importance of subjective reality, the source of individual choice, it is never humanistic, but rather tyrannical. A tyranny can be exerted similar to that seen in severely dysfunctional families, in closed-system dogmatic religious groups, and in dictatorial political regimes. This is important for all researchers and clinicians to consider.

REFERENCES

1. VON BERTALANFFY, L., *General Systems Theory*, New York, George Braziller, 1968.
2. GRAY, W., DUHL, F. J., and RIZZO, N.D. (Eds.) *General Systems Theory and Psychiatry*, Boston, Little Brown, 1969.
3. BUCKLEY, W., (Ed.), *Modern Systems Research for the Behavioral Scientist*, Chicago, Aldine, 1968.
4. HEILBRONER, R. L., *An Inquiry into the Human Prospect*, New York, W. W. Norton, 1974.
5. ROSZAK, T., "Science and its critics: must rationality be rationed," *Science*, 186:925-927, Sept. 3, 1974.
6. VON BERTALANFFY, L., "Systems, symbol and the image of man," in Galdston, I. (Ed.), *The Interface between Psychiatry and Anthropology*, New York, Brunner/Mazel, 1971.
7. MILLER, J. G., "Living systems: basic concepts," in Gray, W., Duhl, F. J., and Rizzo, N. D. (Eds.), *General Systems Theory and Psychiatry*, Boston, Little Brown, 1969.
8. VON BERTALANFFY, L., "General systems theory—an overview," in Gray, W., Duhl, F. J., and Rizzo, N. D. (Eds.), *General Systems Theory and Psychiatry*, Boston, Little Brown, 1969.
9. KORZIBSKI, A., *Science and Sanity*, Lancaster, Pa., The International Non-Aristotelian Library Publishing Co., 1933.
10. GEORGESCU-ROEGEN, N., *The Entropy Law and the Economic Process*, Cambridge, Mass., Harvard U. Press, 1971.
11. SULLIVAN, H. S., *Personal Psychopathology: Early Formulations*, New York, W. W. Norton, 1972.
12. GUNTRIP, H., *Schizoid Phenomena, Object Relations and the Self*, New York, International Universities Press, 1969.
13. LAING, R. D., *The Divided Self*, London, Tavistock Publications, 1960.
14. MEAD, M., "The american family: reality or myth," The Scott Hawkins Lecture, Southern Methodist University, Dallas, Texas, March 31, 1970.
15. LEWIS, J. M., BEAVERS, W. R., GOSSETT, J. T., and PHILLIPS, V. A., *No Single Thread: Psychological Health in Family Systems*, New York, Brunner/Mazel, 1976.
16. BEAVERS, W. R., LEWIS, J. M., GOSSETT, J. T., and PHILLIPS , V. A., "Family systems and ego functioning: midrange families," Scientific Proceedings, 128th Annual Meeting, American Psychiatric Association, Anaheim, California, May 1975.

17. LEVINGER, G., "Basic issues in interaction research," in Framo, J. L. (Ed.), *Family Interaction*, New York, Springer, 1972.
18. WHITE, R. W., "Motivation reconsidered: the concept of competence," *Psychological Review*, 66(5):297-333, 1959.
19. BECK, A. T., "Thinking and depression: I. idiosyncratic content and cognitive distortions," *Arch. Gen. Psychiat.*, 9:324-333, 1963.

*Things fall apart; the centre cannot hold; mere anarchy
is loosed upon the world.*

W. B. Yeats, *The Second Coming*

3

Severely
dysfunctional families

Most of the information about severely dysfunctional (SD) families comes from the study of those families with a process schizophrenic member. This is not to say that SD families produce only process schizophrenics. There is evidence that in such poorly functioning families one may also find extreme behavior disturbances[1,2] and a variety of psychosomatic problems, such as ulcerative colitis[3] and bronchial asthma.[4] In the Timberlawn family research[5] SD families had children diagnosed as psychotic and as severe behavior disturbances.

These diverse individual dysfunctions can emerge from the same family system. For example, a 28-year-old businessman entered outpatient psychiatric treatment with problems related to his marriage. He was emotionally distant from his wife and his two children. Though not conscious of being depressed, he did complain of general vague unease. He described growing up in a family situation in which confusion, chaos, and murkiness were an integral part of his family life. He often withdrew from others and was emotionally arid as he attempted to control and dampen the intensity of interpersonal encounters. He had two older brothers, one of whom had been diagnosed as paranoid schizophrenic since middle adolescence and had been in and out of psychiatric hospitals for 15 years. The other brother, a reasonably successful college teacher, suffered from severe ulcerative colitis, which was endangering his life. Characteristically busy with many complicated money deals, he had only a few treatment sessions before he was indicted for illegal stock manipulation and, as his legal difficulties mounted, he aborted treatment.

Here were three siblings; one suffered from ulcerative colitis, another was process paranoid schizophrenic, and the third (though successful for a time) was convicted of a felony. They were all products of a single family which failed to provide the children with enough ego strength or coping abilities to allow them to function effectively as adults.

This vignette illustrates that failure to develop clear self-definition and adequate abilities to deal with environmental demands are seen not only in those people with a schizophrenic diagnosis, but also in people who will be found in prisons, lawyers' offices, and general hospitals, as well as in psychiatric facilities.

The following descriptions of SD families will depend heavily on clinical and research material from families that have an offspring diagnosed as process schizophrenic, or as a severe antisocial personality (sociopath). These families, though similar in the degree of dysfunction, characteristically have disparate styles, which have been described by Helm Stierlin. In a series of publications[6,7,8] he and co-workers have outlined two patterns of separation found in adolescence and related these patterns to family characteristics and to individual symptoms of emotional illness in offspring. Combining Stierlin's stylistic concepts with the negentropy framework enriches the systems approach and increases its utility in organizing family information.

He terms these two separation patterns *centripetal* and *cen-*

trifugal, and they have the following characteristics: In centripetal families, the family itself holds greater promise for the fulfillment of crucial relationship needs than does the outside world. The world outside the family boundaries is perceived only dimly and appears frightening and threatening. Separation in such a family is, therefore, quite difficult. Characteristically the children lag behind peers in their investment in people and institutions in the larger world. This style binds children to the family.

In poorly differentiated, relatively entropic, severely dysfunctional families, such a centripetal pattern dramatically increases the chances that disturbances in offspring will assume a schizophrenic pattern.

Centrifugal families differ remarkably in basic assumptions and behavioral patterns. Sources of gratification are viewed by this group as existing essentially outside, not inside, the family. Parents and children look beyond the family orbit when frustrated, feeling considerable pressure to distance themselves when family conflict is great and to seek peers as solace. This style expels children from the family. Premature separation is the rule, and early sexual activities characterize the children of these families. Sex mates are usually treated as pawns, and shallow relationships develop frequently and terminate abruptly. In extremely dysfunctional centrifugal families, the children are very prone to behavior that will be labeled "sociopathic" and, as often happens, when institutionalized will be in jail rather than in psychiatric hospitals.

These centripetal/centrifugal stylistic differences may be seen in less dysfunctional families and even in competent ones. As family functioning abilities increase, however, the style is softened and modified by the varied and multiple patterns present. It is only in quite entropic systems that the pure styles are dramatic and pervasive.

CHARACTERISTICS OF CENTRIPETAL SD FAMILIES

The boundary between this family system and the rest of the world is relatively impermeable. There is little openness to the outside, and minimum ability to contribute or receive useful symbolic material from systems outside the family. In addition, the differentiation of subsystems is inadequate. It is often difficult to tell who is parent, who is child, or to distinguish between one and another member of such a family as to beliefs, feelings, perceptions, and wishes. There is a concerted family effort to fight against all differentiation, because it leads to separateness that is terrifying. Third, the purposes and goals are blurred and unclear to all concerned. It is evident that, in our society, a well functioning family "self-destructs." Two people come together and form a family; they develop an ongoing relationship that has continuity, history, rules, and expectations. As children arrive, the system expands with the evolving goal of developing competent human beings who have increasing autonomy, individuality, and shared personal power with the parents. Eventually, these offspring will separate and establish other households. This approach to human development in family structure could be termed horizontal since many needs for support for interactive self-definition are necessarily met by relationships with social structures other than the vertical structure of multi-generational families seen in many other cultures.

Such horizontal interlocking allows for a greater autonomy and a capacity to adapt to a changing social environment, but it makes the family members quite vulnerable to boundary difficulties. In severely dysfunctional families, children receive little help in evolving autonomy. Instead, they are actively prevented from such growth.

In addition, subsystems and individuals within the family are inadequately differentiated. The parental coalition, the "leading edge" subsystem, is characteristically in shambles. Mother and father usually manage to render each other relatively impotent in efforts to make decisions or to exert personal power. They do not communicate well nor are they able to negotiate differences.

Usually the father has little power. Garmezy and Rodnick[9] found that if a schizophrenic patient had a dominant father. this correlated with better premorbid adjustment and a better prognosis. Mishler and Waxler[10] found that a passive and relatively powerless father is usually complemented by a coalition between the mother and the patient. When a child wields greater power in the family than a parent, a breakdown of role differentiation destroys the effectiveness of the parental coalition. In these families, a parent takes a sibling-like role and is both a child and a parent, and yet neither. These "skewed" families (as termed by Lidz, Fleck, and Cornelison)[11] break generation barriers with a potent parent/child coalition. Family confusion, incoherence, and frequent disqualifications of meaning result in the failure of children to accomplish necessary developmental tasks. Lidz, Fleck and Cornelison also noted another disturbed style associated with process schizophrenic offspring which they termed a "schismatic" family. Parents are unable to negotiate differences and set up rival kingdoms in which children are forced to take sides, then are punished for doing so by the other parent. Such preoccupation with intense, conflicted family forces prevents children from investing in normal developmental activities. Peer relationships, individual interests and goals (which are necessary in the evolution of selfhood) do not develop.

Autonomy

The progressive differentiation of family members that is a necessary part of individual self development is not possible in SD families. Closeness in the family is behaviorally defined as thinking and feeling alike. A child or a parent who expresses unique thoughts, ideas, or needs threatens the system. Only in these families do we find any significant number of invasive or mind-reading statements.

In contrast to a family orientation that promotes autonomy, SD families behave much as mutually intimidating members of an illicit gang, checking each other out when a question is posed and making sure that any response from one member is not out of line with the group and does not involve one person's being comprehensively different.

By punishing the expression of personal thoughts and feelings, the family system encourages alienation within one's self and from others. Family members are not aware of how much "group think" they do and how little respect they give to individuals' subjective reality. Bowen labeled this phenomenon an "undifferentiated family ego mass."[12] Wynne speaks of it as "pseudomutuality."[13] Relationships remain undefined and unclear. Laing has termed the communicational qualities resulting from this lack of individuation as "mystification," a chronic confusion in which no encounter makes any sense.[14] All of these terms describe essentially the same interactional deficit: the failure of families to help offspring develop the clear self boundaries that provide a coherent identity. In fact, a useful way to view process schizophrenia is as a desperate attempt to leave the family's murky, quicksand-filled communicational swamp in a radical fashion, since orderly leavetaking is impossible.

The information theorists, Shannon and Weaver, in discussing system models of processing information, stated that if a correction channel containing a memory bank is added to a system, the error in decoding incoming messages can be reduced to acceptable levels, provided the memory bank has a capacity as great as the uncertainty of the incoming messages.[15] If this rather dry engineering observation is rephrased in human terms, it can be quite useful in comprehending the communicational defects of these dysfunctional families. If an individual has enough coherent past encounters recorded in memory, he can usually decode and successfully interpret the relatively ambiguous messages transmitted between people.

In these SD families, children receive few clear messages during early developmental years. Hence, they have stored little information about interpersonal reality, the feelings, purposes, goals, and meanings found in, and with, other people. This severely hampers relationships both within the family and beyond. The child has an ever increasing difficulty in relating to others as he continues his physical growth. He is unable to attend to necessary developmental tasks because of this personal handicap and the anxiety-laden intensity of unresolved family conflict. He is trapped in the family of origin, not because he desires it, but because of stunted interpersonal capability.

Such families use many communicational mechanisms to disrupt expressive clarity, blur self-boundaries, and evade personal responsibility. Some of these mechanisms include:

1) *Invasiveness, the disqualification of another's experience.* Just as individuals in these families treat their own unique thoughts and feelings shabbily, they also show little respect for the worth of another's experience. Invading another's personal life space by speaking for that other person is a powerful method of maintaining a group ego, making it impossible to be separate and acceptable. Invasive communication can be physical, as in infancy, when a mother feeds her child when she herself feels discomfort rather than responding to clues from the child.[16] Continued later into symbolic interaction, invasions destroy confidence in one's ability to know his own mind and body. "You don't really feel that way; you really love your sister. You're not angry at her." "What do you mean, you feel lonely? You've got lots of friends; you are very popular." This verbal style contributes to double binds.[17] If one disagrees, he is ungrateful and uncooperative; if he docilely acquiesces, his unique experience is mangled and pervasive confusion ensues.

2) *Question asking.* Mishler and Waxler found a much higher incidence of question asking in the interaction of families containing a schizophrenic patient.[10] For example, a mother asks, "What do you think is strong about our family, children?" without stating her own opinions, which might serve as a model and invite negotiation. This maneuver forces the other person into a vulnerable position with little threat to the speaker.

3) *Evasiveness.* In interviews with mothers in SD families,[18] there was a high incidence of evasive responses. This mechanism effectively obscures knowledge of the speaker and it contributes to incoherence when pervasive and continuous.

4) *Shifts.* The statement of one's personal subjective view followed by the statement of an opposite position, without any of the necessary glue to acknowledge ambivalence, has been termed a shift.[18] SD family members frequently express ambivalence in this form of naked opposites.

5) *Silence.* A person's value can be diminished by having his

words fall flat with no response. This is an effective means of undermining him without assuming any personal or individual responsibility.

6) *Sarcasm and irony.* These complex communicational methods, with double and triple meanings, are hard to decipher or to confront. If a person is bold enough to challenge such sarcasm or irony, there is an easy retreat with such responses as, "You must have misunderstood. Of course I didn't mean what you are suggesting."

All of these communicational methods allow relationships with a minimum of clarity, personal responsibility, and differentiation of individuals, and they are usual in SD families.

Tasks

The degree of functioning difficulty found in at least one child is well correlated with the amount of difficulty the whole family has in performing group tasks. SD families are unable to perform tasks (such as planning an outing together) that are easy and enjoyable for competent families. The lack of individuality in such families leads to profound difficulties in negotiation; goal direction is lost and the family wallows like a rudderless ship. These families rarely succeed in deciding among themselves what to plan, and they often stop working on the task entirely and begin to discuss past events or dreams of a distant future. Wynne and Singer asked families as a group to interpret ink blots and found that the communicational styles of the family were diagnostic of offspring.[19] An acute lack of family clarity or shared focus of attention was associated with the presence of a schizophrenic offspring.

Mood or Feeling Tone

As one might expect, these families, with their lack of differentiation, extreme difficulty in defining purposes and goals, and marked difficulty in task performance, have the most painful feeling

tone of any group. In the Timberlawn study, the feeling tone subscale was the most definitive of families with psychotic offspring.

In addition to overall mood or feeling tone, there are several
other measurable aspects of feeling. These include the degree of
expressiveness of feelings, quality of empathy (the degree of
awareness and responsiveness to others' feelings), and the degree
of unresolved conflict. SD families scored quite low in all of these
parameters.

I believe *expectations*, that is, the results one expects from
human encounters, are central to these observations. Severely dysfunctional family members believe that encounters inevitably produce a destructive result, that human interaction is necessarily oppositional. To appreciate this expectancy is to understand the result
of disturbed communication patterns: the prevention of genuine
encounter. It also explains the pervasive, unpleasant feeling tone,
since the choice is either to avoid conflict and be alone or to engage in encounters that threaten the self, relationships, and the
family system.

Many researchers have described this negative affective climate
that permeates SD families. Singer and Wynne, using TAT card
stimuli, found that families of autistic children demonstrated pervasive cynicism and deprecating attitudes; parents of young adult
schizophrenics had a mood of depression, hopelessness, and despair.[20] Lennard and Bernstein were impressed by the disparaging
and sarcastic comments and the absence of affirmation in the inter-
changes of families with a schizophrenic member.[21] Riskin and
Faunce[22] and Mishler and Waxler[10] also noted this same painful
discord.

Absence of warmth in these families is striking. Warmth is considered important by almost all professionals concerned with
human growth and development, but often remains undefined, as if
everyone shared the same understanding of its meaning. The definition consistent throughout this book is: Human warmth is human
need, honestly expressed, with the recognition of the limits of the
other person. This definition clearly associates warmth with need.
Many people associate warmth only with giving to another, without

including an awareness of one's own needs; operationally, this error leads to a virtuous, sterile interaction. Even if needs can be consciously acknowledged, however, things can go awry if they are not clearly expressed. Disappointment and frustration, rather than a sense of warm caring, will occur if they are communicated obscurely. Finally, even if one's needs are acknowledged and expressed clearly, but do not relate or mesh with the other person's capacity to meet those needs, then frustration, anger, resentment, and guilt (rather than warm interaction) result.

The SD family members are handicapped in all aspects of relating. Recognition and communication of needs require acceptance of individual selfhood and experience in acknowledging and expressing feelings. Awareness of the limitations of others requires communicational clarity. Hence, depression, despair, and cynicism pervade the SD family.

Trust

Burnham, Gladstone, and Gibson[23] describe a problem of schizophrenic patients that they term a "need-fear dilemma," which is an individual expression of the family system qualities just discussed. Such patients have a great need for sharing with another, but are pathetically inept in doing so and distrust others profoundly.

Of course, the fear and suspicion seen in these family members are striking in degree rather than in kind. All of us have a form of this need-fear dilemma, some hesitation in risking and reaching toward family and friends, even at times when the pain of aloneness is great. Some wariness in choosing someone with whom to share is wise—not everyone will treat us kindly.

But the SD family members have doctrinaire distrust, and have a family system that perpetuates that quality. Whenever there is little or no respect for subjective reality, and separateness is considered terrible disloyalty, a basic developmental task remains unfinished: building basic trust in the world as a potentially safe and gratifying place.[26] In this system a child betrays himself and his family by moving effectively in any direction.

Just as trust is minimal, so is personal choice, for many of the same reasons. In SD families, choice in any but the most elemental activities is almost nonexistent, since it requires fairly clear personal boundaries, an atmosphere of trust, and confidence that subjective matters will be respected.

Mythology

In the Timberlawn studies, families with a psychotic offspring had the most incongruent mythology of all families studied, a finding supported by other research.[25] Therapists who treat severe schizophrenics and their families often observe that the identified patient shows extremely bizarre and distancing behavior, yet other family members consider him "normal," or, at most, obstinate and manipulative. The peculiar tenacity with which they cling to incongruent family myths is a major challenge to a therapist who introduces the possibility of effective change.

For example, in interviews with the family of a schizophrenic adolescent, the mother often stated that the patient was quite capable, in fact, more capable than his father, and that he was simply misunderstood by others. These statements went unchallenged by all family members, despite the child's consistent failures in school and in every interpersonal relationship outside his family.

Families maintain incongruous myths by careful teaching and a variety of mechanisms such as denial, projection, and impermeability. With their shared idiosyncratic perceptions, few corrective mechanisms are available to help individual family members adjust to broader consensual reality. The incongruence is a source, as well as a result, of mixed messages and confusion. Individuals in disturbed families live in two very different realities, the mythic and the observable, and must adapt to both. They must blot out their own perceptions frequently and learn to operate in shared fantasy. A rigid and impermeable family boundary contributes heavily to this learning and reduces the possibility of significant friendships and allies. Like Hans Christian Anderson's child who blurted out, "The king hasn't any clothes on," a comment on observations contradictory to family beliefs might help to increase reality testing, but would threaten the brittle structure of the system.

Time-Binding

Many years ago, Korzibski[26] defined man as a time-binder, and he considered this to be the most important characteristic separating man from other animals. Korzibski meant that each generation could conceivably begin where the last left off; cultures could progress by learning and remembering without re-experiencing. For individuals, time-binding refers to the capacity to have a past, a present, and a future as a part of one's self-awareness, and to be able to focus on any of these at will. (H. S. Sullivan was describing a failure of this capacity when he gave as one definition of schizophrenia the inability to control the contents of consciousness.) This capacity is not equal in all men or in all families because there may be compelling needs to be unaware of the passage of time. Denial, while temporarily alleviating overt pain, leads to greater dysfunction.

The key to the recognition of time's passage is awareness of change. Any device used to measure time is capable of regular change: clock, watch, the sun, the moon. Interpersonal time also requires change. The communicational maneuvers observed in the SD family maximize the difficulty of human encounter, of sharing and of change resulting from such encounter. In order for relationships to produce change, there must be coherence or a shared understanding. When one observes competent family members as they are relating to each other, the shared focus of attention is evident. There are clear responses; things change as the family functions. Through encounters these families acknowledge the passage of time. Children in competent families often say, "I remember when I was little, and I didn't know that." Or, "When I go to high school, I will. . . ," or "When I grow up. . . ." Parents talk of their children's increasing capabilities and understanding, and they contrast such effectiveness with earlier times. Awareness and discussion of time's passage are unusual in severely dysfunctional families; instead, an observer gets a strong impression of a conspiracy to deny the passage of time, to "hold back the dawn," and to fantasize that everything and everyone will remain the same. There will be no growing up, no death; the world of Peter Pan will become the real world.

Here is a description written by a severely schizoid young woman from such a family:

> I lived in absoluteness. My world moved in a slow, unchanging rhythm of a dream. It *was* a dream. Nothing moved in the basic outlines of our existence. Life was an absolute and predictable as the path we had beaten between our house and our grandparents'. Relationships were secure. They were the same when I woke in the morning as they had been when I went to bed the night before. Life was slow then. We lived a rhythm, but it was not based on time. It was based on direction. We moved in a circle. Time belonged to the world, but we belonged to ourselves. We were frozen. I wore that rhythm like a ring around the faithful finger of my life.

Change is an integral part of competent family life and is fueled by biological realities. The "arrow" of time, as entropy has been called, speaks in two dramatic ways: in the presence of human growth and development and in inexorable aging and death. The infant becomes a toddler, who, if fed and cared for properly, becomes stronger than his parents, whose own bodily functions are on the wane. Competent families accept this; SD family systems reject it as a product of, and a reason for, severe communicational disturbances. If one is not a self except as part of a timeless, unalterable family structure, then the threat of loss, from increasing competence of children or failing abilities of parents, becomes devastating.

Object Loss

Searles has written movingly of the relationship between schizophrenia and the fear of death.

> The ostensible prosaic fact of the inevitability of death is, in actuality, one of the supremely potent sources of man's anxiety, and the feeling responses to this aspect of reality are among the most intense and complex which it is possible for us to experience. The defense mechanisms of psychiatric illness, including the oftentimes exotic-appearing defenses found in schizophrenia, are designed to keep out of the individual's awareness—among other anxiety-provoking aspects of inner and outer reality—this simple fact of life's finitude. Various characteristics of our culture serve to maintain our obliviousness to this fact of inevitable death, and the psychodynamics of schizophrenia may antedate the time in the individual's life when death's inevitability tends to confront him. It is the author's impression that this particular deeply anxiety-provoking aspect of reality is one of the major threats which the schizophrenic process is serving to deny.[27]

Searles was speaking of the schizophrenic individual and not of the family system from whence he came. Paul and Grosser,[28] however, have similar views from experiences with family systems with a severely disturbed (usually schizophrenic) member. They see the bizarre communication and disturbances of reality as resulting from a poorly handled loss of a loved one, and they focus treatment on helping family members to grieve properly, and to accept what was previously unacceptable.

The loss of children and parents through successful attainment of adulthood is a ubiquitous source of pain. Some family system characteristics may increase or decrease that pain, notably, the nature of the parental coalition and the ability of parents and children to reach outside the family boundary for self-definition—to have one's identity founded on a larger base.

The SD family fails in both. Its parental coalition is most fragile, and the impermeability of the family boundary handicaps everyone in utilizing outside resources. There is a sad paradox in this tendency to clutch one another and yet fail to comprehend each other.

There are paradoxes in the functioning of all families, of course—the competent as well as the disturbed. For example, in order to be a competent parent, one must not be too enamoured of the role. In order to have satisfactory relationships with parent or child, one must be able to live without the other.

SD family members have a pervasive belief that the basic nature of man is evil, just as is found in the midrange families discussed in Chapter 4, but there is a significant difference in the definition of this evil. Here, the evidence of perversity is the desire to be separate, to have different opinions, feelings, and beliefs. Denial, a basic mistrust, depression, and expectation of treachery result.

PRODUCTS OF CENTRIPETAL SD FAMILIES

The outcome of child raising in these families is somewhat varied, despite the rigid patterns and relative lack of differentiation. Products include process schizophrenics, offspring with no evident emotional illness (here termed the "well" sibling of the process schizophrenic) and borderline personalities. These categories of offspring of severely disturbed centripetal families will be discussed here.

The Process Schizophrenic

It is important to distinguish between "process" and "reactive" schizophrenia. Though evidence suggests that they represent points on a continuum, they represent degrees of dysfunction that differ significantly, and individuals so labeled come from families that are quite different. It is the midrange family, discussed in Chapter 4, which produces individuals peculiarly vulnerable to reactive schizophrenic episodes, while the SD centripetal families characteristically develop children with process schizophrenia.

Langfeldt[29] pioneered in evolving this concept of two varieties of schizophrenia. In 1956, he noted that the classical Kraepelinian label of dementia praecox (later to be called process) was given to individuals with a poorly developed personality (usually introverted), an insidious onset of illness, and an absence of demonstrable precipitating factors.

In contrast, "schizophreniform" (later termed reactive) schizophrenia was applied to individuals with a capable premorbid personality, an acute onset of psychosis, and demonstrable precipitating factors. Assumptions of an organic versus functional etiology have always been a part of such separations of types, and the recent work of Kety, Rosenthal and their associates[30] using this diagnostic separation associated genetic factors with process but not reactive schizophrenia. Zigler and Phillips[31] noted that premorbid social competence was the primary factor in the separation of types and questioned the usefulness of such a separation, since it could interfere with the evolution of a unitary concept of psychopathology. Properly defined and understood, however, the process/reactive orientation can assist in understanding emotional illness as a unitary phenomenon. These two labels relate to preexisting social competence, the degree that an individual showed personal adaptive skills in his premorbid state. This social functioning can be conceptualized as a continuum just as family competence is in the framework provided in this book. Various researchers[1,10,11] offer data suggesting that the severity of schizophrenia is directly related to the degree of disturbed functioning of the family.

A systems focus of research in schizophrenia is not limited to family variables but, by its very nature, includes all variables found to be important in self-definition. For example, Goldfarb[32] offers compelling data from his studies of childhood schizophrenia that some children who receive a diagnosis of schizophrenia have evidence of neurological damage. These children have families with no evident communicational aberrations. On the other hand, schizophrenic children with no evidence of organicity usually have families with severe communicational pathology.

Kety and Rosenthal, in their study of offspring of Danish schizophrenic patients adopted as newborns, impressively document a genetic influence in the most severe schizophrenic states, and it would be unwise to assume that the correlation of family systems characteristics with the psychopathology in offspring rules out organic biologic and genetic factors.

As an individual tries to master the developmental tasks of childhood and adolescence, there are many critical factors. There is ample room in a systems approach for the inclusion of biological and genetic factors, though the primary focus here is on family interactional factors.

Case Example: Charles, age 14, entered the adolescent ward following a bizarre attempt to hold up a food store with a toy pistol. The hold-up, poorly planned and poorly executed, was interpreted as a cry for help by the arresting officers who brought him to the hospital. On admission, Charles was rambling and incoherent, remarkably unconcerned and offhand about his plight, and carried himself something like a displaced Polish aristocrat: haughty, aloof, and grandiose. He portrayed himself, initially, as unusually capable in engineering and architecture. When invited to select a project in occupational therapy, he showed an inability to put his thoughts and ideas into a coherent goal-directed activity. First, he wished to build a draftsman's table for himself, and after a few ineffective weeks with encouragement and help from the occupational therapist, he created a rather shabby, lopsided but recognizable shoepolish box. His relationships with other patients were almost nil, and the patient group viewed him as eccentric and odd.

Charles was the oldest of two children. His father was a mild and passive clerk, his mother an obese, domineering woman who usually spoke for her husband and son. The mother had many hostile encounters with the hospital staff; she insisted there was nothing wrong with her son and that the staff was crazy for keeping him in "a looney bin." Though the mother presented herself as powerful, she retreated into obvious disorganization when any decision was necessary, and deferred to her husband. She presented a shifting, evasive and relatively incoherent communicative style, and the father, though quietly effective outside the family, had little overt power in relating to her.

Family therapy was instituted for the father, mother, and remaining younger son; Charles was hospitalized for two years with the therapist's goal to assist him in developing some social competence and self-definition. A follow-up five years later found a somewhat subdued 21-year-old who worked regularly as a helper in a diner, with a rather pleasant, shy and "kooky" demeanor which allowed him only peripheral contact with his fellow man. A marriage of several weeks' duration had been the only break in a monastic, lonely life-style. His younger brother, defined by family and society as adequate, was doing reasonably well in college.

Here I would like to offer a unitary definition of emotional illness used throughout this book: Emotional illness results from a deficiency of satisfying, coherent, self-defining experiences with meaningful others. It is, regardless of diagnosis, a deficiency disease, one that results from failures (usually early) of family-child interaction that prevent a child from integrating the experiences necessary to provide adequate trust, self-definition, and ego skills. Such a definition includes both biological and social system factors; the relative personal failure may be due primarily to organic deficit and/or to environmental lacks. This is analogous to a computer which may err if its transistors are defective, or if its programming is deficient, or if there is a combination of such factors.

I focus on environmental factors in this book, for it is written to show the interpersonal qualities significant in ego development both in families and in psychotherapeutic situations. This is in no way to be construed as a de-emphasis of biological factors, the neurological, genetic, organic, and familial contributions to a particular person's success or failure in developing capable personhood. Any adequate evaluation of an emotionally ill person must include careful evaluation of the physical self.

People diagnosed as schizophrenic, whether the qualifying adjective is childhood, adolescent, or process, as well as those who are given the label "borderline personality," have a profound deficiency of human relationships experienced and remembered as coherent. Their boundaries between self and others are tenuous, their basic trust in self and the world is minimal. In addition, these patients have a profound difficulty in resolving ambivalence and making choices.

The modal process schizophrenic is an adolescent who has a history of interpersonal failure falling in one of the two groups described by Arieti many years ago as "schizoid" and "stormy."[33]

The *schizoid* personality is withdrawn, shy, and unaggressive. He attempts to be as inconspicuous as possible. He is easy to intimidate, easily frightened, and tied to his family of origin. He accepts such anchoring with little overt struggle.

The *stormy* personality, equally trapped in the primary family, does not accept this fate easily, and flails ineffectually at family and the outside world. He tries many behavioral patterns during early childhood and latency, and will be described as "hard to raise" by parents, just as the schizoid child will be described as a "marvelous child who never gave us any trouble." Neither personality type has satisfying peer relationships, since the children are so mired in the family's conflictual morass.

Viewed from an information-processing standpoint, both patterns derive from a deficiency of self-defining experiences and represent chronic overload of information that cannot be processed. The schizoid person attempts to reduce the pain of incomprehensible interaction by diminishing this interaction, while the stormy child attempts active control of a puzzling world and frequently looks like an agitated, organic patient whose orientation is poor due to environmental overload.

Neither pattern is effective in obtaining positive emotional responses from others, the necessary preparation for separating from the family. Sooner or later, profound despair descends upon the patient-to-be, and even further withdrawal or agitation results, beyond the capacity of the family to accept. At this point, all the classical symptoms of the schizophrenic state become manifest.

The Schizophrenic State

The following is an interactional description of the schizophrenic state. A schizophrenic person is, at a basic level, despairing and without hope of communicating successfully with others due to his previous experiences in family life. He is alone and unable to believe that he might have a coherent, satisfying identity in any social system.[34]

A conventional definition of schizophrenia is "one of a group of psychotic reactions, often beginning after adolescence or in young adulthood, characterized by fundamental disturbances in reality relationships and concept formation, with associative, affective, behavioral, and intellectual disturbances in varying degrees and mixtures. These reactions are marked by a tendency to withdraw, inappropriate moods, unpredictable disturbances in stream of thought, regressive tendencies (to the point of deterioration), and often hallucinations and delusions."[35] The schizophrenic process consists of severe alienation, self-fragmentation, childlike regression, and difficulty in coherent communication. In standard psychiatric texts schizophrenia is referred to as a "thinking disorder," even though the original primary characteristics of the disorder, described by Bleuler (who coined the term), did not refer predominately to thinking. His classical "four A's" (affective disturbance, ambivalence, autism, and associational difficulties) describe feelings and relationship phenomena in three of the four categories.[36]

Many studies have attempted to describe the disturbances in thinking (supposedly limited to schizophrenic patients), but to date there is no evidence that these disturbed people have specific changes in brain substance, or in the functioning of their minds, that are responsible for their strange methods of communicating. Clinical studies[37,38,39] suggest that schizophrenia is not primarily a thinking disturbance, but a disturbance of relationships. To be most effective with the schizophrenic patient, a therapist addresses himself to the development of a satisfying and meaningful human relationship between himself and the patient. If such a relationship develops, the patient no longer shows evidence of "thinking disorder," but communicates comprehensibly. He may continue to have grave difficulties in relating well to others, but his thinking (or his talking, or writing, or behavior, which are the ways all of us share our thinking) is no longer bizarre and strange.

Let us examine some of the formal difficulties most frequently ascribed to such patients: blocking, condensation, loose association, ideas of reference, and "paleologic thinking." Blocking, the break in orderly thought processes that temporarily inhibits communicative efforts, is also seen in highly anxious sane people, and it can be understood as a result of overwhelming anxiety.

"Loose associations" and "condensations" are more specific for schizophrenia and are not so easily explained as resulting from a feeling state. "Loose associations" are shifts in subject matter as a person moves from one thought to another; the clinician hears incomprehensible ideas and allusions, and he labels the patient psychotic. The labeling is a social process, whether in a clinical interview or in psychological testing. One human, as the expert, classifies another ill because the interaction is incomprehensible. Sophisticated clinicians learn to correct for their major social deficiencies and are aware that, for example, a middle-class, Midwestern, Protestant physician, interning in Bellevue in New York City, must be extremely careful when calling another person schizophrenic because of communicational difficulties if that person is an overwrought Catholic, Puerto Rican, lower-class young woman speaking of religious concerns. That this correction process, learned primarily by "clinical experience," may be inadequate is suggested by surveys[40] showing that schizophrenic diagnoses increase directly as patients come from lower and lower economic groups. Clinicians must reach further to comprehend those who fall outside their own social experience in order to diagnose individual rather than social deviance.

"Condensation" refers to the telescoping of several ideas which would be understandable if shared sequentially, but are incoherent when stated without necessary elaboration. These quirks in speaking result from despair. For any person to communicate effectively with another, both speaker and hearer must expect that the other is receptive and "tuned in"; otherwise, the discourse is, at best, formal and ritualized, and, at worse, pointless. A schizophrenic person has suffered a long series of unsatisfying, disappointing, and frequently mystifying encounters with others, including family members. These experiences lead him to be quite hopeless about finding significant people who can understand. He therefore feels there is little use in trying to communicate his thoughts in detail.

To illustrate, a young woman, hospitalized with an acute schizophrenic episode, told me of her early life in Arkansas, of moving to Little Rock at the age of seven, where she began to have stomach pains "like the piano player." I did not understand at all what she meant, said so, and asked if she could help me understand. "Oh . . . well, today at lunch in the hospital one of the patients was banging on the piano instead of eating. He was trying to get attention, just like I was doing as a child. When I had all those stomachaches. I was trying to get the attention of my parents because I was scared, and I didn't want to get involved with the other kids." Suddenly, something quite eerie became comprehensible. What was the difference? I believe it was that someone had reached out and aggressively urged her to make sense. Her interpersonal set changed as she experienced a flash of hope that another person might understand.

"Ideas of reference" are expressed beliefs that events taking place in the ordinary world have special meaning and significance to that person. For example, a patient who believed, for religious reasons, that he was not supposed to eat certain foods, observed that when he began to eat forbidden foods other patients around him made unusual noises or signals, such as dropping a fork, presumably to chide him for transgressing. He believed wholeheartedly that these other patients knew of his private religious views and were signalling him. His erroneous assumption was a result of feeling isolated, unable to communicate effectively with others. Ideas of reference serve as assurances that "I am not really alone." There is a sense of belonging in the world when there are clues, however strange and unreasonable, from others indicating that people are concerned and interested. This patient later observed that, as he became capable of talking with others, the strange signals disappeared. He discovered that ability in ordinary discourse eliminated the need for magical means of sharing.

Arieti described what he considers a fundamental disturbance in the thinking of schizophrenia as paleologic or predicate thinking, the Von Domarus principle.[41] This occurs when the schizophrenic makes identification by predicate rather than by subject (as normal people do). He uses the example of a young schizophrenic woman who says, "I am the Virgin Mary," with the logic as follows: Mary was a virgin, I am a virgin; therefore, I am the Virgin Mary. At first glance, this may seem crazy and qualitatively different from the thinking patterns of the sane. However, Sarbin, Toft, and Bailey,[42] examining the methods psychiatrists use to arrive at diagnoses, suggest that they employ what might legitimately be called predicate thinking: "Jones has a flat affect. Jones has ideas of reference and loose associations; therefore, Jones is a schizophrenic."

It is conventional to consider a group of attributes found in an individual and diagnose from these characteristics. Any single feature is not sufficient; it requires several for this identification by predicate to be made. Novice clinicians, if inept and frightened, may slip over into pathological predicate thinking: "Jones is hallucinating, schizophrenics hallucinate, therefore Jones is schizophrenic."

Fear, loneliness, despair, and inadequate information can cause such misidentification in normal and psychotic individuals. Nearly everyone, on a busy street in a strange city, has seen the familiar figure of a friend, hurried to catch up with him, only to draw back in embarrassment from a total stranger. The tilt of the head, the structure of the jaw, the carriage of the shoulders were similar, but not the same. From a distance, loneliness or emotional need caused a mistake. Such an experience illustrates why humans reduce the number of predicates necessary to make definitions. Our critical evaluations of judgments are inversely related to the magnitude of our human needs. We use fewer clues and make more misidentifications when we are lonely. Pathological predicate thinking can occur when a person is devoid of coherent satisfying human relationships, as the person grasps at straws in an attempt at self-definition.

"Delusions" are firm beliefs not substantiated by others' observations. They can be a desperate attempt to make personal and subjective sense of one's world, even though one is too alone to develop shared, consensual explanations. For example, a delusion that "somebody is after me," or "the people in my boarding house talk about me and are plotting my destruction," expresses the desperate hope that "somebody cares." Even though a delusion may be painful and frightening, it is reassuring in that it provides a world aware of one's existence.

Hallucinations (sensory experiences not shared by others in the social environment) are in many ways similar to delusions. Sensory isolation experiments show the susceptibility of any person to the fabrication of sensory experience if he is deprived of relationships and input clues.[43]

It is quite reasonable to consider that schizophrenia is not an incomprehensible intrusion from a dangerous outside world nor simply a biochemical aberration, but rather a manifestation of a profound life crisis, with the temporary or permanent loss of a sense of belonging in any social structure. This loss of a coherent sense of self is an expression of aloneness and despair due to the great disparity between the individual's needs (especially for intimacy) and his social skill in gratifying those needs in his particular current environment. It is not surprising that many adolescents succumb to the schizophrenic state, since there is a powerful combination of stronger internal drives and greater social demands for autonomous choice-making during this developmental period.

"Well" Siblings of the Process Schizophrenic

A question often asked when family systems concepts are presented is, "How can family factors be so important in severe individual pathology, when frequently only one child is found to be so disturbed?" Indeed, how do the siblings of process schizophrenics survive and (presumably) do well if the family rules are so discouraging to self-development?

To respond, I wish to refer to the multiple factors involved in developing an adequate self: the genetic endowment, the intrauterine life (without essential food items, the brain cannot function adequately),[44] birth factors (prematurity, for example, is more common in children later to be diagnosed as schizophrenic),[45] and constitutional factors that are somewhat more vague (the monozygotic twin, later to be diagnosed schizophrenic, is usually the smaller, more timid, less physically powerful of the two).[46]

But it is inadequate simply to invoke biology when systems concepts falter. It is more useful to try to understand the well siblings of schizophrenic patients without invoking such significant but often nebulous factors.

It is important to keep in mind that all children in any family, though close in age (even monozygotic twins), are subjected to very different family influences and are expected to play quite different roles in the family drama.[11,12,47] The child who becomes schizophrenic usually is one chosen as especially important in an unresolved parental conflict, and he is offered up as a sacrifice to assuage the pain of the difficult parental relationship. He has a demanding, complex family task which requires attention and energy that are needed for developmental tasks. The full force of the confusing, mystifying family pattern is centered in this special child.

The "well" sibling of such patients may also show severe emotional disburbance, though he functions adequately in school and career. Characteristically, this person is emotionally blunted and constricted and insensitive to feelings and nuances; he has great difficulty with close relationships. He usually resents family involvement and tries to stay out of family interaction. After he has left home, for example, if a research study attempts to pull him back, he resists; he expresses relief at being out of the system and a strong desire to stay away.[46] He may have been less trapped in the family's cognitive swamp only at the cost of constriction of his emotional life. Since he was less caught up in the struggle than an ill sibling, he was able to develop some relationships outside the family. The well sibling identifies with peers and learns from them, finding more support outside the family than within.

In clinical work with "well" siblings of schizophrenics in adulthood, I have found them quite susceptible to depression, alcohol abuse, and interpersonal problems that are expressed in unhappy marriages or multiple divorces. Though these children from SD families find some confidence in remaining distant from the intense, unresolved family conflict, and can establish a beachhead in the outside world, they are handicapped in defeating loneliness. They learn one lesson quite well: to get involved is to be destroyed. They maintain a viable and coherent self only by denying themselves much in the way of intimacy.

The Borderline Personality

A discussion of families that produce severely emotionally disturbed children with various types of difficulties should include the concept of borderline personality. Though it is not found in official diagnostic nomenclature, there is a body of literature describing this syndrome and attempting to relate it to etiological factors and treatment requirements. This category of patient and family could just as easily have been placed in the chapter on midrange families and their products. Functionally this group is truly borderline; it encompasses the upper limits of the severely dysfunctional group and the lower limits of midrange group of families.

It is also a very muddled category. A recent review[48] describes a confusion which could lead one to believe that it covers so much varied psychopathology as to be of questionable utility. Nevertheless, there is some consensus by several authors[49,50,51] of characteristics of this syndrome that was described years ago by Schmideberg[52] as a combination of psychotic, behavior disorder, neurotic, and normal behavior patterns, shifting from one to the other in a stable but unpredictable fashion. In other words, a person who is accurately described as a borderline personality stubbornly refuses to stay in any category of competent or incompetent human functioning, but, using a variety of defenses and coping mechanisms, manages to display the characteristics of all these categories at one time or another. Various authors have noted the borderline's tendency to integrate anger into a relationship,[51] his perplexing vagueness in interaction,[53] and his brief excursions into frank psychosis.[50]

The borderline patient frequently experiences a stormy life, but nevertheless presents a certain vagueness, blandness, or smoothness in style. Borderlines vary widely in social and vocational skills, from those with a history of substantial social and vocational accomplishment who are in adult outpatient therapy to those adolescents who are markedly inept in social and academic roles. Upon close inspection, one observes a dire poverty of interpersonal relationships. The borderline may have a series of stormy relationships or a more stable set of superficial ones, but will not experience long-term intimate encounters except for a peculiar kind of symbiosis with a parent.

Looking at borderline patients from another point of view, one sees a quartet of life-history characteristics: 1) A marked inability to tolerate anxiety; 2) poor impulse control, either chronically or episodically; 3) few channels for effective sublimation of drives; and 4) primary process thinking in the area of interpersonal relationships in an otherwise non-psychotic individual.[54]

Once such a category is accepted, there are unanswered questions as to the family characteristics of such a person. Masterson[55] offers a clinical impression that borderline adolescents come from borderline parents. His observations suggest that the families would be at the less functional end of the midrange group, possessing some areas of competence, with a markedly dominant style of functioning that often crumbles into chaotic interaction with no family member in control. Family research on this concept is hampered because criteria for diagnosis vary so widely.

Singer and Wynne have noted that the degree of illness of offspring (ranging from normal, to neurotic, to borderline, to remitting schizophrenia, to non-remitting schizophrenia) is associated with a parallel increase in the likelihood that parents receive a borderline diagnosis.[56] These observations suggest the association of family competence (determined both by the individual member's functioning and by the family's functioning) and the occurrence of borderline personality in an offspring. Refining the syndrome and evolving a shared definition will contribute to a greater understanding of family variables associated with the development of borderline personalities.

Case History: Carol, a 24-year-old dental hygienist, married, with a two-year-old son, entered the hospital because she could not function as a mother or wife. She mistrusted hospital personnel and alternated between withdrawal and poorly directed, highly emotional outbursts. She had ideas of reference, believing that ordinary actions of other patients and the staff were directed toward her and were derogatory, hostile, and contemptuous. Her childlike sweetness and little-girl seductiveness alternated rapidly with imperious and hostile verbal attacks. She was not actually delusional, but was disorganized and quite alienated. When asked to date the onset of her illness, she said impatiently, "I'm just like I've always been— I've never had anything, and I've always had to get everything for myself. I can remember when I was seven, walking around the grade-school play yard after everyone had gone home and picking up dried bits of orange peel and thinking they were delicious. That's the way my life has always been." At ages six to eight, she had a fantasy of a spanking machine which would beat and punish her for her many transgressions. Her view of the world and of herself had changed little; she saw herself as evil and the world as a place for punishment. The only child of alcoholic parents, she was placed in a foster-care unit at age two. She was retrieved at age four when her mother temporarily improved, and then later was placed with various relatives until the age of ten. Her mother died of cirrhosis when she was seven.

At ten, she went to live with her then severely alcoholic father. She remained with him as a kind of combination child, parent, and wife until he died when she was 13, and she went to a boarding school. She felt despairing, lost, and inept until she learned to pretend. She was able to mimic the social skills of her classmates and changed from a rather isolated adolescent to an apparently socially effective, vivacious girl. "I wasn't really any different, but I learned to act like the other kids." She entered training in dental hygiene following boarding school and graduated, although frequently on probation for misbehavior. Once again she began to live an isolated life and decided that she wanted a baby for company. She began to date and found a rigid and lonely accountant with whom she began to have regular sexual intercourse. She purposely avoided contraception, since her conscious effort was to have a child, someone to be close to. She became pregnant and delivered, showing no interest in marrying the father. Though he insisted on marriage and she complied, she had little to do with him following the birth of her son, and occupied herself with baby care. When the boy was 18 months of age, she became increasingly unstable, alternating between screaming attacks and guilt-laden attempts to reinstitute their symbiotic relationship. She sought psychiatric help first on an outpatient basis and later in the hospital for a three-month period. Carol changed little during that hospitalization except that her emotional outbursts were muted and her suspiciousness diminished some. In the following 12 years, she has had many therapists and several short hospital admissions, but has functioned in her profession.

CHARACTERISTICS OF CENTRIFUGAL SD FAMILIES

Information about the interactional characteristics of centrifugal SD families comes from clinical work, the Timberlawn study, and reported studies of families with delinquent offspring.

The severe boundary problem in this group of families is diffuseness, rather than impermeability, as in the centripetal group. The definition of family itself often becomes vague as parents separate, and father or mother surrogates shuffle in and out of the children's lives. Children often move early out of family settings by running away successfully or being placed in detention homes.

Family interaction is characterized by teasing manipulation and frequent open discord. In addition, family members manipulate the outside environment. Family organization is unstable, with no clear role definitions. Members frequently compete for roles and often abdicate expected ones. The father, especially, is apt to abdicate leadership, and no one else effectively assumes it.

In contrast to the centripetal SD families, there is evidence of pseudo-autonomy in the absence of effective relationship skills. Parents and children frequently go off on individual tangents, both verbally and behaviorally, with a resulting chaotic, disorganized effect.[1] Open quarrels are frequent with many hostile, "I" statements ("I won't—"; "I think—") and attacking, blaming statements, ("You always—"; "You never—"). Though the conflict is open rather than covert, as in the centripetal families, there is no greater ability to resolve it. Behavioral patterns parallel verbal ones and individuals often leave for extended periods of time, but are usually unsuccessful in finding sustained relationships in the outside world. When they return, they possess no more ability to function within the family than they had before leaving. Individual family members are quite concerned with their own satisfactions, but are usually frustrated, angry, depressed, and generally deprived, since they have so little ability to satisfy human needs which are met through sharing.

In these families, just as in the centripetal group, members take little personal responsibility, especially denying tender feelings. Angry feelings are usually claimed.

Neither parent consistently accepts nor abdicates power and responsibility. They frequently bicker and attack one another. Because of their inability to cooperate, the children have many opportunities to manipulate either parent for a momentary advantage. Effective parent/child coalitions are unusual, however, since these require more system stability. Discipline is attempted primarily through intimidation and direct control, which are doomed to fail because of the shifting power structure and the lack of cohesive emotional bonds. Family members are an undisciplined, rather surly crew, and an observer can sympathize with an individual member who futilely shouts for order.

These families, like the centripetal SD group, have very disordered communication with frequent incoherent topic shifts and an overall lack of clarity, though individual statements are usually comprehensible. There is great impermeability to each other's communicative efforts. In individual psychological tests, such family members reveal impaired ability for conceptual abstraction.

Family task performance is quite poor. The disorganization, ineffective discipline, and hostile, attacking behavior are so pervasive that negotiation is impossible; goals cannot be defined, much less attained.

An underlying depressive atmosphere is masked by intense conflict. Positive feelings, when expressed, often have syrupy, counterfeit quality. Empathic abilities are poor, and there is little warmth in family interaction. This deficit is for different reasons than in the SD centripetal group. Here, individual needs and wants are loudly proclaimed, but with such a pathetic unawareness of the other's reality that the result is frustration and attack rather than gratification. Their frequent self-punitive behavior implies severe individual guilt, though it is rarely voiced.

Family members have no greater ability to handle object loss than do those in centripetal SD families. There is painful, unmourned loss from the premature separation of children from their parents; in addition, the quarrelsome, conflict-ridden interaction and antisocial behavior of the children seem to be directed at warding off grief over emotional deprivation.

These families seem to view man as evil just as do the other SD families, but here the belief is lived out daily by members, rather than compulsively denied. Discipline is both harsh and hopelessly sporadic, reflecting a "what's-the-use?" attitude. Stabenau and co-workers[1] reported that parents of delinquents, in response to TAT cards, told stories of parents who were impersonal, strict, demanding, coercive, and punitive, and of children who submitted docilely. This suggests that such parents believe humans to be evil in essence, with salvation to be gained only by harsh, unempathic control.

PRODUCTS OF CENTRIFUGAL SD FAMILIES

The Antisocial Personality

The labels change, but this personality type persists. Like some other psychiatric syndromes, such as manic states, depression, and acute psychosis, this psychiatric syndrome reverberates through human history. Socially correct members of many cultures have described, moralized over, and futilely attempted to control these miserable people. Once they were termed "morally insane."[57] Later the term psychopath was applied.[58] For some time the label of sociopath was used to describe this severe behavioral aberration,[59] but in the current Psychiatric Diagnostic Manual the syndrome is covered under antisocial personality.[60]

The Manual describes the bare bones of the disorder: "basically unsocialized and whose behavior pattern brings them repeatedly into conflict with society. They are incapable of significant loyalty to individuals, groups, or social values. They are grossly selfish, callous, irresponsible, impulsive and unable to feel guilt or to learn from experience and punishment. Frustration tolerance is low. They tend to blame others or offer plausible rationalizations for their behavior . . ."

This official description includes themes usually associated with this syndrome: observable behavior that is emotionally immature and hostile to community rules, judgmental moralism ("selfish") in the labeler, and inferences of a lack of guilt.

Most often, the sociopath develops in a centrifugal SD family, which offers little affirmation of tenderness, gentleness, and honest expression of vulnerability, though they can be found as scapegoated members of centripetal, midrange families (a phenomenon discussed in Chapter 4). In a family structure with shifting power, incoherent communication, and overall rejection of the subjective and the tender and vulnerable, a child finds no way to be loved by obeying rules, no behavior patterns that are consistently rewarded by closeness and caring. As one consequence, he is in grave danger of being defined as "unsocialized" in adulthood.

With his efforts to perform in a way that promotes shared love rejected by caretakers, he develops a facade of, "I don't care," that, when superficially evaluated, makes him appear guilt-free.[58] Actually his guilt is pervasive but useless; he cannot show his inner feelings with any hope of reward, so he feels damned. Such irrevocable guilt directs action in destructive pathways, and the resulting socially unacceptable behavior invites responses that confirm his self-loathing.

He provokes rejection and punishment; the severity of his disorder can be determined by the degree to which this self-punitive quality is manifested. He creates a personal hell on earth deserved only by the totally evil. He believes in his own depravity and lives out this belief. Experience in the primary family teaches the sociopath-to-be that his feelings, impulses, and needs are so unacceptable that he must forever be outside the warmth of human relationship systems.

Self-defeating behavior expresses rage to an uncaring world. Premature death from suicide, drug abuse, or accident is a common behavioral expression of his tormented inner world.

RELATING FAMILY-SYSTEM INFORMATION TO TREATMENT EFFORTS

Treatment of the Schizophrenic

A psychotherapist who attempts to treat a schizophrenic patient does well to attend to system or contextual factors that relate to himself as well as to those surrounding his patient. Does the therapist have reasonably good sources of personal gratification (friends, family, and professional relationships)? These allow him to have an active, satisfying life outside his relationship with the despairing patient. Increasing self-definition is accomplished by experiencing relationships with others who are hopeful and possess the openness that comes from reasonably good self-esteem.

In addition, does the therapist have a considerable degree of social power in the treatment setting? It is difficult, if not impossible, to treat a patient who is isolated from, and distrustful of, the broader society unless the therapist possesses overt social power. Though such power is frightening to the patient, he is also reassured that he is negotiating with a valuable person.

With personal satisfactions and social power, the therapist may offer the schizophrenic person an opportunity to develop a *lateral base*, that is, a relationship of potential trust, not controlled by the patient's family, nor by the therapist's hospital or particular ideology. The question, "Whose agent are you?" looms large with these frightened, extremely distrustful and overwhelmed people. The therapist's assessment of his role and definition of his obligations are crucial. He will not be trusted—not for a long time, but it is important that he be trustable and clear in his allegiances. He must define his relationships clearly to patients, peers, and the institution, or this necessary lateral base will always seem to his suspicious patient to be a fragile lily pad.

The demand for openness, honesty, spontaneity, and a sense of humor (a sense of perspective and appreciation of context) is nowhere greater than in the task of working with severely dysfunctional people. Whitehorn and Betz observed, "In the relationship between schizophrenic patients and their physicians, certain kinds of physicians are more effective than others in evoking constructive efforts at problem-solving and social participation. The difference lies in certain attitudes and interests of the physician, whether these are, on the one hand, attitudes that tend to expect and respect spontaneity and thereby evoke activity and self-respectful social participation; or on the other hand, attitudes that tend to restrict spontaneity by preference for conventionalized expectations."[61] To foster ego development in schizophrenics, the therapist needs an open system of thought and relationship.

The centripetal SD family, with its fear of genuine encounter, its lack of respect for subjective reality, its timelessness, and lack of individual self-definition, produces offspring who are terribly deficient in these areas. An effective psychotherapist "has a grasp of the personal meaning and motivation of his patients, a clear concept of goals related to the person's individual assets, and he in-

volves himself in interaction with active personal participation."[61]
These observations of successful therapists' interactions dovetail
with the qualities lacking in patient's family environment. Obscuring mechanisms must be replaced by directness. The therapist's
motives must be as clear as humanly possible; he should combine
the openness of a child with the strength and responsibility of an
adult. A high respect for individual subjective reality and personal
boundaries is essential. Attention to the patient's choice and accomplishments is the foundation for fostering his ego development.

Milieu Treatment. For hundreds of years mental hospitals have
been attempting to provide an atmosphere conducive to successful
treatment. They fail at least as often as they succeed, and there is
no clear evidence of institutional improvement as the centuries un-
fold. Bochoven, in a careful history of mental hospitalization in the
United States found that "moral treatment" (based on enlightened
humanistic tenets) of the insane, prevalent in the early 19th century, was quite successful in rehabilitation and indeed superior to
subsequent institutional efforts from 1840 to 1956.[62]

From a systems standpoint, a treatment environment needs a
greater degree of negentropy (coherent, flexible, and adaptive
structure), than that found in the patients' primary families. Just as
individual therapists are most effective when they are open, spontaneous, and pragmatically goal-oriented, so are institutions. The
authoritarian medical-surgical hospital as a model for a psychiatric
hospital is antithetical to such efforts. Unless hospital environments
are divided into small units with considerable autonomy, a rigid,
dehumanized system results, which usually increases a patient's already profound despair.

Successful intervention in process schizophrenia requires
meticulous attention to the patient's need for encounters with
trustable and comprehensible caretakers in order that an easily
overwhelmed person (one with a small memory bank of coherent
satisfying relationships) can grow in social capabilities. Several
small therapeutic communities have been established in recent
years by founders who hope to establish a pattern for the future.
Laing established a small unit in England, enthusiastically manned

by volunteers. Initially it was successful, but then foundered, apparently because larger system factors (adequate economic support and community acceptance) were ignored.[63]

More recently, Mosher developed such a community in San Francisco with federal financing and a strong effort to evaluate treatment results.[64] Without sacrificing coherent structure he encourages an egalitarian atmosphere, spontaneity, and genuineness in patient and staff interaction. This is a real effort to evolve a negentropic community. Such projects can increase our clinical information about ways to develop adaptive skills as well as reduce symptoms by creating treatment environments which do what severely dysfunctional families cannot do, that is, provide coherent and satisfying experiences with others who become cherished, but not irreplaceable.

The Treatment of the Sociopath

To speak of intensive treatment of sociopathic people is a bit like describing the domestication of the African lion. It is possible; it has been done, but not often. Few people have wanted to make such activity a career choice. The reason is clear; sociopaths handle emotional pain by open conflict and by leaving the field of play, and psychotherapists have tended to treat people who come to them, stay, and cooperate in the work.

Most capable, ambitious helpers view sociopathic patients even more warily than they do severe schizophrenics. Nevertheless, there may be those who wish to engage in the struggle of treating these people, and an understanding of their family dynamics may be helpful.

Since conflicts are handled by distancing, a therapist must have his patient hospitalized or expect to visit him in places of confinement, at least intermittently, throughout treatment. A fundamental defense against suicidal despair and hopelessness in these patients is movement; it is taught by the family and reinforced by their failures in relating. The most useful thing that a growth-oriented therapist can offer—the possibility of satisfying, coherent, self-defining encounter—is viewed by the sociopathic patient as a threat nearly as frightening as death itself. He is the living embodiment of the gingerbread man who will run, run, as fast as he can, hoping never to be caught.

If a therapist is tenacious in his role-definition (as the patient's parents were not) and if he develops a modest treatment alliance, he will then encounter the patient's carefully taught dilemma: "Using other people as things is evil, but occasionally fun; caring about them and being known are disaster." When a relationship is attempted, the patient's sense of worthlessness emerges with profound pain and suicidal guilt.

At this point, the therapist will find that he is treating a psychotically depressed individual, brought back to the time of infancy when the hope of being loved was almost snuffed out by the family's view that fear, loneliness, and a desire to be loved were causes for rejection. It will then be necessary to mourn with the patient, sharing a sense of the absence of loving, capable parents, an acknowledgement that the real parents were also deprived, and the acceptance of an overwhelming need for relationships that has long been denied.

If the alliance survives these heavy demands, more equal negotiation can follow. A close relationship requires empathic reciprocity, and a therapist's concern for his patient is no less important than his own respect for and expression of his legitimate needs in relationship to his patient. In order to teach such a patient trust and trustability, the therapist's vulnerability and limits will need to be accepted by himself and then (through example) by the patient. Personal self-esteem and the expectation of being treated with dignity were sorely lacking in members of his family of origin.

Using this relationship as a model, the patient, no longer sociopathic, can begin to experiment with others by risking openness, by sharing and negotiation with specific people who have gifts to give and needs of their own. As with schizophrenic patients, treatment requires that a therapist provide the sociopath with the experiences missing in his original family setting that led to the failure to develop a successful self.

REFERENCES

1. STABENAU, J. R., TUPIN, J., WERNER, M., and POLLIN, W. A., "A comparative study of families of schizophrenics, sociopaths, and normals," *Psychiatry*, 28:45-59, 1965.
2. STIERLIN, N., "A family perspective on adolescent runaways," *Arch. Gen. Psychiat.*, 29:56-62, July, 1973.
3. JACKSON, D. D. and YALOM, I., "Family research on the problem of ulcerative colitis," *Arch. Gen. Psychiat.*, 15:410-418, Oct., 1966.
4. REES, L., "The significance of parental attitudes in childhood asthma," J. Psychosom. Res., 7:181-190, 1963.
5. BEAVERS, W. R., GOSSETT, J. T., LEWIS, J. M., and BARNHART, F. D., "Family systems rating scales," Scientific Proceedings, 127th Annual Meeting, American Psychiatric Association, Detroit, Mich., May, 1974.
6. STIERLIN, H., LEVI, L. D., and SAVARD, R. J., "Parental perceptions of separating children," *Fam. Prac.*, 10:411-427, 1971.
7. STIERLIN, H., *Separating Parents and Adolescents*, New York, Quadrangle, 1972.
8. STIERLIN, H., LEVI, L. D., and SAVARD, R. J., "Centrifugal versus centripetal separation in adolescence: two patterns and some of their implications," in Feinstein, S., and Giovacchini, P. (eds.), *Annals of the American Society for Adolescent Psychiatry*, Vol. II, New York, Basic Books, 211-239, 1973.
9. GARMEZY, N. and RODNICK, E. H., "Premorbid adjustment and performance in schizophrenia," *J. Nerv. and Ment. Dis.*, 129:450-466, 1959.
10. MISHLER, E., and WAXLER, N., *Interaction in Families*, New York, John Wiley and Sons, 1968.
11. LIDZ, F., FLECK, S., and CORNELISON, A. R., *Schizophrenia and the Family*, New York International Univ. Press, 1965.
12. BOWEN, M. A., "Family concept of schizophrenia," in D. D. Jackson (Ed.) *The Etiology of Schizophrenia*, New York, Basic Books, 1960.
13. WYNNE, L. C., RYCKOFF, I. M., DAY, J., and HIRSCH, S. L., "Pseudomutuality in the family relations of schizophrenics," *Psychiat.*, 21:205-220, 1958.
14. LAING, R. D., "Mystification, confusion, and conflict," in Nagy and Framo (Eds.), *Intensive Family Therapy*, New York, Hoeber, 1965.
15. SHANNON, C. E., and WEAVER, W., *The Mathematical Theory of Communication*, Urbana, Ill.: University of Illinois Press, 1949.
16. BRUCH, H., "Falsification of bodily needs and body concept in schizophrenia," *Arch. Gen. Psychiat.*, 6:18-24, Jan., 1962.
17. BATESON, G., JACKSON, D. D., HALEY, J., and WEAKLAND, J., "Toward a theory of schizophrenia," *Behav. Science*, I:251-264, 1958.
18. BEAVERS, W. R., BLUMBERG, S., TIMKEN, K. R., and WEINER, M. D., "Communication patterns of mothers of schizophrenics," *Family Process*, 4:95-104, 1965.
19. WYNNE, L. C., and SINGER, M. F., "Thought disorder and family relations of schizophrenics," *Arch. Gen. Psychiat.*, 9:191-198, Sept. 1963.
20. SINGER, M. F., and WYNNE, L. D., "Differentiating characteristics of parents of childhood schizophrenics, childhood neurotics, and young adult schizophrenics," *Am. J. Psychiat.*, 120:234-243, 1963.
21. LENNARD, H. L., and BERNSTEIN, A., *Patterns in Human Interaction*, San Francisco, Jossey-Bass, 1969.
22. RISKIN, J., and FAUNCE, E. F., "Family interaction scales," *Arch. Gen. Psychiat.*, 22(6), 504-537, June, 1970.
23. BURNHAM, D. L., GLADSTONE, A. F., and GIBSON, R. W., *Schizophrenia and the Need-Fear Dilemma*, International Univ. Press, 1969.
24. ERIKSON, E. H., *Childhood and Society* (2nd Ed.), New York, W. W. Norton, 1963.

80   *Psychotherapy and Growth*

25. FERREIRA, A. J., "Family myth and homeostasis," *Arch. Gen. Psychiat.*, 9:457-463, 1963.
26. KORZIBSKI, A., *Science and Sanity*, Lancaster, Pa., The International Non-Aristotelian Library Publishing Co., 1933.
27. SEARLES, H. F., "Schizophrenia and the inevitability of death," *Psychiat. Quart.*, 35:631-664, 1961.
28. PAUL, N., and GROSSER, G. H., "Operational mourning and its role in conjoint family therapy," *Community Mental Health Journal*, I:339-345, 1965.
29. LANGFELDT, G., "The prognosis in schizophrenia," *Acta Psychiat. Neurol.*, Supp. 110:1-66, 1956.
30. KETY, S. S., ROSENTHAL, D., WENDER, P. H., and SCHULSINGER, F., "Mental illness in the biological and adoptive families of adopted schizophrenics," *Am. J. Psychiat.*, 128:302-306, 1971.
31. ZIGLER, E., and PHILLIPS, L., "Social competence and the process-reactive distinction in psychopathology," *J. of Abnormal and Social Psychol.*, 65:215-272, 1962.
32. GOLDFARB, W., "An investigation of childhood schizophrenia," *Arch. Gen. Psychiat.*, 11:620-634, Dec., 1964.
33. ARIETI, S., *Interpretation of Schizophrenia*, New York, Brunner, 1955.
34. BEAVERS, W. R., "Schizophrenia and despair," *Comprehensive Psychiat.*, 13(6):561-572, 1972.
35. BLAKISTON, P. and Son., *New Gould Medical Dictionary* (2nd Ed.), New York, McGraw-Hill, 1956.
36. BLEULER, E., *Dementia Praecox, or the Group of Schizophrenias*, New York, International Universities Press, 1950.
37. FROMM-REICHMANN, F., "Basic problems in the psychotherapy of schizophrenia," *Psychiatry*, 21:1, 1958.
38. HILL, L. B., *Psychotherapeutic Intervention in Schizophrenia*, Chicago, University of Chicago Press, p. 26, 1955.
39. SULLIVAN, H. S., *Schizophrenia as a Human Process*, New York, W. W. Norton, 1962.
40. KUHN, M. L., "The interaction of social class and other factors in the etiology of schizophrenia," *Am. J. Psychiat.*, 133(2):177-185, Feb., 1976.
41. VON DOMARUS, E., "The specific laws of logic in schizophrenia," in Kasanin, J. S. (Ed.), *Language and Thought in Schizophrenia*, p. 104, University California Press, Berkeley, 1944.
42. SARBIN, T. R., TOFT, R., and BAILEY, D. E., *Clinical Inference and Cognitive Theory*, New York, Holt, Rinehart, and Winston, 1960.
43. DAVIS, J. M., McCOURT, W. E., COURTNEY, J. and SOLOMON, P., "Sensory deprivation," *Arch. Gen. Psychiat.*, 51:84, 1961.
44. DOBBING, J., and SMART, J. L., "Vulnerability of the developing brain and behavior," *British Medical Bulletin*, 30, No. 2, 164-168, May, 1974.
45. VORSTER, D., "An investigation into the part played by organic factors in childhood schizophrenia," *J. Ment. Sci.*, 106:494-522, 1960.
46. STABENAU, J., and POLLIN, W., "Early characteristics of monozygotic twins discordant for schizophrenia," *Arch. Gen. Psychiat.*, 17:723-734, 1967.
47. DAY, J., and KWIATKOWSKA, H. Y., "The psychiatric patient and his 'well' sibling," *Bull. of Art Therapy*, Winter, 1962.
48. GUNDERSON, J. G., and SINGER, M. T., "Defining borderline patients: an overview," *J. of American Psychiat. Assn.*, 132(1): 1-10, Jan. 1975.
49. KERNBERG, O., "Borderline personality organization," *J. of the American Psychoanalytic Assn.*, 15:645-685, 1967.
50. PFEIFFER, E., "Borderline states," *Disease of the Nerv. System*, 35:212-219, May, 1974.
51. GRINKER, R. R., Sr., WERBLE, B., and DRYE, R. C., *The Borderline Syndrome*, New York, Basic Books, 1968.

52. SCHMIDEBERG, M., "The borderline patient," in S. Arieti (Ed.), *American Handbook of Psychiatry*, Vol. I:398-418, New York Basic Books, 1952.
53. DEUTSCH, H., "Some forms of emotional disturbance and their relationship to schizophrenia," *Psychoanalytic Quarterly*, 11:301-321, 1942.
54. KERNBERG, O., *Borderline Conditions and Pathological Narcissism*, New York, Jason Aronson, 1975.
55. MASTERSON, J. F., *Treatment of the Borderline Adolescent: A Developmental Approach*, New York, Wiley-Interscience, 1972.
56. SINGER, M. T., and WYNNE, L. C., "Schizophrenic families and communication disorders," presented at American College of Psychiatry meeting, San Diego, California, Jan., 1976.
57. PRICHARD, J. C., *A Treatise on Insanity and Other Disorders Affecting the Mind*, Philadelphia, Haswell, Barrington, and Haswell, 1837.
58. DONNELLY, JOHN, "Aspects of Psychodynamics of the psychopath," *Am. J. Psychiat.*, 120(12):1149-1154, 1964.
59. AMERICAN PSYCHIATRIC ASSOCIATION, *Diagnostic and Statistical Manual of Mental Disorders*, 38-39, Washington, D. C., 1952.
60. AMERICAN PSYCHIATRIC, ASSOCIATION, *Diagnostic and Statistical Manual of Mental Disorders, Second Edition (DSM II)*, 43-44, Washington, D. C., 1968.
61. WHITEHORN, J. C., and BETZ, B., *Effective Psychotherapy with the Schizophrenic Patient*, New York, Jason Aronson, 1975.
62. BOCHOVEN, J. S., *Moral Treatment in American Psychiatry*, New York, Springer, 1963.
63. GORDON, J. S., "Who is mad? Who is sane? R. D. Laing: In search of a new psychiatry," in Antonio, R. J. and Ritzer, G. (Eds.), *Social Problems*, Boston, Allyn and Bacon, 1975.
64. MOSHER, L. R., and MENN, A. Z., "Community residential treatment of schizophrenia," (abstract) Scientific Proceedings, American Psychiatric Assn., Washington, D.C., 1976: 220.

Whether 'tis nobler in the mind to suffer the slings and
arrows of outrageous fortune,
Or to take arms against a sea of troubles
And by opposing end them?

William Shakespeare, *Hamlet*

4

Midrange families

The concept of family competence as a continuum, from severely dysfunctional to optimal, focuses attention on functioning ability of family systems and reduces a tendency often found in family literature to characterize according to diagnoses of individuals, for example, "schizophrenic family," "neurotic family." However, in describing family qualities typical of various levels of functioning, it is useful to have some points along the continuum defined in detail; hence, the phrase "midrange family" is introduced.[1,2] This phrase refers to a large group of families who evidence a considerable amount of pain and difficulty in functioning. In addition, at least one member has received a diagnosis of emotional illness. Midrange families usually produce sane but limited offspring who can be categorized under two general headings: neuroses and behavior disorders.

Neurosis is defined as illness in which an individual has emotional pain, such as depression or excessive anxiety, without evidence of chronic psychotic symptoms or without much difficulty in conforming to society's rules of conduct. Behavior disorder is also defined as an illness in which the sufferer has emotional pain, no evidence of chronic psychotic symptoms, but continuing difficulty in following the rules of behavior expected in the world beyond the family. In addition, midrange family members are susceptible to reactive schizophrenic illness, which typically is a short-lived psychosis with recovery. They develop a clear, coherent, self-definition, narrow and limited, which can disintegrate under stress. Srole and his co-workers[3] suggest that there are more individuals who are emotionally disturbed than are asymptomatic. If this be so, then this midrange group is probably larger than any other group, including healthy families, no matter how generously defined.

GENERAL CHARACTERISTICS OF MIDRANGE FAMILIES

Boundaries

The midrange family does not have overwhelming boundary problems. The boundary between family and non-family is neither so rigid and impermeable as that found in the severely dysfunctional centripetal families, nor so vague and tenuous as that found in the severely dysfunctional centrifugal families. This midrange group is not seen as odd, nor is it rejected by other people. Its members are not extremely withdrawn, isolated, or terribly disturbing to others.

Within the system, intragroup boundary problems are less dramatic or overwhelming. A reasonably clear distinction is made between family members and some cohesiveness is present, in contrast to both centripetal and centrifugal SD families. In system terms, the midrange group has a greater degree of negentropy, with some differentiation and effective feedback loops. These families neither clump in an amorphous ego mass nor fly apart under stress.

Further, the midrange family has differentiated sufficiently that parents accept role definitions significantly different from children. There are generational boundaries; coalitions between parent and child are shaky and covert or intermittent. Though the parental coalition is compromised, it does exist.

Power Issues

While the severely dysfunctional families fail most profoundly in the evolution of coherent selfhood, with resulting ego diffusion and confusion, the midrange family structure contributes this basic learning, but defines relationships as necessarily entailing continuing power struggles. There is an incessant "war in the nursery" pervading family life. Power issues and equal relationships are unresolved puzzles. Differences in subjective reality, the core of ego integrity, are comprehended, but never accepted. Family rules are riddled with "shoulds" and "oughts" which encourage intimidation rather than negotiation in family interaction.

The parental coalition is never equal in overt power. Respect for the spouse is modest, and negotiation is difficult. A dominant/submissive pattern is characteristic of centripetal families with one parent consistently deferring to the other. This leads to a variety of subversive means of being effective. In centrifugal families, there is a continual, unresolved parental control battle.

The Family Referee

Midrange families behave as if an invisible "referee," a shared external authority, is present. This referee may be abstract or personified. In many families it is a "they," the faceless order of "good" people who have controlled themselves properly and, therefore, possess social power. In others, it is a formal religious code adhered to with perfectionistic inhumanity. Currently, we see a few families who make science a tyrannizing lawgiver. Frequently, however, the referee is personified—a powerful grandparent or a dominating parent; he is controlled and trapped by the system also. The referee, abstract or concrete, subjugates all family members with standards of thought, behavior, and feelings that are pathetically insensitive to people's needs. The referee system does not limit its efforts to behavioral control, but disciplines feelings and thoughts, continually trying to bring everyone's inner life into agreement with the rules. Feelings rarely come out openly, spontaneously, and without pain. If the feelings are "good," they are likely to be expressed sanctimoniously. If the feelings are "bad," they will be hidden or expressed with defensive hostility, shame, or guilt. Much of the self must be expressed in forbidden fantasy or illicit behavior rather than in real interaction with others.

This family referee concept is related to the familiar Freudian concept of superego. The superego does not, however, encompass the shared quality of the "shoulds" and "oughts" and the incompletely differentiated ego boundaries present in midrange families. The marked contrast of these family members to those of optimal families (described in Chapter 5) dramatically illustrates that, though all will have individual superegos, the tyrannical systems referee is characteristic of the midrange group. This referee, not the presence of the individual superego, destroys respect for individual subjective views of reality and encourages an oppositional set in human encounter. The referee system reduces the autonomy of all members. All individual thinking, feeling, and acting are suspect. These people walk a tightrope between resentment and guilt, leaving little room for any satisfaction or pleasure in life.

Autonomy in Communication

The peculiar incoherence of family communication observed in the SD families is absent in midrange families. Invasiveness or mind-reading comments that are so damaging to self-definition are no more frequently found in this midrange group than in normals.

Individuals from this group do not show significant thinking disturbances in formal testing.

Though communication patterns are not bizarre, there are definable deviations from those of competent families. Typically, midrange family members resist taking personal responsibility for feelings, thoughts, and actions. They avoid responsibility by shrouding pronouncements under the cloak of the inhuman referee. "You should never talk that way about your teachers." "I'm only punishing you for your own good." Blame and attack can effectively obscure personal responsibility: "You've got me so rattled, I forgot." "How can I say what I mean when everybody's talking?" "You're always interrupting." "You're wasting our time." Midrange family conversation is characterized by impermeability and obliviousness of verbal and behavioral messages, particularly if the content is unacceptable to the referee.

Mythology

Raters viewing interaction in midrange families judged that they had a mythology more incongruent than that found in healthy families. Shared distortion is a device used to bring the family apparently closer to the referee's dictates. Examples of family myths include such beliefs as: father is only interested in his business; mother is a saint without any hostility; one child is spiteful and mean, while another is always kind and cheerful.

Timebinding

Midrange family members are capable of timebinding. Biological time and its passage are distorted, but not obliterated. Children's growth and development, parents' aging and death are accepted, though usually with conflict and pain. Mothers often compete with adolescent daughters to be sexually attractive, or submerge themselves in premature asexuality and dowdiness. Similarly, fathers may vie with sons, or depressively and passively withdraw from what they perceive as inevitable conflict.

An old psychiatric joke defines a psychotic as one who thinks two and two are five, and a neurotic as one who knows two and two are four, but *he can't stand it*! Midrange family members recognize life's progression and its finitude, but accept such awareness gracelessly and with pain.

Feeling Tone

Midrange families express a variety of unpleasant feelings. Open conflict produces angry competition, or hidden conflict creates a depressed atmosphere with little spontaniety. Although the parents of acting-out children tell hostile TAT stories, they are without the sadism of those told by parents of childhood schizophrenics. Parents of withdrawn neurotic children tell stories with a subdued mood, without open hostility, warmth or joy.[4] These parents are midrange in affect as well as in child-rearing effectiveness—able to get by, but constantly frustrated.

Task Efficiency

Despite the unresolved conflict due to an unrelenting focus on control through intimidation, tasks are accomplished far more effectively than by severely dysfunctional families. Both the ongoing task of child-raising and the specific shared tasks presented in family research indicate a higher degree of competence, but a high level of conflict.

Beliefs About the Nature of Man

Common to this group of families is an implicit, occasionally directly stated belief that man is essentially evil, his very core willfully antisocial. This concept of the basic destructiveness of people becomes a self-fulfilling prophecy. In families, as in larger social groups, when individuals are over-controlled, their thoughts and feelings monitored and attacked, there are two potential responses: submit or rebel. Either response is taken as "evidence" of the correctness of the original assumption. A submissive child means that the course of control is proper; a rebellious child illustrates that coercion is inadequate. The premise is a necessary cognitive companion to the constant effort to control and the use of a family referee to overcome base instincts.

In these families, the definition of what is good or acceptable often excludes much that is human. To be angry is bad, to have sexual feelings is often unacceptable, and even to be ambivalent is strongly disapproved. This last is extremely damaging to the possibilities for pleasant interaction and peace of mind. Rather than accepting that ambivalence itself is neutral and is at the heart of being human, midrange families perceive it as part of the willful and evil self that must be dealt with by further efforts at personal and interpersonal control.

In viewing interaction in any family group, a quick way to judge the overall effectiveness of the system is to determine the system's expectations. Do family members expect an affiliative encounter with shared goals and purposes, and to what degree? Or, do they consider human interaction as necessarily oppositional, requiring coerceive control? In midrange families, the oppositional expectancy is not so crippling as that of severely dysfunctional families (where fear of encounter requires avoidance). They acknowledge individual sovereignty, a subjective reality, and make a game try at interacting, but most efforts to be intimate are spoiled by overt intimidation or efforts to induce guilt.

These assumptions of the willful, evil nature of man, the oppositional expectation of human encounter, and the absolute character of truth represented by the family referee create great resistance to negotiation and to change. In this midrange group, however, there is usually hope that change does not always signify deterioration and that life could be more satisfying "if only . . ." Generally this sentence is left unfinished as limits to individual freedom extend even to conscious dreams.

Object Loss

Both styles of midrange families, the centripetal group which binds children to the home and the centrifugal group which expels children in premature separation from family, have significant difficulty in handling object loss.

Whether premature or delayed, separation is incomplete, and mourning is denied. A therapist finds the products of midrange families still caught in a frustrating, conflict-ridden relationship with parents, or ineffectually grieving an idealized parent long dead.[5] In developing new relationships, an offspring usually recreates the interpersonal patterns of his original family.

Personal Stereotyping in Midrange Families

The structure of family relationship that gives a growing child a sense of self, of being a separate person, yet related to his world, is essential to his successful maturation. But in the process, there is a varying loss of potential (to be somebody, one cannot be everybody). Along with self-definition and ego skills, forbidden and denied areas evolve. Longings and rebellious feelings, diffuse or sharp and poignant, exist in all of us due to the suppression of aspects of ourselves that do not fit into our particular family or our specific society.

The midrange family, with its simplistic solutions for human problems, its oppositional orientation, its referee system, and its belief in absolutes, places an added burden on a developing child, and results in narrow self-definitions with larger repressed areas of a subjective self. Their stereotyped roles, whether played out or rebelled against, constrict identity.

A frequent expression of this personality constriction is the stereotypical male and female sexual role models accepted as "correct." Men are expected to be powerful, stupid about relationships and feeling, action-oriented, aggressive, and monetarily successful. Women are to be weak, intuitive about feelings, emotive, and dependent. Centripetal families are proud as they carry out these limited self-definitions; centrifugal family members are apt to be ashamed and to have lower self-esteem, since parents and children generally fail to attain these role models satisfactorily. Neither group identifies the unquestioned narrowness as a source of severe personal problems, and psychotherapists' offices are filled with the products of midrange families suffering from the pain of trying to deny large parts of themselves in order to fit the mold. A man as an imitation "Roman centurion," free from "feminine" weakness, does not make a capable lover or even an adequate organization man. Neither does a docile plantation house servant make an adequate wife, parent, or person. Few therapists would deny that these images, duly transmitted from families, exist in the minds of emotionally wounded people and operate as powerful "resistances" to growth and competence.

Severely dysfunctional as well as healthy families are less susceptible to this limited self-definition from culturally defined sexual models: the severely dysfunctional group because of the idiosyncratic, closed-system quality that limits the expectations of acceptability in the larger world, and healthy families because of their greater sympathy with subjective reality, choice, and wishes.

There are, in addition, many idiosyncratic personality stereotypes implanted in individuals growing up in midrange families: "John is our conservative, hard-working son." "Sally is the goof-off in the crowd." "Bill is a Mama's boy who can't compete." "Jane has always been hard to handle and tries to spoil everything for the rest of us." These limited and limiting roles are the results of approaching child development with a coercive, control orientation. Developmental variations—timidity at two, stuttering at three, unusual boldness at four—become hardened into narrow self-definitions. Self-fulfilling prophecies abound and, although modestly useful in providing a child with a coherent identity, leave him firmly convinced of limitations made real through enduring family myths.[6]

The war in the nursery goes on interpersonally and in the minds of the family members, fixing behavioral patterns and self-definition at modest levels of capability. Neuroses and behavioral disturbances are the result.

Contrasting Midrange Family Styles: The Centripetal and the Centrifugal

In the centripetal family, rigidity of structure is maintained. As the submissive parent, usually the wife, accepts the overt power of the spouse, the family system is relatively stable, especially while children are small. Children are effectively coerced into accepting the rules imposed by the ubiquitous referee, "If you do, think, and feel what you are supposed to, you are good; if you don't, you are bad. When you hide your feelings and behave properly, you have the hang of it" (then you are a successful fraud).

In contrast, the centrifugal families lack an effective parental coalition. Both parents have a sense of inadequacy and a fear that they cannot do what is "right." Even though they share with all midrange families the idea that there is a right way to behave, they habitually and ineffectually battle for the control of the children and blame each other for their failures. The mother is typically less invested in her parental role and is engaged, along with other family members, in seeking satisfactions outside the family. The children have greater emotional deprivation, but are freer to explore the world on their own. With continued conflict between parents, unstable, illicit alliances between children and one or the other parent are common. Children in these families grow to adulthood with greater cynicism. They become good at playing one parent against the other, but are doubtful, as their parents are, of their own acceptability (they do not know how to become successful frauds).

The two types of midrange families differ in the nature and

number of crises. Centripetal families have a great fear that the pain in their family will be exposed to the broader community, and when such a family seeks treatment, it is usually by having one individual who defines himself as at fault and attempts to change. Abuse of prescribed drugs such as tranquilizers, amphetamines, and sleeping medications is common. Alcohol abuse is occurring more frequently as it becomes more generally culturally approved. Centrifugal families, in contrast, have flamboyant and repeated interpersonal crises spilling over into the larger community. These dramatic episodes serve to maintain equilibrium in the centrifugal family system. Children often run away from home, not in order to get away, but to dramatize the parent's lack of caring. A parent may retreat into flagrantly drunken behavior, hoping to make the other family members feel remorseful. When a family seeks help, the overall effort is not to change, but to establish the essential badness of a current family scapegoat. Although both groups share a belief that people are essentially evil, the centripetal families consider a person socially acceptable if he will only abdicate and deny his "true nature." To be a socially powerful person, one must give up his sense of authenticity. In contrast, centrifugal families have little hope that their members can fool the world, and they are more likely to exhibit behavior unacceptable to the larger social system.

Centripetal families make a strong effort to adhere to the sexual stereotypes. The centrifugal group, while giving cognitive allegiance to these stereotypes, characteristically fails in performance. The father often shows helplessness and dependency, frequently with the assistance of drug abuse. The mother, in her efforts to find pleasure outside the family, may reject the submissive and nurturing role of the parent and show an aggressive behavioral style. As an illustrative example, Blum et al., studying families of drug-using adolescents, found that the number of traffic tickets received by the mother was significantly correlated with family risk for adolescent difficulty.[7] To believe in absolute behavioral standards and then to violate them does not produce change and growth, but rather overt conflict and ineffectual guilt.

AN OUTLINE OF MAJOR DIFFERENCES BETWEEN THE TWO STYLES

Centripetal (CP)

I. Social and Historical
   1. More in middle-upper socioeconomic classes.
   2. When family not under stress, more effective functioning outside the community.
   3. With family stress, low community visibility— strong attempts to keep problems within family.
   4. Binding pattern—children separate from family later than expected norm.

   5. Parents search for satisfaction within the family.
   6. Excessive use of prescription (sanctioned) drugs.

II. Interactional Qualities of Family System
   1. Acceptance of status quo in parental coalition usually involves a dominant/ submissive pattern.
   2. Parental control over children consistently attempted and generally effective.
   3. Efforts to have children "close by" promoting guilt.

Centrifugal (CF)

I. Social and Historical
   1. More in lower socioeconomic classes.
   2. When family not under stress, less social accomplishment, less community visibility.
   3. With family stress, more community visibility, conflict is spilled out into the larger social structure.
   4. Expelling pattern— children have premature separation and early pseudo-autonomous interaction with the larger community.
   5. Parents seek solace outside the family.
   6. Excessive use of nonprescription (nonsanctioned) drugs.

II. Interactional Qualities of Family System
   1. Parental coalition is chronically unresolved, with open conflict and competitiveness.
   2. Parental control inconsistent and ineffective.

   3. Efforts to blame problems on the child as explanation of failure.

4. Less clear on open expression of feelings; conflicts subdued.

5. Negative feeling tone, typically anxiety and depression.
6. High value placed on words, less attention to body language.
7. (Implicit) Though people are evil, they can appear first-class by repression.

III. Special Problems in Treatment
   1. Words are magic; "insight" rather than behavioral change is frequent.
   2. Immobilization, chronic indecision.

   3. A wish to please—making the therapist the referee and being nice.
   4. Uses authority as an intrapsychic club, converting suggestions to "should's" and "ought's."
   5. Desperately needs acceptance of own limits and awareness of others' power to help.
   6. Tendency to "settle in" and hand problems to the therapist.

4. Feelings, especially if negative, are openly expressed; conflict is open and intense.
5. Negative feeling tone, typically anger which masks depression.
6. Low value placed on words, strong emphasis on behavioral expression.
7. (Implicit) People are no good and this inevitably is exposed.

III. Special Problems in Treatment
   1. Talking distrusted; the behavior of therapist is especially important.
   2. Action-oriented; anger often expressed by absence.
   3. Fear of therapist as referee with defiance or superficial compliance.
   4. Uses authority as a club over other family members to blame, not change.

   5. Desperately needs awareness of the effect that one's behavior has on others and of others' limits.
   6. May flee before real involvement occurs.

A MODEL OF FAMILY STYLES AND COMPETENCE

Stierlin et al., in their presentation of centripetal and centrifugal family patterns, noted that there were contributions to the outcome of individuals, not only from systems, but also from the personal characteristics of the individual offspring. Not all children of centripetal families become schizophrenic or neurotic, nor do all children of centrifugal families become sociopathic or behavior disorders. There is an interplay of system and individual, with varied results.[8]

In addition, Stierlin et al. saw this centripetal/centrifugal schema as a continuum with many families having both characteristics. They described one mixed pattern which produces children "delegates" who are allowed and even encouraged to leave the family orbit, but controlled, with a mission, so to speak. A delinquent girl may be expected to have sexual escapades, but come back to titillate the family with the exciting details. Or, an adolescent boy runs away to a certain area in the Mexican wilderness, a place which his father had infused with tales of the romantic life of Indians and horsemen.

The most clear-cut, unalloyed styles will be found in the most entropic families with the least amount of flexibility, differentiation, and variation. It is in the midrange families where one will see these combinations of centripetal and centrifugal patterns most frequently with the various qualities of expelling and binding children.

Figure 1 displays the continuum of family competence and the stylistic qualities of centrifugal and centripetal families.

This diagram is a simple way of expressing that which is close to my experience with families—it categorizes them in a functional manner without using individual pathological labels for family systems which have often been confusing and contradictory. It communicates the notion that emotional illness is related to family characteristics, and that various types of individual psychopathology are related to other types.

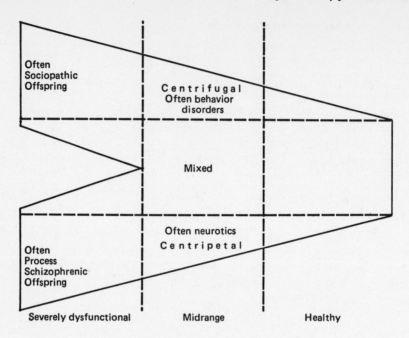

Figure 1. A diagram of family function and style

TWO ILLUSTRATIVE SYNDROMES IN MIDRANGE FAMILIES

In order to illustrate midrange family styles further, two which are often seen in clinical practice are described. The first is termed "saint syndrome," not so frequently encountered as the hysteric-compulsive match described next, but unforgettable when encountered.

The Saint Syndrome

This fascinating family type is one in which there is a member who all the family agrees is more gracious, more loving, more generous, and more self-sacrificing than ordinary mortals. He or she is, in fact, a saint among humans. Remarkably, the family member possesses no negative traits (according to the family myth), and would be capable of even more fabulous performance if not surrounded by venal, immature, willful, misguided, and inept souls who are more to be pitied than openly attacked. The saint is sometimes the mother, who not only operates in a spectacularly capable fashion at home, but also has good work outside which she carries out with humility and public adulation. Or, it may be the father, a brilliant, benign dedicated physician whose patients worship him. The saint adheres to a transcendent value system with such precision and clarity as to awe those around. This value system, though often a formally religious one, may be entirely secular (such as scientific objectivity). Whatever the system, his service to it is selfless and beyond criticism. Such an individual is a part of the typically disturbed family pattern. The saint can relate only to children (innocent, but bumbling), and to sinners (people who lose their way, who must be supported and suffered because of their weaknesses). The spouse of the saint may be seen as a child or a sinner, but never as a responsible adult. Many saintly professional men's wives slip from one to the other as they grow older. The childlike ingenuousness of their youth gives way to drug- and alcohol-induced sin. Such transitions never disturb our saint, of course, since he is able to relate to either the child or the sinner without altering his basic pattern. The children of saints rarely aspire to sainthood themselves, though this is one possible role available to them. If such aspirations are supported, the saint must be unusually unpossessive of the exclusive rights to the role. The children of such a marvel can never leave the family—when chronologically adult, they still warm their hands by the fire of this superior spirit and use his power and money as well. They dare not leave, for fear of threatening the foundation of the family, of the saint, and their own identity as well.

Genet, in *The Balcony*, expresses the complementarity of these roles: "Then the judge explains to the girl, 'You've got to be a model thief, if I am to be a model judge. If you are a fake thief, I become a fake judge. Is that clear?' And he says to the executioner, 'Without you I would be nothing.' And then to the thief, 'You too, my child. You two are my perfect complements.' "[9] For a saint to have any identity, he must live in an interpersonal world of lesser beings. Alcoholism, delinquency, sociopathy, chronic depression, and martyrdom are all individual patterns compatible with the saint syndrome. Autonomy, personal responsibility, and open expression of negative feelings without loss of social power are foreign to the system and are vigorously resisted.

As a psychotherapist, I never see the saint initially as the patient. I encounter him when I insist upon seeing the whole family. However, I see numerous family members from such a system, because sinners and children often hurt and cry for help. Lawrence Kubie's separation of neuroses into "onion" and "garlic" categories applies here.[10] He describes people with onion neuroses as those who hurt inside and want to suffer less; saints are the garlic type, those who feel well themselves, but wither anyone who gets close. Often, a therapist can only hope, at most, to help the identified patient separate from his family system and develop new and more satisfying relationship skills with others outside the family. This family is hard to alter because of the multiple paradoxes involved. The saintly person, selfless and dutiful, is not powerful, but humble; yet he controls all around him. His love is boundless; yet his touch poisons those he loves. If one attempts to be proud, effective, and strong in such a system, he is defined as being ungrateful, foolish, and willful.

The key to the saint syndrome, of course, is selflessness— obtaining power by denying oneself, being both more and less than human. This ethic builds a lie factor into the family. Acceptable gratification of sexual and aggressive desires must always be in the framework of doing for others; if it is not, then it is childlike or evil.

The Hysteric-Compulsive Match

Another variety of midrange family pathology is the hysteric-compulsive match, a very frequently encountered wife/husband pattern. Because of cultural and social factors, the wife usually plays the role of the hysteric neurotic, and the husband the compulsive neurotic. Basically, the hysteric woman is looking for mothering from a man, since she did not receive enough acceptance and warmth from her mother. She became disillusioned with this mother as a possible source of gratification of her own human needs and turned to her father for satisfaction, either in reality or in fantasy. In later years, she turns to other male figures who she hopes will represent the warm and mothering father. This reaching out, however, is not seen as a necessarily equal relationship with a quid pro quo (a swapping out as adults do) to meet each other's needs. Instead, the fantasy continues that a good husband is like a good father—self-reliant, needing nothing, and able to give to her all that she has missed as a child.

The compulsive male, on the other hand, denies his own needs for mothering, though he also came from a family structure where affirmation from his mother was minimal. He attempted to resolve this human pain by repressing his unmet needs and becoming "responsible."

The hysteric splits fantasy and reality. Unlike a healthy person who is able to infuse her daily life with some of the excitement of fantasy, she invests a great deal of energy in a fantasy life entirely separated from interaction with others, and only reluctantly accepts real people present in her life. Reality is seen as an impediment to obtaining one's heart's desire, so the modal hysteric enjoys exciting and dreamy things, drama and make-believe where people are engaged in an effort to blot out reality and reach for the stars.

The compulsive neurotic also makes this split between fantasy and reality rather than integrating them, but he tries to blot out much of his fantasy life. When it pops through, and he becomes conscious of weird or exciting dreams or fantasies, he is frightened and somewhat guilty. This responsible and duty-bound compulsive neurotic looks at the world through feces-covered glasses.

The hysteric uses "fluid-drive" control mechanisms. By fluid-drive, I refer to the way that some cars hook the power of the engine to the back wheels. Instead of a direct contact, there is a fan immersed in fluid that spins rapidly and, through such spinning, causes another fan to turn, and, hence, the car moves. In a similar way, the hysteric person is frightened and needful and makes tremendous efforts to control others. Since the self-image is one of relative helplessness in direct confrontation, then emotionality and dramatic behavior—"fanning the air"—are major methods of coercing others. Emoting powerfully, generously displaying sexual, or angry, or depressed, or anxious feelings, she is able to suck others into her turmoil and produce results. In the fable, Chicken Little became powerful with her dramatic cry, "The sky is falling." The hysteric, like Chicken Little, controls others by drama, but the result of such control is mentally painful.

The compulsive neurotic, on the other hand, prefers direct drive. He wishes the clutch plate to press firmly on its opposite, and to force movement directly. He is concerned with mastery, control and absolute precision.[11] The emotionality of his encounters is diminished because emotion is always imprecise and not easily measured or controlled. He is concerned with *performance* in himself and others, and he attempts to gain binding contracts with penalty clauses. It is important to note that both of these neurotic characters see people as objects as they perform in their neuroses and attempt to relate to fellow human beings as if they were things. The hysteric uses feeling in a manipulative fashion to control, and the compulsive tries to deny the presence of meaningful, significant feelings in himself or in others.

Now, why would these two different styles attract one another? The hysteric is profoundly aware of her dependency and helplessness; in fact, these qualities are a part of her self-image (of which she is somewhat proud). She, therefore, perceives a strong, duty-bound, controlled man as a needed tower of strength. With his self-definition, it is important to demonstrate perfection in himself, and he encourages her to believe that he can be both mother and father and that he has few needs of his own other than to care for others.

The compulsive neurotic looks at the hysteric as a man dying of thirst in the desert might look at water; his duty-filled, dreary, and mechanical way of operating causing him to be intrigued by her apparent vibrant enjoyment of life. At a superficial level, the hysteric neurotic appears to appreciate people, activities, parties, excitement and drama, and the dreary compulsive feels that if he can only *possess* such a person, his life will be complete.

Unfortunately, the very same qualities that draw these two together drive them apart. The tight control and repression of feelings found in the compulsive, seen initially by the hysteric as evidence of strength, become a pivotal point of dissatisfaction. The wife feels that the husband does not care for her, understand her, or have needed sensitivity or awareness. Further, his only interest in her is his desire for sex! On the other side, the compulsive male finds his exciting female toy quite depressed at times and frighteningly unpredictable. He fears that she doesn't really care about him. She wants only to be a little girl and have him do for her. He begins to see behind the dramatic style and becomes worried about her depressive episodes. He bought a firefly and assumed that it would pull a plow; he is most disturbed when it does not.

With increasing frustration, the hysteric wife begins to use her fluid-drive mechanism. She attempts to force her husband to care more for her in the only way that she knows, by using her body in a dramatic and usually flirtatious fashion. She tries to make her husband jealous of other males, saying in effect, "These men care for me; why don't you?" Unfortunately, this increases the agitation of a compulsive male who has a great need to master and control. He is threatened since he no longer possesses her. He clamps more controls, more rules, restrictions on styles of dress, or on the amount of money she spends. In whatever areas possible, he increases controls in a vain effort to get his needs met. This increases her use of the fluid-drive mechanism, and we see an escalating battle with each using the only weapons he or she has.

There are several courses such marriages can take. Some remain in this dangerous territory, with a kind of Mexican stand-off, by developing rule systems that keep each partner from going too far; some divorce (to repeat the pattern with other partners). Some seek therapists, whose job it is to diminish the stereotyped patterns described and to increase the flexibility of both members of the match, helping them to develop some genuinely warm and human interaction that is not so stereotyped and fraught with disappointment.

The children of such a match are prone to develop the same kinds of character pathology found in their parents. A female child does not find her mother particularly warm since the mother is somewhat shallow, frequently depressed, and usually engaged in emotionally draining battles with her husband. Such a daughter turns to her father for warmth and loving. She frequently finds it, since the father sees the childlike sensuality in his little daughter more attractive than the same attitudes found in his aging wife. Male children respond to the relative maternal deprivation and the somewhat chaotic environment by imitating father and isolating their feelings and by becoming concerned with controlling their world and their feelings. They are well on their way to perpetuating the pattern.

PRODUCTS OF CENTRIPETAL MIDRANGE FAMILIES

Neuroses

The natural pattern of midrange CP families is to produce a new crop of adults restricted in emotional expression and behavior, with an implanted family referee and subject to considerable emotional pain. This is a description of the classic neurotic long appreciated by psychotherapists. He comes to treatment regularly, pays his bills, and does not get into much trouble, at least with social institutions beyond the family.

These neurotic personalities present themselves essentially in two types—the compulsive and the hysteric. Differences between hysteric and compulsive patients are primarily those of style in expressing personal conflict rather than any core individual or family system difference. This is not surprising since they develop from the same type of family system, often from the same family. Most of the introjected family rules are identical—the primary difference being in the degree of overt social power the person was expected to possess in his primary family. If the midrange centripetal family relates to a child with the expectation that he is to be effective, significant, and powerful, then that child grown up will show obessive-compulsive behavior. If the family relates to the child with little expectation that he is to be capable and powerful, the child grown up will present with hysteric symptomatology.

In our Western culture, there is relatively clear sex difference in overt social power. Males are expected to succeed materially and have power over others, and females are expected to be grown-up children who depend on others for significance. Therefore, we would expect a predominance of male compulsives and female hysterics. In the future, one might predict greater parity between the sexes in each diagnosis as current social effort to equalize overt power between the sexes continues. In our observations of midrange and healthy families, the more effective a family, the more equal the parents are in overt power, and the more likely that characterological personality traits will be a function of birth order, not sex. Birth order, as related to individual character patterns, has been explored by Toman,[12] who described and expected greater social power in first-born children and less in last-born. Midrange families, with their greater effort to follow social norms, have unequal parental power, and hysteric and compulsive behaviors are significantly correlated with gender.

The relative superficiality of either the hysteric or the compulsive diagnosis is known to most intensive psychotherapists who find it impossible to maintain a relationship with a neurotic patient over a period of time without having the diagnostic clarity disappear.[13,14] It is often true that if a therapist starts by treating an obsessive-compulsive, he finishes by treating a hysteric, and vice versa. People with either diagnosis have trouble with choice and with autonomy, fostered by the family of origin's false assumption that all human encounter must be resolved by power plays that end with one person victor, the other loser.

Such an assumption, expressed in ongoing behavior patterns, limits the neutoric patient in his efforts at intimacy. Whether one wins or loses a power struggle, distancing and defensiveness result in vulnerability, a sense of aloneness, and relative isolation.

Behavior Disorders—Internal Scapegoating

Scapegoating is defined as the process of choosing a person or people within or without a group as unacceptably bad, and attacking that person or group with virtuous hostility. All of one's own denied qualities can be projected onto this scapegoat. I have never seen a family, competent or dysfunctional, that does not do some scapegoating. The most benign type is *external* scapegoating— ascribing to some one or group outside the family those things considered bad, and having the family boundary represent an entrance into relative enlightenment, goodness, and humanity.

Internal scapegoating is a disastrous family mechanism and precludes success in producing competent offspring if the activity is continuous. Centrifugal families, with their continual power struggles and unstable, shifting behavior pattern, are poorly designed for consistent scapegoating. These families rotate the scapegoating function by blaming first one member and then another. In the midrange centripetal family, however, with its control orientation, its relatively rigid structure, its fixed parental power relationship, and difficulty in accepting ubiquitous ambivalence, there is a structural invitation for the development of consistent internal scapegoating of one member. That member, usually the child who has the greatest aggressive drive and who was most needful of strong parental control to force him into the expected centripetal structure, has all of the family rules reversed for him. He is ignored when he performs well, since that does not fit the family myth. He is rewarded by lessened group anxiety and by attention from parents and siblings as he becomes "incorrigible," that is, as he accepts this family role. Internal scapegoating of one family member produces a behavior disorder in a centripetal family. This is the most common family structure of behavior disorders of adolescents hospitalized in a private setting, though the pattern is seen much less frequently in public adolescent wards.

Usually, as a needed opposite to the scapegoat, there will be another child who can do no wrong, a "goody two-shoes" who is as unerringly good as the scapegoat is bad. Together they seem living evidence to family members that there is no need to deal with ambivalence. One can love a good child wholeheartedly and reject a bad one with comfort. Such a narrowing of self-definition is damaging to the goody two-shoes also, and emotional illness will be manifested in this individual as neurosis.

If the family that scapegoats internally has reasonable strengths and some warmth and mutual caring in addition to this pernicious pattern, the child victim is usually treatable. If the scapegoating occurs in conjunction with a great amount of rigid, black-or-white relationship qualities, the behavior disorder may be so severe as to be eventually designated sociopathic, and the person encounters the criminal justice system more often than he does psychiatric facilities.

Case example: John, the 17-year-old son of a civil service worker, was hospitalized in a psychiatric unit after threatening repeatedly to shoot his father with a deer rifle. The boy was an expert marksman and had become violently angry on many occasions when his father had attempted to discipline him. He came from a highly controlled, somewhat depressed family whose only overt conflict or turmoil had been struggles with this boy since he was three. The father, 47, and mother, 45, had one other child, a daughter of 19 who had, according to the parents, always been dutiful and sweet and had given them no trouble.

John had been on the edge of family toleration since he was six, lying, stealing, and insulting others. As he grew into adolescence, he was known by the police in his community and had been handled for minor infractions of the law such as cursing loudly on downtown streets, appearing drunk, and repeated traffic violations. The family members had a strong belief in a clear-cut right or wrong, and none was comfortable with ambivalence in himself or others. Both father and son expressed the belief that to think a thing was the same as doing it in the eyes of God, and John gave this as his reason for his strong desire to kill his father since he couldn't stop thinking about doing so and was already damned.

In the hospital, John was contemptuous of therapists and staff, bullying other patients, and continually boasting. He thoroughly alienated himself and stated that he was only waiting for his 90-day commitment to run out.

When told he was to be in the hospital indefinitely, he arranged to smuggle in a .38 revolver, and he roamed the hospital basement threatening to kill anyone who interfered with him. His therapist, noting that John had made no move to escape, gingerly approached him and took the gun. Following this dramatic invitation to be controlled, the young man was quite different in appearance and behavior. He spoke of always feeling worthless and bad, citing many times when he had let his mother and father down. In Jekyll/Hyde fashion, he fluctuated for some weeks between his previous state of sneering hostility and the newer, hesitant, guilt- and shame-ridden person. The reversions to an "I don't care" attitude became less frequent. Following a long period of individual and family treatment, John passed through a period of depression, then began to socialize and relate warmly on family visits. On hospital discharge, he and his parents continued in treatment with the therapeutic aim of increasing family members' acceptance of ambivalence, of the right for people to have individual thoughts that are quite different from behavior, and of the importance of individual choice. John continued for two years to have moderate difficulty in functioning (brushes with the law, two potentially lethal car accidents). Now, nine years after hospital admission and six years after termination of treatment, he is considered healthy by himself, his wife, and his friends.

The alterations in family dynamics were geared to lessening the scapegoating style and encouraging previously projected parental guilt to be accepted and at least partially resolved. In the process, both father and mother became more aggressive, changing their locale and broadening their interests. They bought a small farm and began to have greater respect for their own needs and their own personal satisfactions.

PRODUCTS OF THE CENTRIFUGAL MIDRANGE FAMILIES

Behavior Disorders

Midrange centrifugal families, whose members look to the world outside for emotional gratification, will characteristically produce children who behave poorly. Growing up, they have difficult interpersonal relationships, various uncomfortable and unpleasant moods, and behavioral problems in social and work situations. The norms of other social groups are difficult for them to accept just as their ineffective and conflicting family rules were. Their families had grave misgivings about the value of following family rules and gave little emotional reward for doing so. Standards of proper behavior were made unattainable by self-definitions of inadequacy, selfishness, and inferiority. Parents disappointed each other and their children; the children learned this pattern.

The centrifugal family appears to be increasing in number in the United States as the culture becomes criss-crossed with varying and contradictory mores, as parents' certainty of the correctness of their way of raising children is no longer fortified by a broad social consensus, and as more women are drawn into the full-time job market. Often, young children are placed in day-care facilities of widely varying quality. The CP family, with its intense emotional ties and delayed separation, becomes less frequent under these circumstances. Psychotherapists are called upon to be more ingenious and energetic in developing treatment alliances with patients who are suspicious of authority, view close relationships with fear, and have great skepticism about the power of words. These characteristics are common in the usual product of the centrifugal family.

Neurotic Personalities from Centrifugal Families

Typical centrifugal midrange families may produce a seemingly "self-made" neurotic offspring. In the midst of turmoil and endless marital battles, one child retreats into the relative quiet and predictive structure of his own dreams and rules. Such a person usually sees himself as the "odd duck" in his family. He attempts to control his own feelings, thoughts, and behavior, looking to outside authority to reward him, and characteristically excels in school and is more future-oriented than other family members.

Case example: Sarah, a 24-year-old female medical student, was admitted to the psychiatric unit of a general hospital after taking a nearly lethal amount of a prescribed sedative. She was the second child of a career Army officer and his volatile wife. This couple had been married and divorced three times, in addition to innumerable separations. Their son, three years older than Sarah, had been a low achieving, hostile boy who had joined the Army at 17 as an alternative, in the parents' eyes, to further difficulties with the law.

Sarah had shown an early interest in reading and schoolwork and was often teased by her brother and mother for being bookish and having no friends. She avoided boys through adolescence and considered her early sexual development embarrassing and undesirable. She felt ashamed of the dramatic emotionality and continual arguments of her mother and father, and rarely brought her friends home. She began dating in medical school, and it was after terminating a relationship in which there was a good deal of sexual activity that she made the suicide attempt. She could accept herself only when hostility and sexuality were totally repressed. When these strong feelings came into awareness, she was thrown into a guilt-laden, severely depressed state. She then identified with her mother whom she consciously rejected. The parents were not amenable to treatment, and the patient received individual therapy for only a short time following her hospital discharge.

Six years later, she had successfully completed a residency in internal medicine, married, and entered treatment again because of a rather severe pattern of drug abuse. She had attempted to make herself totally subservient to her husband, to become a "model" wife, and had built up a large store of unacknowledged anger, especially toward her husband. Outpatient treatment was successful in broadening her acceptance of her feelings and in increasing her behavioral repertoire of skills for more capable social functioning.

A Product of Mixed Centripetal and Centrifugal Midrange Styles—The "Delegate"

Because of the greater negentropy of midrange family systems compared with the severely dysfunctional ones, styles are more often mixed—with several themes apparent to the observer of family interaction. Stierlin described these families with mixtures of centripetal and centrifugal styles, and termed the children "delegates" who respond to both binding and expelling pressure within the family.[15]

These children are caught in a powerful family web created by parents who are themselves ambivalent about obtaining emotional satisfactions within or without the family. The delegates are entrusted with a mission and, hence, are sent out of the family; yet they are expected to return and fulfill unmet parental needs, a binding maneuver. Stierlin categorizes these missions by whether they meet the parents' id (affective) needs, ego needs, or superego needs.

Affective needs are met by the child's becoming a "thrill provider," ego needs by providing support for embattled parents or acting as a scout to do the experimenting for a parent too anxious to reach beyond the family, and superego needs by playing out a parent's unrealized aspirations or becoming the embodiment of a parent's disowned "badness." Regardless of the mission, however, the self-definition of the child is severely narrowed, and he feels guilty when he strays from his directed task. Such an internalized gyroscopic control may direct the child to become either a useful citizen or an acting-out behavior disorder. In any case, he generates a tremendous internal conflict when he attempts autonomous choices. The concept of delegate is not unlike that of "life scripts" described by Berne.[16] A person is encouraged to appear separate, yet he is programmed for a life pattern which is unchosen and unconscious.

REACTIVE SCHIZOPHRENIA, A THREAT IN ALL SANE BUT LIMITED PRODUCTS OF MIDRANGE FAMILIES

The reactive schizophrenic patient is characterized by a relatively good premorbid adaptive pattern when compared with process schizophrenics. He has had a greater degree of success in living beyond the boundaries of his family of origin. The onset of psychosis is relatively sudden, usually with a clear precipitating event such as a loss, concrete or symbolic, which may have derailed his adaptive capacity. His affect is quite labile, usually with some degree of depression. Flagrant disorganization of thinking and disorientation are usual. In such reactive schizophrenic episodes there are no signs of organicity nor evidence of significant genetic factors in the etiology.

Whether the patient's family is centripetal, centrifugal, or mixed, it is midrange, able to raise children with limited, narrow, but coherent self-definition. Because of this limited definition, the offspring are vulnerable to disorganization when stressed excessively by environmental demands. Large parts of their human feelings and thoughts have been repressed in order to operate successfully within the family. As one result, there is a great amount of guilt (in both the neurotic and the behavior disorder) which works actively to prevent unconscious material from erupting into consciousness and disorganizing the self defined so narrowly.

This child, grown to adulthood, has usually used his limited interpersonal skills to separate physically from the family, to go to college, or to obtain a job, and perhaps marry and have children, but he is quite vulnerable to stressful events, contexts, and relationships. When minimal needs are not met, or when demands are too great, withdrawal, depression, and psychosis can result. This acute schizophrenic break may be short in time, as little as two hours, two weeks, or two months, and there is reasonably good opportunity for reintegration, reentry into the social structure, and full recovery. Fortunately, this group of people is the most numerous of those diagnosed schizophrenic. It is this category of patient to whom the treatment environment is crucial in determining outcome. If the psychotic experience can be seen by those involved in the patient's environment as an opportunity for evolving a broader self-definition and greater social skills, the patient can indeed become "weller than well," as Karl Menninger's phrase has it.[17] If schizophrenia is seen uniformly as a tragedy, indicative of loss of hope and value, then the individual diagnosed schizophrenic at a vulnerable period of his life becomes subject to the possibility of unnecessary iatrogenic chronicity. In many hospital environments in the United States, electroshock is used routinely with such patients. This tends to confirm the view of the patient and his family that he must redouble his efforts to control his inner feelings to keep the hidden and the unacceptable from erupting. Often, the use of large doses of phenothiazines is routine. Although such antipsychotic drugs are extremely important in the treatment of reactive schizophrenic illness,[18] for the therapist to rely on medication exclusively produces a response in the patient similar to that found with electroshock: It is a behavioral message that what has been uncovered cannot possibly be useful and must be hidden again. It is fortunate that, in spite of such behavioral messages, in many treatment environments most patients suffering from reactive schizophrenia recover and return to social functioning.

Case history: Sam, a 27-year-old water-meter reader, was admitted to the hospital following a bizarre episode in which he took control of the city attorney's office, placed his feet on the attorney's desk, and imperiously issued orders. He removed his clothes and placed a call to God, with whom he stated he had a special relationship. During inpatient therapy, a picture emerged of a shy bachelor living with a rommate almost as inhibited as he. He viewed his mother as a controlling individual and his father as passive and relatively impotent in the family. Sam had managed to leave his home following high school, obtaining a job and an apartment, and he had lived quietly and independently until the incident resulting in his hospitalization. He was quite inhibited in the expression of strong feelings, but his job as a water-meter reader allowed him to be almost invisible, and in leisure hours he remained obscure, watching television and rarely dating. A limited life, but a sane one.

This fragile status quo continued until a promotion came his way. From being a meter reader, he was elevated to bill collector for the water company. As such, he was required to encounter people and let them know that if they did not pay their bills, their water would be cut off. For the first time in his life, he was forced into a situation demanding aggressiveness and forcefulness. First, in an effort to adapt, he tried to use techniques of friendliness, obsequiousness, and pleading, "If you don't pay your bill, I'm liable to lose my job." With such modest interpersonal tools, he was failing in his new job, and this led to the dramatic and bizarre behavior resulting in hospitalization.

Here was a man who had to go mad to get mad (angry). His self-image, developed through family interaction, did not include the necessary aggressiveness nor the ability to deal with power, and he could not intimidate. His psychosis was a vivid expression of the hidden and repressed parts of being human that he was incapable of expressing sanely (initiative, anger, special power, and even arrogance). True, all these were within him, but could find expression only through an acute reactive schizophrenic episode. His psychosis was of three weeks' duration, though he stayed in a hospital somewhat longer. He was able to reintegrate and, with the help of a social worker, obtained his previous satisfactory position as meter reader.

Case history: Paul, a 29-year-old accountant, was the eldest of three children. His father was a cabinet maker with rigid fundamentalist religious views, and the mother was seen by Paul as dominant in the family. The children grew up to be effective, but restricted, adults. Paul remained at home after his father's death and was living with his mother at the time of his acute illness. He dated infrequently and had a restricted social life. He had become a competent accountant, and when he began to talk of leaving his job and becoming a minister, he received no support from any of his family. He had always felt that he was closer to his father, and longed for greater socialization which he hoped theological school might offer. As the family resisted this change, he withdrew from all social contact, became depressed, and talked vaguely of going away and collecting his thoughts. He then developed two symptoms that caused his family to insist on hospitalization: He believed 1) that people could read his thoughts and would use this ability to help him; and 2) that he could make women pant when he was in their presence.

After Paul entered a psychiatric hospital, it became evident that both of these delusions were attempts to redefine himself and to reduce his sense of helplessness and aloneness. He gained strength with the notions that others understood his problems and were going to help and that he possessed sexual magnetism. Initially, he was confused, with a poor time sense, some ideas of reference, and some depressive features. The therapist arranged that, in order that his social power should be diminished as little as possible, he spend only one week full time in the hospital, and, though still delusional, return to work, coming back to the hospital at night. The basis for this arrangement was that Paul's major social strength seemed to be in his professional life. With small doses of promazine and regular treatment encounters, the delusions disappeared over a four-week period. After locating a bachelor apartment, he left the hospital. As he told the therapist, "I figured you'd never let me out of this damn hole until I left mother." In the ensuing nine months of outpatient therapy, his redefinition of himself as both more powerful and more sexual continued in a realistic fashion. He began to date more and enjoyed his new-found freedom from maternal control, entered a theological school and performed outstandingly. A follow-up several years later found him functioning successfully, with no evidence of emotional illness.

A reactive schizophrenic episode in a sane but limited person can further his development as an effective individual. Although inordinately risky, the shattering experience of ego disintegration renders one vulnerable to influences in the immediate environment. With adequate assistance, the potential in the psychotic episode may broaden the patient's self-image, allowing him to reclaim elements in himself which family limits had forced him to repress. Such a patient claims a broader self-definition and views the world as having greater possibilities. Since all sane, socialized members of a culture have limits imposed by their families (some necessary, some not), it is not surprising that people in the broader world respond ambivalently to the reactive schizophrenic with feelings of contempt, hostility, curiosity, awe, and reverence. A response of "He is less than I" is usually expressed in some way. Yet, because of dim memories of distant past, there is an undercurrent of "He knows something that I have forgotten." It is this potential of broader self-definition to which a growth-oriented therapist must attend. If he does, he can help a patient attain greater power and fewer restrictions than the family of origin could provide.[6]

RELATING FAMILY-SYSTEM INFORMATION TO THE TREATMENT OF NEUROSES AND BEHAVIOR DISORDERS

Emotional illness is a unitary disease. Regardless of type, it is due to a deficiency of coherent, satisfying, self-defining experiences with meaningful others. Midrange family products, sane but limited, usually have coherence (except for reactive schizophrenic episodes), but gravely lack satisfaction in relating, and are unable to achieve intimacy as power struggles interfere.

Specific needs of the patient from the midrange family include a lateral base, a place to stand in order to increase social functioning. A therapeutic alliance provides such a coherent system which assists the patient in further efforts in individuation. He can reduce the tyranny of family rules compulsively followed and increase the opportunities of personal choice. Such an alliance is more readily developed in products of midrange families than in offspring of the severely dysfunctional group. Basic trust in human encounter, though flawed, is greater than that found in the process schizo-phrenic or the sociopath. A therapist finds neither the pervasive amorphousness of boundaries nor the intense fear of relationship, and issues of trust center around problems of power and control. Neurotic and behavior disorders demonstrate ambivalence on two sides of the same perceptual base: a wish for, as well as a fear of, control by someone more powerful than they. If a human en-counter with some elements of mutual respect and caring occurs, a lateral base is established which provides the therapist with the role of midwife, engaged in the process of delivering a unique in-dividual into the world. The successful, growth-oriented therapist makes an effort to reduce the power of the tyrannizing referee sys-tem and provides human concern rather than another rigid system. Midrange families believe that caring means controlling, and a good therapist fights this internalized message with a new ethic, that caring means providing for individual choice. A degree of au-tonomy can be evolved in a relatively trusting and caring relation-ship with the highest priority given to personal choice and its at-tendant responsibility. I have never found the need to encourage patients to "accept their responsibilities." Once choice is experi-enced, the responsibilities of being a finite and limited, needful but unique, human being become painfully evident. In fact, I encour-age patients to take no more responsibility than they are stuck with by being alive; this is enough for anybody. *No referee is needed.*

Once a working partnership is established, issues of power and control become vivid and prominent. Products of midrange families continually try to control or be controlled. I do not view these ef-forts as resistance, but rather as attempts to stay sane by using re-lationship models learned in the primary family. Such skirmishing may be seen as "transference," and rightly so if the therapist has an open system with the freedom to have all his pet beliefs and prac-tices open to question and negotiation. However, if the therapist insists on having a greater degree of overt social power than his patients, he may relieve the patient of his family tyranny only to offer him a new one, half-desired and half-resisted by the patient. Autonomy and differentiation may be as impossible a goal in this new alliance as in the old. Later in the book (Chapter 11) these power issues are dealt with more completely,

Overthrowing the Tyranny of the Referee—Autonomy and Guilt

These patients are caught in introjected referee systems. If they come from a centripetal family, they conform; if from a centrifugal family, they accept the referee, but their behavior is inconsistent with its rules and they feel second class and chronically ashamed. This referee system is more than an individual superego. It is interpersonal and historical, and a growth-oriented psychotherapist will spend much time helping the patient to sort out the residual of past family rules to distinguish them from present reality. Is the wife, husband, lover really a carbon copy of a parent? Or, is the particular genius of neurotics and behavior disorders—the ability to make new people behave like past family—being demonstrated?

However, if the therapist himself has a "referee system"—unquestioned beliefs from a closed ideology—then what is often interpreted as transference or projection is a new, unacknowledged reality. Many patients who courageously seek help for their incompletely developed selfhood find themselves in the position of a prisoner who digs a tunnel to freedom only to find he arrives in another cell. Many therapeutic systems are relatively closed and hostile toward new input from patients or from research. If the growth-oriented psychotherapist does not transcend the limits of his system, he will unwittingly thrust a new referee onto the vulnerable patient. Then, a pathological system masquerades under the heading of treatment. If treatment is marked by right interpretations, right behavior ("you're acting out again"), and a fear of admitting confusion, uncertainty, and doubt, the patient cannot move further than midrange in functioning unless he is able to transcend his therapist's limitations.

Efforts by a well-meaning therapist with a closed system ideology can assist a patient over a rough spot, but unfortunately cannot help him become more fully human since the limits of the treatment system are quite similar to the limits of midrange families. If the belief that science can provide absoluteness and certainty (the 19th century view of science) is held by a psychotherapist, he becomes even more likely to insist that his patient swap one referee for another, which results in stylistic change rather than emotional growth.

Midrange families provide two beautiful illustrations for growth-oriented therapists of what to avoid. Negotiation is made difficult by certainty adhered to in preference to other's subjective truths, and no one can bargain in good faith, with pleasant results, when he is burdened with the belief that, at the core, he and his fellows are mean spirited and evil. If the therapist possesses similar beliefs, he cannot assist his patient to make a qualitative move toward optimal functioning.

Midrange families define a part as the whole; many treatment systems do the same. For example, some treatments emphasize cognitive understanding, others emotiveness, and still others insist that behavioral change from whatever origin is all that is needed.

It is not unusual to see obsessional styles of therapy utilizing extremely intellectualized discourse; such treatment can go on indefinitely with patients who had a similar cognitive style in their original families. Encounter groups may provide education in expressiveness without contextual integration of such emotiveness; the patients may have many emotional binges without increasing their capacity for intimacy.[19] Some therapies focus on behavior (more assertiveness, more heterosexuality, less bed-wetting, less nail-biting), with a view similar to that of midrange families that if you behave according to the referee, you'll get along fine.

Splitting the patient into thoughts, feelings, and behavior and focusing on one may help patients reduce symptoms, but usually reinforces narrow definitions of selfhood.

Guilt, a socially derived, profoundly subjective phenomenon, reflects aspects of the conscious self, the unconscious introjected interpersonal reality of family, and values of a larger society. It may be either useful guilt or useless guilt. Useful guilt may be defined operationally as not lasting more than five minutes and producing behavioral change that benefits the guilty person and/or others. This is the internalized version of a family vignette in which a child purposefully spills milk, Mother gets angry and says, "Clean it up." The child does so with absolution, and good feelings return. Useless guilt lasts forever and produces no behavioral change; it produces psychic pain and/or socially unacceptable behavior that is damaging to the guilt-ridden and to others.

The classical Freudian views guilt as resulting from parent/child interaction of a relatively late period of development—four, five, and six years—when the Oedipal conflict rages.[20] Guilt develops as the desire to possess the parent of the opposite sex is repressed, but not renounced. This concept does not square completely with clinical realities. The most guilt-ridden individuals a therapist encounters are in diagnostic categories considered to represent regression or fixation at periods of development earlier than the Oedipal. Schizophrenic patients, generally considered to be at an oral level of functioning,[21] are bedeviled by guilt; the schizophrenic voices, spokesman for his hidden self, the "not-me," described by Sullivan,[22] often berate and taunt him for his evil qualities and he usually sees his essential nature as evil.

Further, the obsessive-compulsive neurotic is presumably stuck at a pre-Oedipal anal phase; yet he is similarly tortured by guilt. He is terribly concerned with obligation and duty and defends against his guilt with complex rituals, undoing, and reaction formation.

This is a theoretical problem. The most guilt-ridden patients are concerned with developmental riddles considered by classical analytic view to be prior to Oedipal conflicts, yet the Oedipal phase is assumed to be the originating point of guilt. How does one extricate himself from this theoretical perplexity? One way out is to consider the data and constructs of superego development offered by Melanie Klein. Data from the analyses of young children led Klein to conclude that the Oedipal triangle appears quite early in infantile development. "The fact that we assume the Oedipus complex to reach its zenith around the fourth year of life and that we recognize the development of the superego as the end result of the complex, seems to me in no way to contradict these observations (of early manifestations of the Oedipus complex in her patients). These definite, typical phenomena, the existence of which is in the most clearly developed form we can recognize when the Oedipus complex has reached its zenith, and which precede its waning, are merely the termination of the development which occupies *years*. The analyses of very young children show that as soon as the Oedipus complex arises, they begin to work it through, and thereby develop a superego. The effects of this infantile superego upon the child are analogous to those of the superego upon the adult, but they weigh far more heavily upon the weaker infantile ego."[23]

Another view is to separate neurotic guilt from issues of Oedipal conflicts entirely. It is quite possible to consider neurotic guilt as reflecting introjected family patterns of distancing and punishment for disclosing the inmost self. The Oedipal complex is ubiquitous; we cannot appeal to the phenomenon itself for an explanation of any pathology. Instead, we must look to specific interactions and patterns which encourage or discourage modification of the primitive, punitive, infantile superego and allow it to become, in Fenichel's words, "more amenable to the ego, more plastic, and more sensible."[24]

The system factors of a family or a therapist most important in such modification include:

1) *Love*. A valuable, succinct definition of love is H. S. Sullivan's: "caring about another's well-being almost as much as one cares about one's own." Of all the factors that ameliorate a punishing superego, this is the most important. It seems impossible for any individual to see himself as neutral. He may consider himself as bad, good, bad and good, but never neutral. Being considered important, valuable, *loveable*, is necessary to counterbalance early guilt.

2) *Acceptance of the instinctual drives possessed by the child or the patient*. Without this, a child tries to become acceptable to himself and others only at the expense of alienating and repressing large portions of the self that generate neurotic guilt.

3) *Clarity of expectations*. Interaction that allows an individual to

feel successful and be rewarded for expected behavior is important.

4) *Models whose own superegos are sensible with whom the child or patient can identify.* The individual can then develop a hierarchy of values: Killing is more reprehensible than stealing food when one is hungry; lying is worse than making honest mistakes. The superego becomes a usable guide rather than destroying self-esteem. With a relentlessly painful, damning, punishing superego, the outcome is either endless suffering or a strong effort to ignore the whole thing. Thus, neurotics suffer continually, and behavior disorders often act as if they have no superego at all, since it is of little use.

This conceptual system fits with clinical experience. The punitive superego, found early in even the most fortunate children, can be modified by virtue of the love and social education of parental figures. Without such loving care, the child is doomed to extremely low self-esteem. The least socially adept are the most guilt-ridden. Schizophrenia is a hell of self-reproach: obsessive-compulsive neurotics suffer terrible guilt; hysteric neurotics constantly feel inadequate and attempt to assuage pervasive guilt by attacking those who are presumably more powerful. Behavior disorders express this useless guilt as well. Franz Alexander pointed out years ago that people who behave poorly (he termed their diagnosis "character neurosis") have no less guilt than did classical neurotics.[25] They express it, however, by bringing punishment upon themselves rather than by internal suffering.

Because of their rigid referee system, midrange families encourage guilt that is useless. Their belief in the essential evil of man and their view of relationship are coercive. Effective psychotherapy for the midrange product must challenge all referee systems, question the reality of man's depravity, and offer experiences of intimacy without coercion. Sharing in an atmosphere of equal power reduces useless guilt. A patient can learn that he can think and feel anything; further, he can do that which he will take responsibility for and does not need to blame his fate on others. This is ego-building and esteem-promoting work that reduces useless guilt.

Closed therapeutic systems with a new source of external author- ity do not reduce this useless guilt, but merely rearrange it. As a therapist challenges the particular referee system of the patient's family by encouraging personal choice, a pragmatic, functional self begins to emerge that can experience satisfaction.

These treatment issues, brought into focus by study of midrange families, are intended to be provocative rather than exhaustive. Discussion of scientific psychotherapy in later chapters adds to the concept that therapist/patient interaction must go beyond the limi- tations of midrange family patterns in order to be optimally effec- tive.

REFERENCES

1. BEAVERS, W. R., LEWIS, J. M., GOSSETT, J. T., and PHILLIPS, V. A., "Family systems and ego functioning: midrange families," Scientific Proceedings, 128th Annual Meeting, American Psychiatric Association, Anaheim, California, May, 1975.
2. LEWIS, J. M., BEAVERS, W. R., GOSSETT, J. T., and PHILLIPS, V. A., *No Single Thread: Psychological Health in Family Systems*, New York, Brunner/Mazel, 1976.
3. SROLE, L., LANGNER, J. S., MICHAEL, S. T., OPLER, M. K., and RENNIE, A. C., *Men- tal Health in the Metropolis: The Midtown Manhattan Study*, New York, McGraw-Hill, 1962.
4. SINGER, M. T., and WYNNE, L. D., "Differentiating characteristics of parents of child- hood schizophrenics, childhood neurotics, and young adult schizophrenics," *Am. J. Psychiat.*, 120:234-243, 1963.
5. PAUL, N. L., "The use of empathy in the resolution of grief," *Perspectives in Biology and Medicine*, 11:153-169, 1967-68.
6. BEAVERS, W. R., "Schizophrenia and despair," *Comprehensive Psychiat.* 13(6):561-572, 1972.
7. BLUM, R. H., and Associates, *Horatio Alger's Children*, San Francisco, Jossey-Bass, 1972.
8. STIERLIN, H., LEVI, L. D., and SAVARD, R. J., "Centrifugal versus centripetal separa- tion in adolescence: two patterns and some of their implications," in Feinstein, S., and Giovacchini, P. (Eds.), *Annals of the American Society for Adolescent Psychiatry*, Vol. II, New York, Basic Books, 211-239, 1973.
9. GENET, J., *The Balcony*, Frechtman, B. (Trans.), New York, Grove Press, 1958.
10. KUBIE, L. S., "The eagle and the ostrich," *Arch. Gen. Psychiat.*, Vol. 5, August, 1961, 109-119.
11. SALZMAN, L., *The Obsessive Personality*, New York, Science House, 1968.
12. TOMAN, W., *Family Constellation: Its Effects on Personality and Social Behavior*, New York, Springer, 1969.
13. SUSSEX, J. N., "Drugs in the therapy of the neuroses," in Usdin, G. L. (ed.), *Psychoneurosis and Schizophrenia*, Philadelphia, J. B. Lippincott, 1966.
14. EHRENWALD, J. JR., *Neurosis in the Family*, New York, Hoeber Medical Division, Harper & Row, 1963.
15. STIERLIN, H., *Separating Parents and Adolescents*, New York, Quadrangle, 1972.
16. BERNE, E., *What Do You Say After You Say Hello?*, New York, Grove Press, 1972.

17. MENNINGER, K., MAYMAR, M., and PRUYSER, P., *The Vital Balance*, New York, Viking Press, 1964.
18. MAY, P. R. A., *Treatment of Schizophrenia, A Comparative Study of Five Treatment Methods*, New York, Science House, 1968.
19. LIEBERMAN, M., YALOM, I., and Miles, M., *Encounter Groups: First Facts*, New York, Basic Books, 1973.
20. BRENNER, C., *An Elementary Textbook of Psychoanalysis*, New York, International Universities Press, 1957.
21. NUNBERG, H., *Principles of Psychoanalysis*, New York, International Universities Press, 1955.
22. SULLIVAN, H. S., *Clinical Studies in Psychiatry*, New York, W. W. Norton, 1956.
23. KLEIN, M., *Contributions to Psychoanalysis*, 1921-1945, London, Hogarth Press, 1948.
24. FENICHEL, O., *The Psychoanalytic Theory of Neurosis*, New York, W. W. Norton, 1945.
25. ALEXANDER, F., "The neurotic character," *International J. of Psychoanalysis*, Vol. XI:292-311, 1930.

*Once the realization is accepted that even between the
closest human beings infinite distances continue to exist,
a wonderful living side by side can grow up, if they succeed in loving the distance between them which makes it
possible for each to see the other whole against the sky.*

Rainer Maria Rilke

_____ **5**

Healthy families

Mental health professionals develop a fantasy of health for individuals and families that is derived from observing disturbed
people, and they carry this definition in their heads as an ideal,
with few supporting data. The usual mental health professional will
stoutly deny that his family of origin was normal, and he has great
doubts about the health of his friends' families! We are not unlike
energetic and enthusiastic missionaries who encourage others to be
good Christians, but have knowledge only of sinners. Perhaps
many of us, like wise missionaries, recognize that the fantasy is just
that, a construct, possibly useful to urge ourselves and others toward a laudable but eternally unattainable goal. If we do not recognize the abstract quality of the fantasy of health, our work with
struggling individuals can be discouraging. My hope is that information about successful families' struggles through developmental
crises, efforts at attaining intimacy, and pangs of separation will

provide a beam of light in the fog, helping parents and therapists do a better job by demythologizing emotional health.

The following material about healthy families is derived primarily from the six-year Timberlawn study reported elsewhere.[1] It is central to the purpose of this book as it details the systems developed by the primary helpers, the parents, in the most effective family systems that we could find. The research emphasis is on functioning, not pathology, and on systems and interaction rather than on an artificial isolation of individuals for study. Past family research has studied dysfunctional families and extrapolated to presumably healthy patterns. Moreover, few of these studies were interactional; families containing an identified patient were evaluated from patient data and from interviews with family members. In recent years, attempts to correct the limitations of such research led to interactional studies, many of which have been referred to in the preceding two chapters. In addition, several research projects, focusing on pathological family systems, used non-pathological families as controls.[2,3,4,5] That these data are consistent with ours is not surprising, since the studies were similarly constructed, using family interaction rather than individual information as the base.

The simplest way to define a healthy family is negatively: Health is the absence of emotional illness in family members. If a family has an emotionally ill member, it is not healthy; if it has no one so diagnosed (and generally such definitions are qualified by time limits, for example, for the last two, three, or five years), then it is healthy. This is the first of four perspectives on normality or health described by Offer and Sabshin.[6]

A second perspective on normality is that of optimal functioning, determined by a theoretical system. This could be a step forward or it might lead us back to the good-Christian-or-sinners approach. In this chapter we move from the first definition to the second, but with the theoretical system derived from a data base.

A third definition of normality is statistical: It is the average. With this orientation, midrange families would probably be closer to the normal than the families to be described in this chapter. Optimal families are as deviant from the mean as are the severely dysfunctional ones at the other end of the negentropic continuum.

Offer and Sabshin's fourth definition of normality is that health is a process, recognizing growth, adaptation, and change through time as an integral part of getting and staying healthy. Longitudinal studies are necessary to bring data to this perspective. Though the data are incomplete and not yet integrated in the summary statement, the families in the Timberlawn study are being followed in such a fashion.

After absorbing, sifting, and evaluating the data from healthy families, the Timberlawn research group arbitrarily divided the sample into two groups, which were termed "optimal" and "adequate." Though the two groups differ significantly, there is a continuum, and an arbitrary breakpoint was chosen to separate these two. Both quantitative and qualitative differences between these two groups were determined at three different levels of study: clinical, rating scale, and microanalytic data.

ADEQUATE FAMILIES

Though this chapter is concerned primarily with the optimal group, the information obtained from studying adequate families was useful as well. All healthy families, adequate and optimal, showed little invasiveness, a high degree of members' taking personal responsibility for feelings, thoughts, and actions, and a relatively small amount of unresolvable family conflict, when compared to families possessing an identified patient. These variables were not significant in distinguishing the two healthy groups. In several other ways, however, the adequate families were more similar to midrange than to optimal families; that is, they showed an unequal overt power structure, the parental coalition was relatively weak, the family members were deficient in permeability to each other and in empathic qualities. Further, the adequate group was handicapped almost as much as were midrange families in negotiating and in performing tasks. These adequate families lacked spontaneity compared to the optimal group; there was little pleasant laughter and a great deal of tension or depression.

Role stereotyping of various kinds, especially sexual, was comparable to that found in midrange families, and there was clear evidence of a family referee, which diminished their respect for subjective reality and reduced potential for personal growth and development. Adequate families were often caught up in rather grim control efforts just as are symptomatic families, and the fear of normal human drives was quite evident. A somewhat oppositional set was apparent, though the degree that adequate family members could break through this and find shared human warmth was greater than in any pathological group. Though individual boundaries were clear enough for members to have a coherent self, self-definition was usually at the cost of considerably distancing oneself from the family group and a reduction in joyful sharing.

These adequate families illustrated that family goals and purposes can be attained even in the presence of stereotyped roles, limited interpersonal skills and considerable obliviousness to feelings. Painful, repetitive, and game-like behavior can be observed in family members who are raising competent children. Strained parental coalitions with unresolved Oedipal struggles, dominant/submissive parental roles, and even confusing communicational sequences can exist along with adequate functioning.

From individual interviews it seemed that the mother in our adequate group suffered the most pain. She was the most likely to have periods of depression, to rely on tranquilizers, and to doubt her own adequacy. The family functioned at the expense of interpersonal pain centering in and expressed by the wife and mother.

Maladaptive patterns existed; problems were frequent in the family, yet function was maintained. What contributed to this toughness, this tenacity in survival and functioning? Predictability of structure, perhaps. There was a greater trust of the known difficulties in the family than in the unknown dangers of the outside world. In addition, real self-esteem was apparent in all these family members. The parents valued their parenting roles, and, though their skills were modest, they persevered. Further, each family was headed by a father with vocational ability in which he took pride, and he provided economic security and comfort; this freed his wife to meet, in some fashion, the children's emotional needs.

Parents' consistent presence and their belief that the job of parenting is important compensated for deficiencies in interpersonal skills. It appears that *trying* is important if that trying is consistent.

OPTIMAL FAMILIES

These optimal families showed the characteristics of a highly negentropic system. The structure was definite and clear, yet flexible, and it was carried lightly. Family members concerned themselves with functioning. Change in methods, goals, and choices did not threaten the family; even the youngest children contributed to family plans. These families enjoyed negotiations and welcomed new input. This input was examined and evaluated, but the family members viewed it positively. They respected human biological drives. There was little embarrassment when a family member showed fear or anxiety, and anger was considered a sign that something needed to be corrected; it had less of the impotent or intimidating overtones seen in less effective families. Sexual interest was considered a positive force, both in parents and in children. We did not observe any of these optimal families concerned with masturbatory activities in their children. (Our findings were compatible with those of Westley and Epstein, who found that frequency of parental sexual intercourse correlated positively with the emotional health of children!)[7] When a system, whether person or family, is not at war with itself and is able to accept and affirm its basic qualities, an adaptive and differentiating state can develop.

In these optimal families one could see the same stylistic differences described in the severely dysfunctional and in midrange families that were termed "centrifugal" and "centripetal." There were striking variations in family styles; it appears that as the family systems become more competent and healthier, their styles are more varied, less stereotyped. The classification could have been continued, placing some families in the centripetal category, others in the centrifugal, and still a third group in the mixed category. However, this did not seem particularly useful, since these stylistic differences were subtle and did not hinder the development of offspring.

Two Optimal Families*

A description of two optimal families' interactional qualities may illuminate these concepts.

The *Comfort* family consisted of parents in their mid-thirties and three children ages 11, 13, and 14. Overall, this family's interaction seemed capable, easy, understated, and somewhat bland. Though the family was clearly quite happy and effective, and they did command the observer's attention, their style was rather like that of a Cadillac idling: there was strength and power, but little variation. The family did not make difficult challenges for itself. Hence, it had potential power, with all the members content to enjoy their ease and not extend themselves. They were skilled at avoiding painful anxiety.

The Comforts evidenced a striking sense of "we-ness," an expectation of affiliative encounter. They supported, affirmed, and frequently reached out to each other. Oppositional exchanges were nearly nonexistent.

The family had a clear and obvious deference to outside authority. They were able to meet their needs within what they considered a proper and benign social order, and viewed people who deviated from that structure as being either foolish or threats to the community. This may explain their small concern about changing or affecting the larger world. They saw themselves as important and took care of themselves and each other, but they believed the *"real"* authorities were other people who make the rules, wisely

---

*Names and other identifying characteristics of each family have been altered. Reprinted by permission from *No Single Thread: Psychological Health in Family Systems*, Jerry M. Lewis, W. Robert Beavers, John T. Gossett, and Virginia Austin Phillips, New York: Brunner/ Mazel, 1976.

and benignly, and that was perfectly all right. The Comforts were reminiscent of the Betas in Huxley's *Brave New World*—defining themselves as better than most, but not at the top. Their family system incorporated a very strong sense of right and wrong in a most humane way.

This family had the most continually overall positive mood of any family studied. In interacting with each other, these family members illustrated a belief in human dignity. They respected each others' world views, though that world was small. They did not have a great deal of interest in disparate views outside the family; since they related only to those they considered similar, they remained affiliative in almost all of their activities. Their feeling tone was strikingly warm and caring, optimistic and cheerful. There was little evidence of unresolved conflict and no evidence of continued anger or underlying depression.

They were verbally open. The children were direct about their feelings, and expression of anger was acceptable in the system. Each child's superego structure was not foreign and isolated, but skillfully integrated into everyday functioning. Rather than inhibiting their ability to be themselves, it seemed to be a framework around which they distributed their self-definition. This allowed leeway in expressing feelings. Although this system did not encourage individual thinking, it was otherwise so rewarding that no one needed to be deviant.

There was a very capable coalition between the parents, with no evidence of favoritism for one or another child. The family was father-led, but father's attitude towards his wife was one of interest, concern, and respect, with no attempt to subjugate or to flaunt his power. Mother's efforts to be autonomous or to lead were minimal, but not to the point of inefficiency.

The family did not talk about abstract concepts. However, their understanding of complex human motivations and needs was clearly revealed in their behavior.

This family handled some functions less well. Because of the powerful, though integrated, superego structure in the family system, there was a conventional tone to the family. Very little surfaced in the way of unique views of the world. This was not due to modest intellect, since both parents were college graduates, and the father had built a business with a good income. Their intellect had been used to make life comfortable. This conventionality did, however, reduce spontaneity.

The family was socially active and especially involved in organized sports. Though showing no interest in activities having to do with ideas or concepts, they had a great deal of ability and shared their enjoyment of the world with others who were similar.

Mr. Comfort was a sensitive, sturdy, and flexible man. He expressed feelings easily, was physically relaxed and quite responsive to others. The other family members had similar evidence of personal capabilities. It was clear that the parents found adulthood pleasant and gratifying, and they rewarded their children by allowing them more grown-up activities. This was most significant in the growing family. Father stated that the main thing he wanted to impart to his children was respect and consideration for others. He saw the reason for problems in the world as personal immorality. This orientation produces adaptive human beings, though perhaps few great achievers.

The *Powers* family consisted of parents in their early thirties and three children 14, 13, and 9. The father, an aggressive, successful businessman, set the tone of the family interaction. Though he often tried to dominate, Mrs. Powers presented herself as competent and usually held her own with him. The oldest child was quiet; the middle and youngest children were active and aggressive, much like their father. Family members had a warm responsiveness to one another, and a truly affiliative orientation, interspersed with some chafing at father's great power and occasional outright dominance. Though generally pleasant and positive, the family had a high level of anxiety. They operated well with this anxiety level, and it seemed to be a spur for all except, perhaps, the oldest child, who was quiet and somewhat unaggressive and tended to respond to anxiety by moderate withdrawal. The family accepted this difference, and he was not scapegoated. They showed reasonable empathy, but also some concern over this child's difficulty in making friends.

There was definite respect for different viewpoints in this family, whose tolerance encouraged a vigorous marketplace of ideas. Father usually stated his position directly and aggressively. He really attended to other family members and responded to their communications, both verbal and behavioral, but they must scramble for the floor. Mrs. Powers was an energetic person who, encouraged by her husband, was furthering her education. Mr. Powers had a family tradition of active women, so his wife's activity outside the home was quite consistent with his view of the world. Overall, there was a high degree of respect for each others' perceptions and feelings.

Communication in this family was open and direct with little confusion or obscuring. The one apparent exception to this was the oldest child who was a "marginal commentator." For example, when one of the interviewers asked him if he ever got angry with his father, he responded, "Well no, not really." Then he went on and in a pseudo-dutiful fashion remarked, "They get angry with me for good and just cause," and then also commented, "Yes, only for just cause," with an ironic inflection that was not lost on the rest of the family, and it was accepted. There was a game-like quality in the way the oldest child presented himself as one-down to his siblings and the world in general, but it was a pleasant game; he was able to enjoy himself and seemed to have adequate self-esteem. There were no sarcastic, cutting messages.

There was a firm parental coalition in this most physical couple of all of the families seen. When together they moved toward one another and touched in a warm way; no evidence existed of favoritism of one child over another, or unresolved oedipal feelings. Generation barriers were clear. Mother, though involved outside the family circle, was most invested in the family. She often seemed to be the family cheerleader.

The family was insightful and verbal with great appreciation of human complexity and an excellent capacity to express this understanding both in behavior and words.

There was an unusual degree of spontaneity and the unexpected was almost anticipated. Each person was a well differentiated individual, and there was a prevailing presumption of autonomy. Two areas of repetitive, stereotyped interaction centered around father's power and the oldest child's withdrawal. Mother seemed a bit hard-put to keep up with the aggressiveness of her husband, and the oldest child tended to fringe family interaction as he apparently fringed outside groups. He was, however, quite witty and a major contributor of the unexpected.

This family was the most constructively aggressive of any family in this group. Contrasting with the Comforts, a family equally high in competence, their capabilities were due not to skillful avoidance of intrafamily friction, but rather to keeping friction moderate while reaching out into the world. They were movers, doers, and changers.

Both parents had impressive individual characteristics. The father was driving, aggressive, creative, and never really content. Mother also showed this pushing quality in her considerable outside activities. The two younger children were also active and aggressive; but the oldest marched to a different drummer and came across as different rather than inferior. This was a kinetic, striving group, offering each other enough mutual support for the struggle to be rewarding.

EIGHT VARIABLES IMPORTANT IN FORGING A COMPETENT SELF

From all of the process-oriented clinical and research study of families, but especially from the formal systems research of optimal families, eight variables emerged that I consider most important in environments that attempt to develop human competence, such as families, settings for the treatment of emotional illness, and educational situations. These are: 1) a systems orientation; 2) boundary issues; 3) contextual clarity; 4) power issues; 5) encouragement of autonomy; 6) affective issues; 7) task efficiency; and 8) transcendent values.

Some of these variables are continuations of those developed at the beginning of our research in family systems, and others evolved through the years of study. Each is described here in detail; together they represent a place to stand to evaluate and enrich intensive growth-promoting psychotherapy systems.

1) *A Systems Orientation*

Observing families of widely varying competence attempt to work together in accomplishing assigned tasks, I have some identification with every member of each family. I was aware of having at times behaved and felt similarly to each parent and each child. As I identified now with a schizophrenic adolescent, then with a rigid parent, or a capable child, or a satisfied adult, my "objectivity" and even my coherence were threatened. It was hard to classify, judge, and evaluate, possessing such a sense of shared humanness and relative perplexity in adapting to the human condition. Thus it became apparent to me that the tasks of the researcher, a psychotherapist/psychiatrist, a parent, and a child are in many ways comparable: to make sense out of what is going on in the relationship in order to have individual definition, social power, and a sense of purpose compatible with the system in which one is enmeshed. I was judge and victim, controller and controlled, definer and defined, just as family members are. I had to be oriented, and orientation depended on organizing the overwhelming reality surrounding me. Engulfed in human struggle, I was constantly redefining myself. What was it that I wanted? What could I achieve? How was achievement to be defined? By whom? Many models of performance and cognition were available to me as an expert and a reasonably sane person, just as they are available to family members. The boundary between me (as observer) and the families (as observed) would become clear, then collapse, with resulting confusion and anxiety. Input overload was an ever-present threat. I remembered with fondness and relief the passage from Wilder's *Our*

Town as Emily came back to earth to view a morning with her family:

> I didn't realize. So all that was going on and we never noticed—Oh earth, you're too wonderful for anybody to realize you. Do any human beings ever realize life while they live it?[8]

I felt the pull to blot out information, to deny meaning, purpose, and direction, just as severely dysfunctional family members do. Sometimes, when less stressed, I could identify with midrange families and reach for a referee. I would use what I was taught and "explain" things to myself and others in the psychoanalytic framework, my particular historical cognitive structure. Maybe I would learn little that was new, but at least I could survive and be judged well by my peers.

Occasionally, when quite comfortable in my interpersonal context and self-definition, I could identify with optimal family members, accept the limitations of my past, maintain coherence with openness to the unknown, and see this unknown as a gift rather than a terrible threat. People in their buzzing, confusing reality can be benign teachers rather than depriving dangers; openness to the new can be satisfying rather than painful. In such periods of lucidity, I began to understand emotionally the orientation of optimal families. Such an orientation can be described as an open systems view of the world.

This view includes at least four basic assumptions:

> a) Any individual needs a group, a human system for individual definition of coherence and satisfaction.
> b) Causes and effects are interchangeable.
> c) Any human behavior is a result of many variables rather than one clear-cut single cause.
> d) Humans are limited and finite. A social role either of absolute power or of helplessness prohibits many of the needed satisfactions found in human encounter.

The optimal family members knew that people do not prosper in a vacuum; human needs are satisfied in an interpersonal matrix. As a child develops and matures, he leaves one system—the primary family—not for isolated independence, but for other human systems. Whether he enters college or marriage, the military or the swinging singles, he will continue to need community, and must develop interpersonal skills to adapt to the next system.

Some theoretical concepts of man give short shrift to this reality, just as disturbed families do, defining maturity as hypothetical independence, close in meaning to aloneness. The optimal families did not make this error but instead defined maturity as the evolution of new relationships that provided reciprocal satisfying intimacy. Adults possessed skills in meeting needs of others as well as their own. Humans were accepted as social animals who grow up, leave home, and necessarily establish new reciprocal relationships.

This awareness promoted an open system, one with rules compatible with (though not necessarily the same as) those found in the larger society. Members of an aberrant family with peculiar rules find it harder to leave and are more vulnerable in their passage into the larger world. Compatibility of rules increases the chances of success for any system, whether family, school, or treatment environment. This is a system phenomenon which is ignored only to the detriment of those being assisted.

The second hallmark of a systems view of the world, recognition that causes and effects are interchangeable, is equally significant. Severely dysfunctional family members are awash in confusion, looking vainly for clear identifiable causes for their frustration and pain, and often retreating to vague or mystical answers, such as fate or destiny, for explanations of personal and family problems. Midrange families seek answers for human problems in simple causes, for example, a bad seed within the household (the scapegoat), or human perversity (evil drives), and they flounder forever in their efforts to control these perverse forces.

The optimal families knew that, for example, hostility in one person promotes deception in the others; deception promotes hostility. Efforts at tyrannical control increase the possibility of angry defiance, just as uncooperative defiance invites tyrannical control.

Stimuli are responses, responses are stimuli, in a process with shape and form, but no clearly defined individual villains or victims.

The third assumption, that human behavior results from many variables, is striking by its absence in dysfunctional families. Much of my time as a psychotherapist is spent in increasing patients' abilities to change sets, move out of linear ruts, attain more of a systems viewpoint, and thereby become more competent in relating. The members of optimal families already possessed such knowledge, taught since infancy by rewarding relationships.

An example may assist in comprehending the difference. A child of three spills milk at the table. There are a number of possibilities as to why the milk is spilled. Perhaps it is accidental and no motive should be attached to the behavior; or, perhaps it has interpersonal meaning, that the child has a score to settle with Mother; or, a third possibility, the child has hostile destructive drives unrelated to Mother that must be expressed and controlled; or possibly, he is tired or anxious and therefore apt to make mistakes; or, it is mechanical—the glass is too large and his little fists are unable to hold on to it. Each of these approaches is used almost exclusively by one or another type of dysfunctional family. Depressed and poorly behaving families assume that things are random and accidental and nothing means very much, or that things happen because of evil drives in individuals. Paranoid families automatically assume hostile purpose, "You meant to do it, to me," and families with hypochondriacal members assume high anxiety or physical causes. The optimal families used all of these concepts and more; they were not locked into stereotyped responses from theories of simple causation and their responses to an event varied with the context in a highly pragmatic fashion.

An interview with the father of an optimal family revealed the following story: The oldest daughter, now 18, had at 13 become rebellious and oppositional to her mother, to the point of stating that she wished to kill her. The father rather shamefacedly confessed that he physically threatened and even slapped his daughter in an effort to force her to shut up and straighten out. At the same time, he and his wife reviewed their interaction with the child and decided they had put too much pressure on her. When they then drastically reduced performance demands, the girl became more comfortable, her anger abated, and the relationship between daughter and mother improved. Intuitively, these parents responded to a stress with both coercion and relaxation, seeing the girl as needing both limits and reduced unrealistic expectations. Their use of two models simultaneously was a pragmatic success.

Finally, a systems orientation includes awareness that humans are finite, limited in power, and that self-esteem lies in relative competence rather than in omnipotence. Success in all human endeavor depends on variables beyond anyone's control; yet if one possesses goals and purpose he *can* make a difference in his life and in others'. This is an eternal tension which one can accommodate to, but never overcome. Here we see the resolution of the impotent/omnipotent behavioral patterns described in Chapter 3. One is terribly vulnerable if he tries to control another absolutely. Negotiation is essential for success in human enterprise, and individual choice must be taken into account.

As I work with parents of disturbed adolescents, I must often begin by offering a harsh reality: The child can go to hell in a handbasket if he or she so chooses, and there is *nothing the parents can do about it*! This approach is a dramatic attempt to bring the family to a realization which every optimal family possessed. A person can be adequate and fail in any endeavor that requires the participation of others. Power is relative. A human will feel despairing and impotent unless he realizes this stark fact. Trust is relative, whether that trust is in oneself or another. Absolute trust is a fantasy that may be placed in superhuman entities, but not in any limited, vulnerable parent or child, friend or lover. This knowledge promotes a milieu that helps a child develop far beyond the initial impotent/omnipotent relationship. His competence is rewarded, his failures accepted as a part of human effort. Failure is sad and painful, but it does not indicate evil drives, malevolent intent, or basic inadequacy.

2) *Boundary Issues*

A useful parallel to the external boundary of an optimal family system is that of a living cell. It possesses enough strength and integrity to allow highly negentropic interaction within its borders, yet it is permeable to the outside world, allowing effective interchange. The interchange includes getting and using valuable information and material from the outside world, and discarding outworn patterns and beliefs that are no longer adaptive. Optimal family members were actively involved in the world beyond the family and related to it with optimism and hope. From these encounters, they brought varied interests and excitement into the family. Some families accented intellectual activities, others were social, some political, and some physical (as in enthusiasm for tennis, golf, baseball, or biking). All multiplied the satisfactions of family interaction by investing in other inclusive social systems.

This openness to other viewpoints, life-styles, and perceptions contributed to the congruent mythology seen in optimal families. Observations of raters coincided with family members' assessment of their strengths and weaknesses. There was little of what might be called family autism in the more entropic closed-system families. Openness to the world increased their ability to alter views of themselves and their family and eliminated the need to live in two worlds, the mythic and the unacknowledged "real" (the interactional reality as seen by outside observers).

These optimal families had clear (intrasystem) boundaries between members. It was easy to determine how Mother felt as compared with Father, or how one child viewed a specific situation as compared with another. Respected differences flourished. Negotiation consisted of accepting those differences and working toward shared goals. In such a differentiated family unit, individual choice was expected. Family members spoke up; even the youngest were respected as significant sovereign individuals whose contributions were valued. Usually the parents made a special effort to share their power with these small children, bringing them into deliberations and helping them to express viewpoints. These people offered a valuable model for groups of any sort that wish to meet both group and individual needs.

Respect for individual boundaries allows intimacy. Members of optimal families had the delightful opportunity to share their innermost selves with others who were different but empathic. In deciding on plans and goals, compromise was usually unnecessary as family members considered individual and family goals compatible. Negotiation is qualitatively different from compromise, since compromise suggests an oppositional set with an acceptance of "half-a-loaf." Optimal family members accepted that the whole system must function for individuals to prosper, and they considered the negotiating process an aspect of being an individual rather than an incessant compromising of personal goals.

As I work with rigid midrange families in psychotherapy, I find they often see compromise as a heaven just out of reach, thwarted by the selfishness of a parent or child. I spend much time offering the optimal family's viewpoint that compromise is usually unnecessary. If one accepts finite humanness and a finite family system, his goals are quite dependent on other group members' having their needs met also. Negotiation can consist of meeting reciprocal individual needs effectively. A major lesson from the family studies was that affiliative, compassionate, and accepting relationships support clear individual boundaries. Self-abnegation is not useful in obtaining intimacy.

Invasiveness, the aggressive defining of another, might appear opposite to submissive self-denial, but it is close to the same phenomenon. If one respects his own unique feelings and thoughts, he is equipped to respect his spouse's or his children's. If he is prone to self-abnegation, he is also insensitive to the other's need for self-respect. Optimal family members did not invade; they presented their own subjective world view. These most fortunate families attained intimacy by skillful communication and the awareness of individual needs and boundaries, avoiding the quandary of SD families who look vainly for consensus, or MR families, who struggle for control.

3) *Contextual Clarity*

In optimal family interaction it was generally clear to whom comments were addressed and the relationship of the speaker to his audience. Body language was congruent with verbal messages and was attended as avidly as was speech. In discussions, all family members possessed a shared theme. Under-the-table discussion, common in midrange families and carried on with body language and quick asides, seldom occurred in the optimal group. To continue conversation with a shared focus of attention over a period of time is a remarkable achievement.

Optimal family members had a clear definition of generational boundaries; though overt power was shared freely, there was no question as to who was parent and who was child. Clear definition of generational boundaries clarified roles for both parents and children. No parent felt obligated to throw away his or her adult power, and no child felt called upon to assume a premature responsibility. Such comforting clarity was bought at the price of *renunciation*. Parents renounced any exploitation of children; children renounced the exclusive possession of a parent.

A central aspect of adequate resolution of the Oedipal conflict, made possible in health by the confluence of family-system qualities, is renunciation. A four-year-old child says, "I am going to grow up and marry Daddy (or Mommy)," and the parent smiles, unperturbed. Such fantasies are expected in early years. As the child grows older, he is capable of apprehending triangles and limitations, and he has assistance in accepting these limitations from parents who present clear role definition and a solid coalition.

Why is renunciation so necessary in resolving the Oedipal conflict? One can have a parent, one can have a lover, but one cannot have a father or mother and a lover in the same person. If it is not clear whether one has a parent or a lover, he has neither. Here is another central human paradox: By renouncing, one can receive. Closeness and warmth can reside only in the finite limits of a clear relationship.

In any social context, whether family, friendship, or therapist-patient relationship, there is a useful rule of thumb in defining the degree of craziness present: How clear is the context? There was generational clarity in optimal families and a reasonable acceptance that father could enjoy his daughter, but he could not be her lover. Mother could enjoy her son, but he could not replace her lover/ husband. If a child and the opposite-sexed parent have a confused and unclear relationship, the result is pain and unmet need in all aspects of mother, father, child interaction, and the resulting sticky mess complicates all other family relationships. Unless necessary renunciation is relatively complete, as in these optimal families, the opportunities for contextual confusion and continued fantasies are infinite.

This contextual clarity began with a strong parental coalition, both in functional and affectional terms. It was also aided by relatively equal parental overt power, which intensified the generational contrast. Such clarity made it possible for pleasure to be obtained in open, licit, above-board interaction and reduced dependence on illicit behavior to satisfy human needs.

In Chapter 4, I described the tendency of sane-but-limited midrange families to have family role stereotyping, especially sexual. At first glance, such stereotyping might seem to be in the service of context clarity (Mother is soft, sweet, and ineffectual; Father is insensitive, hardworking, and dutiful). Not so, however—stereotyping does a disservice to human complexity, and therefore invites a blurred context. If acknowledged reality and power do not include enough individual capabilities and needs, these go underground and become illicit. Illicitness may be expressed within the family or with similarly needful people in the outside world. Optimal families had the least amount of stereotyping. A wide range of human feelings and perceptions was acceptable in all members. Discipline was not a preoccupation, but usually a minor issue in these families. If the context between family members is clear and complex human needs are acceptable, intimidation is unnecessary. Most of the interesting qualities and needs of family members can be expressed without being forced to seek forbidden outlets.

4) *Power Issues*

When a human is frightened, he seeks some kind of power. Two choices are available: a) the power of a loving relationship with a meaningful other—reaching for another without coercion and expressing needs directly; b) the power of coercive control over the environment, one's inner self, and others. Disturbing examples of relying on control include autistic children who are indifferent toward human objects and attempt to relate to mechanical parts of the world which seem controllable, and the chronic schizophrenic who finds that he cannot control the non-human world or other humans, so retreats to fantasies which are more amenable to his control. More effective, but still painful and lonely, methods of adaptation include those seen in neurosis and behavior disturbance. People with these difficulties distrust themselves and others, and they feel so vulnerable that they must intimidate rather than risk open negotiation. In the various dysfunctional families such control efforts are evident. In optimal families a different picture emerged. There was a clear hierarchy of power with leadership in the hands of the parents who formed an egalitarian coalition. The children were less overtly powerful, but their contributions influenced decisions. Incessant and self-defeating power struggles seldom occurred, and family tasks were undertaken with good-humored effectiveness. These fortunate individuals had learned that the royal road to enjoying humanness is through closeness and sharing.

Optimal families had the majority of parental coalitions scored as equal in overt power. Such a finding is relevant to the broader social issues currently raging about the rights of women and the possible threat to males as women's roles become more powerful. Equal overt social power is beneficial, not damaging, if there are complementary rather than symmetrical role relationships. In both long and short time frames (months and years as well as minutes and hours), the optimal families demonstrated complementary parental roles—such as teacher and taught, speaker and listener, aggressive role definer and supportive partner, breadwinner and homemaker, volatile reactor and calm dampener. This complementarity allowed for more equal overt power without hostile competition and rivalry. Complementary roles need not be stereotyped; they need not slavishly follow prescribed cultural expectations, but they must exist in order that relating is shared enjoyment rather than a fight.

Current cultural definitions of female equality sometimes insist on a rather referee-oriented symmetrical role; for example, both partners should work and share the housework and child care equally. None of the healthy family systems studied had such symmetry, though symmetrical relationships are found frequently in the midrange families, along with continued unresolved conflict. Long-term and short-term complementarity and role differentiation seem necessary to allow pleasant interaction with shared dignity. This is analogous to a sport such as basketball. On unskilled teams everybody tries to get the ball and shoot baskets; on very skilled teams, players cooperate with complementary roles. While some authors[9][10] have used complementarity to mean an unequal power differential, this is not how the term is used here. Overt power is one dimension of family interaction; role definition with role complementarity or symmetry is another.

Optimal family members recognized and utilized the two different kinds of power described earlier—relationship and coercive control. Authoritarian control was occasionally used to enforce family rules. It was neither compulsively denied nor virtuously touted. This allowed the family under pressure to revert to a more control-oriented style if necessary. However, they had enough skills that they were not usually under great stress, and could enjoy relating intimately by throwing aside overt power differences and sharing as fellow humans.

This group of families showed clearly that closeness and shared power are essentially intertwined—a parent is no more powerful than a young child if he wishes to have closeness with the child. Personal attacks between parents and children were rare. Anger was expressed openly, but it was usually goal- or behavior-directed rather than person-directed ("I don't see why we can't go to Galveston, we took two weeks' vacation last year," rather than, "You never let us do anything that's fun."). There were no instances of generational role reversal, with a child assuming a parental role. Power was shared, not abdicated.

Although the sexual stereotyping found in midrange and adequate families (with overt power related to sex) was not present in the optimal group, there was a significant relationship between the children's social power and birth order. The oldest children were somewhat more controlled in emotional expression, well disciplined, and more achievement oriented. Second children showed more affective openness and spontaneity, and less concern with achievement, order, and personal discipline. The youngest children were often slightly immature for their age. These qualities did not suggest emotional illness.

One of the striking features of the optimal group was the high degree of individual initiative, drive, and performance found in almost every individual. Because the members did not fear moving toward others or moving into the world, they found rewards in active solutions to life's problems. Observations of families of varied competence suggest that the most passive and inhibited individuals develop not so much from biological variation but from family systems that cripple initiative.

5) *Encouragement of Autonomy*

Our society places a premium on behavioral manifestations of a personal sense of autonomy. The autonomous person knows what he feels and thinks, and he takes responsibility for his behavior. He interacts with others with a reasonably clear notion of where his symbolic, feeling self ends and another's begins. He has clear ego boundaries. He is able to think, most of the time, in terms of cause and effect; only in unusual circumstances does he rely on magical explanations of interpersonal phenomena. Westley and Epstein stated, "Autonomy seems to be essential to the development of a satisfactory ego identity, for one must be permitted to consider oneself a separate person and to experience oneself as such, to find an identity. Without such autonomy, it seems likely that the child will be unable to solve the basic problems of separation from his family of orientation and will remain overdependent."[7]

System encouragement of autonomy includes several specific characteristics: ability of family members to take responsibility for individual thoughts, feelings, and behavior; openness to communication from others (obliviousness is a strong sign of a threat to individual identity); respect for the unique and different subjective views of reality found in any group of people, and minimum reliance on an inhuman, omniscient family referee. Optimal family members expressed feelings and thoughts clearly. Speech mannerisms provided clues to family functioning. Muttering, incoherence, and poor enunciation occur with low self-esteem and little autonomy. As families move toward negentropy, speech is clearer. Optimal family members showed a striking absence of blaming and personal attack, and no internal scapegoating. Since they were comfortable with uncertainty, ambivalence, and disagreement, members could be visible and known. The family system recognized people as mistake makers; parents could issue pronouncements that later proved in error with little loss of face; children could fail without being scapegoated or defined as inadequate. They could be open, candid, and vulnerable. This flexibility led to coherent expression of views and feelings. Also, honesty was possible, with resulting family trust. If one is not punished for telling the truth as he knows it, lying is unnecessary.

The absence of invasiveness allowed each member a respected and secure internal life space. There were minimal efforts to control others' thoughts and feelings. Though there was considerable attention to behavior within the family, an observer seldom heard coercive statements about family members' behavior beyond the family circle. It was assumed that individual members would like to do well in the outside world; if they did poorly, family members tried to help. They did not criticize motives.

Though there was no scapegoating of family members, there was a pattern of external scapegoating, comparing the family favorably to people and groups in the world beyond the family. Some scapegoating is found in all families studied; it seems to be a necessary part of family interaction. If it is external, it adds to group cohesiveness ("we are better than they").

These optimal families did not attack outside authorities such as church or government officials, nor racial or ethnic groups. External scapegoats consisted of unspecified families who "let their children run wild" or whose "kids use dope." Generalized wrongdoers were attacked by the children as well as the parents.

These most capable families showed an impressive responsiveness to others; even fragments of sentences were attended and incorporated in the ongoing negotiations within the family. Mishler and Waxler found in healthy families the highest incidence of complete acknowledgments of member communications even though there was also the highest incidence of fragmented sentences and unscoreable remarks.[2] Fragments and coherent responses were a part of a highly flexible, open, and effective communicational system.

Family members were consciously aware that children grow up and leave home, that being in a family was being a part of an evolving and changing enterprise that eventually self-destructs. Their warm and optimistic orientation was attained not through denying, but by accepting responsibility for developing capable and autonomous individuals who were not tied to the family by helplessness, fear, or guilt. Autonomy was facilitated by an ingrained respect for their own subjective view of reality and for that of others. These families had a delightful capacity to listen with interest and respect, and intimidation was rare. They were aware of the essentially tentative and subjective quality of perceptions. (How well these people incorporated the view presented in Chapter 1 of science as a dialogue in which no one is ever proved right!)

When subjectivity is respected, spontaneity is possible. These families, with their unpredictability, fantasy, and humor, were fun to observe. They gave strong indications of being more flexible and adaptive than adequate families who were hampered by more restricted and stereotyped roles. Though the adequate families were effective in child raising, their referee system and rigid patterning inhibited the joyful and spontaneous. I worry a bit about such nonpathological families, which are so predictable and rigid. If their environment changed markedly, it is questionable if the system could adapt. I have no such concern about the optimal families. Their members were unafraid to deal with the new.

As we view the spectrum from entropic family systems to the most negentropic ones, we see marked change in respect for subjective reality. Severely dysfunctional families invade and attempt to distort individual reality. Midrange families believe in external absolutes and attempt to control by intimidation and coercion. Only the optimal families showed many areas free from efforts at thought control.

This progression is analogous to that which has occurred in man's efforts to understand himself and his universe. Prior to the introduction of science in the Western world, truth was considered absolute, and it was obtained from authorities who kept change at a minimum through invasive and coercive efforts at thought control. With the beginnings of scientific method, a split between mechanistic body and spiritual soul allowed some autonomous exploration free from a refereeing external authority. Later, science, as it became more powerful culturally, was the source of a tyrannical new authority which rejected subjectivity as unworthy and built a temple to a spurious god of objectivity. Only recently has science identified itself as limited, uncertain, and probabilistic, and discarded objectivity as a myth.

In every family there is a core of belief, unquestioned and unchallengeable, a shared authority that I have termed a family referee. Optimal families exhibited this phenomenon; the difference between them and less fortunate families was quantitative, not qualitative. It would have been aesthetically pleasing to find that optimal families did not have this core, that they held all beliefs open to negotiation; but such was not the case. Though the fixed and inflexible core of the referee diminishes as family systems improve in effectiveness, a minimum of this unyielding structure seems either necessary or inevitable. Perhaps it is essential to group identity of any sort. A family's beliefs are a part of its unique identity, just as an individual's beliefs are a part of his identity. There will always be a tension between loyalties to family or group and loyalties to oneself which can be useful and growth-promoting in an open system.

Autonomous growth and development lead to emancipation, not isolation. One can judge family competence reasonably well by determining if children have a dignified and satisfying way out of the family structure. Is leaving disloyal? Are thinking one's own thoughts and choosing different directions considered traitorous? The optimal families taught individual members that conflict can be resolved and goals attained; this provided a matrix for choice.

6) *Affective Issues*

Feeling Tone. The optimal families had both an engagingly warm, optimistic feeling tone and a striking emotional intensity. These people were *involved* with each other. They were interested in what each had to say. Transactions reverberated with affirmation; members had a conscious knowledge of personal worth that was intensified by the value seen in others. Caring, warmth, and hope for the future characterized the interaction without censoring expression of anger or disagreement. Most of the families studied gave up afternoons or weekend time to be a part of the research project, and some children expressed anger about missing out on cherished activities. Their anger was accepted within an overall framework of agreed-on family purposes. This openness to individual feelings promoted the overall positive feeling tone. Anger was expressed, acknowledged, and whenever possible adjustments were made. Non-hostile humor was frequent and served a powerful purpose: It allowed dealing with the ambiguities and mixtures of feelings that occur inevitably as people function in a group. Parents made fun of their own tendencies to be controlling, and children joined in with a shared awareness of human limits. Recognizing that wishes always reach beyond performance frequently evoked light laughter.

For example, in one of these families the father described himself as a hard-nosed tyrant who laid down the law. His children referred to him as "Archie Bunker," whose bark was worse than his bite, and he shared in the laughter. "He doesn't really mean it," said one child, and there was more laughter. These families, with a humorous perspective, acknowledged that relationships are too complex for simple reflex responses. As this family interacted, it became clear that the father was quite sensitive and aware of his children's needs and responded to them. He needed his tough talk, but it was not taken too seriously.

Raters scored the optimal families high on judgments of empathy, a significant factor in their competence. Empathy goes beyond the acknowledgment of, or permeability to, another's communicative efforts; it includes sharing another's subjective experience without the loss of individual self-boundaries. To experience another's anger without in turn becoming angry, or to share another's sadness without losing morale, is to participate in human interaction at a highly differentiated level. These optimal family members accomplished this to a degree that challenged and humbled the researcher/clinicians.

The accuracy of empathy can be determined only by respectful negotiation with another, so that projective mind-reading, a destructive interpersonal maneuver, can be sharply distinguished from empathic judgments. For example, a statement such as, "You seem depressed," can be projection, empathic perceptiveness, reaching out, or even attack. Dysfunctional families do not give sufficient respect to subjective reality to check out the accuracy of such observations; optimal families did. Empathic skills can augment, but can never take the place of, valued communication in which inquiries about feelings are made. A low regard for mind-reading and frequent attempts to elicit expression of feelings from others develop skills in empathy.

Conflict—Resolvable and Irresolvable. Every family interaction has conflicts, just as individuals possess various wishes and goals requiring choice. If the family can and does negotiate, their conflict is limited and resolvable. As one observes such system conflicts, the responses indicate family competence; poor responses to immediate disagreement lead to festering resentment, which then pervades the atmosphere and makes future encounters painful. Optimal family members were sensitive to individual feeling states and responded with concern and action; this encouraged closure, with a group decision. It allowed new conflicts to arise and be resolved, unhampered by suppressed and seething unfinished business.

In these fortunate families there was a strikingly affiliative orientation: an expectation that human encounter would produce satisfaction, that responsiveness to others and clear expressions of feelings would be rewarded. Expectation is most important in family functioning. When positive, it pulls individuals into interaction, involvement, and investment in others. If there is an oppositional set, a shared belief that conflict is inevitable and irresolvable, obliviousness and guarded expression are the only logical tools for maintaining relationships. An oppositional attitude promotes distancing, isolation, resentment, and chronic fear, and leads to a variety of confusing communicational patterns. A group's affiliative or oppositional set is a shared prediction of what will happen in encountering others. Assessment of this attitude is based on a complex synthesis of behavior, voice tone, verbal context, and communicative patterns. Attitudes strongly influence family effectiveness; humans exist in an imperfect world where others are never totally rewarding, and predictions help to bring about cooperative, creative interactions, or painful, hostile ones.

The optimal families, with their affiliative set, behaviorally rejected any ideas of man's being essentially evil. In order to approach relating to spouses, children, or parents with affiliation, one must assume that man's essence is at least neutral or possibly kindly. Parents who have a benign view of man, or at least of themselves and their children, can guide and direct their children and expect them to follow family rules without recourse to intimidation. Power can be shared and negotiation is pleasurable. In the optimal families, there was a belief, tacit or expressed, that "of course my child (parent) will do the best he can; why shouldn't he?" With a view of man's nature as benign, human needs for intimacy, sexual expression, and assertiveness are embraced with a minimum of fear and apprehension.

There was considerable variability in the extent to which people in the world beyond the family were included in this benign assumption, but all of the optimal families included at least their own members. The family data support the view that man's nature is not hostile/destructive in essence but becomes so if children are exposed to developmental environments that make such a prediction. Coercive measures create the need for them, producing behavior that justifies the tyranny. If a person feels reasonably benign in intent, becoming a parent reinforces this view and children are included in this compassionate orientation.

7) *Negotiation and Task Performance*

In interactional tasks the optimal families showed the greatest capacity to: a) accept directions; b) organize themselves to respond to the task; c) develop input from other members; d) negotiate differences; and e) provide a coherent and effective response to the challenge. The functioning of the family was smooth. Typically, the father operated as "Chairman of the Board," bringing out others' opinions, then voicing his own. Mother alternated with him in a complementary fashion. Ideas from everyone were integrated, and a response evolved that was satisfying to all members. All of the variables considered important in family systems came into play as the family approached a task: An affiliative orientation with trust in the essence and motives of others allowed for openness and responsiveness; viewing group goals as compatible with individual goals allowed for resolution of conflicts without rancor; relatively equal power with respect for subjective reality prevented exclusion of any member.

In the systems studies, family performance in specified small-scale tasks was correlated with overall competence in child raising. It is clear that competent family functioning is associated with differentiation of individual family members, the acceptance of unique selfhood which promotes a child's progression through necessary developmental tasks.

8) *Transcendent Values*

Underlying all the family systems variables discussed thus far is the ability of family members to adapt to the inevitable losses from growth and development, aging, and death. Capable families self-destruct: Parents no longer provide living necessities for their children; children become adults; parents grow old, have failing functions, and die. These stark realities can be accepted only by individuals who have a reasonably clear self-definition that does not depend on unchanging relationships. To love is to lose; yet to remain aloof is never to live at all. Browning's question, "Can we love but on the condition that the thing we love must die?" suggests this poignant, intimate relationship between closeness and the awareness of human finiteness and death.

If parents feel capable, are able to live without clutching a particular relationship (whether parent, spouse, or child), then they have no need to blur reality, to live in fantasy, to insist on the perpetuation of unbroken ties between generations. The strong parental coalition seen in healthy intact families allows parents to break excessive bonds with their own parents and sets up the opportunity for generational boundaries in their own developing families.

However, the demands of living are only partially met by a gratifying husband-wife relationship. The ability to have meaningful encounters and relationships in the broader environment is vital to competent family systems. These relationships, reaching into the wider community, are sources of stimulation to the family structure and put adaptive strength into the system. They augment the ability of parents to accept their own aging and the developing autonomy of their children.

Optimal family members were able simultaneously to love and to risk, acknowledge the arrow of time, and prepare for change and loss. Children were not seen either as crutches or competitors, and their increasing competence was viewed with pride. Children's accomplishments were celebrated.

It has become apparent to me that in order to accept the maturation of children, in addition to the capable parental coalition and involvement in the larger world, a third factor is necessary—the possession of a transcendent system of great personal value which allows self-esteem without clutching particular relationships, without denying biological fate. Transcendent (defined as something beyond the limits of experience or knowledge) beliefs are necessary for enjoyable, optimistic, and hopeful living. People must view a day's reality in the light of a conceptual and relationship system broader than themselves or their families in order to make sense of events, to accept losses of loved ones, and live with human consciousness encased in a finite, aging body which must die. Without investing in such a transcendent belief system, no human exists without hopelessness and despair.

Every viable culture has the task of providing mythic truths that touch each member of that society, drawing them together in a comprehensible whole that provides some trusted relationship to a benign universe. The essentially secular Western society produced by the scientific revolution is no exception. Its "liberated" members invest faith and trust in nations, in science as a religion, or in belief systems ranging from capitalism to Communism, from natural foods to the eventual triumph of technology.

The ability to accept the loss of loved ones is intimately related to accepting the idea of one's own death. Freud was aware of this intertwining threat when he stated, "I therefore maintain that the fear of death is to be regarded as an analogue of the fear of castration, and that the situation to which the ego reacts is the state of being forsaken or deserted by protecting superego (introjected parents)—by the powers of destiny—which puts an end to security against every danger."[11]

A child experiences the threat of annihilation as the loss of necessary supporting figures, and concepts of death are hazy until considerable development of the self occurs. If adults have not experienced opportunities for successful maturation and self-definition, the fear of personal annihilation remains as a threat of loss. Denying the passage of time and being unable to let children or parents go are related to the inability to accept one's own mortality, starkly epitomized in the reality of personal death. A meaningful transcendent value system allowed the optimal family members to accept their inability to control the future and to have trust in a coherent universe.

All the optimal families came from conventional religious orientations, and I might consider them special cases except for my clinical psychiatric experience. I have yet to treat a patient with intensive psychotherapy who did not become intensely aware of a need for personal coherence in relating to his community and to his world. A valued transcendent meaning system allows a person to center himself in the universe, to define his activities as meaningful, without depending on unchanging relationships to make them so. Sometimes such centering is found through conventional religion, but often it is more individual, with various humanistic goals incorporated in a self-definition that includes transcendent values. When such symbolic meaning reaches beyond the confines of one's physical self, a dying person (as we all are) can invest in living with purpose, without crippling despair.

Becker offered that, "The human animal is characterized by two great fears that other animals are protected from: the fear of life and the fear of death."[12] It is only in using our human capacity for symbolism and defining ourselves as part of a meaningful whole that these threats can be met openly and courageously.

Every system is related to others at lower and higher levels of functioning. No individual person can be viable and purposeful without relating to a larger social system—usually a family. No family offers sustenance to its members without relating to more comprehensive systems, both social and symbolic. It is not my intention to shift from a discussion of systems qualities found in a successful development of a self to a treatise on religion, but I am forced to speak of transcendent meaning that provides personal goals and purposes as a necessity for emotional health.

This is one of the most significant of the lessons taught by optimal families—accepting loss is related to possessing a system of transcendent values that provides hope, trust, and meaning when human helplessness is overwhelming. I believe that psychotherapeutic efforts frequently assist a patient to arrive at the point of realizing the need for such transcendent values, and then often fail in one of two ways. The simple way is to shrink from this realization, to ignore or ridicule such needs. Psychic or social engineering is attempted with a studious avoidance of the depths of the human condition. The second way to fail is (in spite of opening oneself to the pain and perplexity of the patient, entering his tension-filled depths of feelings and thoughts) to define therapy as providing answers to paradoxes—definite interpretations and specific responses to questions answerable only by the individual self. Indoctrination takes the place of necessary exploration by the patient. Intensive psychotherapy is often portrayed, with some validity, as attacking religious thought or, conversely, as creating a rigidly secular religion.

Neither mistake is necessary. Patients are not children to be kept away from the depths that might drown them, nor are they to be told the "right" answers to existential questions. The psychotherapist's job is both simpler and more complex: to develop an environment comparable to that found in optimal families where individual choice evolves with an awareness of human limitations.

In addition, family studies suggest a way to evaluate transcendent systems that are valued by individuals who wish to grow in relationship competence. If a belief system acknowledges and offers support for both individual choice and for human vulnerability and limitation, then it is compatible with the rule systems of optimal families. Though many varieties of beliefs can offer support and meaning, those that discourage individual choice and decision making or encourage a hopeless quest for perfection (if taken seriously) will discourage the evolution of ego skills.

REFERENCES

1. LEWIS, J. M., BEAVERS, W. R., GOSSETT, J. T., and PHILLIPS, V. A., *No Single Thread: Psychological Health in Family Systems*, New York, Brunner/Mazel, 1976.
2. MISHLER, E., and WAXLER, N., *Interaction in Families*, New York, John Wiley and Sons, 1968.
3. LENNARD, N. L., and BERNSTEIN, A., *Patterns in Human Interaction*, San Francisco, Jossey-Bass, Inc., 1969.
4. RISKIN, J., and FAUNCE, E. F., "Family interaction scales," *Arch. Gen. Psychiat.*, Vol. 22(6):504-537, June, 1970.
5. BLUM, R. H., and Associates, *Horatio Alger's Children*, San Francisco, Jossey-Bass, 1972.
6. OFFER, D., and SABSHIN, M., *Normality*, New York, Basic Books, 1966.
7. WESTLEY, W. A., and EPSTEIN, N. B., *The Silent Majority*, San Francisco, Jossey-Bass, 1969.
8. WILDER, T., "Our Town," in *A Treasury of the Theater*, Vol. III, New York, Simon and Schuster, 1951.
9. BATESON, G., *Naven*, 2nd Edition, Stanford, Stanford U. Press, 1958.
10. WATZLAWICK, P., BEAVIN, J. N., and JACKSON, D. D., *Pragmatics of Human Communication*, New York, W. W. Norton, 1967.
11. FREUD, S., *Civilization and its Discontents*, London, The Hogarth Press, 1969.
12. BECKER, E., *The Denial of Death*, New York, The Free Press, 1973.

II

A FAMILY

SYSTEMS PERSPECTIVE

. . . only life knowledge produces competence in living.
Only the family can teach the most basic knowledge
there is: how to live.

Leontine Young

_____ **6**

A teacher of
psychotherapy looks at
family systems issues

JERRY M. LEWIS, M.D.*

Although it is always a pleasure to be asked to contribute a chapter to a friend and colleague's book, the request leading to this chapter is of particular significance for this writer. In part, this reflects the years of collaborative work on our study of family systems[1] and the manner in which that effort has influenced my own work as an individual therapist, supervisor, and teacher. In addition, however, I am struck by how W. Robert Beavers and I have

_____

*Director of Research and Training, Timberlawn Foundation, Dallas, Texas

arrived at much the same position about the processes underlying effective psychotherapy from what seem to be different starting points. My perception and understanding of his track is that it started with a significant emphasis upon theory, a group of ideas and constructs growing out of his own therapeutic work which were then influenced by the data from the study of healthy or optimally functioning families and their communication patterns.

My track has been different in that it involved a greater initial emphasis on psychotherapy processes and how to teach them. My dissatisfaction with the teaching and learning of psychotherapy led to a seminar for first-year residents which focused on experiential learning of specific psychotherapeutic skills. Although empirical in origin, my concern with process and technique led, of course, to increased interest in theory. The course of study evolved over an eight-year period and will be described in this chapter. It, too, has been influenced both by our work with healthy families and by the many research contacts and friendly talks Beavers and I have had about psychotherapeutic process. It intrigues me that we started out so differently and arrived at essentially the same position.

The course for residents started with a concern about supervision and led to my request that residents tape-record all of their psychotherapy interviews. They wrote summaries of the interviews, and we listened to the recordings and focused upon those aspects of the interviews that the residents did not report in their summaries. Shortly thereafter, I taped some of my own psychotherapy interviews and requested the same of several trained professionals whom I was supervising. At this early stage, attention was focused on therapy that seemed to be at a standstill. On review, it was clear that many such psychotherapy interviews were very cognitive. Although the therapist may have felt initially that this was the patient's use of intellectualization, it emerged as a process in which both patient and therapist participated. These cognitive dialogues, which seemed to disregard feelings, gave the interviews a flat, sterile quality.

My interest in ways to increase therapists' sensitivity to affect led to the literature on empathy and a search for teaching methods that might increase a therapist's empathic capacity. The work of Rogers,[2] Truax,[3] and Carkhuff[4] was the basis from which the training in interviewing skills evolved. The training included the residents' responses to audiotaped patients' statements, their open discussion within the group and, later in the course, interviewing hospitalized patients. The literature regarding empathy was introduced and, as a result, the concept of empathy was enriched by the writings of several psychoanalysts.[5,6,7,8] At this point, the course was one hour each week, and the focus was almost exclusively on empathy. It has been described in an earlier publication.[9]

Gradually, the scope of the course broadened to include other aspects of the psychotherapeutic relationship. At first, this involved those dimensions the Rogerian writers considered necessary and sufficient for effective psychotherapy: therapist's warmth, respect, and genuineness, the use of clear and specific (as contrasted to abstract) language, the indication for and technique of confrontation, the complexities of therapist's self-disclosure, and a focus on the here-and-now of the patient-therapist relationship. As the residents observed each other's interviews, the use of simple rating scales for these dimensions seemed to sharpen observational skills. Other dimensions of the psychotherapeutic relationship which were added included: listening for chains of associations; recognition of increased affect (seen as "tips of the iceberg"); awareness of nonverbal cues (the patient's, one's own, and the nonverbal, motor interaction or interpersonal ballet); recognition of mechanisms of defense; knowledge of the patterns of the interview (its cadence, depth, and distance); use of clarification and interpretation; the therapist's use of signals from within himself (feelings, memories, fantasies, variations in attention); and the skills required in formulating observations and hypotheses about the patient from interview data.

We start with audiotaped patient material, add videotaped patient material, and employ actors to simulate patients so that each resident can interview the same "patient" and observe the striking differences in these videotaped interviews (which presumably are in response to the differences in the therapists). We observe vid-

eotapes and films of eminent therapists and discuss their widely dif-
fering styles. Each resident interviews several patients behind the
one-way mirror and later participates with colleagues in dissecting
the interview.

Currently, the course occupies a prominent place in the first-
year curriculum, involves four hours per week, and precedes the
residents' inauguration of individual psychotherapy with inpatients.
It does not, of course, replace psychotherapy supervision, but
rather introduces the beginner to a variety of very specific skills
and techniques. The course has come to focus on the process of
psychotherapy, and has crystalized around several key constructs:

1) Psychotherapy is a collaborative enterprise, the aim of which
is to explore the patient's behavior, that is, feelings, thoughts,
memories, fantasies, and actions. The therapist's primary function
is to facilitate the patient's self-exploration by having the direction
of the interview responsive to the patient's feelings and associations
and, whenever possible, focusing on affect. The therapist is collaborative rather than directive, helping the interview to spring
from the patient. He avoids being an authoritarian director of the
interview who relies extensively on his own preconceptions. An excellent indicator of whether a therapist is directive or collaborative
is the amount and type of verbal activity by the therapist (the more
active, the more likely directive).

2) Each psychotherapy interview is interactional, and the
therapist must be sensitive to the multiple ways he influences the
nature of the interaction. If he is unaware of the ways his behavior
either encourages or discourages certain patterns of patient response, his formulation of the patient's dilemma will reflect the
response patterns he elicits, and often will seem to fulfill the
therapist's preconceptions or hypotheses.

3) A central, and in some ways overriding, influence in each
psychotherapy interview is the therapist's balance of intimacy and
detachment. The therapist must be capable of closeness—of feeling
deeply "with" his patient—and, in the next moment, of stepping
back and analyzing in a much more "objective" way the
phenomena in which he has participated. Therapists who lack

either the capacity for intimacy or the capacity for detachment are incapable of helping many patients and may harm some. It is the struggle to maintain a balance involving both intimacy and detachment which offers the therapist a continuing opportunity for personal growth.

With this brief description of the evolution of this training in interviewing skills, I would like to describe in greater detail each of the psychotherapeutic skills or constructs and then attempt to relate them to the eight variables Beavers has extrapolated from the study of healthy families to individual psychotherapy.

EMPATHY

There is considerable variation in the ways in which therapist's empathy is described, but most writers acknowledge that it is central to the function of a psychotherapist. It may be one of the few characteristics essential to a therapist, parent, or teacher (that is, any helper). Empathy may be seen as a continuum, with those processes which are essentially observational and communicational skills (the ability to hear precisely what another is feeling and to let him know his feelings have been perceived) at one end. This orientation, primarily Rogerian, has been termed "cognitive empathy." Processes characterized by the therapist's more active use of himself, in which the therapist allows or encourages himself to feel what the patient is feeling, have been described as "affective empathy" or "compathy."[10] This is considered a momentary ego regression in the service of "being with" and understanding the patient. This type of empathy is described most often by psychoanalytic clinicians.

Because empathy is considered a cardinal therapist characteristic, considerable time and energy are spent on exercises designed to increase residents' appreciation of their own empathic capabilities. Initially, the focus is on cognitive empathy, the therapist's recognition and verbalization to the patient of his messages, both content and affect. Affective empathy involves the residents in a "letting-go" process, a change in their usual method of disciplined thinking and experiencing. Such a departure is frequently felt to be risky. One helpful technique is introducing the group of residents to "forced fantasies"; each member writes down a fantasy that incorporates a given stimulus (picture, word, or videotape). This appears to encourage the therapist's freer use of himself. Nevertheless, in my experience, the capacity for affective empathy develops slowly, and some residents remain very limited in this area. Cognitive empathy, on the other hand, can be learned rapidly and easily. It is far less risky. Its emphasis during the early part of the course appears to increase the sensitivity to affect of all the participants.

GENUINENESS

In asking colleagues how they might select a therapist for themselves or members of their family, I have been impressed that therapist's genuineness is a characteristic frequently mentioned. First-year residents, on the other hand, are most frequently anxious, frightened, and stilted. A common tendency is to adopt a severely professional role, and to be silent, serious, and safe. This essentially defensive posture is meant to hide their fear, but it also obscures their unique humanness. Getting from this starting point to a position of feeling naturally themselves as therapists is no easy accomplishment, and it takes time. That time can be shortened by training exercises that both call attention to a mechanical and stereotyped manner and also encourage the development of a more natural style of interviewing. Hearing their own audiotaped responses to patient material and observing themselves on videotape are powerful tools in the encouragement of such movement. By defensively hiding themselves, beginning therapists may present ambiguous or conflicting messages and, hence, a very blurred image to the patient. If the patient responds with (understandable) defensiveness or confusion, it is apt to be considered a part of his psychopathology, a deficit in his capacity to relate to others. In observing the interviews of skilled therapists, residents quickly respond to whether or not the therapist "seems to be" natural and himself. However, achieving this state is a difficult and hard-won battle.

WARMTH

A therapist variable related to empathy and genuineness is warmth. How much does the therapist appear to be interested, concerned, and caring about the patient? That this factor is often noted by colleagues in their responses to my question about what they look for in a therapist testifies to the important, perhaps essential, role of *caring* in all helping relationships. This ability to value another is, by itself, however, not sufficient. Most beginning residents are warm, caring, and people-oriented, but the anxiety associated with learning to be a therapist often leads to a defensive façade which hides this characteristic quality. Focusing on this aspect of the therapist-patient relationship appears to encourage beginners to be less defensive. Many are surprised by the sound of their recorded voices or their images on videotape.

Although the remote, detached defense is more common, one needs occasionally to deal with a beginning therapist who defends himself by an overly solicitous or seductive manner. As attention is focused on this style, most residents are able to find their own ways of communicating warmth, caring and interest in the patient's dilemma.

SELF-DISCLOSURE

The therapist's concern with genuineness and warmth leads to a more complicated and controversial aspect of therapist-patient relationships, the therapist's self-disclosure. Two positions are frequently articulated in this matter. Some[11] suggest that a therapist should disclose personal and intimate aspects of his own life if it is "in the interest of the patient." Others[12] suggest that a therapist should maintain as neutral or bland a position as possible in order to understand and deal with transference material. Often the question of what, when, and how a therapist discloses is not asked. In the training being described, the resident is taught to consider self-disclosure only as it relates to the here-and-now of the patient-therapist relationship. This type of openness provides the patient with important feedback about his impact upon another person. The disclosure of details of the therapist's personal life or past experiences is only rarely in the interest of the patient, and generally to be discouraged. The course does not present rigid guidelines, but encourages the group members to consider and discuss their own feelings about self-disclosure openly.

IMMEDIACY

Some students of psychotherapy suggest that explorations of the evolving patient-therapist relationship itself offer an unusual opportunity for clarification and resolution of the patient's difficulties. For some, interest in this dimension is concentrated on the reactions of the patient transferred from earlier relationships; for others it is the here-and-now relationship between therapist and patient. These writers[13] have termed this dimension "immediacy," and they suggest that therapists should strive to achieve high levels. This presents considerable difficulty for the first-year residents who may be comfortable in perceiving the interview only as an instrument by which a patient's disease is exposed. To focus on the here-and-now of human interactions in which they participate often seems strange or dangerous. Models for this type of therapeutic activity, in the form of interviews by the instructor and films or videotapes of other therapists, can be useful.

SPECIFICITY

This characteristic has to do with the therapist's use of language which is explicit and deals concretely with issues. It is, in a sense, the opposite of language that is generalized, abstract, and often ambiguous. It is one of the more easily learned dimensions, and presents little problem for most residents. Occasionally, a resident clings to what appears to be an entrenched defensive use of language that is vague and blurs his communications. When feedback from the group, observing himself on videotape, and listening to audiotapes have little impact, such a resident has real difficulty in becoming an effective therapist without undergoing a basic change in these character defenses.

CONFRONTATION

Confrontation can be understood as the capacity of the therapist to face the patient with his perception of discrepancies in the patient's communications. Often, this involves a disagreement between the verbal and nonverbal segments of the message: "Although you say you feel happy, you're frowning, and there seem to be tears in your eyes." There are other types of discrepancies that may suggest the need for direct feedback, but the term confrontation, as used here, is not to be confused with a hostile demand or the "heroic confrontations" a therapist may use when deeply alarmed about his patient's behavior.

Once residents have learned to recognize discrepant communications, it is not difficult for them to learn to confront patients. The critical problem is to be able to be direct without being disrespectful, and without implication of censure.

LISTENING FOR CHAINS OF ASSOCIATIONS

If he keeps in mind his own impact upon the therapeutic dialogue (avoiding explicitly directing what the patient talks about by focused questions or by a more subtle signaling), the therapist can learn much by listening to the flow of the patient's associations. This is not the "free associations" of classical psychoanalytic technique, but rather the awareness that, if the therapist does not intrude, he can improve his understanding by following closely the patient's train of thought. This willingness, at times, to "track" the patient's thoughts passively is related to the psychoanalytic concept of evenly suspended attention. To complicate the process further, skilled therapists must also listen "inside"; that is, they must at the same time attend to their own thoughts, feelings, fantasies, and memories. Because this dual listening often seems impossible to beginning therapists, we start by stressing listening only to the patient's associations.

RECOGNIZING TIPS OF AN ICEBERG

As one part of listening intently and following the patient's thoughts, the beginning therapist must come to recognize those points in his patient's communications when there is a suggestion that strongly charged or conflicted material is close to the surface. A variety of behaviors may signal such points in an interview, for example, an unusual word choice,[14] a change in the speed or intensity of the patient's voice, a sudden change in posture, or autonomic phenomena such as blanching or dilation of the pupils. Each resident is taught to note such behaviors, but always to explore in his own mind the possibility that the patient may be responding to some behavior of the therapist.

AWARENESS OF NONVERBAL COMMUNICATIONS

Early in the course, residents are introduced to the significance of nonverbal communication. Facial expression, posture, and body movement are emphasized. Relevant literature is assigned, and the use of videotapes without the sound emphasizes this mode of communication. Initially, the focus is on the patient's nonverbal communication, but it soon includes the therapist's as well. Gradually, the interactional aspects of the patient-therapist communication are explored. If this aspect of the interview is not viewed as a kind of pas de deux, or if one person's nonverbal communication is analzyed as if it occurred solo, the therapist may make erroneous interpretations. When understood in context, those nonverbal communication acts which do appear unrelated to the interaction, that is, seem to spring mostly from within, come to assume particular importance as indications of stress, strong affect, or conflict.

THE RECOGNITION OF DEFENSE MECHANISMS

Although increasing emphasis is placed upon the interview as an interactional process and on the resident's need to recognize patient behavior that he either invites or discourages, the resident is encouraged to perceive and identify the patient's defense mechanisms. Vaillant's[15] hierarchy of adaptive ego mechanisms, which assigns certain levels of health or pathology to individual defenses, is introduced as an orienting schema. Denial, suppression, intellectualization, projection, acting out, and other defenses can be recognized in exploratory interviews. The resident is cautioned, however, to avoid inviting a particular response and then labeling it as a pathological defense. An example might be the resident who interviews a patient at a very cognitive level. He pays no attention to affective cues and relies on questions of the "how, what, why, and when" variety. If, in his formulation, he stresses the patient's reliance upon intellectualization, he comes to understand that he is labeling the very responses he invited, which is insufficient basis for concluding that the patient relies on intellectualization.

THE USE OF SIGNALS FROM WITHIN THE THERAPIST

The capacity of the therapist to attend his own feelings and use the information obtained in his efforts to help the patient is felt to be a significant characteristic of the skilled therapist. Experienced therapists continue to learn about themselves in this way. Whether it is the attempt to feel what the patient is feeling (as in affective empathy), or the awareness of the therapist's own responses, such as boredom, inattention, irritation, or the intrusion of personal material (fantasies, reveries) into the therapist's mind, the foremost question is how it relates to the understanding of the patient and the ongoing patient-therapist relationship. This ability relates to the therapist's awareness of himself and his own psychopathology and is a capacity which is achieved gradually. The course for beginning therapists can only introduce the construct and help the participants become more comfortable with the use of signals from within. Discussing fantasies and feelings openly with other residents in the seminar setting is a most helpful exercise.

AWARENESS OF THE THERAPEUTIC INTERACTION

The beginning therapist must not only perceive the verbal and nonverbal signals from the patient and his own thoughts, affects, defenses, and fantasies, but he must also be aware of the verbal pattern he and the patient establish. This type of awareness is, in many respects, the most difficult to achieve. How does one listen intently, suspend attention, attend to the signals from within himself and, at the same time, perceive the pattern of the two-person interaction in which he is participating? To beginning therapists, these tasks often appear overwhelming. Awareness of the interaction itself can be augmented by focusing the resident's attention upon three interactional variables: the cadence of the interview; the depth of the interview; and the complex assessment of interpersonal distance.

The cadence of the interaction has to do with the pattern of verbal activity. Residents are taught that meaningful exploration is more apt to be occurring if the cadence involves a pattern of brief verbal activity by the therapist, followed by longer verbalization by the patient:

    T: xx
    P: xxxxx
    T: xx
    P: xxxxx

The reverse pattern:

```
T :xxxxx
P: xx
T: xxxxx
P: xx
```

suggests that the therapist may be involved in directive or supportive activity, but the likelihood that he and the patient are involved
in a collaborative interaction that explores the patient's feelings,
thoughts, or conflicts is lessened. A cadence of nearly equal verbal
activity:

```
T: xx
P: xx
T: xx
P: xx
```

is more difficult to interpret. It may reflect either the therapist's
use of focused questions inviting brief "yes," "no," or statements of
fact, or the patient's resistance to exploration.

Awareness of the depth of the interaction refers to the therapist's
ability to assist the patient to explore his disturbance below the
surface presentation. The interactional aspect of this variable is an
interface between the patient's resistance to exploration and the
therapist's ability to facilitate exploration. Some patient-therapist
interactions are characterized by the mutual avoidance of deeper
levels of exploration. Sometimes, the therapist may not wish to
facilitate deeper exploration for well-considered reasons, but on
many occasions the therapist is not aware of his own part in a superficial exchange until he has the opportunity to review the recorded interaction. If deeper exploration is not invited by the
therapist, it is patently misleading to ascribe the avoidance to the
patient's resistance.

Kagan's work[16] with the Interpersonal Process Recall Technique
explores the unspoken thoughts and fantasies of patient and
therapist and suggests that both individuals are influenced by their
needs for, and fear of, closeness and acceptance. From this viewpoint, it is possible to conceptualize some segments of a patient-
therapist interaction as movements to decrease interpersonal dis-

tance, which are usually followed by retreat, a withdrawal by one or both participants and, hence, greater distance. This accordian-like effect may or may not be associated with postural changes that influence the actual distance between the participants. More often, it is reflected only in a sense of interpersonal closeness or distance felt by one or both participants. This interactional variable is subtle and elusive, and awareness of it is not easily taught. Its introduction through the use of the Interpersonal Process Recall techniques assists the beginning therapist to become sensitive to this interactional dimension.

CLARIFICATION AND INTERPRETATION

These closely related types of therapist activity are frequently associated with psychoanalytic therapy. The beginning therapist, influenced by distorted, popularized presentations, may think initially of these processes as wondrous pronouncements of an all-wise therapist who speaks commandingly from a mountain top. The course, to the contrary, teaches that, optimally, therapy is a collaborative interaction and that the more an interpretation is the work of the patient, the greater the likelihood the resulting insight will modify the patient's feelings, thoughts, or behavior. "How do you put all of that together?" is seen as an example of a therapist's high-level interpretive response. At a different level, "Considering these feelings along with what we discussed last time about your mother, can you find a common thread?" is another example. This type of exchange is collaborative and suggests that both participants are competent and effective. Authoritarian, "from-the-mountain-top" therapist's interpretations are useful only in those rare instances in which the therapist is concerned about the patient's survival (if his behavior isn't modified), or, occasionally, frightened about what is going to happen to the therapist (if the patient's behavior is not modified).

These 14 constructs are central to the course of study. Although there is some reading and lecturing, the course itself is mostly experiential. Most of the hours are spent with the residents responding to audiotaped material, being videotaped interviewing an actor, watching a film of a Rogerian therapist or a training analyst, or interviewing a patient behind a one-way mirror. The emphasis is always upon what the group can add to what the individual resident observed or felt. The climate of the seminar is one of openness, critique without attack, acknowledgment of mistakes, and awareness of shared human imperfections. There is a strong emphasis on always using data from three systems: the patient, the therapist, and the therapeutic interaction. What, then, does the course have to say about the relationship between the eight variables Beavers extrapolated from our studies of healthy families and effective individual psychotherapy? Let us examine each of the eight variables from the viewpoint of the resident training course and what it hopes to teach.

SYSTEMS

Beavers makes four basic points about the concept of systems as it has evolved out of family research. The first is that life is essentially interpersonal; that is, it consists of countless interactions with others (who are real whether they exist separate from us or incorporated within us). The second point concerns the complex nature of causality and the fact that a linear concept of A-leads-to-B causality only rarely offers an understanding of human behavior. The third point is a related one concerning the difficulty of separating causes from effects. Each influences the other, and within the system a single event is often both effect and cause. The final point stresses the limitation of power for any one participant in the system. Each participant has multiple methods of influencing the system, and even in rigidly structured and controlled systems there are both active and passive responses which moderate or undo the influence of the controlling participant.

These system constructs play a central part in the seminar for first-year residents. Psychotherapy is presented as a collaborative enterprise: a human, problem-solving interaction in which the therapist is not only highly attentive to his patient's behavior, but recognizes that he is actively involved in the interaction and must always struggle to be aware of the multiple ways in which he influences the patient's behavior and the totality of the interaction. He listens to the cadence and depth of the verbal interaction, and actively attempts to sense the variations in interpersonal distance. His behavior encourages the patient to ascribe meaning, and he treats with respect the patient's hypotheses about his own behavior. The therapist's interpretive comments must be tentative in order to allow the patient to modify or disagree. The therapist presents a model of understanding that searches for multiple determinants and conflicting ideas, but rarely for certainty. Except in unusual circumstances, the choice is the patient's. The therapist may help explore options, but the final decisions belong to the patient. In this way, the therapist hopes to involve the patient in a way of relating in which collaboration rather than the arbitrary use of power is the model in problem-solving.

These concepts are not new, and a number of students of the psychotherapeutic process have commented on them. Many psychoanalytic writers seem to have moved toward the position of Sullivan in emphasizing the need for the analysis to occur in the context of a "real" relationship. Namnum,[17] for example, in a recent essay on activity and personal involvement in psychoanalytic technique, stresses that the "so-called anonymity" of the analyst facilitates projections onto him and may induce regressive mechanisms in the perception of external stimuli. This is not, however, transference. According to Namnum, transference can develop only in the climate of a relationship which is to "some degree reciprocal." Complete masking and absolute neutrality do not offer optimal conditions for analysis of transference phenomena. The analyst's personality, like other aspects of reality, is always present, though in the background.

Strupp,[18] a long-time researcher in the field of psychotherapy, emphasizes that the therapist, as a participant, becomes subject to the principle of indeterminacy; that is, he cannot make observations in the interpersonal field without altering that field in important ways. He goes on to state that in regard to the patient-therapist relationship there is an increasing tendency to deal with the dynamics of the relationship in process terms, "to think of transference and countertransference as phenomena along continua instead of regarding them as either 'positive' or 'negative'."

Students of psychotherapeutic process from both the clinical and research directions are increasingly concerned with the therapeutic relationship as an interactional system. Recently, Luborsky[19] reported the direct study of therapeutic alliances. He indicated that the outcome of treatment is only slightly determined by the initial characteristics of the patient, the therapist, and the match of patient and therapist as evaluated before treatment. One turns, therefore, to an assessment of the patient-therapist interaction as a determinant. Luborsky found that patients who improved in therapy entered an alliance that emphasized a shared responsibility for working out treatment goals very early in treatment. His data suggest that both patient and therapist contribute to the evolution of helpful alliances. From our viewpoint, there does seem to be a growing interest in the study of the nature of the interactions that are associated with positive outcome of psychotherapy. This can be understood as an increasing clinical and research concern with the system properties of a psychotherapeutic relationship.

BOUNDARIES

Members of healthy families clearly define themselves as individuals by openly expressing their feelings and thoughts. The observer has little cause to wonder "what does he really mean?" This degree of separateness or individuation allows closeness to evolve, for there is no threat of fusion or loss of identity. At the same time, healthy family systems encourage high levels of permeability; members of such families acknowledge or are receptive to each other's feelings and thoughts. Clarity of individual boundaries, the development of closeness, and the high level of permeability are cardinal characteristics of optimally functioning family systems.

There is much about the course for beginning therapists that relates to these family characteristics. Students are encouraged to use concrete, everyday language, to be clear in what they say, and to avoid abstract, ambiguous, or fuzzy statements. They are encouraged to disclose their own reactions to the here-and-now of the transactions. In other words, they are asked to present clear self-boundaries to their patients. At the same time, we encourage a style of intense listening, along with frequent acknowledgment to the patient that his feelings and thoughts are heard and (it is hoped) understood. If a patient's feeling or thought is not clear, the resident is instructed to request clarification. In many ways, the student is prompted to attempt consistently to establish a relationship in which both his and his patient's individuality is clear.

At a different level, the therapist must have a personal model or system of understanding human behavior. There are two potential difficulties in this area. First, since all people (whether or not they are aware) have some basic ideas about what makes people human, the therapist who is not open (at least with himself) about his values may be caught up unknowingly in repetitive attempts to fulfill his own unarticulated hypotheses. The second difficulty involves the therapist who clings so rigidly to his model that he is not open to new information. The course attempts, at the minimum, to introduce each resident to the impact of his core values upon the psychotherapeutic process. A therapist, for example, would respond differently to a patient's rage depending upon whether he sees the patient as a tenuously controlled beast with murder in his heart, or as a person whose anger is related to underlying feelings of pain, helplessness, or impotence.

The literature in this area is spotty. In recent years, there is certainly less of the "therapist-as-a-mirror" type of writing. Rogers and other non-directive therapists[20] have stressed the need for the therapist to be clear and use specific language. They also have emphasized the importance of the therapist's genuineness, which is part of presenting clear boundaries. Others have studied therapist characteristics, although not necessarily directly within the therapeutic interaction. An example of this type of work (although not confirmed by a replication study)[21] is the classical work of Whitehorn and Betz.[22] They identified personality characteristics of successful therapists of schizophrenic patients. My interpretation of their findings is that successful therapists are more apt to present themselves clearly. Strupp's study[23] of patients following psychotherapy also suggests that a therapist's genuineness and humanness are recalled by patients as important factors in their improvement.

CONTEXTUAL ISSUES

In healthy families, the context is marked by the clarity of roles and expectations. Parents behave as responsible leaders. Although not authoritarian, they are in charge and make no demands on the children for a premature adulthood. The children are not expected to live out parental fantasies. There are no emotionally charged parent-child coalitions which trangress generational boundaries. Indeed, confusion or blurring of roles or unrealistic expectations within the family are evidence of system pathology.

In the psychotherapy seminar, the emphasis on a comparable clarity of context starts with the importance of establishing a clear contract in which each participant knows what to expect from the other. The necessity for the therapist to have both a capacity to care about the patient and an ability to understand psychodynamics—that is, the characteristics which contribute to his expertness—only increases the demand for contextual clarity. The therapist must be comfortable in what has been called "disciplined intimacy." He must repeatedly contend with transference distortions which, if not attended at the time they arise, understandably lead to changes in what the patient expects from the therapist. The residents are taught that lack of contextual clarity may lead to heightened expectations and, ultimately, a full-blown regressive transference neurosis or psychosis. Although transference phenomena are ubiquitous, a transference neurosis or psychosis is to be avoided. It is the intent of classical psychoanalysis to induce a transference neurosis (not psychosis), and the emergence from such a state not only requires a skillful analyst, but a patient with considerable ego strength.

Indeed, the research literature[24] does not suggest that the deliberate induction of intense transference states (brought about by the failure of the therapist to keep the context—that is, roles and expectations—clear) is associated with better outcomes. I can find, in fact, no studies in which this process variable has been examined as a determinant of outcome.

POWER

The parents in healthy families share power in the family system. We see neither a pattern of dominance and submission nor an unending conflict over who is in control. Although either parent may appear to be the negotiating leader, most often the situation determines who has the greater influence. It is precisely because this power is shared that intimacy is possible. Hidden thoughts, intense feelings, or daring ideas can be shared with real freedom only if the relationship is of nearly equal power. To be afraid to reveal oneself for fear of censure or loss of approval is to preclude intimacy.

In the psychotherapy seminar, considerable attention is paid to the many aspects of power. The students are encouraged to think of psychotherapy as a collaborative effort characterized by negotiations. The therapist is not like the surgeon operating on a passive patient. Rather, therapist and patient are partners in solving the patient's problems. This is reflected in many ways; the therapist encourages the patient to take the lead in the explorations of self. The therapist is a facilitator rather than someone who maintains control of the interview by directing its focus through multiple questions. He is tentative, invites disagreement, and provides a model of negotiation. His interpretations are framed as suggestions or questions rather than as authoritarian pronouncements.

There is little to suggest that we understand the basic processes of effective psychotherapy. Indeed, this deficit in our understanding has led Beavers to draw attention to the lessons therapists may learn from healthy families. I do not know of any studies that investigate directly the issue of the distribution of power in the patient-therapist relationship as it relates to the effectiveness of therapy. It may be that more studies of helpful alliances,[19] with shared responsibility (and, inferentially, shared power), may help us to know with greater certainty if the equality which seems so central to the effectiveness of the parental marriages in healthy families is of equal importance in the patient-therapist relationship.

AUTONOMY

Healthy families are characterized by a number of interactional processes that encourage the development of autonomy: clarity of individual boundaries; permeability to each member's communications; respect for the unique subjective reality of each member; flexible rules; the freedom to have all kinds of feelings; high levels of empathy; and negotiation and compromise as the model of solving problems. This type of interpersonal system leads to individuation, separation, and ultimately autonomy.

There are many parallels between these processes and the model of therapeutic interaction the seminar focuses upon. The beginning therapist is encouraged to listen attentively, acknowledge the patient's multi-level communications, and respond empathically to the patient's feelings. Problem-solving in the therapeutic relationship is seen as relying on negotiation and helping the patient to clarify his options. The ultimate decisions must be the patient's, and rigid rules are not applied except in life-or-death circumstances. This type of essentially collaborative work is seen to encourage autonomy and growth. There is, however, to my knowledge no research literature which directly approaches these issues other than the work on therapeutic alliances previously noted.

AFFECTIVE ISSUES

The healthy family is highly expressive of feelings (both positive and negative), generally reflects a warm and caring tone, reveals a high proportion of empathic responses, and deals with conflict early and effectively. These characteristics of healthy families are so clear and so distinctly differentiate them from dysfunctional families that life itself has a different quality in their presence. Mental health professionals, upon viewing videotapes of such families, respond in a variety of ways. Some recognize the processes of health, while others search for some underlying pathology. Many acknowledge how long it has been since they experienced a family that appeared to be spontaneously warm, caring, and humorous.

There is an obvious relationship between these affective variables and the process of psychotherapy as it is presented in training residents. The effective therapist is interested and attentive to the patient from the very start. He is not afraid to express his warmth and compassion openly. He uses his empathic capacities to understand and be "with" the patient. He attempts to create an affective tone that becomes genuinely friendly. He is both friend and expert.

Strupp reported that patients who do well in therapy recall their therapists as warm, caring, and understanding. Frank[25] has stressed that to be effective, the psychotherapeutic relationship must be one of high affective intensity. Truax and Carkhuff[3] have correlated high levels of therapist's empathy with increased depth of exploration and better outcomes. Psychoanalytic writers[26] focus increasingly on the "real" relationship and suggest that empathy is the cornerstone of the therapist's capacity to be helpful. The importance of affective vectors in psychotherapy is widely recognized in the professional literature.

NEGOTIATION AND TASK EFFICIENCY

Healthy families approach problem-solving with a basic reliance upon negotiation. Their negotiations are a splendid process to observe—the give-and-take, the search for consensus and, often, the willingness to compromise. At the same time, such family systems are efficient; they get each job done; there is an evolving closure. This system characteristic is in striking contrast to the two patterns of problem-solving frequently seen in dysfunctional families: the inefficiency resulting from the chaotic communication pattern seen in severely disturbed families, or the absolute domination of one family member that stymies negotiation in the rigid midrange dysfunctional family.

The translation of the optimal family model of negotiation in problem-solving to the psychotherapeutic relationship involves several of the processes focused upon in the seminar. The therapeutic contract itself makes the goal of joint work explicit. The entire focus of the course is on collaboration, and breakdowns in the progress of the joint effort are examined (both from the viewpoint of intrapsychic resistances and as interaction blocks).

Perhaps the scanty research in this area reflects both the difficulty in knowing the "right" research questions and the problem of operationalizing and measuring the appropriate dimensions.

TRANSCENDENT VALUES

Beavers suggests that one way of considering the family is as a mechanism for the learning and communication of shared values, some of which transcend the life of any individual. These may be formally identified as religious, but not necessarily so. Truth, honesty, and fidelity are examples of such values which may or may not be experienced within a formal religious framework. The study of healthy families suggests that the communication of values is very clear, but is more apparent in the transactions and processes which occur within the family day by day than in any precisely verbalized set of basic beliefs.

The issue of the impact of value systems on the psychotherapeutic process is a complicated one. There is, in my opinion, no value-free therapy. The problem is whether the therapist's awareness of his own values (and the multiple ways in which they can influence his participation in the therapeutic process) is enough, or whether, as suggested by some,[27] the therapist's values are so potentially powerful that they should be stated openly at the start of treatment. Currently, the course is oriented around the basic notion that it is impossible for the therapist not to have a set of core values about the nature of man and the universe. It is his responsibility to think clearly about "where he is" in regard to such issues and to be constantly vigilant to the potential impact of these core values upon his response to his patient's dilemma.

At the present time, there is an understandable tendency for beginning residents to think of man primarily as a biological organism dominated by the same chemical imperatives which seem to be involved in lower animals' territoriality, hoarding behavior, and bar-pressing for food. Eisenberg's succinct essay[28] on "the human nature of human nature" is an antidote and, therefore, the first reading assignment in the seminar.

As I hope I have made clear, I find much with which to agree in Beavers' hypothesis that healthy families have something of importance to say about individual psychotherapy. My own concern about teaching and learning psychotherapy led to an increasing interest in more theoretical issues. There are many unanswered questions. The comprehensive review of psychotherapy research by Meltzoff and Kornreich[24] demonstrates that the outcome studies are substantial: Psychotherapy *is* effective. The process studies are inconclusive: We do not know "how" psychotherapy works. The way in which healthy families relate and communicate can point the way to asking the right questions.

REFERENCES

1. LEWIS, J. M., BEAVERS, W. R., GOSSETT, J. T., and PHILLIPS, V. A., *No Single Thread: Psychological Health in Family Systems*, New York, Brunner/Mazel, 1976.
2. ROGERS, C. R., "The necessary and sufficient conditions of therapeutic personality change," *J. Consulting Psychol.* 21:95-103, 1957.
3. TRUAX, C. B., and CARKHUFF, R. R., *Toward Effective Counseling and Psychotherapy: Training and Practice*, New York, Aldine, 1967.
4. CARKHUFF, R. R., *Helping and Human Relations*, 2 Vols., New York, Holt, Rinehart, and Winston, 1969.
5. GREENSON, R. R., "Empathy and its vicissitudes," *Intern. J. Psycho. Anal.*, 41:418-424, 1960.
6. SCHAFER, R., "Generative empathy in the treatment situation," *Psychoanal. Quart.*, 28:342-373, 1959.
7. MADDALONI, A., "The meaning of empathy," *American Imago*, 18:21-33, 1961.

8. HALPERN, H. M. and LESSER, LEONA N., "Empathy in infants, adults, and psychotherapists," *Psychoanal. Review*, 47(3):32-42, 1960.
9. LEWIS, J. M., "Practicum in attention to affect: a course for beginning psychotherapists," *Psychiatry*, Vol. 37(2):109-113, May, 1974.
10. PAUL, N. L., "The use of empathy in the resolution of grief," *Perspectives in Biology and Medicine*, 11:153-168, 1967.
11. JOURARD, S. M., *The Transparent Self*, New York, Van Nostrand Reinhold Co., 1971.
12. GREENSON, R. R., *The Technique and Practice of Psychoanalysis*, New York, International Universities Press, Inc., 1967.
13. CARKHUFF, R. R., *Helping and Human Relations*, 2 Vols., New York, Holt, Rinehart, and Winston, 1969.
14. VOTH, H. M., "The analysis of metaphor," *J. Am. Psychoanal. Assn.*, Vol. 18(3):599-621, July, 1970.
15. VAILLANT, G. E., "Theoretical hierarchy of adaptive ego mechanisms, a 30-year follow-up of 30 men selected for psychological health," *Arch. Gen. Psychiat.*, Vol. 24:107-118, Feb., 1971.
16. KAGAN, N., *Studies in Human Interaction*, 3 Vols., U. S. Dept. H.E.W. (ED017946), Dec., 1967.
17. NAMNUM, A., "Activity and personal involvement in psychoanalytic technique," *Bull. Menninger Clinic*, Vol. 40(2):105-117, March, 1976.
18. STRUPP, H. H., *Psychotherapy: Clinical Research and Theoretical Issues*, New York, Jason Aronson, Inc., 1973.
19. LUBORSKY, L., "Effective psychotherapy," *Psychiatric News*, XI(9):33, May 7, 1976.
20. ROGERS, C. R. (Ed.), *The Therapeutic Relationship and Its Impact*, Madison, University of Wisconsin Press, 1967.
21. STEPHENS, J. H. and ASTRUP, C., "Treatment outcomes in 'process' and 'non-process' schizophrenics treated by 'A' and 'B' type of therapists," *J. Nerv. Ment. Dis.*, 140:449-456, 1965.
22. WHITEHORN, J. C. and BETZ, B. T., *Effective Psychotherapy With the Schizophrenic Patient*, New York, Jason Aronson, 1975.
23. STRUPP, H. H., et al., *Patients View Their Psychotherapy*, Baltimore, Johns Hopkins Press, 1969.
24. MELTZOFF, J. and KORNREICH, M., *Research in Psychotherapy*, New York, Atherton Press, Inc., 1970.
25. FRANK, J., *Persuasion and Healing: A Comparative Study of Psychotherapy*, Baltimore, Johns Hopkins University Press, 1961.
26. MUSLIN, H. L. and SCHLESSINGER, N., "Toward the teaching and learning of empathy," *Bull. Menninger Clinic*, 35:262-271, 1971.
27. HALLECK, S., *Politics of Therapy*, New York, Aronson, 1976.
28. EISENBERG, L., "The human nature of human nature," *Science*, Vol. 176, April 14, 1972.

——————————————————————————— 7

Using the family variables to critique the Freudian psychoanalytic system

If my position in evaluating a treatment system is uncommitted and not doctrinaire, there must be both positive and negative comments. The vantage point of this critique will be the eight qualities described in Chapter 5. My comments, though developed through responsible research effort, are not presented as "objective." There is no such thing as objectivity in human encounter, in scientific theory, or in observations; there is either admitted or unadmitted bias from the personal history and subjective experience which are brought to events. The discussion of treatment systems will set the stage for the synthesis of material on psychotherapy to be found in the third section of this book. The sources of that synthesis include the family systems data, research in psychotherapy, and a descrip-

184

tive evaluation of psychotherapeutic systems presented in this and the following chapter.

A critique of a system which is as continually controversial as psychoanalytic theory and technique could offend some who are invested in protecting or attacking it. Freudian psychoanalysis has polarized as many mental health professionals as has any theoretical system extant. I will stand on the family systems material, a position that has no a priori targets or icons in treatment systems. There is a bias, stated earlier in this book, toward systems solutions to human problems, which I believe to be supported by the family data.

It is hard to imagine someone stoutly maintaining that he is an Oslerian (a follower of Sir William Osler), who becomes extremely indignant if someone questions Osler's tenets; conversely, it would be strange to hear someone attacking Osler for his efforts to treat human ills. The various forms of the psychoanalytic movement have had the characteristics both of a scientific endeavor and of a religious cult. I believe it will benefit therapists and patients to consider a scientific psychotherapy utilizing the best of psychoanalytic contributions and discarding cultist qualities. In Chapter 8, I will use the family variables to evaluate several other systems of psychotherapy with the goal of synthesis. In approaching this task, I feel a bit like Mort Sahl, the politically oriented comic, who, after ten or fifteen minutes of his dialogue, would look around and ask, "Is there anybody out there I haven't offended?" Fortunately, increasing numbers of mental health professionals are searching for ways to synthesize useful treatment techniques rather than for ways to pit one therapeutic system against another. Therefore, I believe the number who are seriously offended will be small.

I would like to make a contract with the reader: Give me no more and no less power than you yourself have to consider the beliefs found in various treatment systems. If my opinions differ from yours, perhaps the text will stimulate dialogue with colleagues and patients. If you feel that any treatment systems discussed in this and the next chapter have optimal family systems characteristics that I indicate to be modest or lacking, well and good. It is only if the family systems qualities described are considered unimportant that we will have real disagreement. I do not wish to attack, but to affirm qualities that seem significant in the effort to further growth and competence in others. It is only a true believer who insists that his theory and technique have all the ingredients necessary for optimal results; such a belief is the hallmark of the cultist, of the closed system. We will view various treatment systems with an open mind, beginning with Freudian psychoanalysis.

Freud developed the first treatment of emotional illness that attempted to be both scientific and humanistic; it was revolutionary in inviting a partnership between patient and therapist. After all the years since his major contributions have been absorbed by the Western world, Freud's concepts are still fresh and valuable. He developed the most profound and meticulously complete psychotherapeutic system ever conceived. If I had to forego all synthesis and choose one treatment system, his would be my choice of a theoretical home. Fortunately, such a choice that in years past plagued the field of psychiatry is no longer necessary.

Freud was a bold, adventurous researcher/physician, determined to be famous. After a number of false starts, he found a secure niche in history with his tenacious efforts to treat neurosis. His daring theories challenged some of the basic intellectual assumptions of the 19th-century Western world. He was a self-defined conquistador, bounding into uncharted territory with the daring of a Cortez, leading a small, rather ragtag band of confederates in an ambitious effort to conquer a world.

There are several qualities of his approach to patients that indicate his genius and deserve emphasis. First, Freud listened to his patients. He took their communications seriously and attempted to make sense of them rather than dismissing them as nonsense as his medical colleagues had done before him. Second, he took careful notes of family interaction as seen by him directly, or as described by the patient, or, occasionally, by relatives. His report of Dora is a magnificent pioneering observation of family interaction.[1] Third, he related psychological illness more directly than anyone before him to the characteristics of normal human development. Fourth, he reduced the distance between doctor and patient in a manner quite unusual for his time and locale. Fifth, Freud insisted on the importance of early life experience to later success or failure in adulthood. Sixth, by focusing on unconscious aspects of man's life, he encouraged a multicausal, non-linear approach to understanding the human condition. Finally, Freud brought sexuality, especially childhood sexuality, from the near exclusive consciousness of the lower classes into powerful intellectual circles. Ernest Jones, in his delightful autobiography, spoke of the knowledge of sexuality that every Welch street-child had at an early age and of the difficulty found in possessing such knowledge and having respectability and social power.[2] This focus on human sexuality emphasized that humans are animal, and that the real understanding of man must include an appreciation of his fleshly mammalian beginnings.

Freud was both scientist and dogmatist. He had great respect for the truth and pursued it to the best of his ability throughout his long and productive life. However, he also had a deep and continuing mistrust of others' efforts to search for the truth, and he was constantly concerned with heresy and betrayal.[3] He therefore forged a hierarchical power base different from scientific groups but having much in common with religious movements. Freudian psychoanalysis is a coherent theoretical orientation that defines the nature of man, and provides a method of treatment of emotional ills; it is also an institution that admits, initiates, indoctrinates and disciplines novitiates. It rewards approved behavior with upward mobility in a hierarchical structure.

I will address myself to the first two of these aspects of psychoanalysis—the theory and the technique of treating emotional illness. This presentation is not intended to be comprehensive but rather a cursory outline. I expect that most readers will be familiar with Freudian concepts; for those who are not, I would recommend, as a beginning: 1) Greenson's *The Technique and Practice of Psychoanalysis*;[4] 2) Brenner's *An Elementary Textbook of Psychoanalysis*;[5] 3) Fenichel's *The Psychoanalytic Theory of Neurosis*;[6] 4) Freud's *New Introductory Lectures on*

Psychoanalysis;[7] and 5) Freud's *A General Introduction to Psychoanalysis*.[8]

FREUDIAN THEORY AND TECHNIQUE

The theory is explicitly based on a notion of man and of science that embraces a belief in objectivity and a reductionist concept of science which rejects as infantile any supra-rational faith. When Freud was 75 years old he said that Brücke, his physiology mentor in medical school and in his brief career as a researcher in neurophysiology, had been the most important influence upon him. Brücke followed the doctrine of Helmholtz, which taught that man was precisely the sum of his parts. The doctrine is deterministic, antivitalistic and materialistic in that it attempts to explain the higher by the lower.[9] This viewpoint is responsible in large measure for providing Freudian psychology with scientific respectability in the early 20th century; it is also responsible for many of the limitations of the system.

Early in his work, Freud developed two fundamental hypotheses which remain the cornerstones of psychoanalysis. First was the principle of psychic determinism. There are no meaningless slips of the tongue or body, but all are dictated by significant patterns and forces. Second, consciousness is the unusual and not the regular or expected part of psychic processes, many of which are unavailable to awareness. In addition, psychoanalysis includes instinct theory. After considerable evolution, two instincts were considered elemental and intrinsic in man—the sexual or erotic and the aggressive. Instincts arise from sources of stimulation within the body, operate as a constant force, and have a source, an object, and an aim. This instinctual orientation tilts orthodox psychoanalytic theory toward essentially fixed biological explanations for human behavior, a necessarily socially conservative position.

The theory of psychosexual development is an important aspect of psychoanalysis. Libido, a biologic contribution, is invested at different foci during a normal infant's development. The child moves from oral to anal to genital libidinal cathexis or investment. This concept led to the notion that fixation or regression is involved in pathological states. Fixation occurs when there is a failure in the orderly progression of libidinal energy from one developmental focus to the next; regression occurs as an individual reintroduces earlier behavior patterns and earlier sources of gratification. For example, a child of four whose new baby brother threatens his security may regress by reverting to thumb-sucking.

As normal development continues, sexual energy is invested in the genitals and the Oedipal period ensues. Children have murderous fantasies toward the same sexed parent and a desire to possess the opposite sexed parent. Castration fears in males and penis envy in females are considered inevitable. The sexually intense Oedipal period is responsible for the development of individual superego and guilt.

Abstractions of intrapsychic structure are characteristic of psychoanalysis. Freud developed the concept of the conscious, the preconscious and the unconscious. Later a structural hypothesis evolved that included the id, ego, and superego. The id is the psychic representation of drives, the superego is the sequestered part of the ego initially derived from the introjected parental voices (later including moral principles obtained from the world beyond the family), and the ego is the mechanism that negotiates between id, superego, and outside reality. After this structural hypothesis evolved, neurosis was described as resulting from intrapsychic conflicts between, for example, the id and the ego.[5] These abstractions are now firmly established and are often spoken of concretely. Theorists frequently describe these structures and their interaction with a precision rivaling that of anatomists.

This intrapsychic world of id, superego, and ego can be viewed as an abstraction of a Victorian midrange centripetal male-dominated family placed inside the universal human's head. A powerful, controlling father (superego) keeps willful children (id) under control as mother (ego) scurries about trying to serve both. The introjection of family into the psyche is analogous to the projection of family relationships into the cosmos with a resulting theology.

Another significant theoretical concept is that of anxiety. Freud's

original theory considered anxiety to be a damming up of libido—
quite biological. Later, he defined a more interpersonal or existential theory: Ego anxiety results from object loss, loss of love, fear of
castration, or the disapproval of superego. A tremendous contribution of analytic theory was the recognition of the ubiquity of ambivalence. Since the theoretical structure is predominately biological, ambivalence was defined primarily in sexual terms. Freud believed humans to be essentially bisexual with developmental maturity requiring the resolution of such ambivalence.

In recent years, ego functioning has occupied a larger place in
Freudian theory. Wilheim Reich, though later rejected by the orthodox, focused psychoanalytic thought on character patterns and
ego functioning;[10] Anna Freud developed concepts of ego defenses;[11] in recent years theorists such as Hartmann[12] and Kris[13]
have carried psychoanalysis further by their focus on ego. Ego
psychology assists in comprehending the interaction between
human biology and human culture. Eric Erikson, without formally
discussing systems concepts, weaves together psychoanalytic, anthropological, and sociological aspects of human development,
character formation and emotional illness.[14,15]

Ego functioning is closely allied with reality testing. Freud early
contrasted primary and secondary thinking processes. The primary
process (found in the very young child, the dreamer, and the
psychotic) possesses no opposites, no time sense, no conditionals or
qualifiers. Through interaction with the environment, the child develops secondary process thinking—adult rationality. In some normal adult activities, as in slang, humor, and poetry, one sees remains of primary process; maturity consists of repressing but not
eliminating childhood thinking processes.

Emotional illness is closely related to defects in reality testing
and ego functioning. Brenner, an orthodox Freudian, defines reality testing: "To be able to distinguish between stimuli rising from
the outer world and those from wishes and impulses of id."[5] Normal development and maturity are dependent on the necessary
mastery of instinctual drives. The concept of transference—
misidentifying a present person and considering him to possess

characteristics experienced or longed for in times past—captures the sense of instinctual drives and previous experience as interfering with the comprehension of present reality.

Treatment is posited on the assumption that emotional illness results from a perseveration of infantile wishes attempting to impose themselves on and override an outer objective reality—a deficiency of ego. Psychoanalysts attempt to increase the amount of psychic functioning available to consciousness and reduce the amnesia of childhood. Effort is made to redistribute the energy available to the ego, making it possible to deal with realistic needs and conflict resolution with less energy spent in repression. In addition, the psychic structure is modified, increasing its adaptiveness, and developing a better coordination between drive and object.

A consistent treatment goal is to help people grow beyond their premorbid state. Greenson, a contemporary analyst, believes that only psychoanalytic therapy produces constructive and progressive change in the ability of a human to adapt. The methodology used for such alterations in the intrapsychic structure consists of interpretations made by the therapist to a patient admonished to give up any pretense of social conversation. The patient should allow himself, as far as possible, to state whatever comes into consciousness without censorship or restriction. The therapist's work consists of observing and interpreting resistance, and interpreting material produced after resistance is overcome. In addition, a transference neurosis is encouraged in order to facilitate bringing significant fantasy material to consciousness; to assist in this, therapists strive for anonymity. As Greenson stated some years ago, "The less the personality of the analyst intrudes upon the patient, the more likely it is that the patient will relive the whole gamut of his repressed emotions with the person of the analyst."[16] It is assumed that regression isolated in the therapeutic environment will be efficacious.

Of course, very few patients are treated by classical analysis anymore, and relatively few psychiatrists consider themselves orthodox Freudians. "Psychoanalytic psychotherapy" is a phrase used frequently, implying movement toward synthesis and a shared science with psychoanalytic principles as a base. As Lebesohn noted in a recent discussion of psychiatric practice, "Psychoanalysis has unquestionably had profound influence on American psychiatry. . . . What is not so generally recognized, however, is the extent to which general psychiatry has influenced the practice and theory of psychoanalysis."[17] This critique, however, will understandably address itself primarily to the orthodox position, since changes and developments move in many different directions and overlap with many other treatment systems.

PSYCHOANALYSIS VIEWED FROM A
FAMILY SYSTEMS VANTAGE POINT

1) *A Systems Orientation*

Optimal family members approached human problems in a systems fashion. They assumed that a) people must have a viable ongoing social system for essential needs to be met; b) causes and effects are interchangeable; c) causes of human problems are multiple, not single; and d) people are limited and finite.

The orthodox Freudian focus on biological drives and intrapsychic structure produces a psychology with only minimal concern for systems issues. Though critical aspects of theory and treatment deal with interpersonal phenomena, e.g. mother/infant interaction, Oedipal conflicts, and transference phenomena, the analytic therapist directs his attention to the intrapsychic representation of external objects.

This was not always so. Early in Freud's career as a psychotherapist he proposed that sexual abuse by fathers was the cause of his female patients' hysteria.[18] When subsequent evidence appeared to prove him wrong, he retreated from this family systems theory of causation and from then on never deviated from a biological approach. As we now know, there are many ways to "rape" a child. The rape of women of Victorian society was no fantasy. Had Freud been able to demythologize the language of his patients in the light of social forces affecting them, he might have added even more to his gifts to the world. However, it is probable that his theories would have been even less acceptable to his society had they espoused interpersonal causes of emotional illness rather than intrapsychic and biological ones.

Considering the cause of emotional illness to be essentially biological, but treatable through changing intrapsychic abstractions through the development and the resolution of transference by interpretations, offers somewhat sterile ground for the development of systems approach. The mechanistic concept of science Freud held throughout his long career encouraged a retreat from understanding illness in relation to environmental contacts. This is a pity since Freud had an unusual gift for shrewd descriptions of family interaction.

The orthodox psychoanalytic structure has evolved in this regard, however. Franz Alexander wrote of the importance of the "corrective emotional experience" found in the interaction of patient and therapist,[19] a modest advance toward a systems view. Recently Greenson emphasized the real relationship between therapist and patient as being significant in treatment and encouraged psychoanalysts to be aware that therapeutic interaction is real, as well as distorted and interpretable. "In addition to transference feelings, Michael also had a non-transference relationship to his analyst. This formed a basis for a working alliance, kept him in analysis and opened the door for continuance in effective work."[20]

Judd Marmor is another friendly contemporary voice urging the psychoanalytic system to become more open and rely on scientific uncertainty rather than dogmatism.[21] Such openness can allow a melding of biologic, family, and social factors in emotional illness and health. Treatment strategies can then become much more responsive to research and clinical input.

Non-negotiable insistence on biological origins of such patterns as male and female character traits, and the tendency to interpret questioning and criticism from patient or colleague as unconsciously motivated hostility rather than as honest efforts for open system dialogue must be abandoned if psychoanalytic system is to become open and reasonably negentropic.

Emphasis on unconscious factors helps increase awareness of the complexity and multiple causation of human behavior. It has promoted the humanistic treatment of social deviants. For example, punishment, a linear response frequently found in family and society to combat complex behavioral maladjustment, has severe limits. Psychoanalytic theory has helped many people understand that punishment for those who are depressed and self-destructive can invite poor behavior rather than deter it. However, the concept of psychic determinism, if deified and used as a single explanation for human behavior, can be a powerful defense against system change. For example, if treatment is unsuccessful, the patient can be blamed; he must be masochistic or anxious to keep his symptoms—or, alternatively, perhaps his therapist possessed too much countertransference. Concepts of the unconscious can increase one's understanding of the human condition, but they also can be a way of rationalizing inadequate methodology. Ineffective treatment methods can continue for many years with the use of such logic. If a tool does not do the job well, it may need sharpening. Blaming unconscious factors is analogous to man's blaming his gods or his sins—the notion might be right, or perhaps other factors are worthy of consideration. Behavior therapists often criticize this tendency of psychoanalytic therapists to blame patients for failures. There is a great difference but a small leap from, "You have choices that can never be taken from you," to "Whatever you are doing you have chosen." Using the unconscious to explain treatment impasses moves the therapist back to linear thinking that psychoanalytic theory has the potential to reduce.

Scapegoating the unconscious reduces the chance that the therapist and the patient will realize that humans are finite and fallible and so are the theories and methods that they create.

2) *Boundary Issues*

External Boundaries. The optimal family boundary had enough integrity to maintain definition, yet was porous enough for productive interchange with the outside world, bringing in new material useful in adaptation and discarding patterns and thoughts no longer effective. Freudian theory early developed definite boundaries but it has had a continual struggle to remain open to different ideas from outside that boundary. Closed system qualities are evident in sluggish technical and theoretical change, a mistrust of research data that do not confirm previous belief, and a tendency to confuse theories and hypotheses with absolute "fact." The prolonged period of indoctrination and control in the training of psychoanalysts encourages conservatism and orthodoxy. Festinger, in his theory of cognitive dissonance, has documented the relationship between costly and public adherence to a belief system and the tendency to ignore any information that challenges it.[22]

Intrasystem Boundaries. Optimal family members have clear and differentiated individual boundaries without distancing. There is respect for uniqueness and individual sovereignty. Here the psychoanalytic style is comparable to the midrange family model. There is a laudable awareness of the sovereignty of individuals; indeed, with the heavy emphasis on intrapsychic integrity, the individual seems at times to be surrounded by a moat! However, to consider humans as aggressive/destructive causes continual efforts to control patients, fellow practitioners, and students to make sure they have the "right" understanding.

The psychoanalytic social and ideological system has unfortunately adhered to Freud's pessimistic view of man: "I have found little that is 'good' about human beings on the whole. In my experiences most of them are trash, no matter whether they publically subscribe to this or that ethical doctrine or none at all. . . . If we are to talk of ethics I subscribe to a high ideal from which most of the human beings I have come across depart most lamentably."[23] The history of psychoanalysis is replete with internal conflict and attacks on heretics. Such attacks are partly a result of seeing man as trash or essentially destructive; different opinions must come from invidious motives.

Adler, Jung, Reich, Horney, Sullivan, and Perls were split from the parent body and carried on their individual explorations by evolving new schools. The orthodox may suggest that these people were acting out patricidal wishes and eliminated themselves. Just as a severely dysfunctional family views individuality as betrayal, a closed system must always seek unanimity and rationalize human diversity as having destructive origins.

Here we have a central issue. Is rebelliousness inevitable, to be repressed with force in order for a system to survive, or is it a result of the closed system that forces either homogenization or alienation? An important aspect of the myth of Oedipus, often overlooked as it is used as an analogy for all human families, is that his father tried to kill Oedipus first! In order to understand the behavior patterns of subsystem members it is important to be aware of the qualities of the whole system. It is only in the rigid midrange family systems that we see the generational fights and the bitter "inevitable" parent/adolescent struggles. In an undifferentiated system, rebellion is necessary for maturation. In flexible open systems there is no need to kill or to dominate offspring, who can grow to adult equal power without rebellion or alienation.

In treatment efforts, this mimicking of midrange, father-dominated families, encouraging "proper" views, may be limiting but not disastrous. However, if the patient's world is quite different from the "average expectable environment" (a phrase used by Hartmann),[24] treatment failure or worsening of function can occur rather than a simple limitation of results. An open system allows the therapist to be wrong, to learn from the patient, to have clear boundaries with the permeability to receive new and useful input. Reality and the patient are better served. Emancipation is missing from the emotional vocabulary of midrange centripetal family members because it requires greater trust in people than in external authority. To determine how open a human system is, it is important to see how members respond to those with different opinions. How does the church-going family respond to the 18-year-old daughter who decides to live with her boyfriend? How do orthodox psychoanalysts respond to the female psychiatrist who renounces penis envy as a meaningful concept? An open system adapts and rarely needs to reject its members. A closed one defines difference as rebellion.

3) *Contextual Clarity*

Craziness or sanity in a system is closely related to context clarity. Further, sanity has less to do with what an individual thinks in absolute terms than with the extent to which his views are understood and shared by others who have power within the culture. For example, a lone adolescent who insists that he knows the wishes of Jesus Christ and who follows those presumed wishes though they differ markedly from those of his parents will often be considered disturbed and be placed in a mental hospital. However, if this adolescent shares his views with members of a group (e.g., The Children of God) who have money and access to lawyers, then operationally he is not sick but different.

A family helps an infant develop a sane self by relatively clear interaction, feeding his memory bank with comprehensible relationship experiences. Optimal families were effective in this effort largely because of clear contexts within the family. Their parental coalition was strong, generation boundaries were clear, and individual competence was expected and rewarded with respect and caring.

The psychoanalytic theoretical emphasis on Oedipal phenomena is a great strength of the system, capable of encouraging therapists and parents to strive for context clarity. Generational boundaries, role definitions, limitations of individual power (licit competence, no illicit impotent/omnipotent relationships) are all involved in this concept.

The complex and potentially confusing triangle of mother, father, and child that must be mastered in normal development is a part of an infant's experience from birth, and only becomes more evident during the "Oedipal period." Krebbs reported a family experience reflecting his four-week-old infant's ability to thwart parents' efforts to resume sexual intercourse. Each time the father made sexual advances, the infant began to cry; this pattern continued for two months. When the same phenomenon occurred with his next child, Krebbs postulated that sexual arousal in his wife produced lactation which aroused the child.[25] Mother, father, and child were actors in an emotionally powerful drama requiring each to face conflict and make choices. The anecdote describes the rivalrous feelings of a frustrated husband and his fantasies in grasping for coherence in the strange experience of competing with a nine-pound rival, a peculiar struggle which can increase awareness of relationship subtleties. Here is an Oedipal system—father threatened and perplexed by his own child, mother torn between two powerful wishes, and the child probably unconcerned about triangular subtleties and wishing exclusive rights to mother.

Many years ago as my wife and I drove on a long journey with our 18-month-old son in a back seat crib, I put my arm around my wife and immediately felt a pair of firm, goal-directed small hands attempting to remove my arm from his mother. There was little question that he would feel defeated if unable to reduce our contact, and successful if he could. Such exchanges, common long before the "Oedipal period," suggest that family contextual issues are ongoing and continuous. Mother, father, and children each have vested interests, and clarity is needed so that each can know what to expect and what must be renounced. Enlightenment, awareness, hostility, and frustration are not exclusive to parent or child but are thoroughly mixed into each individual's reality. In the optimal family these triangular relationships are negotiated without assuming eternal opposition. Parents recognize that limited possession is a part of any relationship, and sharing is not only necessary but desirable. This affiliative model begins with the parents, and as children come on the scene, the parents can experience pride without being invested in jealousy and rivalry.

However, a frequent family stress seen in clinical settings is the birth of the first child. Desertion, alcoholic episodes, physical attacks, occurring in the period shortly after, suggest the difficulties many males have in dealing with this triangle. Such occurrences are powerful testimony to the parental portion of the Oedipal story—resentment and frustration of father and conflict in mother. With little experience in family negotiation, the mother may believe an either/or decision is necessary, requiring the choice between the role of mother or that of wife.

In competent families the infant has a model at an early age of shared possession and learns that *renunciation* is necessary to have gratification in close relationships. No one person can meet all the needs of another, not lover or spouse, child or parent. This knowledge is communicated to a child only if the parents possess it. If they do, then the child learns to deal with triangular demands by negotiation, and can give up the impotent/omnipotent power mode. The child learns that mother needs others, and therefore those others are not enemies but allies. He learns this as he experiences himself not as a dangerous intruder but as a welcome addition to the parental relationship.

Emotionally disturbed people usually remember contextual confusion in their families. As one result, patients often hope for a therapist/lover/father/child combination. Here the precise clarity of roles found in the psychoanalytic technical model is most useful; the therapist takes pains to define relationship limits, and this emphasis on contextual clarity promotes the developmental task of renunciation. The therapist clearly defines what he cannot deliver. Acts that might be interpreted as seductive—touching, compliments, even sympathy—are eschewed. Contrasted with the current proliferation of faddish techniques which promise quick cures by blurring context and denying relationship limitations, the psychoanalytic position stands as a rock.

But there are other problems in contextual clarity. A treatment method that ignores symptom concerns by redefining treatment goals in abstract and intrapsychic terms invites confusion as to the contract between patient and therapist. The question, "What are you doing in treatment?" often meets with notably unclear responses from psychoanalytic patients. If this confusion persists, and especially if it is considered virtuous, treatment can be interminable.

In addition, if a therapist feels responsible for determining when a patient has completed treatment (if the criteria of cure are presumably known more by the expert than by the patient) this is a source of contextual confusion. Here the psychoanalytic therapist may bear a heavier burden of responsibility that is necessary, useful, or wise. The goals are to resolve transference, and to assist patients in assuming adult responsibilities, and yet these patients are not expected to decide for themselves when they are well. "I decide when you are mature" is a power message with a built-in contradiction inviting subservience or rebellion.

The orthodox practice of seeing only the identified patient and no others can both clarify and confuse context. Behavior that clearly answers the question "Whose agent are you?" is to be applauded, when compared to less disciplined therapists who see family, lovers, spouses indiscriminately, and often seem unaware of the meaning of such meetings to the participants.

For example, I was seeing a female married patient who was having an affair with a man, also married, who was in treatment with a "modern" psychotherapist. I was startled to have a request transmitted to me from my patient's lover's therapist that this rather odd couple get together with their respective therapists for "treatment." Such flagrant and even bizarre disregard for needed context clarity will never occur using orthodox psychoanalytic principles. But the principle of seeing only one person in a system may also create contextual problems. For example, seeing only one member of a marital pair may imply that the spouse is less or more sick, less interesting or valuable. It can inadvertently encourage further rupture of a weak parental coalition; a therapist/spouse coalition can become as strong as any parent/child bond. Clarity of context cannot be obtained by simplistic formulae or rigid rules which produce their own confusing ambiguity.

Another booby-trap in the effort to obtain clarity is the attempt to develop a transference neurosis, an intense, ambivalent, one-sided relationship in which the therapist is fantasied as being extremely powerful. Orthodox psychoanalysts believe this to be essential for successful treatment, although no research supports this contention. In the throes of a transference neurosis, a patient regresses and contextual clarity disappears.

4) *Power Issues*

In moving from entropic to negentropic system, family power changes from a style in which nobody is effective, to a rigid control-oriented structure with overt power battles omnipresent, and then finally to optimal family systems where overt power is coherently shared, and family member roles are complementary, not symmetrically competitive.

By its strong focus on the individual patient's history, psychoanalytic technique encourages the patient to have overt power in the relationship. If the problem relates to his unique past, the alert efforts of both patient and therapist are required for cure. This approach is far ahead of the ancient model of stereotyped treatment of mental illness based on diagnostic categorization (much as electroshock is sometimes administered even today).

On the other hand, encouraging transference and considering the patient's feelings toward the therapist as irrational, to be interpreted by the therapist, lead to a marked overt power differential. The patient can submit, rebel, or fight back, much as submissive marital partners do, with sneaky, indirect, impotent/omnipotent behavior. Transference, though ubiquitous, is negative; it should not be fostered but fought. If equal overt relationship power is a goal, it is a dangerous misjudgment of therapist strength and patient weakness. An overt power differential is a cause for what is treated because symptoms of emotional illness are associated with impotent/omnipotent behavior forms. Transference and overt power differences reduce the patient's opportunity to experience competence in the relationship.

As family competence increases, the overt power of male and female parents and children becomes relatively equal. In effective families, role stereotyping is minimal. Men can be gentle, women competent, and not threaten the family but strengthen it.

Psychoanalytic theory bears some responsibility for continuing and giving presumed biologic support for anti-female themes already common in the Western World. Male theorists speculate about proper mothering and infant/mother interaction, often without direct data and certainly without personal experience. Women are presented as envious, angry, and inferior, and yet are expected to become nurturing mothers who do not take out their frustrations on helpless children.

The similarity of such a theoretical view to a type of pathology found in neurotic males—the madonna/prostitute complex—is hard to overlook. In both, there is double vision about women, seeing them as both more and less human (or male), which precludes the development of intimacy.

No two people, whether in families, peer groups, or therapist's office, can be intimate without possessing relatively equal power. If a parent wishes to be close to his child, to share an intimate moment, he intuitively drops to the child's eye level, a behavioral statement that any power difference is renounced for the moment and two humans can be together and share. It is the ability to become intimate and to remain so for periods of time that is conspicuously lacking in all emotional illness. Therapy aimed at helping individuals attain a level of maturation reached by offspring of optimal families must assist them in experiencing intimacy.

Such learning could conceivably occur outside the patient/therapist interaction, with the therapist acting as something of a non-playing coach. If so, equality between therapist and patient would not be necessary. However, most psychotherapists today believe that emotional, experiential learning is important in treatment and that the quality of patient/therapist interaction is significant.[4,26]

5) *Encouragement of Autonomy*

Optimal family members expressed feelings directly, were open to others' expressions, respected individual subjective reality, and took personal responsibility for thoughts, feelings and behavior. The psychoanalytic system similarly supports autonomy by listening respectfully to a suffering human, taking seriously what he has to say, attempting to understand and to avoid judgments. However, the theory is flawed by viewing man's essence as lustful and aggressive/destructive, possessing drives which must be controlled by society in order for the person and society to survive. Such a belief encourages therapist behavior similar to that seen in mid-range families. Obstructionism and resistance are expected and found, and a marked overt power differential (the transference neurosis) is considered necessary to defeat this resistance.

A technique that encourages anonymity operates much as a mid-range family referee, decreasing the therapist's inclination to be open, spontaneous, and forthright. Such behavior also decreases the patient's movement toward spontaneity through identification and role modeling. Psychotherapy research provides no evidence for the value of such stereotyped, distancing behavior; as discussed in Chapter 11, there are indications that anonymity and the encouragement of transference are counterproductive. Therapists learn these tactics through indoctrination, the acceptance of a system of presumably certain authority. Unequivocal allegiance to any ideological system is damaging to autonomy, and one cannot give to another what he himself does not have. Only those who understand the difference between open and closed systems, and, if psychoanalytically trained, who transcend its relatively closed system limits can help patients develop autonomy greater than that found in midrange families.

Subjective reality. The strong biological orientation of psychoanalytic theory, coupled with its reductionist view of science and truth, provide a powerful framework for absolutes and "objectivity" rather than helping emotionally ill people to see human truth as incomplete, relative, and defined by social interaction. In short, psychoanalytic theory, if taken too seriously, acts as a referee that threatens an individual's subjective reality and forestalls the learning of negotiation quite as well as absolutes found in disturbed families. Such absolute reality always emanates from a social structure that considers some people closer to the source of truth than others; questioning authority leads to highly charged moralistic attacks.

Recently, I was one of a group of psychiatrists who heard Paul Chodoff, a somewhat unorthodox psychoanalyst, make some irreverent remarks about libido theory in his humorous, friendly, but earnest manner. After his talk, the ranking psychoanalyst in the audience asked, in all seriousness, "Do you believe in the unconscious?" After the group's shock and surprise had leveled off, I realized the question was based on the notion that anyone who challenges any substantive area of psychoanalytic theory has probably lost the faith entirely. Family therapists are sometimes in situations with a disturbed family that are similar to that of Chodoff amidst his colleagues. For example, a therapist may try to deal with a father's adamant attack on his hospitalized adolescent son's cigarette smoking. If the therapist suggests that this might not be the most pressing issue, the father reacts with outrage and quite honestly believes that the therapist is trying to destroy his beliefs and his family. This is a common response when absolutes are the basis of rationality.

6) *Affective Issues*

Optimal families had an intensity of interaction marked by shared focus of attention and absence of boredom. This intensity was generally pleasant, though anger was permitted by the family rules. Among family members, conflict was resolvable and empathy was high.

Jerome Frank lists as one of the universal qualities of successful psychotherapy the development of emotional arousal.[27] Psychoanalysts have continually struggled with the need for intense, yet reasonably positive, feelings in the patient/therapist interchange. Over the years, many heretics have disagreed with the orthodox on how to attain this emotional intensity for maximum therapeutic potency. The pesky assumption of essentially destructive drives is an enormous obstacle in working toward affiliative (rather than oppositional) possibilities and intense human encounter.

Psychoanalytic technique requires more cognitive than affective input by the therapist, and discourages dialogue that includes powerful feelings from the therapist. In its place the technique includes free association in an atmosphere of permissive acceptance. This frequently produces emotional intensity in a patient, as he recaptures and expresses highly charged material. In addition, the transference neurosis allows the therapist to become endowed with highly distorted positive and negative qualities, which also can result in emotional intensity. Both technical devices reduce the significance and the intensity of the current patient/therapist relationship and rely on memory for the affect. Hence, even if a psychoanalytic therapist works through the problem of defining man as destructive, relying on history for emotional intensity invites hostile and negative feelings toward the therapist, whether overtly or covertly expressed. People with emotional illness have had rather painful early experiences, and encouraging transference increases resistance as it increases primarily negative affective expression. (So-called positive transference, usually of an erotic nature, is negative in its results and basic intent.)

Conflict—Resolvable and Irresolvable. In human interaction, conflict is inevitable, but optimal family members had an impressive ability to resolve these conflicts. They had an affiliative, optimistic set; negotiation was the rule, and differences were seldom settled by naked power plays.

Many assumptions of psychoanalysis are remarkably like those of the midrange family—man is evil, males and females are in permanent conflict. Envious women resentfully provide love to males through submission, children invariably wish to kill their parents (though apparently not the reverse) and successful socialization consists of inhibiting basic drives. These self-fulfilling prophecies produce eternal irresolvable conflict. The belief system tends to dampen enthusiasm for intimacy in encounter and encourages a formal, somewhat stereotyped interaction, hard to distinguish from that of compulsive neurotics.

All systems of psychotherapy with which I am familiar acknowledge that conflict, sometimes bitter and painful, occurs during treatment. Patients, by definition, are unhappy, relatively socially inept, and confused. Their painful memories have produced a pessimistic, or at least a highly mistrustful, set. However, I know of no data indicating that such conflict is irresolvable, and the family studies suggest the reverse.

Brenner dramatizes the issue here as he speaks of Oedipal phenomena: "By no means all of the child's directly incestuous and murderous impulses toward his parents are abandoned. On the contrary, at least a portion of them are simply repressed or otherwise defended against . . . it is the intensity of the child's own hostile impulses toward his parents during the Oedipal phase that is the principal factor in determining the severity of the superego rather than the degree of the parent's hostility or severity toward the child."[5]

Research in child abuse (discussed in Chapter 9) has produced data indicating that parents who abuse their children were themselves abused in childhood. Destructiveness toward others with the resulting overwhelming useless guilt, so often seen in these child-abusing parents, comes from their experiences, not their drives. This is a happy circumstance where data provide hope that speculative theory does not.

Some psychoanalytic researchers, for example, Lyman Wynne, Theodore Lidz, and Stephen Fleck, have gone far beyond these orthodox limitations in their studies of family interaction. Researchers and clinicians can and do transcend theoretical limits, just as optimal family members transcended the limitations of their religious belief systems.

There is an interesting parallel between this assumption of irresolvable human conflict and an assumption of opposing forces in the psyche. Freud considered that "it is necessary for us to destroy some other thing or person in order not to destroy ourselves, in order to guard against the impulsion to self-destruction."[28] Irresolvable conflict *between* humans is related to irresolvable conflict *in* humans.

Finally, the concept of penis envy as a ubiquitous part of female development assumes an eternal male/female struggle. The conflict between Freudian theory and concerns about human dignity for both men and women has been present since the earliest days of psychoanalysis. It is a male oriented psychology assuming a dominant/submissive sexual relationship that was common in the middle classes at the turn of the century. Complementary equal power with role reciprocity is not included in the biological theorizing about social behavior. (Marmor reports finding breast envy and womb envy in male patients in recent years as the social system changes.[29] He toils continually to lead the psychoanalytic system into openness.)

Just as family capability can be determined by its position on an affiliative/oppositional expectation continuum, treatment theories can be similarly evaluated, using the views they present of man's nature and of the expected results of encounter.

Empathy. The optimal family members were capable of feeling with, of being emotionally tuned in to each other.

The psychoanalytic system began thus, but encountered the problems found in midrange families. It is hard to feel with someone else if you mistrust his essence and yours. The Freudian system, taken neat, is soft on obsessionalism. The normal is apt to come across as a cognitive, control oriented, socially powerful person who mistrusts people and distances himself from them. Living always with a "necessary" basic mistrust of humanity, he obtains security by following proper rules of conduct and remaining within an honorable hierarchy—a sane but constricted pattern, apt to diminish empathy. However, many practicing psychoanalysts have transcended the limits of their cognitive system and can express the warmth and empathy necessary for treatment progress; they and dissenters have made technical and theoretical changes which augment the possibilities for empathic involvement with patients.

7) Negotiation and Task Performance

Optimal families not only fared well in the task of raising children, but accomplished assigned tasks with zest and good humor, using excellent feedback loops among the members and resolving conflict quickly. They attended to individual thoughts, wishes, choices, and feelings, as well as to overt acts, as they developed and maintained shared goals and purposes.

The psychoanalytic system gets mixed reviews in task efficiency. Its focus on the patient's verbal productions and its concept of the developmental origin of neurosis reduces the tendency for simplistic efforts at symptom relief and encourages attention to the task of growing up. However, its emphasis on cognition and intrapsychic constructs and the diversion of attention from symptoms—if compounded by an overt power differential—can produce an inefficient, non-negotiating system without coherent, shared goals. If the therapist is seen as authoritative interpreter of cognitive material produced but not assessed or interpreted by the patient, the therapist can reinforce a patient's introjected family rules (for example, never encounter, never confront, never take personal responsibility). Negotation then is nil and task efficiency poor. Erikson credits Freud with contributing to psychotherapy the establishment of a treatment contract. If this contract between the patient and therapist is clear and frequently updated and not forgotten in the pursuit of "deep" (i.e., not immediately relevant) associations, the shared task can be efficiently accomplished.

8) *Transcendent Values*

Optimal family members accepted loss better than those from symptomatic families. This ability is related to individuation—to a self-definition with goals and purposes not dependent on unchanging family relationships.

Purpose has both system and meaning implications. Von Bertalanffy considers purpose as a necessary part of evolved systems, providing support for the idea that optimal families are negentropic systems. In addition, family purpose is related to a shared meaning implicit in daily activities—a religious concept if one defines the search for meaning as a religious quest.

Freudian psychoanalysis has long been hostile toward religious beliefs, viewing them as evidence of emotional illness, or at least poor reality testing. Freud commented in 1933, "A Weltanschaung (an intellectual construction, which gives a unified solution of all of the problems of our existence in virtue of a comprehensive hypothesis . . .) based upon science has, apart from the emphasis it lays upon the real world, essentially negative characteristics such as that it limits itself to truth, and rejects illusion. Those of our fellow men who are dissatisfied with this state of things and who desire more for their momentary peace of mind, may look for it where they can find it. We shall not blame them for doing so; but we cannot help them and change our own way of thinking on their account."[28]

Becker has discussed the predicament of Freud—needing a transcendent system of value, as all humans do, but rejecting religious belief as illusion; relying on science, but seeing its truths as essentially negative, and finally deifying his own conceptual framework.[30]

The interpretation of religious belief as sickness continues in the psychoanalytic system. Brenner comments, "Religious beliefs in general reflect the general unreliability of the capacity of our egos for reality testing."[5] Freud's orthodox followers have continued the European intellectual tradition of attacking the tyranny of organized religion. The attacks are somewhat similar to those of Marx; whether opiate or illusion, religion is believed to hold man back rather than hold him together.

There is a peculiar irony in this psychoanalytic intolerance of Western religious institutions, since their views of man's nature are similar. Man as essentially antisocial is compatible with some 19th-century Christian interpretations of original sin. Concepts of narcissism can substitute for many Christian views about the evils of selfishness. Frequently I have heard psychoanalytic psychiatrists use the term "sick" in reference to a public figure or a colleague in tones reminiscent of ministers using the term "sinner." The common denominator is a pharisaic manner—an effort to control the other by defining him from a closed system viewpoint.

If shared meaning and purpose are necessary for competent individuals and families, then the reductionist, "nothing but" of pseudo-objective science can never offer food for this hunger. In my experience, when a patient has been freed of much of his "private religion" (the neurotic stereotyped maladaptive attitudes and behavior), he feels a great restlessness, a desire to develop clearer purpose, to have a life with greater shared meaning. Successful treatment of emotional ills seems to develop religious people then, in this sense. I believe that a treatment system can approach the effectiveness of optimal families in producing emotionally healthy people only by accepting the human need to be a part of a community defined by shared purpose and values. When this is achieved, every act and every interaction with others can transcend the immediate and practical, and become a part of a meaningful whole. Far from being immature and emotionally ill, such skill is necessary for adulthood.

COMPLEMENTING PSYCHOANALYTIC THEORY WITH FAMILY SYSTEMS CONCEPTS AND DATA—THE SCHREBER CASE

The Freudian system has made many valuable contributions to growth-oriented psychotherapy, but much useful material, particularly of a systems nature, needs to be added in order to provide a more complete theoretical base.

A way of illustrating the value of adding a systems orientation is to re-evaluate a theoretically important family, that of Dr. Daniel Goetlieb Moritz Schreber (1808-1861). This family produced one of psychiatry's most famous and often cited patients—Daniel Paul Schreber (1842-1911), who wrote a somewhat bizarre book, *Memoirs of My Nervous Illness*, published in 1903. In 1910 the *Memoirs* came to the attention of Sigmund Freud, who then published, in 1911, the "Psychoanalytic Notes on an Autobiographical Account of a Case of Paranoia."[31] In this paper, Freud used Schreber's memoirs to develop the theory that paranoia has a sexual etiology and "what lies at the core of the conflict in cases of paranoia among males is a homosexual wishful fantasy of loving a man."

Schreber, a distinguished lawyer who held several judicial posts, had an attack of severe hypochondria at age 42, necessitating a six-month hospitalization in the Leipzig Psychiatric Clinic, where he was treated by Dr. Paul Emil Flechsig. Following his appointment as presiding judge of the Supreme Court of Saxony, Schreber had a second illness which began with hypochondriasis, but assumed a violent force for two years, manifesting mutism, stupor, hyperactivity, suicide attempts, hallucinations, delusions of persecution by his physician and by God, delusions that miracles were performed on his body, compulsive and obsessive symptoms, and transvestism. Though Schreber began his journal to acquaint his wife with his experiences, he later thought that many people would be interested in his ordeal and his supernatural insights; against family resistance he published the book that Freud discovered.

Utilizing only this material and with no knowledge of the family, Freud developed his renowned etiological theory of paranoia, relating it to denied homosexual wishes.

Freud assumed a reasonably benign family and an unusually capable father: "His memory is kept green to this day by the numerous Schreber associations which flourish especially in Saxony. . . . (He) exerted a lasting influence upon his contemporaries . . .

"His great reputation as the founder of therapeutic gymnastics in Germany is still shown by the wide circulation of his *Arzliche Zimmergymnastik* (Medical Indoor Gymnastics) in medical circles and the numerous editions through which it has passed . . .

"Such a father as this was by no means unsuitable for transfiguration into a god in the affectionate memory of the son from whom he had been so early separated by death."[31]

In the intervening years, however, more information is available concerning the family, especially the father. Schreber the elder was a famous orthopedic surgeon and pedagogue. He was also a dangerous, sadistic, and severely disturbed man who ruled his household with an iron fist and chose his two sons for special attention. He used them, but not his daughters, as guinea pigs to try out cruel physical insults under the guise of improved child development techniques which he advocated as an expert. The medical reports of the Sonmenstein Asylum where the son was confined state, "The father (founder of the Schreber Gardens in Leipzig) suffered from compulsive manifestations with murderous impulses." The father also wrote an apparently personal report of an episode of insanity which included delusions, attacks of melancholia, brooding, and tormenting criminal impulses.

It is evident that Freud assumed that the public face of Schreber the elder was the actual one rather than the private face known to his family.

There were five children in the family: Anna, the eldest; Gustave, the second child, three years older than the patient who also had a severe psychosis and killed himself by gunshot in 1877 at age 38; the patient, and two younger sisters. Both male children were extremely disturbed, while all three daughters apparently escaped obvious emotional damage and lived out their span uneventfully.[32] Here we have the phenomenon of well siblings of severely psychotic individuals and a dramatic illustration of how family environment for one child is much different than for the next. In this case markedly different handling depended on the sex of the child.

Schreber the elder developed a great reputation as an expert on child raising, ironically undiminished by his having two psychotic sons, one of whom committed suicide. His books preached household totalitarianism in a systematic attack on children's developing selfhood.

Schatzman[33] provides material from the father's writing which dramatically illustrates his viewpoint. For example: "When the man can support his opinions by reason of demonstrable truth, no wife with common sense and good will will want to oppose his decisive voice." "If one wants a planned upbringing based on principles to flourish, the father above anyone else must hold the reins of upbringing in his hands. The main responsibility for the whole result of upbringing always belongs to the father . . ." "Training should start early, at five or six months. Suppress *everything* in the child. Keep everything away from him which he should not make his own, but guide him perseveringly toward everything to which he should habituate himself. If we habituate a child to the good and the right,

we prepare him to do the good and the right later with consciousness and out of free will." Schreber the elder aimed to develop self
reliance and free will in children by denying them any self expression or any family respect for their own subjective reality. "One
must look at the moods of the little ones which are announced by
screaming without reason and crying. . . . If one has convinced
oneself that no real need, no disturbing or painful condition, no
sickness is present, one can be assured that this screaming is only
and simply the expression of a mood, a whim, the first appearance
of self-will—One has to step forward in a positive manner; by quick
distraction of the attention, stirring words, threatening gestures,
rapping against the bed—or when all of this is of no avail, by moderate intermittent bodily admonishments consistently repeated
until the child calms down or falls asleep—such a procedure is
necessary only once, or at most twice, and one is the *master* of the
child *forever*. From now on, a glance, a word, a single threatening
gesture is sufficient to rule the child. One should keep in mind
that one shows the child the greatest kindness in this, and that one
saves him from many hours of tension which hinder him from
thriving and also frees him from all those spiritual torments which
very easily grow up vigorously into more serious and insurmounta-
ble enemies of life."

Tenderness or expressions of love by a child's caretakers are considered destructive and damaging to proper child rearing. "If the
child is lifted from the bed and carried around each time he makes
noises, without checking if there is really something wrong, and is
calmed by gentleness of one kind or another, this may often lead to
the appearance of the emotion of spite later in the life of the child.
I wish mothers and nursemaids would recognize the importance of
this point!" "Here is only a small experience from my own family
circle: The nurse of one of my children, generally a very sweet
person, once gave a child something between his meals even
though having been told explicitly not to. It was a piece of pear
which she herself was eating. She was without any other reason
dismissed from the service at once because I had lost the necessary
trust in her unconditional correctness." Following such behavior,

his reputation spread, and he said he had "no further trouble with any other such maids or nurses." "Parental control over the inner life of the child, including thoughts, feelings, and motives should be complete." No negotiation here! Schreber the elder never ex-presses any awareness that a child may at times know his own needs better than does his father.

As a training exercise, Schreber advises that children of three to five years old should be induced after punishment to feel what the parent thinks he should feel. "It is generally salutatory for the sen-timents if the child, after each punishment, after he had recov-ered, is gently prodded (preferably by a third person) to offer to shake the hand of the punisher as a sign of a plea for forgiveness—from then on everything should be forgotten. After this prodding has occurred a few times, the child, feeling his duty, will freely approach the punisher. This insures against the possibility of re-sidual spiteful or bitter feelings and mediates the feelings of repentance—If one were to omit this procedure altogether, one would permit the punished child the right of anger against the punisher which is certainly not consistent with an intelligent pedagogic approach." The denial of individual feelings is made con-tinuous and explicit. "The art of self denial: each forbidden desire, whether or not it is to the child's disadvantage, must be consis-tently and unequivocally opposed by an unconditional refusal. The refusal of a desire is not enough though. One has to see to it that the child receives the refusal calmly, and if necessary one has to make this calm acceptance a firm habit by using a stern word or threat, etc. Never make an exception from this." In this disturbed man's plan for rearing children, we find a storehouse of explicit di-rections for developing a severely dysfunctional family system. Power is monopolized by the father and yet denied—his avowed purpose is to develop the child's "free will," yet he sees autonomy as the ultimate evil. Individual feeling expression is suppressed, and objections to the suppressions are also suppressed forcefully and with self-righteous vengence. Communication is one-way inva-siveness from parent to child. Unpleasant feelings are to be denied, repressed, or ignored; individual subjective responses are defined as willfulness and spite.

A child should learn never to trust his own feelings, and as the final blow to any residual trust in himself, should put his faith in his persecutor. Individual choice does not exist in such a family.

Data from disturbed families suggest that such a reversal of loving common sense, with the careful avoidance of authentic human encounter, will develop offspring unable to make choices, with little effective ego functioning.

It is fortunate for the female children of this family that Schreber the elder focused on his sons, and fortunate for students of family interaction that we can see in this ghastly experiment the results of such a program. The father was apparently able to persuade his compliant wife to assist in his destructive activities. Neiderland quotes Anna, his eldest: "Father discussed with our mother everything and anything; she took part in all his ideas, plans, and projects. She read the galley proofs of his writings with him and was his faithful, close companion in everything."[34] Apparently the two sons were unable to turn to their mother for rescue.

Schreber the elder developed a wildly imaginative torture chamber of restrictive devices which he used on his male children, including restrictive shoulder straps, chest restraints, restraints across the body used with a sleeping child, head halters, chin bands, and the like, all of which he advocated for the proper growth of the children of Germany. Neiderland and Schatzman painstakingly compared the father's torture with the son's delusions, and have illustrated their parallel nature. Judge Schreber suffered from memories of real events and a faulty sense of time; he also lacked the necessary ability to deal with object loss (specifically the death of his persecutor father) characteristic of children from severely disturbed families. This description of family characteristics of psychiatry's most famous patient speaks to the value of exploring family data in understanding a particular individual's emotional illness, its etiology and manifestations.

The information concerning Judge Schreber, his father and his family is also useful for those who might wish to look at the next level of social systems, the society beyond the family. In a series of careful expositions, Erikson provides data about Martin Luther,[35] Mohandas Gandhi,[36] Adolph Hitler, Maxim Gorky,[14] and their social milieus, supporting his view that an individual's personal dynamics can elevate him to major social influence if they reflect similar (isomorphic) dynamics in the larger society. It is not too fanciful to consider Schreber the elder as one of these significant men; it is possible to see his popularity during his own time as causally related to the later popularity of Adolph Hitler, who expressed vengeful hate toward father figures and attempted to replace them with the image of the eternal rebellious adolescent who conquers all tradition but inevitably uses the same inhuman methods as the hated father. In fact, Schreber the elder's biographer, Ritter, described him as the spiritual precursor of Nazism.[32]

The case of Schreber goes far beyond an intrapsychic mechanism of excessive homosexual love for a parent. With the added data concerning the family, particularly the father, it offers a dramatic and memorable family case history with a formula for raising children who are deprived of psychic freedom and subject to psychosis. The recognition that psychotic delusions can be related to experiences and faulty time sense rather than to instinctual drives suggests potentially useful treatment approaches.

REFERENCES

1. FREUD, S., "Fragment of an analysis of a case of hysteria," *Colllected Papers*, Vol. 3, New York, Basic Books, 1959.
2. JONES, E., *Free Association; Memories of a Psychoanalyst*, New York, Basic Books, 1959.
3. THOMPSON, C., with Mullahy, P., *Psychoanalysis: Evolution and Development*, New York, Grove Press, 1950.
4. GREENSON, R. R., *The Technique and Practice of Psychoanalysis*, Vol. I, New York, International Universities Press, 1967.
5. BRENNER, C., *An Elementary Textbook of Psychoanalysis*, New York, International Universities Press, 1957.
6. FENICHEL, O., *The Psychoanalytic Theory of Neurosis*, New York, W. W. Norton, 1945.
7. FREUD, S., *New Introductory Lectures on Psychoanalysis*, New York, W. W. Norton, 1933.
8. FREUD, S., *A General Introduction to Psychoanalysis*, New York, Permagiants, 1949.
9. YALOM, I. D., "Existential factors in group therapy," *J. of the National Association of Private Psychiatric Hospitals*, 6(3):27-35, Fall, 1974.
10. REICH W., *Character Analysis*, New York, Orgone Press, 1949.

11. FREUD, A., *The Ego and the Mechanisms of Defense*, New York, International Universities Press, 1946.
12. HARTMANN, H., *Essays on Ego Psychology*, New York, International Universitites Press, 1964.
13. HARTMANN, H. and KRIS, E., "The Genetic Approach in Psychoanalysis," in *The Psychoanalytic Study of the Child*, Vol. I, 1945.
14. ERIKSON, E. H., *Childhood and Society*, 2nd Ed., New York, W. W. Norton, 1963.
15. ERIKSON, E. H., *Insight and Responsibility*, New York, W. W. Norton, 1964.
16. GREENSON, R. R., "The Classic Psychoanalytic Approach," in Arieti, S. (Ed.) *American Handbook of Psychiatry*, Vol. II., p. 1409, New York, Basic Books, 1959.
17. LEBESOHN, Z. M., in Marmor, J. (Ed.) *Psychiatrists and Their Patients*, Washington, D. C., Joint Information Service of APA and NAMH, p. 174, 1975.
18. JONES, E., *The Life and Work of Sigmund Freud*, Vol. I., New York, Basic Books, 1953.
19. ALEXANDER, F., *The Scope of Psychoanalysis*, New York, Basic Books, 1961.
20. GREENSON, R. R., *The Technique and Practice of Psychoanalysis*, Vol. I., New York, International Universities Press, 1967.
21. MARMOR, J., "The future of psychoanalytic therapy," *Am. J. Psychiat.*, 130(11):1197-1202, Nov., 1973.
22. FESTINGER. *A Theory of Cognitive Dissonance*, Evanston, Ill., Row Peterson and Co., 1957.
23. FREUD, S., *Psychoanalysis and Faith: Dialogues with the Reverend Oskar Pfister*, New York, Basic Books, 1963.
24. HARTMAN, H., *Ego Psychology and the Problem of Adaptation*, New York, International Universities Press, 1958.
25. KREBBS, R. L., "Interruptus," *Psychology Today*, 3(8):33, 1970.
26. STEINZOR, B., *The Healing Partnership*, New York, Harper and Row, 1967.
27. FRANK, J., *Persuasion and Healing: A Comparative Study of Psychotherapy*, Baltimore, Johns Hopkins Press, 1961.
28. FREUD, S., *New Introductory Lectures on Psycho-analysis*, New York, W. W. Norton, 1933.
29. MARMOR, J., *Psychiatry in Transition*, New York, Brunner/Mazel, 1974.
30. BECKER, E., *The Denial of Death*, New York, The Free Press, 1973.
31. FREUD, S., "Psychoanalytic Notes upon an Autobiographical Account of a Case of Paranoia (Dementia Paranoides)," *Collected Papers*, V. 3, New York, Basic Books, 1959.
32. NEIDERLAND, W. G., "Schreber's Father," *J. of the Am. Psychoanalytic Assn.*, V. 8, 1960.
33. SCHATZMAN, M., "Paranoia or persecution: the case of Schreber," *Family Process* 10(2):117-212, June, 1971.
34. NEIDERLAND, W. G., "III Further data and memorabilia pertaining to the Schreber case," *Int. J. of Psychoanal.*, 44:203, 1963.
35. ERIKSON, E. H., *Young Man Luther, A Study in Psychoanalysis and History*, New York, W. W. Norton, 1958.
36. ERICKSON, E. H., *Gandhi's Truth*, New York, W. W. Norton, 1969.

Upon this gifted age, in its dark hour,
Rains from the sky a meteoric shower
Of facts . . . they lie unquestioned, uncombined.

Wisdom enough to leech us of our ills
Is daily spun; but there exists no loom
to weave it into fabric . . .

From *Collected Sonnets of Edna St. Vincent Millay*

8

Using the family variables to critique other psychotherapy systems

The previous chapter provided a critique of the Freudian system. In this chapter, I will summarize the divergent views of two early Freudian followers—Adler and Jung—and of five currently popular schools of psychotherapy. Then, I will discuss these schools using the eight variables derived from family systems study. There is no attempt to describe these schools in detail; the interested reader may refer to definitive presentations of their theory and techniques referenced in the text. Rather, I will define treatment principles found in these systems and describe an emerging historical and logical synthesis pointing toward the evolution of a broad-based, open-system, scientific psychotherapy.

ALFRED ADLER

By 1912, Freud had developed most of the fundamental concepts of psychoanalysis—unconscious motivation, repression, resistance, transference, and anxiety. He considered the sexual instinct all-important in the etiology of neurosis, and psychoanalysis stood or fell on this belief.

It was in 1911 that Alfred Adler was severed from the psychoanalytic group because of his inability to accept the theory of sexual etiology. He was much more impressed with power issues in neurosis and pioneered in considering ego factors, or social skills, as crucial in determining whether a person became emotionally ill.[1]

Extrapolating from his studies of individuals with specific organic inferiority, Adler noted that all humans who, as small children have a sense of helplessness and feel inferior, continue to struggle with these feelings. One method of coping is through compensation, by gaining power over others. This aggressive (he called it "masculine" in both men and women) reaction often leads to recognized achievement and success. A person may also cope with these inferiority feelings by using "feminine" patterns of passivity, submission, and retreat, likely to be termed neurotic. Unlike Freud, Adler considered male and female roles to be culturally influenced rather than of simple biological origin. In Adler's view sex, rather than being the core of people's lives and patients' neuroses, is useful in the struggle for power. He presaged the orthodox analytic development of the aggressive drive, but never defined it as narrowly biological or destructive.

Though Adler called his school of therapy an individual psychology, he was most insistent that man is a social animal, and he defined treatment as necessarily involving social context as well as individually defined goals. He believed that no human could be mentally healthy without self transcendence and social interest.

Since Freud believed at that time that all ego functioning is conscious, he considered that Adler was no longer dealing with unconscious material and, therefore, was not a psychoanalyst. Much later, Freud's opinions changed to recognize that much of ego functioning is unconscious and that the aggressive drive is most important. Seemingly momentous theoretical clashes often move toward agreement.

Adler altered Freudian treatment methods considerably, dispensing with the couch and assuming an active teaching role. He frequently interrupted patients; free association gave way to a therapist-directed interview. Patients were seen less frequently and less formally; also, treatment was less lengthy.

Adler's psychology, viewed from the vantage point of the family system variables, has some strong features. If Freud, Adler, and Jung could have remained within the same system, a non-cultist and scientific psychotherapy might already exist.

Adler intuitively conceived of systems factors influencing the developing self; he had a lifelong interest in child development and defined emotional health as necessarily concerned with relationship, purpose, goals, and choice. He was acutely aware of power issues and correctly considered them central in self-esteem. Probably before any other psychoanalyst, Adler comprehended the meaning of autonomy and its importance in human functioning. His masculine protest and neurotic submissiveness are somewhat close to the impotent/omnipotent concept, and he defined an optimal adaptation in terms that could be used to describe competence. Finally, his appreciation of the need for a transcendent value system, though it made him suspect as a real scientist in his time, gives him a distinctly modern flavor.[2]

C. G. JUNG

Jung's break with Freud followed soon after Adler's. Though he had never been as wholehearted as other psychoanalytic disciples in his acceptance of Freud's ideas or control, the ostensible reason for this break was disagreement about libido theory. There really was not a great difference between the two here; Jung accepted the primal libido, but considered it to be undifferentiated energy rather than specifically sexual. Their split was emotional and harsh, but Jung and Freud continued to have many concepts in common. Jung's explication of the collective unconscious, the source of much of his treatment's unique characteristics, was accepted by Freud and, though not elaborated in detail, became an accepted part of orthodox psychoanalysis. Jung considered the unconscious to be a powerful force for personal development rather than a repository of antisocial drives. He saw patients as having been thwarted and damaged by early environment with limits that can be overcome with competent psychotherapy. He was the first analyst to emphasize that parents' emotional problems are significant in the etiology of emotional illness. He, in effect, predicted one result of the family studies—the quality of the parental coalition is related to the children's emotional health.

Jung developed a character typology quite different from Freud's. Rather than being based on sexual development, it was founded on male and female characteristics present in all people, their variations leading to introversion or extroversion, and a balance being necessary for health.

Jung believed that a patient could not grow beyond the capabilities of the therapist, but that a patient could help a therapist develop and mature, an interpersonal concept expanded many years later by existentialists. Jung's therapy, like Adler's, accented the future and the possibilities within the patient. He also considered that people need a religious attitude.

Unfortunately, Jung's treatment system developed aspects of a religion with indoctrination of patients resulting from his belief that the wisdom of the collective unconscious is greater than that of the individual.[1]

Jung's therapy gets good marks in some aspects of systems variables; man is rooted in his family, social, and symbolic reality, and his innate symbolism makes him a part of all mankind. Because of Jung's optimism about people and expectation of growth, his therapy does encourage a kind of autonomy.[3] However, the mystical side of Jungian treatment promotes a kind of self-conscious isolation similar in style, if not in content, to that of an orthodox Freudian patient who expects cure from intrapsychic reshuffling.

Power issues are not examined closely, especially those related to the treatment environment.

Adler and Jung were harbingers of the controversy, vituperative conflicts, and dramatic splits that have been a part of psychoanalysis in the years since. In 1924, Otto Rank made a final break with Freud, attacking his nihilism. He believed Freud placed too much emphasis on the past, resulting in sterile intellectual analysis and ignoring potentially therapeutic emotive life. Rank advocated a more active therapy and encouraged patients to assert themselves. He was concerned with *will*, and evolved treatment designed to help the patient transfer negative expressions of will into positive and creative ones. He experimented with time limits in therapy and emphasized the flexible, adaptable, and patient-centered nature of the therapeutic process. He presaged the greater democratization of treatment later found in Sullivanian and Rogerian therapies.

Sandor Ferenczi deviated from Freud more in his approach to treatment than in any theoretical differences. Ferenczi was warm and human with his patients and advocated that therapists admit mistakes, a therapeutic stance disdained by the orthodox. He took the position, later extended by Franz Alexander, that the therapist should be as different as possible from the depriving parent in relation to whom the patient developed his neurosis. The therapist should try to be a "good" parent who accedes to as many of the patient's wishes as possible. Thus, he went against another tenet of Freudian analysis, that frustration is a necessary condition for treatment.

In the 1920's, psychoanalytic concepts continued to evolve under the leadership of Freud. This evolution had little impact, however, on treatment methods and maneuvers. Changes in technique were developed by the dissenters. Freud became disinterested in improving treatment effectiveness and used his conceptual framework to look at the broader society. In fact, his belief in psychoanalysis as therapy wavered more and more as his biological orientation led logically to pessimism and doubts of treatment efficacy.[1]

Wilhelm Reich broke with Freud in their controversies over the death instinct and instinctual masochism. Reich was attempting to maintain optimism about psychotherapy; he was more intense than other psychoanalysts in the fervor with which he advocated libido theory. In fact, he was a source of embarrassment to the Freudians, not by his deviation, but by his fundamentalist zeal. He became a bit strange (and some say psychotic) in his later years as he emphasized orgastic potency as the cure of emotional illness, using an apparatus called an orgone box as a means of treatment. Before he became monomanic in this approach to therapy, Reich made important contributions to psychoanalysis in describing character defenses and character analysis, expressing the concept that analysis of character defenses is needed before interpretation of id wishes.[4] Reich foreshadowed the later emphasis of Freudian psychoanalytic theorists on ego mechanisms.

FIVE CURRENT SYSTEMS OF THERAPY

H. S. Sullivan's Treatment System

In the 1930's, a group of psychoanalysts led by Harry Stack Sullivan, Karen Horney, and Eric Fromm modified Freudian theory and therapy to include a greater emphasis on social factors. Horney and Fromm both immigrated to the United States in this period; Harry Stack Sullivan was the first unusually competent and widely recognized American psychiatric theorist since Adolph Meyer, who was one of Sullivan's teachers. Though Horney and Fromm were creative and influential, Sullivan made the most complete explication of the change in psychoanalytic focus from biology to interpersonal relationships.

A most empirical theorist, he stayed close to what could be observed, referred to theories that could not be disproved as "doctrines," and encouraged psychotherapists to distinguish between dogma and data. Sullivan presented the most thorough and coherent theory of human development since Freud's. He described the phases of infantile development with exquisite sensitivity to the mother-infant relationship, downplaying the importance of instinctual drives in emotional illness. In Sullivan's view, psychiatric illness is due to peculiarities of relationships in a patient's formative years and in the cultural pressures impinging on the family duly communicated to the child. He parted with Freud most dramatically in his perception of the nature of man. Whereas Freud saw the human unconscious as a cesspool of sex and aggressive/ destructiveness, essentially threatening to society, Sullivan saw people more as frightened rabbits, without fang or claw, requiring the caring and approval of others. As he saw it, man lives with anxiety which arises from the threat or actual withdrawal of this approval. The content of the unconscious is developed from this need for approval; the repressed does not consist of any uniform, instinctual drive force, but rather of that which is unacceptable to significant others. Like Jung, Sullivan was impressed with the significance of the peculiar behavior patterns and emotional difficulties of parents in influencing child development.[5]

Sullivan believed people have two decisive goals: the pursuit of satisfaction and the pursuit of security.[6] By the pursuit of satisfaction, he recognized those biological factors which Freud emphasized, but he focused equally on the individual's need for the interpersonal environment in order to maintain personal security. The self arises from the infant's relating to significant others; it is made up of their "reflected appraisals." Therefore, transcending one's culture is quite difficult; Sullivan emphasized society's making the man rather than man's making his society. To Freud, society and man are always in a battle; to Sullivan, the social structure is necessary to bolster the weak and anxious human. Clara Thompson, an adherent of Sullivan, stated this position well: "The conclusion from the study of comparative cultures is that man is not biologically endowed with dangerous, fixed animal drives and that the only function is to control these. Society is not something contrasted to man, but something at the same time created by man and creating man."[1]

The self system, then, arises and is maintained by continuous interaction between the individual and needed others. A *me*—the part of the self acceptable to others—and a *not me*—the part rejected by significant others—evolve. This *not me* must be kept from consciousness to avoid painful anxiety, and the process by which this is accomplished is termed selective inattention. This phrase refers to the ability of humans to become unaware of aspects of themselves and others that would threaten personal security, and covers phenomena that Freud would call suppression and repression. It is closely related to dissociation, which Sullivan considered an extreme form of selective inattention, dramatic rather than "suave."

Sullivan used the term "parataxic distortion" for phenomena subsumed under transference in the Freudian scheme. Parataxic distortion refers to the series of projections that emotionally disturbed people place on others. This distortion is related to earlier life experiences, and though comparable in some ways to transference has significant conceptual and practical differences. Parataxic distortions occur immediately in new relationships; they need not be developed. The problem for the therapist is to assist a patient in reducing the degree of this distortion.

Sullivan rarely mentioned reality; rather he spoke of "consensual validation," the reality of consensus in a social group, emphasizing the subjective nature of reality and the relativity of truth. This was a great theoretical advance with significant treatment implications. Sullivanian treatment consists of a therapist who recognizes his reality in the patient/doctor relationship, who is a participant, yet who steps out of the thick of things to function as an observer. Such a therapist needs to be sensitive to the ways that human interaction may produce crippling anxiety in people who are forced to be unaware of much that is true about themselves. He will carefully and respectfully begin to reduce a patient's distortions by offering coherent feedback. The feedback is provided by therapeutic dialogue; monologues by either patient or therapist are not considered helpful in the correction process. Treatment is active, with frequent therapist input. Though Sullivan encouraged a more active therapeutic stance than that advocated by orthodox psychoanalysts, he was never able to accept the greater degree of emotional participation some existential schools advocate.

As the patient finds that the therapist, and then other people, can approve of him, he uses less selective inattention and operates more in the syntaxic mode—that is, with more present consensual validation. There is no purposeful development of a transference neurosis. In fact, the reduction of parataxic distortions means attempting to reduce such transference whenever it appears. This approach decreases the overt power differential between patient and therapist. Expecting dialogue and assuming no absolute truth, the therapist cannot make an interpretation in an authoritarian fashion, but is open to negotiation and consensual validation within the treatment session.

Cure is considered to be the development of new adaptive ways of relating as increased self awareness and shared (consensual) perceptions of others allow greater need satisfaction and security. "Insight" means not merely an intellectual understanding of personal difficulties, but the loss of a wish to act in old maladaptive ways.

Sullivan was a systems theorist before Von Bertalanffy developed the science, describing the self as a "unitary system" which cannot be separated from its necessary environmental milieu without ceasing to be a living organism. He made an effort to integrate psychoanalytic understanding with modern sociology and anthropology; his theory parallels the greater attention paid to ego factors by Freudian psychoanalysts in later years. In addition, Sullivan's empirical approach and his attention to the interpersonal reality of therapist and patient foster a scientific psychotherapy that respects subjectivity. From such a base, new concepts, such as information theory and communication theory, are easily integrated. Sullivanian theory is second only to that of Freud in offering the modern, growth-oriented therapist tools with which to work.

Horney and Fromm were also leaders in using analytic insights without the rigidity or pessimism of a biological preoccupation. Horney was dissatisfied with the notion that biology dictated Victorian masculine and feminine traits. She was an early contributor to the leavening of psychoanalytic theory with a new respect for women and the development of a theoretical base for equality of the sexes.[7]

Fromm was particularly interested in carrying psychoanalytic insights into the broader society, and for many years has written on interpersonal power themes and the possibilities of individual freedom in any culture. Like Adler and Reich before him, Fromm insists that societies differ in the opportunities they provide for individual growth and development; he suggests that one can judge societies just as one can judge the competence of individuals within a given society.[8]

Classical Existential Therapy

Existential psychiatry originated at the turn of this century, but has had an uphill struggle to obtain recognition, becoming relatively popular only after World War II. Existential psychotherapy, though quite different from existentialist philosophy, shares with it the effort to break away from positivism, functionalism, and objectification—concepts that have been associated with science in American psychology. This has made its acceptance in orthodox academic circles difficult. The phenomenological point of view advanced by these therapists has been anathema to American psychological science, while Freudian concepts are relatively more attractive because of their apparently greater objectification of experience lending itself more easily to hypotheses, data gathering, and conventional research.

In spite of such handicaps, existential psychotherapy is reflected in at least three flourishing treatment systems. These are Fritz Perls' gestalt therapy, Carl Rogers' client-centered therapy, and classical existential treatment. Though these therapies are different in technique, they all minimize the use of developmental history in formulating causes of problems and directions of treatment, are extremely wary of diagnosis as objectifying and distancing, and emphasize the immediate, emotion-filled, and unique therapeutic relationship as the primary healing force.

Carl Jaspers wrote the earliest (1913) classical existential psychiatric text expressing the theme that a therapist must participate sympathetically in a patient's experience in order to understand him. Binswanger followed closely in advancing this position, and modern advocates of the existential position include Medard Boss[9] and Victor Frankl[10] in Europe, and Rollo May[11] and Leston Havens[12] in the United States.

Classical existential therapists assume that emotional illness results from a sense of estrangement from others and that successful treatment must assist the patient in having authentic encounters with his therapist. Perhaps because of their wariness of classification and objectified structuring and their emphasis on the unique patient/therapist interaction, formal description of the existential technique is hard to come by. The following summary is derived from Leston Havens, and though it may not fit all of the activities of those who consider themselves classical existential therapists, it is a clear definition of his conception of the process.[13]

Treatment consists first of being, or arriving, or reaching—an intense effort on the part of the therapist to be where the patient is. This goal contrasts with the psychoanalytic method of collecting memories and associations as well as with descriptive psychiatry's search for accurate observations in historical detail, and with the Sullivanian method of attempting to discover parataxic distortions.

The mental state of "keeping looking" is basic to the clinician engaged in existential work. This requires that every temptation the patient offers, or the therapist finds, to *conclude* be pushed away. To conclude is anathema to an existential therapist. It makes a patient a thing, it diminishes the authenticity of the encounter between patient and therapist, and it distances. Therefore, the second necessity of existential therapy is "keeping looking." Havens contrasts this to the goal of psychoanalysis, which is to make contact with the analysand's mental life—to continue to listen. Analytic interest is in the similarities that reverberate in the therapist's mind (patterns); the unique is almost put aside. Comparable to this "keeping looking" of the existential therapist is the Sullivanian "knowing what transpires." The Sullivanian asks himself, "What is the patient's current feeling about my attitude?" "How is the patient misperceiving me now?"

Staying is the third necessity. To stay with the patient, to maintain contact in encounter, inevitably means that the therapist will have strong feelings. Therapists must make their feelings known to the extent that such expression promotes being and staying. If a finite mortal, well-trained and competent as a therapist, has an authentic relationship with a patient who is infuriating, he will either become infuriated or withdraw in an austere, stereotyped, distancing manner—a position of safety, but one that offers little help to the patient. Existential treatment consists of maintaining the relationship, come pleasure or pain, with the confidence that such an endeavor will promote intense feelings and treatment progress. To see treatment as being and staying, keeping looking, never distancing or deriving conclusions about the other increases treatment utility. Havens contrasts this intensity in existential therapy with the client-centered therapy of Rogers: "Sometimes the goal of client-centered therapy seems to be only the revelation and perception of the client and his world with a relatively neutral therapist. This falls short of the existential method."

The classical existentialist is willing to drop the protection of the aloof expert and engage in caring interaction with emotionally ill people. He expects that greater authenticity in relating will kindle positive emotions and attitudes in the patient and result in improvement or cure. By avoiding pseudo-objectivity and neutrality, the therapist changes along with the patient. Sanity and basic moorings do not consist of absolute truth nor correct context; a therapist at times may be as needful as the patient. This treatment framework, so terribly demanding of a therapist's awareness of his own feelings and comfort in expressing them, along with awareness of his vulnerability as a human, can be subverted in the service of countertransference. Havens notes that "existential techniques *could* become an excuse for emotional license in the patient's presence, just as analytic technique could fall into the excessively neutral, aloof, passive hands of some therapists." The discipline required for such work is a flexible one which does not depend on a power differential or on fixed stereotyped behavior to define therapist responsibility and avoid countertransference. It depends rather on courageous honesty in clarifying, changing contexts, and attending to the patient's needs, choices, and direction at all costs. Though such discipline sounds rigorous, it has many compensations. One can laugh with patients, experience ecstasy as well as despair without feeling illicit or burdened by the guilt of a presumed countertransference.

Classical existential therapy relies on subjective reality; it suggests that poor results accrue from power differentials and objectification. If a therapist, in his need to be powerful and sane, is impatient and contemptuous of another's subjective truth, he may reject valuable human reality to his own and his patient's detriment. Coupled with a strong sense of personal responsibility and clear ego boundaries, the existential message can add a great deal to treatment effectiveness.

Gestalt Therapy

Fritz Perls is the spiritual leader of the gestalt therapeutic movement, a rather peculiar fruit of the existential tree. It is peculiar in that Perls defined his treatment as existential, with a focus on the subjective here-and-now, yet his technique was quite authoritarian in a fashion abhorrent to classical existential therapists. Perls attempted to dramatically separate his treatment from orthodox Freudianism, yet his conceptual framework is strongly reminiscent of Freudian analytic theory of the 1920's. Perls saw the individual human as necessarily opposed to society. He spoke of a "natural existence," reminiscent of Rousseau, that conflicts with social existence and causes confusion. He was strong in his belief that frustration was necessary for treatment to progress. Using the concept of projection rather than transference, he considered the therapist a projection screen having no real relationship with the patient but only a fantastic one. Further, his view of instincts versus experience in producing pathology is quite reminiscent of the early orthodox psychoanalytic view. He stated "All the so-called traumata of infants are all lies."[14] His theoretical system is a throwback to pre-Sullivanian psychoanalysts.

Perls could use this dated and questionable developmental theory since his gestalt therapy almost offhandedly dismisses such etiological intellectualizing and lunges toward effective treatment rather than attempting accurate but ineffectual understanding of causes.

Perls was contemptuous of other psychotherapies because of their ineffectiveness in getting past what he termed the "sick point," the impasse when the patient finds no more support from the unconscious or the environment for maladaptive ways, yet has not achieved authentic self-support.

His therapy appropriated the name "gestalt" from an early 20th-century German research psychology. He believed that humans have a need for patterns, for completeness of those patterns, and that people will go to great lengths to complete them in order to reduce emotional tension and re-establish homeostasis. (Such a concept is reminiscent of Freud's repetition compulsion.) Unfinished gestalts interfere with present adaptive efforts, and existence is painful until the unfinished business of an unresolved past is dealt with.

Perls considered emotional illness due to areas of unfinished business reflected in projections of vital parts of the self. Gestalt treatment consists of finding areas of denied conflict, for example, between patient and therapist or in dreams between one symbol and another, and inviting the patient to claim both parts of the conflict, resolve it, and become whole in the process. A major part of treatment consists of a patient's successfully reclaiming that which he has split off and projected.

Perls described five layers of neurosis: 1) the layer of cliché; 2) the layer of games (the "Eric Berne" or "Sigmund Freud" layer—a synthetic existence); 3) the point of impasse—there is nothing, one is stuck and lost; 4) an implosion which is experienced as a death or a fear of death; and finally, 5) an explosion into grief, orgasm, anger or joy, an authentic existence. Moving past the stage of impasse allows a completed gestalt and the ability to be alive in the here and now.

Treatment technique dramatizes personal responsibility: "Do you want to work?" "Do you wish to get past the impasse?" "Will you claim the images in your dream?" There is, however, no emphasis on equal, overt power of therapist and patient. Gestalt therapists, modeling themselves after Perls, are often authoritarian and echo what Perls once quoted himself saying to a patient, "If you had known what I was about, it (the treatment) wouldn't have worked."

Current gestalt therapy has many specific techniques, usually involving play-acting by the patient rather than autonomous, authentic encounter with the therapist.[15] A common one is the "empty chair technique": a patient speaks to a part of himself to an empty chair, then reverses roles and speaks for the absent person or excluded part of himself. This evolution away from classical existential being and staying can produce an "as if" quality to the treatment, perhaps reflecting a debt to Moreno's psychodrama technique.[16] Working through a neurosis depends on the patient's dramatizing and accepting previously denied attitudes and behavior.

Client-Centered Therapy

Finally, there is an American-made existential therapy, the client-centered therapy of Carl Rogers.[17] Rogers, with a theological background enriched by the educational concepts of John Dewey, is an aggressive phenomenologist. He insists that comprehending another person requires knowing how he feels and perceives. Though Rogers does not admit to dealing with unconscious material in any depth, he considers every person to have a limited phenomenal field with only a small portion of experience consciously held at a given moment. One's self-concept is an organized configuration of these perceptions, and some areas consciously considered unimportant by the individual are left vague and unattended. This viewpoint is closely related to Sullivan's description of selective inattention; it is apparent that Rogers was influenced by Sullivan.

An emotionally ill person has a narrow perceptual field that includes many values taken from significant people in his past. These values are often unintegrated and distorted; they seem to have been experienced by the person himself. The confusion and conflict between authentic and borrowed self-concepts result in emotional pain and maladaptive behavior.

The Rogerian therapist's main task is to provide a treatment atmosphere free of any threat to the client (non-possessive warmth), whereby the patient himself can work out a harmonious integration of the self-system. Any attempt at diagnosis is detrimental to this work. The therapist has enough to do in understanding what the client is experiencing and attempting to work through.

Treatment factors include 1) a consistent effort to understand the client's content of speech and his feelings conveyed by words, gestures, intonations, and body posture; 2) communicating this understanding to the client; 3) presenting a synthesis of previously unintegrated material; 4) occasional defining of limits (statements of context); 5) answering questions and providing information; 6) providing and requesting feedback to insure that the therapist understands what the client is saying and feeling; and 7) eschewing direct promotion of insight, giving of advice or praise, or blaming, teaching, or suggesting activities.

Client-centered therapy differs from other systems primarily in leaving the course and direction of the therapy to the client. The overt power differential between therapist and client is tipped heavily in the direction of the client and the therapist is expected to be non-directive and virtually anonymous. A Rogerian therapist will track the patient and respond to his cues, resisting impulses to offer his own views or involve himself in autonomous participations. Rogers believe that such recommended therapist behavior precludes the development of a significant degree of transference or the existence of a transference neurosis.

Rogers and his co-workers, in addition to evolving this treatment system, have been major contributors to psychotherapy research. They have illustrated that a respect for phenomenology, or the subjective reality of patients, is compatible with a scientific evaluation of therapist behavior.[18]

The Behavior Therapies

The behavior therapies represent a loosely defined school still being developed and formalized. Its practitioners, like Freudian psychoanalysts, often insist that theirs is the only scientific treatment model. Because of its recent entry into the field, it is more difficult to offer a comprehensive thumbnail sketch of its major outlines. As Marks has observed, "There has been no shortage of all-explanatory schools, each trimming the richness of clinical experience to its own Procrustean formula in the name of ideological purity." But recently, several authors, including Marks,[19] Danieli, Loew, and Grayson,[20] and Birk and Brinkley-Birk[21] have tried to wrestle this data-oriented, pragmatic field into some coherent order, and I borrow from them in the following short description.

Behavior therapy approaches psychopathological states as involuntarily learned bad habits which arise from interaction with the environment and which can be modified by new environmental input.[22] Behavior therapists attempt to rid patients of these bad habits and/or have them develop more effective ones. Instinctual drives are given short shrift; concepts such as masochism or innate aggressive/destructiveness are denied or ignored. Assumptions about the nature of man are generally deterministic and mechanistic. Insight is considered a result, not a cause, of behavioral change. Most behavior therapists believe that as a patient performs more effectively, the increasing competence gives him greater self-esteem and it is unnecessary for him to understand the origins of his difficulty.

The therapeutic purpose is usually well defined with the method chosen for the problem of a particular patient executed in a clear and controlled fashion. The treatment approach arose from experimental psychology, and most behavior therapists consider themselves scientists who constantly learn and improve methodology. Operationally defined goals and careful records allow the science to progress.

A behavior therapist will usually take responsibility for the patient's improvement or recovery. If the patient does not improve for whatever reasons—even if the failure seems to be due to a lack of cooperation—the therapist attempts to work out effective alternative approaches and does not state or imply to the patient that he is resisting or is wishing to fail in his treatment.

Behavioral methods have protean forms. As Marks commented, "A cynic might argue that those methods which are found to be effective tend to be called behavioral, and those which are not disowned and given some other name."[19] Nevertheless, there are two main divisions of behavior therapy—classical conditioning and operant conditioning. Classical conditioning employs a variety of techniques that include desensitization, aversive conditioning, modeling of new behavior, and social skills training. Two examples of the conditioning approach are assertiveness training and systematic densitization. Both are predicated on the assumption that the aberrant behavior is anxiety related, and, therefore, treatment must consist of reducing anxiety in situations which are threatening to the patient. Both approaches involve reciprocal inhibition, which is rooted in the notion that if a response which inhibits anxiety can be made to occur in the presence of anxiety-provoking stimuli, this will weaken the connection between these stimuli and the crippling anxiety. The therapist obtains precise information about what produces anxiety and what diminishes it. He may, in common with the practitioners of other schools, inquire into the life history of the patient and learn something of the quality of his personal relationships. When this information is gathered, priority is given to the problem that is of the greatest immediate concern of the patient, and a clear contract is made with the patient and therapist agreeing on the goals of treatment. Advice or reassurance may be given if it is considered to be immediately useful. Almost all behavior therapists consider that one should be empathic with the patient and establish a reasonably trusting relationship. If a patient first needs to confide in the therapist or to be enlightened, specific measures of counterconditioning may be delayed until these pressing needs are satisfied.

If the patient's problems seem to center around a difficulty in asserting himself, assertiveness training is often provided. Here, the therapist explains to the patient that he must express his feelings openly, thereby inhibiting anxiety; repeated feeling expression will lead to a cumulative inhibition of the anxious responses. He in- structs the patient in effectively expressing desires, resentments, and hostilities in various situations. Easy assignments lead to dif- ficult ones, and success experiences are expected to help the pa- tient gain confidence and assertive competence. In order to avoid socially disruptive behavior, there is a test question, "Would an expression of this feeling seem appropriate to circumstances as viewed by an objective observer?" If so, then it is considered self- assertion and not aggression. The therapist who teaches self- assertion may describe a lily-livered, inhibited person who evades life, and this will usually make the patient angry and resentful enough that he will try to overcome his fear of self-expression. As the assertive efforts proceed, the patient is usually asked to keep careful note of his encounters with others and discuss them with his therapist. Behavior rehersal—play-acting, with patient and therapist enacting scenes—is a frequent technique. The therapist may assume the role of his patient and model behavior for him. Most of the patients trained in such self-assertion become aware of their excessive self-restraint. Tentative and clumsy efforts at asser- tiveness lead to increasing skills in self-expression.

If the patient's symptoms occur in situations that result in the avoidance of those situations—that is, if the behavior or problem is defined as a phobia—then systematic desensitization can be used. This usually consists of teaching the patient how to relax and then developing an anxiety hierarchy—a graded list of stimuli that in- corporate different degrees of the features that in the individual pa- tient evoke anxiety. After the patient has been taught to thoroughly relax, desensitization begins. If lessons in relaxation prove insuffi- cient to diminish the anxiety of the patient, some behavior therapists will prescribe sedative drugs. Occasionally, behavior therapists carry out the densitization procedures under hypnosis. In any case, there is a concerted effort to keep the patient in a state of relaxation during densensitization.

Counter conditioning may progress in fantasy, with relaxation and comfort interspersed, as the patient proceeds up his individually developed hierarchy of anxiety producing situations, until mastery of all the disturbing situations evolves. Alternatively or in addition, in-vivo sensitization may be used with a patient being directed to face the feared situation directly.

Aversive therapy may be considered a third type of classic conditioning treatment. In this approach, a negative or punishing stimulus is arranged to be associated with aberrant behavior. Such aversive conditioning can be done in a fantasy situation or with the provision of actual punishment. For example, an exhibitionist might be asked to imagine exposing his genitals to a pretty girl and then to imagine a policeman arresting him, the arrest fantasy acting as an aversive stimulus. Or, a homosexual who has stated his willingness to undergo behavior therapy may receive somewhat painful electric stimuli as he views pictures of nude males, with alternating pictures of nude females being presented with no punishment.

The operant conditioning paradigm, pioneered by Skinner, is a different type of behavior therapy. It consists of "shaping" behavior, the development of a desired behavior by rewarding successive approximations to it. An example of this in the treatment of mental illness is the development of "token economies" in chronic wards of psychiatric hospitals. Here, patients are rewarded with tokens that can be bartered for desirable privileges or material as they perform in a progressively more socially acceptable fashion.[20] Operant conditioning is most feasible in situations where the therapist has considerable control over the environment of the patient, and at present it has less applicability in outpatient psychotherapy.

These approaches developed from an underlying belief that behavior is malleable and that humans, like other animals, respond to positive reinforcement (reward) by increasing rewarded behavior, and to punishment, either physical or symbolic, by reducing the punished behavior.

Though personal history is often taken into account, there is little room in the theoretical structure as yet for changing these fundamental beliefs about behavior alterations in individual cases. Subjective reality may be recognized in determining individual sources of anxiety, but aberrant responses to conditioning stimuli are inadequately appreciated. For example, the characteristics of depressed and psychotic people who have varied, relatively unpredictable, and often perverse personal definitions of reward and punishment suggest the need for greater theoretical sophistication in order to broaden the scope of behavior therapy. Bandura[21] believes that behavioral concepts potentially offer a valuable approach to these complex emotional states.

Lee Birk, an orthodox Freudian psychoanalyst, joined with his wife Ann Brinkley-Birk, a behavioral psychologist, in efforts to integrate behavioral therapy approaches with psychoanalytic individual and group therapy. In this integration, the therapist is very much a part of the reinforcing and punishing environment of the patient, and he consciously tries to be active and expressive. Defining the therapist's role as including the function of behavioral modification encourages an atmosphere of emotional intensity and (inadvertently) encourages the incorporation of much of the classic existential approach. The therapist can function more effectively as a behavior modifier by relating as an authentic specific human who can express tenderness, anger, frustration, and fear. The Birks report great improvement in many patients thus treated, and they are enthusiastic about the inherent potential.[22] However, they seem to express some ambivalence by urging any who attempt such combination therapy to be treated in classical analysis in order to be trusted to perform it. If they were confident that the integrated treatment was superior, then one would expect them to recommend it for therapists as well as patients.

FAMILY SYSTEMS VARIABLES AND TREATMENT SYSTEMS

After this foregoing brief presentation of psychoanalytic dissidents and five currently popular psychotherapies, I will discuss them from the standpoint of their contributions to furthering the eight variables derived from family systems study.

1) *A Systems Orientation*

Adler made an early contribution to systems-oriented psychotherapy by rejecting the libido theory, the purely biological explanation of illness, and by insisting that mental health necessarily included involvement and service to society. He pointed the way to the contributions of Harry Stack Sullivan, who painstakingly evolved the concept that man's sanity is related to socialization, that family relationships are important in the production of neurosis, and that an involvement in larger social systems is necessary for health.

Sullivan's technique depends on a dialogue between patient and therapist for corrections of distortions. This is an active social process utilizing feedback mechanisms; it is a marked change from the encouragement of a regressive transference neurosis with free association and interpretations, reducing communicational feedback loops rather than furthering them.

Sullivan encouraged an open system by his emphasis on data-based theory. Theoretical notions, in his view, are to be held tentatively, and experience with patients is more important than theoretical purity. He defined reality as consensual validation, dramatically shifting psychotherapy from a search for absolutes to assisting patient and therapist in developing social and communicational skills in specific social systems. Absolute truth and insistence on the "right" interpretation give way to relative effectiveness of therapist and patient, and competence is defined for both as being able to hear the other person rather than being or doing "right" according to a referee system.

Classical existential theory, by allowing the therapist to be professional while responding authentically and passionately to his patient, encourages the system concepts that causes and effects are interchangeable and that humans are finite, neither impotent nor omnipotent. A person can be more or less emotionally ill, depending on how he is responded to in the treatment relationship; the doctor's response can be a cause and an effect at the same time.

Rogerian and behavior therapies moved psychotherapy a bit further toward systems awareness by rejecting the orthodox psychoanalytic biological preoccupation. A systems orientation is not a strong suit of Perls' gestalt therapy.

2) *Boundary Issues*

The treatment systems discussed in this chapter have a more open theoretical approach than that found in orthodox psychoanalysis. The empiricism of Sullivan and the emphasis on subjective reality found in the three varieties of existentialism negate a closed system of theory or practice. Behavior therapy's insistence on judging theory and methodology by results is another approach to system openness and permeable theoretical boundaries.

These schools of therapy have also advanced the definition of intrasystem boundaries as illustrated in the clarity of the patient-therapist interface. In Sullivan's method, the therapist is acknowledged as a real person who wants to make his separateness and unique subjective reality clear. Projections—betrayers of separateness and boundary clarity—are always challenged. It is not surprising that there was little advance in the psychotherapeutic treatment of schizophrenia until Sullivan evolved treatment methods that could deal with its prominent features of murky boundaries and identity confusion.

The classical existential approach encourages the awareness of self boundaries between patient and therapist by its intense focus on the subjective reality of both, and the expectation that treatment proceeds as feelings of the therapist as well as of the patient emerge in the relationship. The therapist expresses vulnerability, frustration, and anger as well as the nonpossessive warmth recommended by Rogerians, thus providing needed coherence and role model for patients in their efforts to define themselves.

Gestalt therapy, in considering the treatment relationship essentially unreal in a manner similar to the Freudian system, makes little advance in boundary definition. However, since Gestaltists do not encourage transference, vigorously attack projections, and insist on patient responsibility, boundary clarity is encouraged for the patient.

The active reality-oriented communications of behavior therapists who define reasonable expectations and provide direction to the patient, clearly outlining his part in the treatment process, contribute to intrasystem boundary definition.

3) *Contextual Clarity*

Orthodox Freudianism has been a positive factor in the emphasis on this interpersonal variable in psychotherapy. The system's main difficulty here is its continuance of the belief that the encouragement of transference is helpful since intense transference obscures the realities of the treatment contract and invites contextual confusion. All of the psychotherapeutic systems discussed in this chapter attempt, in their various ways, to reduce transference rather than build it.

4) *Power Issues*

Lessening of overt power differences between patient and therapist is a consistent trend of psychotherapy systems. Freud's approach was more egalitarian than the accepted medical model of his time and place. The early defectors, Adler and Jung, were less authoritarian than Freud (perhaps partly because of their recent brush with the adamant, unyielding Freud!).

Here is another human tension that psychotherapeutic systems inevitably encountered: Giving power to the patient is betting on the drives, on the eternal child. Extreme emphasis on patient power produces a Laingian hostility toward social wisdom, social structure, and the hard-won effectiveness of socially powerful elders. Keeping the patient relatively impotent in the therapist-patient relationship is an alignment with authority, the parents of this world, and indicates a deep suspicion of the child, his questing openness, powerful drives, and unskilled authenticity. Freud began this reduction in overt power differential by being compassionate and respectful of his neurotic patients and listening to them. He was handicapped by being a product of his time, often betraying a blind trust in the social status quo and in parental virtues. His instinctual drive theory explained neurosis in terms of infantile perversity rather than incompetent authority.

Adler was egalitarian and informal in his treatment; he emphasized social power variables in the etiology of neurosis, and he considered patient/therapist power issues significant. Jung decreased the power differential between therapist and patient by emphasizing the value of the patient's repressed material, rather than its destructive horror, presenting himself more as a respectful midwife than a guardian of the gates of hell as he related to the patient's unconscious.

Sullivan, Horney, and Fromm moved further toward trusting the child, re-defining drives as neutral, increasing the importance of social environment in producing personal success or failure and furthering Jung's emphasis on the positive potential of regressed material. With less fear of the patient's innermost feelings, the therapist needs less power advantage. These theorists could see the benefits of having the patient as a partner.

Classical existential therapists have pioneered equalizing patient and therapist power. They do not believe that a demoralized, faltering person with low self-esteem can be healed in the presence of a human who seems to live with no uncertainty, no pain, no vulnerability, but rather apparently endless wisdom and equanimity. The contrast between such a paragon and the patient's ineptness is apt to induce or increase depression, or (if disbelieved) paranoia.

Existentialists of all types, especially gestaltists, urge patients to reclaim abdicated power; in so doing they eliminate transferences and projections and may join the ranks of scared, uncertain, limited but effective humans. Mature people know and accept their limits and have few illusions about the invulnerability of others.

Behavior therapists, especially when doing operant conditioning, can be throwbacks to controlling Victorian physicians. More frequently, however, their emphasis on informed consent and patient choice allows a partnership of relative equality.

Modern psychotherapists of many schools reinforce the equality and human dignity of male and female, rich and poor, black and white. Most tend to deny any presumed scientific or biological support for structured differences found in the larger society. Horney attacked biological justifications of male supremacy; Fromm challenges concepts that the poor and socially powerless are in some way constitutionally inferior, and suggests that men often clutch for tyrants, not out of inferiority, but out of fear. Many experimental psychologists attack old theories of biological racial superiority.

From clinical observations, I have become convinced that unless a person can see other humans as potentially of equal value, whether they be white or black, male or female, rich or poor, intelligent or retarded, then that person is vulnerable to neurosis. The reasons are simple. If he identifies himself with a one-down group, he feels inferior. If he identifies himself with a one-up group, he must hide those personal qualities that are similar to the ones ascribed to the disdained group (e.g. "female" feelings, "black" sexuality or indolence, the impoverished person's vulnerability, or the folly of the ignorant). Emotional illness is intertwined with overt power differentials, consensually validated or individually fantasied.

Most psychotherapists of whatever system recognize the need to respect and care for their patients, but these feeling states can be present along with unequal, overt power. Intimacy, possible only with equal-powered encounter, is qualitatively different from caring or even loving. One can love and exert coercive, intimidating control in the name of that love. With equal overt power in the treatment relationship, intimacy—which is necessary to rid a patient of depression, incoherence, and despair—is possible between therapist and patient. Therapists who emphasize such equal power use such experiences in intimacy as a model which patients can carry into relationships outside the treatment situation.

Behavior therapy is the only modern treatment system that does not consider intimacy significant in healing. Relative trust is important, but symptoms are bad habits to be retrained and a power differential may be considered helpful.

5) *Encouragement of Autonomy*

It seems clear that any system which encourages autonomy will necessarily share the responsibility of defining and reaching goals for its members. For example, placing complete responsibility for goal definition on either patient or therapist is antagonistic to the development of autonomy. There is little autonomy in helplessness or total responsibility; such role definitions promote a perseveration of impotent/omnipotent relationships rather than relative competence. Shared responsibility allows the use of many techniques to further competent self-definition; insight, affective experiences, coherent encounter, identification, and behavior modeling may all be used.

Classic psychoanalytic methods and modern behavior therapies are poles apart on this issue; behavior therapists often see themselves as providing a needed correction for the excesses of Freudian therapists' irresponsibility. Neither, in unmodified form, can be given high marks in promoting autonomy, but a synthesis of the two could rival the Sullivanian and classical existential approaches in this endeavor.

Sullivan believed a therapist to be a real and finite person whose discipline required him to observe and correct projective distortions rather than to play an active, personal part in the relationship. Gestaltists and Rogerian therapists are comparable to Sullivan on this issue. They consider the patient's autonomy is well promoted without the necessity of actively modeling such behavior in the interaction.

Classical existential treatment goes a critical step further in this shared responsibility. Therapists are not only participant observers who care, but they feel and respond with their own autonomous being; it is their professional responsibility to share the burdens and joys of expressing the innermost in treatment encounter, rather than hiding behind professional anonymity, observation post, or emotional withdrawal.

Any theoretical system which is open-ended and uncertain, rather than closed and absolute, more effectively promotes autonomy since its main enemy, at least in sane but limited patients, is the referee, the external authority that intimidates fallible humans and inhibits choice-making.

Many failures in intensive psychotherapy result from an over-controlled therapist slavishly following a closed system model attempting to help an over-controlled patient slavishly following restrictive family rules. All of the therapies described in this chapter provide patients with relative, not absolute, definitions of the truth, and encourage the therapist's responsible freedom in developing a similar responsible freedom in his patient.

Respect for individual subjective reality is such a central issue for autonomy that special attention must be directed to it. Classical existential therapy was an early reaction to an objectifying science. Kraepelinean psychiatry, with its objectification and insensitivity to the patient's world, was a vivid example of 19th-century science running roughshod over human dignity. To objectify the world is to lose sight of the subjective and incomplete perceptions of those finite beings who are doing the defining. Here is a theme found in the family systems studies: *If one does not respect his own unique, erratic, vulnerable, subjective experience, he is unable to respect that of others.*

Sullivan and Rogers continued this existential theme, emphasizing the importance of individual family experience in producing later interpersonal distortions through perseveration—frozen attitudes and expectations. Though the subjective perceptions are not simplistically accepted, they are respected as a necessary beginning of treatment negotiation.

Sullivan's definition of reality as consensual validation sets a standard for challenging objectivity and affirming reality as a synthesis of individual subjectivity. It is only in such an ideological climate that autonomy can blossom. This contribution of Sullivan's influenced the development of ego psychology. If all participants in a social system consider themselves somewhat in the dark, taking responsibility for their individual feelings, thoughts, and behavior, but not for voicing certainty, the group may move toward wisdom.

Behavior therapy, often considered spuriously objective by detractors, frequently respects the patient's subjective reality. Desensitization schedules are carefully tailored and shaped for the individual, relying on his own hierarchy of symbolic threat. Though Skinner would probably demur, operant conditioning shows respect for the subjective view of the experimental subject, whether that subject is pigeon, rat, or human. The experimenter never gives a pigeon tacks or pebbles to reward it for desired behavior, but rather responds to the pigeon's desires by offering small grain. The pigeon's reality, therefore, defines for the experimenter what he must do to change pigeon behavior. In the same way, successful human conditioning requires attention to the subjective reality of the individuals involved.

6) *Affective Issues*

Psychotherapists have long considered emotional intensity important in effective treatment. Many dissenters, including Rank and Reich, left orthodox psychoanalysis complaining that its sterile, intellectual, cognitive approach stifled useful emotionality in treatment.

Sullivan, a rather austere intellectual and cognitive person, did not make significant improvements in this area. The existential therapists emphasized the importance of maintaining a treatment milieu that is loosely structured so that strong feelings arising in treatment are not discouraged. Classical existential therapists almost guarantee emotional intensity by defining treatment as encounter which includes the therapist's feeling expression. Gestaltists aggressively confront and directively suggest, Rogerians offer accurate empathy and reflection. The existential styles differ, but all attempt to maintain affective intensity.

Behavior therapists can provide an intense affective experience by tapping individual sources of anxiety and presenting those stimuli in fantasy or in vivo by providing painful stimuli in response to undesired behavior, or by gratifying desires of the individual following acceptable behavior.

Conflict, Resolvable and Irresolvable. To approximate the optimal family, a treatment system must view conflict as inevitable and irresolvable conflict as pathological and capable of remedy.

Adler was the first defector from the Freudian camp to attack the notion of eternal conflict between man and society. Jung's description of the unconscious as a potential friend and ally pointed toward an integrated personality with resolvable conflict. Sullivan, in denying innate destructive drives, eliminated a major source of assumed irresolvable human conflict.

The classical existential therapist invests wholeheartedly in the belief that conflict is resolvable and therapist and patient can, and should, risk openness with one another. This radical belief in the essential satisfactions rather than dangers of intimate encounter is not matched by any other modern treatment system.

The treatment schools discussed in this chapter emphasize an affiliative orientation. Sullivanians see man as needing society for definition and comfort; classical existential therapists assume that open and honest encounter provides what the patient has missed and needs. Gestaltists consider conflict between patient and therapist as arising from the patient's unclaimed projections; if the patient will take responsibility for himself, he can resolve interpersonal conflicts. Behavior therapists are affiliative with patients since all symptomatic behavior is involuntarily learned. The therapist makes every attempt to assist in new and useful learning—he is not training a perverse animal. If the behaviorist is unsuccessful, he does not view such a failure as due to the patient's innate willfulness, masochism, or other reprehensible trait. He believes only that his methods are not sufficiently evolved.

Concepts of treatment resistance are related to assuming affiliation or opposition in encounter. It is not happenstance that resistance is a central issue in Freudian therapy, a minor issue in Sullivanian and existential therapies, and totally rejected in behavior therapy.

7) *Negotiation and Task Performance*

All of the qualities just discussed are related to the efficiency of negotiation and task performance in treatment systems, just as they are in optimal families. If a clear contract is made between a patient and a therapist who have clearly defined complementary roles and shared responsibility, increasing clarity of communication through adequate feedback loops, and affiliative emotional intensity, the jointly defined task may be accomplished with resulting growth of ego and autonomy.

Though a scientific pluralistic psychotherapy may use aspects and techniques of all the systems discussed, and more besides, it is probable that the difficulty presented by various patients will be more efficiently approached by accenting one or another kind of methodology depending on the problems of the patient. For example, there is little doubt that Sullivanian treatment is especially useful with schizophrenic states, that behavior approaches are valuable in phobic states, compulsive rituals and aberrant appetitive behaviors (e.g., exhibitionism or obesity). The use of psychoanalytic insight-oriented psychotherapy integrated with behavioral modification is advocated by Birk and Brinkley-Birk for stubborn neurotic and behavior disorder states that have resisted other "purer" therapies.

Existential methods go hand-in-hand with the belief that intimacy is a treatment necessity and emotional illness is a deficiency of satisfying, coherent, self-defining experiences with significant others. An existential approach, therefore, is a part of any growth-oriented therapy. As the various schools respond to increasing demands of therapist and patients alike for greater effectiveness, not ideological purity, the passing of unique schools is likely. Greater treatment efficiency results from flexibility and adaptiveness of theory and methodology; these are characteristics of a scientific, open system.

8) *Transcendent Values*

As fervently as Freud disavowed religious systems and claimed them to be not only unimportant to mental health, but evidence of poor reality testing, the two initial defectors, Adler and Jung, each in his own unique way, passionately insisted that investment in shared communal systems of thought and relationship is essential to emotional well-being. The study of family systems indicates that transcendent systems are needed to provide individuals with the self-definition necessary to accept losses from growth and development, aging and death.

One of Sullivan's followers, Clara Thompson, stated this position clearly: "If man is to perserve his sanity, he must have some kind of spiritual relatedness to the world, some form of orientation and devotion, whether he finds it in organized religion, or in some secular institution, or in a comprehensible idea."[1]

Existential therapists are quite sensitive to man's need for purpose and meaning, and a prominent existential therapist, Victor Frankl, has developed a treatment approach based on this search for meaning.[10]

Behavior therapists do not consider this aspect of man's existence. They provide no response to man's peculiar dilemma—a symbol-making self that can fantasize perfection, imagine his own death and non-existence, encased in a decaying animal body. Behavior therapies do not deal with paradox, with the innately tragic, and they offer a valuable and enlightening contrast to other therapies which risk more.

It seems necessary for ego development and growth of the self to struggle with the essential paradoxes of man's existence, to be a responsible behavioral scientist and at the same time respect the patient's search for a transcendent system of personal value.

CONCLUSIONS

In the last two chapters, six systems of psychotherapy theory and practice were briefly reviewed—Freudian psychoanalysis, Sullivanian therapy, classical existential treatment, Perls' gestalt therapy, Rogerian client-centered psychotherapy, and behavioral therapy. There was an attempt to present them in historical perspective and to evaluate them, as currently popular therapies, from the vantage point of the eight system variables derived from family studies.

The underlying thesis is that various schools of psychotherapy will gradually give way to a synthetic, pluralistic, scientific psychotherapy, continuing the strong points of each and eliminating various closed system quirks that have been defended by coercive, intragroup pressures rather than by scientific dialogue and treatment results.

There are at least three lines of data to support this thesis. The first is that all of the systems described are increasingly liberalizing, borrowing from one another, and sharing concepts and approaches. Though there are prominent practitioners in each school who rigidly defend orthodoxy, an ever greater number of therapists consider pragmatic openness a positive quality.

In addition, the systems are not profoundly incompatible with one another—as orthodox psychoanalysis reduces the emphasis on biological causation, absolutism, and the hostility toward religious thought more appropriate to 19th-century intellectuals, it begins to resemble the Sullivanian framework. Sullivan and Rogers had many common concepts. The classical existential emphasis on the unique subjective can be incorporated into all the systems, though the radical demands for "bold, swinging" (Buber) therapist interaction is not acknowledged or formally accepted by the other therapies. Gestalt etiological theory is closely bound to the orthodox Freudian; its techniques are not incompatible with other schools. Behavior therapy is the only system that seems incompatible with the others in theory and practice, and yet even such a widely variant therapy illustrates the third line of data suggesting synthesis— experienced practitioners of any school are more alike than they are different when their activities with patients are studied; this includes psychoanalytic practitioners and behavior therapists.[23]

There are clear trends in the psychotherapies toward 1) the patient as partner; 2) more concern with intimacy, the successful, pleasant sharing of the innermost in the treatment session; 3) efficiency and clear goal definition; 4) individual emotional illness seen as a reflection of group phenomena; and 5) accepting transcendent systems of values as a part of emotional health. These changes are not only reflective of an evolutionary movement toward principles found in competent families (in this culture); they also reflect special human needs resulting from peculiar characteristics of our larger society.

We are more open about sex, and yet more concerned about loneliness, emotional isolation, and pointlessness. In our secularized world, we do not have a strong, dogmatic, and tyrannical church to provide us with structure or a scapegoat; we are forced to hammer out some kind of meaning as individuals. We are becoming ever more mistrustful of and hostile toward authorities of any sort. There is a stubborn wish to deflate the mighty (this desire to point out the clay feet of human leaders also indicates a touching, childlike wish to have giants to worship, a side that will, perhaps, surface later). The current direction of the psychotherapies generally follows these cultural patterns attempting to deal with modern ills with an egalitarian, pragmatic, systems-oriented thrust.

REFERENCES

1. THOMPSON, C., with MULLAHY, P., *Psychoanalysis: Evolution and Development*, New York, Grove Press, 1950.
2. ANSBACHER, H. L., and ANSBACHER, R. R., *The Individual Psychology of Alfred Adler*, New York, Basic Books, 1956.
3. JUNG, C. G., (Ed), *Man and His Symbols*, New York, Dell, 1964.
4. REICH, W., *Character Analysis*, New York, Orgone Press, 1949.
5. SULLIVAN, H. S., *The Interpersonal Theory of Psychiatry*, New York, W. W. Norton, 1953.
6. SULLIVAN, H. S., *Clinical Studies in Psychiatry*, New York, W. W. Norton, 1956.
7. HORNEY, K., *New Ways in Psychoanalysis*, New York, Norton, 1939.
8. FROMM, E., *The Sane Society*, New York, Rinehart, 1955.
9. BOSS. M., *Psychoanalysis and Daseinanalysis*, New York, Basic Books, 1963.
10. FRANKL, V. E., *The Doctor and the Soul*, New York, Alfred A. Knopf, 1957.
11. MAY, R., "The Existential Approach," in *American Handbook of Psychiatry*, Vol. II, 1348-1361, New York, Basic Books, 1959.
12. HAVENS, L. L., *Approaches to the Mind*, Boston, Little, Brown, 1973.
13. HAVENS, L. L., "The existential use of the self," *Am. J. Psychiat.*, 131(1:1-10) Jan., 1974.

14. PERLS, F., *Gestalt Therapy Verbatim*, Lafayette, Ca. Real People Press, 1969.
15. POLSTER, E. and POLSTER, M., *Gestalt Therapy Integrated*, New York, Brunner/Mazel, 1973.
16. MORENO, J. L., "Fundamental Rules and Techniques of Psychodrama," in Masserman, J., and Moreno, J. L. (Eds.), *Progress in Psychotherapy*, Vol. III, New York, Grune, 1958.
17. ROGERS, C. R., *Client Centered Therapy*, Boston, Houghton Miflin, 1951.
18. ROGERS, C. R. (Ed.), *The Therapeutic Relationship and Its Impact*, Madison, Wisc., U. of Wisconsin Press, 1967.
19. MARKS, I. M., "The current status of behavioral psychotherapy," *Am. J. of Psychiat.*, 133(3):253-261, March, 1976.
20. DANIELI, Y., LOEW, C. A. and GRAYSON, H., "Behavior Therapy," in Loew, C. A., Grayson, H., and Loew, G. H., *Three Psychotherapies, A Clinical Comparison*, New York, Brunner/Mazel, 1975.
21. BANDURA, A., *Principles of Behavior Modification*, New York, Holt, Rinehart and Winston, 1969.
22. BIRK, L., and BRINKLEY-BIRK, A. W., "Psychoanalysis and behavior therapy," *Am. J. Psychiat.*, 131(5):499-510, May, 1974.
23. SLOANE, R. B., STAPLES, F. R., CRISTAL, A. H., YORKSTON, N. J., and WHIPPLE, K., *Psychotherapy versus Behavior Therapy*, Cambridge, Harvard Univ. Press, 1975.

_____ **9**

A systems view
of human aggression

As a helper, whether parent or psychotherapist, toward the goal
of individual competence, one must strive for a relationship of
mutual trust. Most psychotherapists find the capacity for relative
interpersonal trust to be desperately lacking in emotionally ill
people, irrespective of diagnosis.

From the family systems studies it became apparent that there
were two major ideological stumbling blocks in evolving trust: the
assumption of an absolute, objective external reality, and the assumption of essentially perverse and destructive human nature.
These two conceptual errors have often been accepted and promul-
gated by behavioral scientists, and have handicapped
psychotherapists in developing treatment systems that rival the effectiveness of optimal families in developing human competence.

Chapter 1 presented a conception of science and the scientific method which challenged any misplaced confidence in an abstract objectivity or reality. In this chapter I raise the question of man's essential destructiveness and offer a systems viewpoint in an effort to reduce scientific support for the damaging concept of man's evil nature.

The view of oneself and others as essentially dangerous, which necessarily requires the development of ponderous interpersonal defenses, would seem to be more a matter of emotional difficulty requiring therapy than a cognitive state requiring education, but, unfortunately, both seem to be necessary. Respected professionals in theology, anthropology, ethology, psychology, and psychiatry, both past and present, promote the notion of humans as basically killers. It is impossible for a therapist subscribing to such a philosophy to alter his patient's maladaptive view of the world. But how, one might ask, with the newspapers filled with reports of killings, rapes, and wars, with genocide having been practiced within our lifetime, could a reasonable person *not* view man as a killer ape? The crucial distinction bearing on potential control of destructive behavior is whether it is present as a biological given or whether it results from experiences with others. A family may be loving and trusting of its own members and still think of many outsiders as dangerous and violent, but no family and no therapist can be trusting of anyone, including themselves, while believing that humans are essentially violent.

What is aggression anyway? Confusion reigns in operationally defining this term, so important to society. The Latin origins of the word do not help much: Aggress means *to walk*, an innocent beginning for such a frustrating word. Webster's unabridged includes both "bad" and "good" (or at least neutral) definitions: "A first, or unprovoked attack, or act of hostility; the first act of injury or first act leading to a war or controversy; an assault; also the practice of attack or encroachment" (encroachment seems neutral).

The word covers too much, too vaguely, and has many moral and political overtones. Twenty-five years of wrestling with the equally controversial term "schizophrenia" embolden me to try for a clear definition.

In various professional and lay articles, aggression has meant: 1) physical violence; 2) intraspecies physical violence; 3) physical or symbolic violence; 4) physical or symbolic interhuman violence; 5) hostility and anger, whether expressed or not; 6) pushy and insensitive behavior (often applied to women). These are "bad" meanings. A "good" meaning is 7) to be active rather than passive, to move out in an effective, assertive way, as in aggressive lover or aggressive salesman.

Each of these concepts is acceptable, but mischief arises from indiscriminately fluctuating among them. Further, no one is out of the semantic woods by separating seven meanings of the word and attempting to keep them straight, for one of the words used in the defining was violence. Though Webster's definition of violence—"the exertion of physical force so as to injure or abuse"—is unambiguous, a 1971 sampling of the opinions of over 1,000 male Americans revealed that 57 percent thought shooting of looters was not a violent act, but 85 percent thought looting was violent, and 58 percent considered draft card burning was violent.[1] Such information indicates that lay people (and I am afraid, many experts) like Humpty Dumpty in *Through the Looking Glass* consider words to "mean just what I want them to mean, no more and no less." This is a convenient tactic in dialogue, but it is confusing and unlikely to increase consensual validation.

Let us clear up as much murkiness as we can. First, no one is particularly concerned about *good* aggression. Parents anxiously desire their children to walk, sales managers advertise for aggressive employees, and most behavioral experts agree that the ability we share with all animal species—movement with a purpose for food, sex, or company—is not pre-programmed aggression/violence.

Definitions five and six (hostility and anger, pushy insensitive behavior) also cause relatively little trouble unless they are confused with the others. Most behavioral scientists agree that hostility, or the experience and expression of anger, is an unconditioned biological given for man. It is neutral as far as the species is concerned, a response to frustration and a potential fuel for action. Like many other human powers, it can be a constructive or destructive force to the individual and to society. The values of the larger society and the values and skills of individual family members are significant in tipping the balance toward the constructive or the destructive. Anger can help a slum youth struggle for an education or power his desire to destroy. Overbearing, pushy, and insensitive behavior, while annoying, is not threatening to society. Insensitivity is learned rather than an atavistic biological given.

The enduring ambiguity resides in definitions one through four. Does aggression include symbolic as well as actual violence, and interspecies as well as intraspecies violence? I will simplify a bit further by dismissing symbolic violence, not because it is of little importance, but because it is of much less significance than physical damage as a basic threat to social order. Speak harshly to your neighbor's plants, but do not squash them. Verbally abuse your dog, but do not beat him. Berate, ridicule, and insult your child, but do not physically harm him. Sneer at minority groups, tell ethnic stories in quaint accents, but do not roam the streets sniping with a 30-30 rifle. One may remain respected and never be considered an example of man's innate aggression/violence while expressing much symbolic aggression. I am not suggesting that symbolic violence is unrelated to physical violence, but the critical issue for parents, therapists, behavioral scientists, and theologians is aggression in the form of *physical violence to other human beings*. Physical violence to other species will always be dealt with lightly. The survival of every species depends on violence to living material of some sort.

Though I do not question that destructiveness to other species may at times be as threatening to the human as killing one's neighbor (our world becomes smaller, and we are becoming more aware of our dependence on many other species), the essential question, with religious, anthropological, psychological and psychiatric ramifications, is found in Arthur Koestler's quaint phrase, "Man—one of evolution's mistakes?"[2] Does he have a screw loose that makes him, willy-nilly, turn on his neighbor in order to preserve some semblance of order?

Or, to the contrary, does the belief produce the evidence? If a social group believes this despairing myth, will the necessary cultural and family defenses against such alleged innate violence *produce it*, just as cornering a frightened animal produces attack, the result of external, not internal bedevilment?

In the subsequent discussion, aggression is defined as aggression/violence, and refers specifically to physical violence to humans by humans. In Chapters 4 and 5, midrange and optimal family systems were found to contrast strikingly in their evident assumptions about human nature. A self-fulfilling prophecy of innate destructiveness produces neurotics and individuals with behavior disorders, who suffer and cause suffering through unnecessary efforts to control, which both cause and result from continued frustration over control. Optimal families illustrated that this basic fear of human motivation is neither useful nor necessary in rearing competent humans. These observations support the belief that evidence for man's innate destructiveness is lacking, since loving or hostile, constructive or destructive children are related, not to immutable drives, but to family relationships.

MAN AS AGGRESSIVE/VIOLENT

On the issue of aggression/violence, as in other issues having moral overtones (sex, drugs, law and order), there is often a polarization into rigid either/or arguments. I will first examine the position that man is basically aggressive/violent, then the opposite view that man is essentially a tabula rasa with no significant biological features that produce violence. Finally, a third view will be offered, the systems view to which I subscribe.

There are many historical precedents for viewing man as having an antisocial essence. A type of Christianity, currently represented by fundamentalists, has always spoken of human perversity and evil, while another Christian concept has presented Christ as absolving people (or at least believers) from essential evil. These different views of man's nature are paralleled in the behavioral sciences. The concept of man as a lustful and violent animal, at odds with society, was unchanged by the Freudians. The "aggressive drive" was considered as innate as the sexual, and "defenses" were a necessary part of character structure—not defenses against a threatening outside world, but against powerful instincts which, if exposed, would threaten a child's world and his happy relation to it. The essence of the instinctual argument is that the power of the world outside is inconsequential compared to the strength of instinctual drives, and aggression/violence arises unprovoked (like lust) without relation to deprivation, ego skills, frustration, or contentment. This was the source of Freud's pessimism in his later years, for such a concept paints man into a corner, with no direction for personal or societal improvement.

This view can prevail if it remains an article of faith rather than a scientific hypothesis to be tested. Hartman, Kris, and Lowenstein, modern psychoanalytic theorists, illustrate this as they state, "We do not forget that the very absence of activity may express aggression in one of its forms."[3] The trick to keep such a concept unassailable is to cycle continually through the seven definitions mentioned previously and have all of them, plus inactivity, as "evidence" for what is really a matter of faith.

Psychoanalytic revisionists of the 30's—as Sullivan, Horney, and Fromm—departed from the concept of man as a lustful, violent stud; they saw him more as a frightened, skinned rabbit who manages to survive through his genius for social organization. Society is more protector than jailer. In that same period, John Dewey sparked a sociological and anthropological study of human nature that discarded the belief in man's innate violence. Such a change in the academic winds prompted Becker, in 1972, to remark, "The social scientist who criticizes the instinct theory of human behavior often has the uncomfortable feeling that he is charging against doors already wide open."[4] A broad psychophysiological view of human behavior is so implicit in Becker's mental set that it seemed inconceivable to him that such antiquated ideas lingered. However, he was banging against stubbornly half-open doors; the residue of old ideas remains.

Without new input, the debate would probably be dormant by

now, at least in scientific circles, had not the ethologists entered the fray. Lorenz,[5] Ardry,[6] Morris,[7] Storr,[8] and Tiger,[9] with different levels of professional competence and knowledge, used animal data to "prove" man's essential aggressive/violent nature. Often not content with articles in scholarly journals, they fired salvos of popular non-fiction, aimed at a mass audience, attempting to convince Western man of his hopelessly depraved state. Information concerning seals, tigers, dogs, cats, chicken, bees, and even fir trees (!) was marshalled to prove that humans possess the instinct for aggression/violence and for tangentially related interpersonal phenomena, such as dominance and territory.

Spitz, a Freudian psychoanalyst distinguished by his efforts to obtain data to support theory, stated that Lorenz was contributing more to the issue of aggression than were psychoanalysts.[10] Other scientists, doubtful about extrapolations from other species, have disparaged the use of animal data to prove man's depravity. Tinbergen made a passionate plea for scientists to apply the ethological *approach* to man rather than to rely on extrapolation of *data*; he insisted that rarely have animal data proved directly applicable to man.[11] Klopfer, a zoologist, reviewed the animal material relating to human aggression/violence and concluded, "It is at least equally plausible that early man showed very little 'aggression.'"[12]

To bring the subject into meaningful scientific (as opposed to polemical) discussion, the central propositions would have to be stated in a way that they could be proved wrong. For example, hypothesis: Violence is familiar to people in all cultures since it is an inborn quality of man, little affected by cultural influences or different attitudes about human potential. Stated in this way, it has respectability as a scientific theory, but it cannot be seriously supported. There are many anthropological reports of societies which have existed far longer than Western culture without wars or other significant intraspecies violence, except as a surprising and bizarre occurrence.[13,14,15,16] Societies, then, have been constructed so that aggression/violence is so infrequent that most members live out their lives without encountering it.

Another valid approach would be to apply the theory within a culture: If aggression/violence is a biological drive unaffected by child-rearing, it will be randomly distributed to offspring of families of all types. Or, alternatively: If the possibilities of aggression/violence are ever present in the human species, families with strict discipline would produce fewer aggressive/violent members, and families that do not induce fear of authority will have more violent members.

Once again, stating the idea clearly provides a scientific framework but exposes its error. The frequency of violence varies greatly among members of different family styles. For example, Ivy Bennett reported that gross environmental disturbances are extremely frequent in the early life situations of children who are aggressive or aggressive/violent toward their fellows. Their histories include unsettled homes, frequent moves, overcrowding, placement in foster homes or with friends and relatives, periods spent in institutions, parents who separated, divorced, or deserted, and parents who have a diagnosis of antisocial personality.[17]

Robins studied the early environment of individuals diagnosed as sociopathic (those who are aggressive/violent toward their fellows) and made similar observations. Their parents' histories were marked by frequent arrest, chronic unemployment, desertion, excessive drinking, failure to support, poor management of money, physical cruelty, and neglected home life. She cited relationship deprivation, rather than failure to provide material comforts and social prestige, as a factor in producing antisocial behavior. Low social status was not a predictor of sociopathy in these children. Rather, emotional deprivation in the family was highly correlated with later sociopathy.[18]

These are but two examples of studies relating early family disturbance to later aggressive/violent behavior. Emotional deprivation is highly correlated with the expression of aggression/violence. Attention to sustained behavioral expression of love and caring by parents is vital to any study of violent behavior, and the presence or absence of such loving relationships in the life of a child is directly related to his propensity for violence. Therefore, it is not true that violence is scattered randomly through family styles.

As to the alternative theory that the most strict and harsh families produce fear of authority and therefore help children to control innate aggressive/violence, data on child abuse indicate quite the opposite.

Parents who abuse children physically were themselves abused and/or neglected.[19][20][21][22] These parents are insensitive to their own children's relative helplessness and their human needs, and generally treat them *as if they were much older*. Like their own parents before them, they consciously espouse physical punishment as a virtuous and proper way to train children to behave. One of a cluster of characteristics found in child-abusing parents was a compulsively rigid, unempathic, and "righteous" attitude toward child-rearing, and specifically toward the abused or battered child.[22] Steele and Pollock believe that strong superego rudiments are developed in the upbringing of parents of abused children by repetitive frustration, impossible demands, and verbal and physical attacks with subsequent identification with the aggressor. If the abuser considers that he is in the "right" and that the child is in the "wrong," he can express extreme aggression/violence: "While the abuser's aggressive drive may not be unusually strong, its release against infants may then be overt and intense."[23] These psychoanalytically oriented investigators possess traditional views concerning aggressive drives, but they observe that the expression of aggression/violence results from a rigid control-oriented cognitive set.

Cultural and family research refutes the notion of innate aggression/violence. One might just as easily consider, as Fromm suggested, "Man is driven by an innate compulsion to flee; he may try to control this impulse by his reason, yet the control will prove to be relatively inefficient, even though some means can be found that may serve to curb the power of the 'flight instinct.' "[24] One might also believe in a drive for love, which will be victorious unless emotional deprivation does overwhelming damage to the evolving self.

Yet, pseudoscientific "proofs" of man's essential evil continue to surface. Why should this be? Possibly it is because in such highly emotionally charged, complex issues, *simple* explanations, not necessarily those that fit the data best or are most effective in solving problems, are attractive. In addition, instinctual explanations for human behavior support repressive counter-measures as well as absolve individual miscreants: "What do you expect from me . . . we're all killer apes!"

Perhaps the subject is not, and never will be, in the scientific domain. The dramatic thrust and counter-thrust of theorists, followed with wide-eyed fascination by the general populace and by vested interests, are not science but vicarious psychodrama.

Since science has assumed authority in a secular world, its power can be perverted to political use. Only our gradually increasing awareness of the limitations of science and of its proper methodology will diminish this misuse. A psychiatrist writing about the increase of murders in the United States,[25] though tangentially sketching the deprived backgrounds of many people who murder, gives reasons for their actions, including "changes in child raising practices (that) have contributed to this holocaust. Permissive parents are less likely to insist that children develop and use internal restraints." This conclusion, offered with no data or comparative studies, was reported with enthusiasm in a mass Sunday magazine and in a periodical that popularizes psychology.

THE TABULA RASA VIEW

Belief in an intrinsic, aggressive/violent drive is a good example of being scientific in 19th-century fashion: providing absolute explanations of abstract man, while ignoring contextual, environmental variables. One can thus create out of one abstraction—human nature—a villain, and of another abstraction—society—a hero, for controlling the beast at times. An opposite way to commit the reductionist error, with equally dreary results, is by the tabula rasa view which compares man's mind to a blank writing tablet, with no genetically endowed attitudes, predilections or directions. Found in Aristotle, this concept was emphasized by John Locke in the late 17th century to oppose Descartes' insistence on "innate principles" and "innate ideas," and was carried into modern times by the "logical positivism" of Auguste Comte, which served as the anti-metaphysical underpinning of 19th-century science.[26]

In the political arena the tabula rasa view was embraced by Marx—understandably, since emphasis on biological destiny encourages political conservatism, and the rejection of genetic attributes furthers the belief that radical political change can develop a new and better human.

Experimentalists, from Watson in the 1920's to Skinner at the present time, espouse a psychology of behavior determined by environmental variables. I have no quarrel with many of the results of such a psychology; behavior therapy has added to the psychotherapist's skills and is a valuable corrective to murky concepts such as masochistic drives and essential aggression/violence. On the face of it, the clean-slate idea seems optimistic, reminiscent of Rousseau; man is kindly, malleable, and often spoiled by mean-spirited society. (These are either/or abstractions, but reversed from the previous ones.) With proper social manipulation, man becomes gentle, happy, and productive.

However, when taken seriously and carried to logical conclusions, the tabula rasa approach is as destructive to respect for human individuals and to the human enterprise as the assumption that man is essentially depraved. B. F. Skinner, who is unusually visible because of his popular writings, ridicules the "myth" of individual autonomy and choice, and denies the usefulness of such concepts as dignity or freedom for individual humans.[27] Skinner eagerly carries the tabula rasa position to its ominous conclusion that social structure should ignore individual responsibility and selfhood entirely, and he pushes the possibility of conditioned societies, à la Huxley's *Brave New World*, or Orwell's *1984*, as a benign dream rather than a malignant nightmare. Forget human individuality and foolish subjectivity and enter a world of peaceful, fun-loving, gratified, cooperative humanoids. Behavioral scientists, when given effective control, will make a new breed of man quite superior to the old model, who, though talking of freedom and dignity, robbed and killed.

Both these simplistic views of man rest on a pre-systems concept of human interaction and on rejecting individuality. The instinctivist says, "The poor beggar can't help himself, unless society intimidates and scares hell out of him." The behaviorist insists that individuality and choice do not exist, and those benighted souls who speak of subjectivity are pre-scientific.

In two recent works,[28,29] Ernest Becker, a social scientist who pursued the knotty problem of the nature of man throughout his career, refutes the tabula rasa view without veering into a doctrinaire instinctivism. He applauds Freud for drawing attention to the animal part of man—his grubby biological nature, his hunger and thirst and evolutionary history—that any comprehensive understanding must include. A theory of man that summarily dismisses this biological essence is trivial. Though man possesses a glorious symbolic self that can soar and leap and imagine perfect worlds or himself an omnipotent god, his needful, decaying, finite body makes him an eternal paradox, poised between biological determinism and symbolic possibility. The tensions are tragic but not hopeless; any environmental manipulation of man is limited both by his animal nature and his symbolic personal definition. Man will kill for food or for preservation of his self definition; his benignity toward his own species is dependent on biological and subjective factors which must be taken into account by those who would eliminate his potential for violence.

The family systems material presented in earlier chapters indicates that parents who are most unconcerned about individual choice—their choices and their children's—do the poorest job of parenting. They are tyrannized and tyrannical, destroying the delight and satisfactions of being human by their marked insensitivity to individual autonomy, subjective reality, and choice. Severely dysfunctional families routinely operate by ignoring the unique individual, quite in keeping with Skinnerian concepts that the environment is everything, freedom and choice are evil fiction. These family systems produce severely damaged offspring. Optimal families place a high value on the subjective reality and choice of each family member.

Family studies illustrate the inaccuracy of considering the human as innately aggressive/violent or as a docile pawn in environmental games controlled by parents, researchers, or politicians.

A SYSTEMS VIEW OF MAN'S NATURE

A vital defect in both these simplistic approaches is the lack of consideration of choice and responsibility for personal behavior. Both views, so different in superficial appearance, deny the significance of the individual. Here is an illustration of the integral relationship of systems approaches and individual selfhood—man is a maze of paradoxes, and all simplistic linear methods of understanding him fail. He is both biologic and symbolic; his identity is both from his animal self and his environmental interaction. Neither is explanatory, and neither can be ignored.

If one rejects the instinctual and the environmental conditioning approaches to understanding man's aggression/violence, what is left? Shall we parcel out percentages, say, 20 percent for heredity, 80 percent for environment, and develop an uneasy juxtaposition of respected but unrelated forces? This would continue a non-dynamic, non-systems view of human reality doomed to be without closure or coherence.

A more productive approach to the nature of man will include two other elements: a systems approach, and an understanding of the symbolic self-system developed as the infant encounters social interactional structure.

First, I wish to deal with the biological contributions to this symbolic selfhood—species specific, genetically determined, and as much a part of man as his opposed thumb and forefinger. The unique aspect of the human animal is his remarkable overgrowth of frontal cortex, a profound biological reality making the human animal as different from other mammals as a bird from a reptile. This overgrown cortical layer, interacting with the phylogenetically conventional midbrain, allows man to symbolize, to conceptualize, and to be a time-binder. The intrinsic possibility that a human can learn all that has gone before him and start from there, rather than being forced to depend on the agonizingly slow process of biological evolution or individual experimentation, is a qualitative difference between man and his nearest species.

Pribram considers that this biological phenomenon requires man to develop an individual reality far removed from raw sensory input.[30] Sensory stimuli are filtered through interpretive circuits, and reality becomes more complex, more subjective, more abstract, and more individual.

When man evolved with this cortical-midbrain symbolizing capacity, not one species but more than ten thousand arrived on the world scene. Humans, in their symbolic richness and their poverty of absolute biological pre-programming, can identify other members of homo sapiens as far more foreign than other animal species. Species identification becomes a learned symbolic process rather than genetically determined. The man from the next valley might be seen as a more dangerous enemy than a bear, a coyote, or a snake. Interactional, socially defined experience programs man's definition and the understanding of his world, including the question of who is like him and who is so different as to deserve destruction.

The capacity for language is (in the main) a human phenomenon that requires the capacity to comprehend and invest in symbols. His symbolizing capacity allows man to develop a conscious self—an abstract concept of an *I* that can be more real than instinctual drives to an individual ("I could not love thee half as much, loved I not honor more"). The soldier who covers a live grenade with his own body to protect his buddies usually sees his act as noble, and is not considered crazy or "not himself" by others.

A self, tenuous (many psychopathologists believe man is the only animal that can go crazy), hard to define, and by its stubborn persistence a challenge to reductionist theorizing, is the essence of humanness.

As science matures, we can discuss this self without fear of being considered primitive or metaphysical. The biologist, Roger Sperry, says, "One of the most important things to come out of our brain research in recent years, from my standpoint, at least, is a greatly changed idea of the conscious mind and its relation to brain mechanism. The new interpretation, or reformulation, involves a direct break with long established materialist and behaviorist thinking, which has dominated neuroscience for many decades. Instead of dispensing with consciousness as just an 'inner aspect' of the brain process, or as some passive 'epiphenomenon' or other impotent by-product, as has been the custom, our present interpretation would make the conscious mind an integral part of the brain process itself and an essential constituent of the action. As a dynamic, emerging property of cerebral excitation, subjective experience acquires causal potency and becomes a causal determinant in brain functioning. Although inseparably tied to the material brain process, it is something distinct and special in its own right, different from and more than its component physical-chemical elements."[31] Gunther Stent, a molecular biologist, writes a precise and moving essay on the limits of science in understanding man. He insists that the self is modern psychological parlance for the soul, and agrees with Descartes that its nature is inaccessible to scientific analysis.[26] I believe these constructs represent a hopeful and sensible forefront of science. Recognizing limits is an indication of maturity, and apprehending that subjective awareness is a necessary part of understanding *meaning* is a quantum leap in scientific theorizing.

A modern scientist, then, can deal with the individual self without embarrassment. He can consider paradox, tension, and tragedy, and incorporate these contextual and value-laden concepts into his work. Paradoxes can become an accepted part of his world view. For example, science deals with patterns and generalizable statements. Yet, if unique perceptions are ubiquitous, then science is interested in them. No human is humanity, yet humanity can only be understood as a collection of subjective, specific selves.

The *I*, the self-system, sometimes called the ego (the consciousness of a specific and subjective myself that views an outside world, tries to understand that world and to obtain satisfaction from it) is the subject of our study. *I* is made up of my body that comes from my biological forebears. *I* can run, but *I* can't fly. *I* can digest meat and fruit, but not hay. *I* want to survive, and *I* would just as soon run as fight, to cooperate as to kill, depending on what *I* consider to be proper for myself, as determined by my fellows, and (if I am capable and somewhat separate from the group that defines me) on my determination of the odds for success, based on my past experiences. *I* was once very small, and *I* always feel vulnerable, so *I* have a weakness for underdogs. This is true unless the group that *I* depend on for my identity convinces me that these underdogs are symbolically not human, and hence as valueless as a cockroach. *I* am always frightened and need friends. *I* must have the approval of others whom I consider important, or *I* am as wounded as if I were physically attacked, so strong is my symbolic, social, and contextual self. *I* am ceaselessly changing in an evolving series of feedback loops between me and my fellows. *I* am a strangely perseverating amalgam with the delightfully perverse quality of not being well defined by anybody.

As we establish the respectable reality of the individual self, developed in interaction with others, we may be closer to understanding the reality of human aggression/violence. As Becker observed, "of all animals, man alone filters his action responses with the conceptual screen produced by culturally learned conventions."[4]

Perhaps aggression/violence occurs as a consequence of the breakdown of continuing relationship and dialogue between man the animal and his symbolic images of self, and between individual selves and the broader social environment of other symbolic selves. Continued dialogue at these interfaces is necessary to maintain an affiliative rather than an oppositional view of the relationship of symbolic self to physical body, of the self and other group members (as family, ethnic groups, nations) and of these groups and others (who can be seen either empathically as brothers or as non-human filth). Aggressive/violent solutions to human needs are therefore related to communicational breakdown. Individuals can turn against their bodies and suicide, turn against their families or strangers and kill, or, allying with a larger group, turn against those outside the pale and destroy them. Destruction does not result from any biological killer instinct, but from the desire to define and maintain a viable self.

I and He, We and They; I and It, We and Its

In the family, an infant learns distinctions which will be significant for the likelihood of later aggression/violence. These distinctions include those of the self and others, me and not-me, mother and not-mother, humankind and animal, family and stranger, valued and abhorred species. These affectively loaded social abstractions are part of self and world definitions.

In a sane self there is a portion considered unacceptable, evil— the *not-me*. This rejected, repressed part is available for projection onto others. Under stress of either group pressure or intense individual aloneness, this part can be mobilized for projective scapegoating. The family system is, therefore, quite important in the potential of an individual for the expression of aggression/ violence. The more the family referee (discussed in Chapter 4) is insensitive to, and out of touch with, physical needs and needs for dignity and self esteem, the more likelihood that family members will show aggression/violence. If a child's dependency, fears, frustrations, anger, sensuality, curiosity, and sexuality are acknowledged and dealt with acceptingly, his conscious self-definition can include them. He will have little need to scapegoat others who are different; they can be, if not *we*, at least *they*, and not *its*— inhuman material that can be destroyed.

The Aggression/Violence of Areté

Koestler, in a glorious paradox, believes the essential reason for man's aggression/violence in his terrible need for love and belonging, his capacity for loyalty.[2] This is certainly a widespread source of defining another as so alien as to justify violence done to him. Many people can remember scapegoating a playmate, secretly identified with, because of the overwhelming need to belong and the fear of becoming an outcast by defending a pariah. The need for others' acceptance and love can produce aggression/violence through the social phenomenon of scapegoating—seeing undesirable characteristics, rejected by the group, as the possession of humans outside that group, rendering them another and inferior species. Wars and pograms depend on this group phenomenon with its submersion of individuals into a sharply defined group.

The experiments of Milgram[32] are illustrative. A subject is told to give ever increasing amounts of painful electroshock to a human "victim," though the victim protests, screams, and begs for mercy. Few subjects defied the experimenter's authority, in spite of the fact that many subjects who continued to shock were profoundly pained by the cries of the victims and there was no obvious personal advantage for them to continue. The need to belong to an authority-defined in-group created aggression/violence in ordinary people.

The herd instinct of man coupled with a symbolic self which can render parts of human reality *not-me*, repressed and available for projection, makes possible the defining of other human beings as *its*—as gooks, wops, devils, gringos, spiks, degenerates—things less valued than cockroaches. In such mass aggression/violence as war, there is a breakdown of possible dialogue between individuals who can empathize with all other poor, powerless humans, and their group whose expectations may include killing other humans in order to belong.

We can thus include *areté* as a source of aggression/violence. I use the term as the anthropologist Goldschmidt defined it—"the qualities a person should ideally possess according to the consensus of his community—every normal community has a set of ideals of human conduct we may call its areté."[33]

Areté is isomorphic in human community systems with the referee found in family systems. Areté is not necessarily what is good for the individual, nor what he likes, nor what he gets or does—it is what he *ought* to be and do, were it not for human frailty, weakness, or accidents of fate. It is a moral imperative that lies within any spiritually unified group.

Just as the family referee system varies in its rigidity or sensitivity to human characteristics and needs, so does the areté of a community vary in the unrealistic demands made on community members. Such variability has a great deal to do with the propensity for organized institutionalized violence in a given society.

For example, the Nazi areté had peculiarly rigid and fanciful requirements for first-class group membership. True Germans were supermen with no cowardice, abject fear, or tenderness toward enemies. Therefore, dialogue between the group and individual Germans (who were scared, lonely, and empathic toward suffering people, just like individual humans everywhere) was almost impossible. Such a breakdown in communication, aided by impossibly high standards of group areté, set the stage for aggression/violence on a large scale.

I list this source of aggression/violence first because it is so important in terms of the numbers of humans who die from it, and because it is ignored in many discussions of human violence. For example, the Presidential Commission on Violence,[34] functioning during the time of the Vietnamese war, never dealt with the issue of war in general or the Vietnamese conflict in particular. Our own areté intervened! As von Bertalanffy noted, if Hitler or Stalin, driven by some innate aggression/violence, had become murderers and run amuck, they would have killed a few or a dozen people before being apprehended.[35] Their terrible danger was their power to define a whole nation's areté destructively.

The most clear and authoritative acknowledgment of the necessity for continued dialogue between individual humans and their communities came from the Nuremberg trials. For the first time, individuals were punished for following leaders, for not refusing to kill because of their own individual consciences. Here was the first official recognition that such communication would reduce violence, the first moral imperative for such communicational sharing. New ground in international law was broken in these trials. From a systems standpoint, the Nuremberg trials underscored the necessity for interacting feedback loops between individual human selves and the powerful representatives of a society in order to reduce aggression/violence.

Even in this awesome group source of aggression/violence, individual ego skills and self-esteem play a significant role. If individuals must communicate the dictates of their conscience in order to alter an areté that promotes violence rather than empathy, it is easy to see that people with minimal trust in themselves, autonomy, or social skills will be grossly handicapped in such an effort.

Once again, we see the necessity for human systems to have a permeable external boundary and individuated subsystems that communicate well with each other in order to be effective. As we move from the family hierarchy to the society, the needs are quite similar.

After many months of garbled, fragmented reports of mass destruction of Vietnamese civilians in a little village called My Lai in 1971, Lieutenant William Calley was brought to trial as the man responsible for a massacre. He was accused of giving orders to shoot unarmed civilians. This historical event dramatized the contextual and social aspects of a coherent definition of aggression/violence. It is a group judgment whether an act is defined as aggression/violence or heroism, as long as the group areté expects individuals to serve by killing other humans. One can be sentenced to 20 years in jail for killing a stranger in a bar or Vietnamese civilians, or for *refusing* to kill a stranger in a jungle. The socially defined virtue or evil of the act depends on its context, not on the essential drives of the person.

Lt. Calley's trial was long and difficult, and his conviction stirred many conflicting responses. An attempt to determine the attitudes of U. S. citizens toward his presumed actions found that a majority approved, and a significant minority felt that he did wrong.[36] Quotes from these respondents are enlightening in terms of what society members consider aggression/violence: "I would shoot because there are no civilians in Vietnam. They are either for you or against you. They all have killing on their minds." Obviously, Calley's actions were not considered evil, since he was faced with a malevolent enemy, and no distinctions can be made. "It is either shoot or be shot, and one must take orders from the commanding officers. I don't approve of killing women and children, but unfortunately in war these things happen." The belief that one should follow constituted authority, as Milgram's studies show, is a powerful force. "I would tell superior officers to go to hell, because it is immoral; the whole war is wrong." Here individual perceptions are attempting to dialogue with society. Ego ideal is communicating with areté. "I wouldn't shoot because I can't imagine old men, women, and children could be a part of the war." Empathy, which is only experienced individually and not by a group or a committee, enters as a potential societal corrective. It requires great personal strength to take stands of this sort. If we deny the pessimism of a fixed aggressive/violent drive, we have only pointed in the direction of the arduous task of making a world without violence of man to man.

Individual Isolation and Ego Deficit

Now, let us look at a personal system interface that affects the expression of aggression/violence—the individual human who kills strangers or loved ones within his own social group.

In my psychiatric career, it has been my lot to examine, and occasionally treat, individuals who have murdered friends, family members and, infrequently, strangers. There is a common pattern in the case histories of these people, both in their family background and in the acute situational crises that led to the ultimate act of aggression/violence.

The family experience of these murderers-to-be was uniformly emotionally deprived. Family mechanisms dealing with basic human needs for intimacy and tenderness were lacking. Physical abuse under the guise of discipline and a rigid, simplistic definition of people as good or bad were common. A sane but severely limited self-system developed which placed many of the biological and symbolic needs in the *not-me*, the denied part of the self. In some, this not-me was successfully hidden from needed others during childhood and adolescence; more frequently, it stubbornly resisted repression and the developing person was defined by the family as relatively unacceptable—bad, willful, selfish, or weird and scary. This person could find no acceptable family role; he was excess baggage.

The acute situation generally included a greater than usual sense of demoralization on the part of the person about to do violence, and a further reduction in the always tenuous communication with significant people in his immediate surroundings. The unacceptable *not-me* was becoming conscious, and this potentially overwhelming experience was averted by projection onto another, followed by attack. Though the projection and violence could occur within a few minutes, the stage had been set by many remote as well as contemporary factors.

Becker observed, "In many situations, aggression might be understood as an inept, sporadic method of creating a positive acting self, of exaggerating or affirming self-esteem—hate-aggression is a moment of paranoia which, by creating a fiction—a hostile environment, permits a positively valued self, along with ongoing action in an encapsulated world. In this sense, it is a creative act."[4]

Another illustration of this phenomenon is found in child-abusing parents. Beating, burning, or killing small children occurs, not from powerful drives, but from dynamics similar to those found in murderers—emotional deprivation, low self-esteem, and a simplistic control-oriented view of the world asserting that people are good or bad, saints or devils. The tremendous pressure of a repressed and evil self that discourages communication with others is easily marshalled into projective identifications. Dependent children can be seen as identical with the rejected *not-me*.

Contextual, Systems-Oriented Animal Studies

Experimental data from sophisticated animal study may prove useful in comprehending human aggression/violence. Azrin et al. found that pain, either physical or symbolic (for example, conflict), was a powerful trigger for inter- or intraspecies aggression/violence in varied mammalian species. For violence to occur, it was necessary that these animals had no way to turn, no opportunity for flight, and that they had no more creative ways of avoiding the pain. If these animals could learn ways to circumvent the painful stimulus (an experimental equivalent of ego skills), the aggression/ violence was averted.[37]

Delgado reported a study involving the implantation of an electrode in what was presumed to be the aggression center of the brain substance of a gibbon. In the laboratory, this caged gibbon would attack other members of his species whenever the electrode was stimulated. However, when given the freedom of a small island in the company of a colony of his fellows, he never showed aggression/violence to any other gibbon, no matter how much the electrode was stimulated by remote control. Instead, he would move around in an erratic manner, and on occasion would attempt to attack the barricaded experimenter.[38] Even with direct brain stimulation, the context made the difference. Aggression/violence to his own kind occurred only when other responses were ruled out by the circumstances.

CONCLUSION

To sum up, a systems view of aggression/violence acknowledges biological givens in man—his animal beginnings—his lust to survive combined with a symbolizing consciousness creating a unique symbolic self that interacts with other. Aggression/violence occurs with the breakdown of effective dialogue at interfaces between physical self and symbolic self, between self and others within the family system and in the larger community. Aggression/violence is not inevitable for either individuals or large groups, but a monumental task awaits those helpers who are interested in increasing the affiliative and reducing the oppositional orientation at these various interfaces. Family and community values must exert great power in encouraging needed communication and high individual and group self-esteem, thereby providing meaning and purpose without recourse to scapegoating and violence.

A psychotherapist with this systems view can better create in his treatment milieu an accepting growth-oriented context comparable to that found in optimal families. He can more effectively assist pa-patients to develop increasing reliance on autonomous competence and to decrease dependence on intimidating control or projective attacks.

REFERENCES

1. U. of Michigan Institute for Social Research, reported in *Time Magazine*, June 14, 1971, p. 49.
2. KOESTLER, A., "Man—One of Evolution's Mistakes?" *New York Times Magazine*, Oct. 19, 1969.
3. HARTMAN, H., KRIS, E., and LOWENSTEIN, R. M., "Notes on the Theory of Aggression," *Psychoanalytic Study of the Child*, 3, 4, 1949, 9-36.
4. BECKER, E., "Anthropological notes on the concept of aggression," *Psychiatry*, 25:4, 1962, 328-338.
5. LORENZ, K., *On Aggression*, New York, McGraw-Hill, 1967.
6. ARDREY, R., *African Genesis*, New York, Dell, 1961.
7. MORRIS, D., *The Naked Ape*, New York, McGraw-Hill, 1967.
8. STORR, A., *Human Aggression*, New York, Atheneum, 1968.
9. TIGER, L., *Men in Groups*, New York, Random House, 1967.
10. SPITZ, R., "Aggression and adaptation," *J. of Nerv. and Mental Disease*, 149 (2), 1969, 81-90.
11. TINBERGEN, "On war and peace in animals and man," *Science*, June 28, 1968.
12. KLOPFER, P. H., "Aggression and its evolution," *Psychiatry and Social Sciences Review*, Vol. 3 (3), March 1969, 2-8.
13. MEAD, M., *Cooperation and Competition among Primitive Peoples*, (Rev. Ed.), Boston, Beacon Press, 1961.
14. BENEDICT, R., *Patterns of Culture*, New York, Mentor, 1934.
15. MURDOCH, G. P., *Our Primitive Contemporaries*, New York, MacMillan, 1934.
16. MACLEISH, K., and LAUNOIS, J., "The Tasaday: stone age cave men of Mundanas," *National Geographic*, Aug. 1972, 218-249.
17. BENNETT, I., *Delinquent and Neurotic Children*, London, Tavistock Publications, 1960.
18. ROBINS, L. N., *Deviant Children Grown Up*, Baltimore, Williams and Wilkins, 1966.
19. GALDSTON, R., "Dysfunctions of Parenting: The Battered Child, the Neglected Child," in John G. Howells (Ed), *Modern Perspectives in International Child Psychiatry*, 571-588, New York, Brunner/Mazel, 1971.
20. FONTANA, V. J., *The Maltreated Child: The Maltreatment Syndrome in Children*, Charles C. Thomas, Springfield, Ill., 1964.
21. MELNICK, B. and HURLEY, J. R., "Destructive personality attributes of child-abusing mothers," *Journal of Consulting and Clinical Psychology*, 33: 746-749, 1969.
22. SPINETTA, J. J. and RIGLER, D., "The child-abusing parent," *Psychological Bulletin*, 77 (4): 296-304, 1972.
23. STEELE, B. F. and Pollock, C. B., "A psychiatric study of parents who abuse infants and small children," in Helfer, R. E. and Kempe, C. H. (Eds.), *The Battered Child*, Chicago, Univ. of Chicago Press, 1968.
24. FROMM, E., *The Anatomy of Human Destructiveness*, New York, Holt, Rinehart and Winston, 1973.
25. LUNDE, D. T., *Murder and Madness*, New York, Charles Scribner's Sons and W. H. Freeman and Co., 1976.

26. STENT, G., "Limits to the Scientific understanding of man," *Science*, 187: 1052-1057, March 21, 1975.
27. SKINNER, B. F., *Beyond Freedom and Dignity*, New York, Alfred A. Knopf, 1971.
28. BECKER, E., *The Denial of Death*, New York, The Free Press, 1973.
29. BECKER, E., *Escape from Evil*, New York, The Free Press, 1975.
30. PRIBRAM, K. H., "What Makes Man Human?" James Arthur Lecture on the Evolution of the Human Brain, The American Museum of Natural History, New York, 1970.
31. SPERRY, R., "Left Brain, Right Brain," *Sat. Review*, 32:30-33, Aug. 9, 1975.
32. MILGRAM, S., "Some conditions of obedience and disobedience to authority," *Human Relations*, 18: 57-76, 1965.
33. GOLDSCHMIDT, W., "Areté—Motivation and Models for Behavior," *in* Galdston, I. (Ed), *The Interface Between Psychiatry and Anthropology*, New York, Brunner/Mazel, 1971.
34. National Commission on the Causes and Prevention of Violence, *Presidential Commission on Violence Report*, 1972.
35. VON BERTALANFFY, L., "Comments on Aggression," *Bulletin of the Menninger Clinic*, 22 (2): 50-57, March, 1958.
36. KELMAN, H. C., "Assignment of responsibility in the case of Lt. Calley: preliminary report on the national survey," *J. of Social Issues*, 28 (1): 177-213, 1972.
37. AZRIN, N. H., HUTCHINSON, R. R., and HAKE, D. F., "Attack, avoidance, and escape reactions to aversive shock," *J. of the Exper. Analysis of Behavior*, 10 (2): 131-148, 1967.
38. DELGADO, J., "Exploring inner space," *Sat. Review*, 32: 21-25, Aug. 9, 1975.

_____ **III**

PSYCHOTHERAPY

I have formerly said that there was but one fever in the world. Be not startled, gentlemen; follow me and I will say that there is but one disease in the world!

Benjamin Rush, *"Lectures on the Practice of Physics"*

_____ **10**

The patients, the problems, and two pathways of treatment

The rest of this book is devoted to individual and group treatment methodology. In this chapter, I will present a general statement about emotional illness and bring into focus the variations found within a coherent, unitary concept of etiology. In addition, I will describe two fundamentally different approaches to treatment—termed the "controller" and the "grower" orientations—that are chosen, whether consciously or not, by all psychotherapists.

WHAT IS THE DISEASE WE TREAT?

Are the varied emotional ailments treated by psychotherapists one disease or many? Is there a relationship, for instance, between schizophrenia and depression, neurosis and sociopathy? If they are qualitatively different, what are their varied natures; if they are related, what is the common thread?

From the early chapters, the reader will be aware that I consider all psychopathology to be related. Every infant must have a reasonably benign match of his biological possibilities with his social system, and both must be at least minimally adequate for him or her to develop into a gratified adult who is accepted by the society beyond the family. The family system is powerful and pivotal in the developmental tasks. If tuned in to human biological and symbolic needs, a family can soften and neutralize some of the more rigid and harsh aspects of a particular culture's areté. For example, harsh and judgmental religions can be de-fanged by a family; love and kindness may be extracted as effectively as a combine separates wheat from straw. However, if a family is alienated from the larger community with emotionally deprived parents possessing little self-esteem, the potential richness of the broader culture is lost on the infant, and ego starvation occurs regardless of that richness or of the infant's biological potential.

Since a systems approach is a multi-factoral one which handles many variables, it can and must include information about a specific patient's genetic qualities, physical defects and strengths, past physical illnesses, and possible sequelae in approaching his emotional illness and determining treatment. These non-interactional factors may, at times, loom large, but any patient is, by his very existence, responsible for integrating his biological self into the social structure. Therefore, I believe that all psychopathology can be productively considered a unitary disease, a *deficiency* disease—a lack of satisfying, coherent, self-defining encounters with meaningful others. In the language of ego psychology, ego is developed through such encounters, and illness consists of "ego deficit."

In addition to being a result of a deficiency of needed human interaction, the various categories of emotional illness 1) are related, 2) are contextual, 3) relate to human development, 4) involve disturbances in consciousness, 5) are interactional, 6) represent the confusion of past with present, 7) represent a problem in effective consensual validation, 8) signify estrangement from others, a lack of intimacy, 9) include a lack of integration of individual fantasy with shared reality, 10) involve a continuing impotent/omnipotent pattern of behavior, 11) result from individual difficulty in dealing with human complexity and paradox, and 12) represent a failure in obtaining and maintaining sufficient social power in close relationships. Regardless of diagnosis, these factors need to be attended by patient and therapist alike if treatment has a good possibility of being successful. Now, let's look at these factors individually.

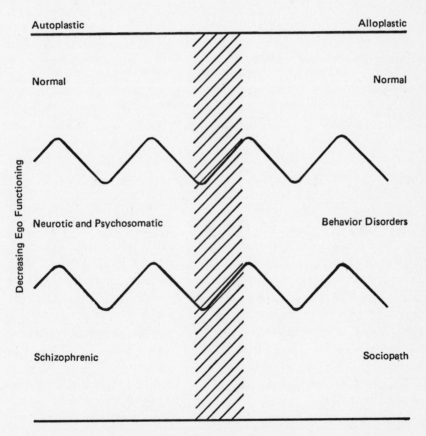

Figure 1. Individual psychopathological states and their relation to each other

1) *The Various States of Psychopathology Are Related*

The diagram, modified from one created by Franz Alexander,[1] presents emotional illnesses as definably different, and yet related. The vertical axis represents a continuum of methods of conflict expression—on the left are the most autoplastic styles which characteristically express emotional conflict by psychosomatic illness or inner conflict and pain, with little in the way of socially disruptive action. On the right are alloplastic styles which characteristically express emotional conflict by engaging the social environment, the social appropriateness of their behavior depending on ego strength. The middle area is drawn hazily because most people have both styles available to them and are not easily pigeonholed.

The vertical axis represents ego strength or coping ability, with the greatest ability at the top of the diagram.

The division between healthy and sane-but-limited neurotic and behavior disorder catagories is drawn wavy, not as a straight line. This represents the reality that the separation is made by individuals and their social groups—family, peers, employers—and its definition varies with the tolerance of these entities. The psychopathologist uses such self and social labeling for his diagnosis; he is dependent on the subjective reality of the patient and on the social context.

The division between the sane-but-limited psychopathological states and the severe disturbances of psychoses and sociopathy is also drawn wavy for the same reasons. This delineation is also an individual or a social determination, though it is more often made by the culture which defines the most dysfunctional groups as socially unacceptable. The delineations are not static, but dynamic; people move from one category to another, depending on environmental stress. In addition, cortical depressants such as alcohol will usually produce a shift to the right; these drugs are quite likely to release behavioral inhibitions.

This diagram emphasizes the relationship of psychiatric diagnoses to one another and relates them to relative ego skills and to characteristic styles of expression. It highlights the fact that divisions are made as much by individuals and the social structure as by diagnosticians.

2) *All Psychopathology Is Contextual*

No individual thought, feeling, or behavior is pathological in itself. It is extremely important for a therapist to understand this. To illustrate I will mention such apparently obvious deviant behavior as murder. If one kills on command, he may be decorated rather than called sick. If one kills strangers on a city street, he is thought to be a dangerous psychotic. The interpersonal social context makes the difference, and this is true for any behavior or expression of thought. A treatment system which considers health to be objectively defined and absolute (for example, possessing orgasmic potency, being in the here-and-now, performing heterosexually, being serene) garbles the reality of psychopathology and its treatment.

3) *Psychopathology Is Related to Unaccomplished Developmental Tasks*

Many interpersonal skills and considerable awareness of one's feeling states and thoughts are needed for successful selfhood. If an individual failed to learn important lessons because of disturbed family interaction, he is highly vulnerable to psychic pain and overt dysfunction. The label of emotional illness, however, is not directly tied to the presence or absence of many of these skills. Many capable people define themselves as ill because of subjective pain, and they enter psychotherapy; others may suffer severe psychic difficulty, dreadful aloneness, or markedly deviant behavior and never seek treatment, escaping the label of emotional illness though severely handicapped in functioning.

4) *Consciousness Is Important in Functioning Ability and Has a Double-Edged Effect on Becoming Defined as Emotionally Ill*

A person with few relationship skills has to exclude from consciousness much internal and external material in order not to be overwhelmed and demoralized. Yet, his obliviousness increases the likelihood of social rejection and diminishes his reaching out for increasing skills. Sullivan once described schizophrenia as the inability to control the contents of consciousness. The resultant loss of time sense, of context awareness, and of goal-directed behavior is dramatic in schizophrenia, but is also a part of other psychopathological states.

Some psychiatrists especially interested in family dynamics believe that the content of an individual's unconscious is largely controlled by his family.[2] We are conscious of what we could *afford* to notice, what we were allowed to notice, in our family of origin. The more areas of human reality which were denied, the greater our vulnerability to illness.

5) *The Disease is an Interactional Phenomenon, Not Something That Occurs Within One Person*

Though people vary greatly in living skills, a non-threatening interpersonal setting may allow individuals with quite modest ego strengths to adapt reasonably well and be accepted. Conversely, if the interpersonal setting is exceedingly ambiguous, demanding, and unrewarding, even a capable person may become ill. This applies to therapeutic environments as well, and every therapist must attend to his own contribution to a patient's symptoms. Refusal to respond humanly to a patient is as sadistic as rude badgering. Trust is essential to a functioning self-system, and mistrust is a function of the behavior of all parties in a transaction, not simply the patient's.

6) *Emotional Illness Represents Confusion of Past with Present*

Freudians speak of transference; Gestaltists concern themselves with projections; Sullivanians deal with parataxic distortions. All are describing a central feature of emotional illness—dealing with the present as though it were identical with the past and thereby becoming vulnerable to psychic pain and/or group extrusion. Assuming that nothing is new and that the broader world is simply an extension of one's own family system can alleviate anxiety, but it handicaps functioning and new learning. Such a closed system approach, resulting in rigidity, adaptive failure, and isolation, is characteristic of all emotionally ill people.

7) *Consensual Validation—the Coming to a Shared View of Important Aspects of Reality with Significant Others—Is Deficient in Any Category of Emotional Illness*

Please note that I do not say that a patient has "poor reality testing." Therapists who misunderstand this point will often be off-target; they may consider the purpose of treatment is to educate, to provide information about an alleged "objective" reality known to the therapist. Patients who lack social skills have difficulty negotiating with others about personal desires and perceptions of the world. Effective negotiation requires that an individual's subjective reality be heard and respected. A good therapist provides experience in negotiating, not in some objective reality.

8) *Just as an Emotionally Ill Person Cannot Bear to Be Aware of Important Aspects of Himself, He Also Hides from Others and Is, in Varying Degrees, Alone*

The terms alienation and estrangement are currently bandied about so casually as to reduce their power and meaning; they nevertheless have great significance in understanding emotional illness. People in all categories of illness are in some degree closed to others and fear rejection if someone knows what they really are, what they really think, feel, and do.[3] Often, this conviction becomes a self-fulfilling prophecy, and inner feeling states are expressed in such a way that rejection follows.

9) *Because of Many of the Foregoing Features, People in All Categories of Emotional Illness Have a Dramatic Split between Their Fantasies and What they Perceive to Be Their Real Existence*

This is characteristic of the disturbed self. People are symbol-makers. This capacity allows for, among many other things, fantasies of perfection in themselves and others. The human environment of failing, limited, conflicted, and ambivalent creatures appears disgusting when contrasted with (rather than integrated into) fantasy. The more painful and unsatisfying our real experience as we develop our self-definition, the more we split fantasy from reality as a needed defense. Children can handle harsh reality in no other way, yet this split is maladaptive for relating to others. For example, people who are labeled schizophrenic have few skills in developing validated reality and tend to withdraw from others, investing in their fantasies. Hysteric neurotics, though remaining in a sane world, invest little in relationships and depend a great deal on fantasy. Compulsive neurotics split off and deny their fantasies and try to live in a reality defined (and therefore experienced) as severe, unmagical, and joyless. Human fantasies are the engine of ourselves, the driving force for joy, action, and accomplishment. They clothe enterprises and people with meaning, shared purpose, and value. As we grow and develop, the magical, the wondrous, changes in content: The three-year-old who sees all of life in a butterfly or earthworm evolves into an adult with complex beliefs, loyalties, and dreams of glory. The dream always precedes and directs. If fantasy and reality are integrated, the result is a healthy, socialized human; if not, the product is emotional illness.

Here cultural values also enter. In Eastern cultures, an extremely aggressive, action-oriented person might be seen as aberrant. In our Western world, we are much more inclined to put those who are heavily invested in dreams into places of seclusion and label them ill. We are geared for action. When one treats a family in which there is a schizophrenic member, one often finds a super-rational individual as a counterpoint. The father, perhaps, has worked in the same place for 30 years, has a terribly restricted emotional life and a monotonous way of speaking. If one listens closely, he will make no more sense than does the identified patient, but his investment in consensual reality, dull as it is when squeezed dry of dreams, allows him society's blessing as normal.

10) *Emotional Illness Includes the Preservation of an Impotent/Omnipotent Relationship Pattern*

This pattern is expressed normally in the interaction of mothers and infants. All of normal development may be seen as having the purpose of eliminating this pattern and replacing it with relative social competence. Hallmarks of the impotent/omnipotent style of relating include: a) helplessness is more powerful than competence, and b) absolute power is a trap depriving the possessor of personal choice. In addition, the impotent/omnipotent mode offers little or no opportunity for negotiation—demands are non-negotiable, control battles eternal. In the process of normal development, children experience family interaction that responds to their needs, rather than to power struggles; negotiation with respect for these personal needs helps the growing child to capture the vision of integrating his wishes and his autonomous functioning. Competence includes the ability to accept human limitations, one's own and those of others, to acquire ego skills, and to function without hope of godlike omnipotence or fear of abject helplessness.

11) *In All Problems of Self-Definition and Adaptation, There Is a Defect in Dealing with Paradox*

Every capable human encounters and masters at least some of the built-in paradoxes of being human. We wish to be kind to those we love; yet sometimes kindness consists of being openly and clearly angry. We must respect another's limitations in order to enjoy him; yet to expect too little of another is to be contemptuous and uncaring—to expect nothing is to defile. The assumption of personal responsibility is the cornerstone of autonomy; yet sharing responsibility is necessary for effective negotiation. Part of loving is to look out for and help others; yet in the most dramatic events of our life, for example, birth, death, and (some say) in the intensity of orgasm, we are necessarily alone. We must learn to rely on our own judgment; yet all humans are fallible so we should be open to others' views. In order to feel significant we need a dream in which we personally participate; yet we must recognize our mortality. Emotionally ill people cannot deal with such paradoxes. They get confused, blot out the data, or try to make the complicated simple by assuming another mortal infallible and following clear-cut, fixed, maladaptive rules.

12) *Finally, There Is Always Failure of Social Power*

The difficult part is that one must have enough social power to satisfy his own human needs. Many people with great power over others are starved emotionally and are truly ignorant of what to do about it. King Midas had great power because everything he touched turned to gold, but he could not eat—a modern counterpart being physical disease resulting from the lack of essential vitamins in people surrounded by food. Often, of course, one sees patients whose social power is limited in every sphere. Emotional illness increases as social class decreases, a testimony to the enduring relationship between social power and emotional health. To be effective, any therapist must appreciate the need for effective social power in abolishing symptoms and increasing morale.

These twelve items are not exhaustive, but serve to illustrate the interrelatedness and complexity of patients' problems. The therapist who oversimplifies problems hoping to render them more easily manageable will often fail to treat, or will even worsen, the patient's life situation.

Though all of the above difficulties may be present in a person defined as emotionally ill, in most instances there are immediate difficulties described as "acute symptomatology." Foremost is demoralization. A person often acknowledges his illness when he loses his previous hope and feels he has nowhere to turn. This demoralization is expressed in one of two general ways: He may become disintegrated, "all to pieces," "unable to pull himself together," or he may become insistent on absolute certainty with rigid thinking and behavior as in paranoid states, depression, and obsessive-compulsive neurosis. These responses to stress may be understood in the framework of systems theory as stages of disorganization.

Figure 2 may help in relating this process of demoralization and regression to some of the labels placed on people at various degrees of functioning difficulty. Conceive of any human population placed on a two-dimensional scale with the horizontal axis representing the degree of consensual validation or shared world view present, and the vertical axis representing gratification or hope of gratification. In the top left-hand portion are those individuals considered healthy. As satisfaction or hope of satisfaction in living is reduced, they will be located on a U-shaped curve, with a loss of a shared sense of reality first corresponding to the loss of hope.

Clinical states of anxiety, depression, and finally psychotic depression will appear as individuals follow this regressive curve. At the bottom of the curve, one finds immobilizing psychic pain—utter despair. Most people cannot remain here, and they will either lunge back into social activity or move further into social isolation. Arieti referred to this as the schizophrenic decision;[4] further reduction in consensual reality and increased investment in fantasy reduce psychic pain but also profoundly decrease social functioning.

Most emotionally ill persons are on the left side of this curve,

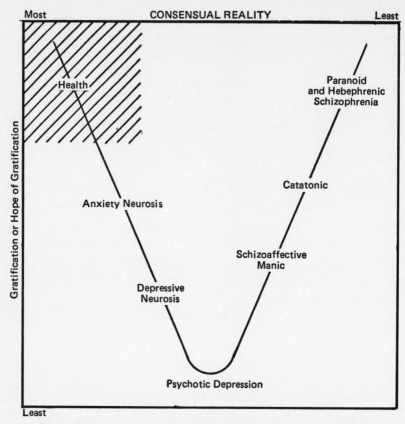

Figure 2. Emotional illness related to gratification, hope, and relationships.

less profoundly isolated; this is fortunate because of the tremendous pain and effort required of both patient and therapist to bring an individual through absolute despair into a resocialized, normal condition.[5]

HOW THE DISEASE IS TREATED

There are many treatment methods for emotional illness, including somatic, supportive, uncovering, directive, non-directive, insight oriented, and relationship. I believe these descriptive labels can be usefully divided into two categories termed the "controller" and the "grower" approaches. The intent of the therapeutic approach is readily identifiable. Both approaches have their advocates and their critics, each has advantages and disadvantages, and I see them as different rather than as superior or inferior. Many people wish to be rid of their emotional pain without concern for increasing their functioning ability; hence they will choose controller treatment methods. Many other disturbed people cannot tolerate the reduction in personal power involved in submitting to these techniques. The therapist's virtue (and probably good results also) consists of matching the desires of the patient with the treatment approach. The therapist's sin (and probably poor outcome) consists of ignoring the patient's choice and giving the treatment the therapist prefers rather than negotiating with the patient.

Examples of controller approaches to healing the mind include electroshock, most drug therapy, hypnosis, and such varieties of psychotherapy as directive, supportive, indoctrination, and some behavioral modification approaches. I know of only four ways for one person to change another's behavior or attitude: coercion, persuasion, empathic sharing, and problem-solving with the other. The controller hterapist uses coercion and persuasion. He is the therapist with the most ancient lineage, the direct descendant of the shaman. He uses social power, magical transference, charismatic personality, and any other means of increasing overt power. In our culture, gleaming instruments, expensive furnishings, positioning the therapist in a higher position than the sufferer, all serve to increase this power differential.

Either therapeutic approach may begin with this marked difference in overt power. The grower must share it with the patient, the controller must keep it. The controller focuses on indoctrination, not dialogue. He wishes to minimize objections or back-talk from his patient, and defines questioning or efforts to engage in a more equal discourse as resistance to treatment. The patient who fights electroshock, who won't take his medicine, questions a directive, or denies an interpretation is seen as prolonging his illness and fighting both the therapist and recovery. The family model for such treatment is parent and infant with enormous disparity between the knowledge and power of the caretaker and the cared for. Certainty is expected of the healer. Empathy and kindness may also be present, but not discussion of alternatives or the provision of significant choice for the ill person. The expert should know what the problem is and what to do; the role of the sufferer is passive. The patient's subjective reality is unimportant except as it gets in the way. Intimacy between therapist and patient is not expected. In fact, any degree of closeness would lessen the chance for cure by destroying the power differential.

There are cultural and class differences in the preference for such treatment. The more a society or a group believes that individuals are controlled by outside forces, the more frequently controller healing is expected. In our own country, the greatest demand for such therapy might be expected at the lowest and highest socioeconomic levels. People in both groups are likely to wish for magical (whether scientific or superstitious) cures out of their common belief that outside forces are paramount in controlling individuals. Very poor people, having seldom experienced much personal social power, look askance at the healer who represents only himself, not some superhuman force, and who implies that the healing power comes from the suffering person. Upper-class people are also likely to demand magic. The statement about the poor is well documented.[6] I offer the statement about upper-class patients as more anecdotal and consistent with shared experiences of colleagues. Often, in upper-class homes, great wealth has been accumulated by one powerful person, and individual members may have as much difficulty with self determination and individual choice as do the poor. The above applies to group tendencies; individual members of all social classes may ask for, and respond well to, growth-oriented treatment.

The controller approach is not only the oldest, but also the most common form of treatment. Though potentially effective in all varieties of acute emotional illness, its one severe drawback is an inability to deal with the root cause (as I have defined it)—the lack of satisfying, coherent, self-defining experiences in a shared group milieu.

The parent/infant relationship was once the model for physician/patient encounters. Medicine was simpler; there were many acute illnesses, and physicians had little to offer in the way of help for chronic disease. Now, however, in all forms of medicine the physician spends more time treating people with chronic illness, i.e., hypertension, arthritis, diabetes, tuberculosis, peptic ulcer, who do not do well if infantilized. Blum[7] showed a positive correlation between malpractice suits and the doctor's personality characteristics of arrogance, godlike certainty, and the taking of power from the patient. It is a necessary and integral part of treatment to establish a mutually respectful partnership in which the patient has responsible choice. In addition, many of the above chronic illnesses overlap with emotional illnesses, and approaches which increase ego strength are desirable. Because of changes in the nature of the illnesses a physician treats, because more individuals define themselves as middle-class and desire to control their own destiny, and because of a rising tide of anti-authoritarianism reflected in general loss of respect for all authority, the grower, equal-powered orientation is increasingly in demand. Physicians are expected to provide the responsible involvement of their patients.

The grower orientation, relatively new on the scene, owes its birth to Sigmund Freud. It is as different from the controller approach as the optimal family is different from a low midrange, centripetal one. The approach is scientific in the sense defined in Chapter 1. It acknowledges that no man or system has the truth, that certainty is evidence of a developmental arrest, and that people's subjective reality is important and worthy of respect. Growth-oriented treatment always strives to equalize the overt power between therapist and patient since the major weapons used to alter behavior and attitudes are the empathic relationship and problem-solving with the patient. These methods flourish in a relationship of mutual responsibility and wither in an atmosphere of unilateral control. Magic and transference are minimized, while sharing and intimacy are emphasized. Interaction is designed, even during the acute phases of disease, to treat the cause, to provide needed self-confirming and self-defining relationship experiences which increase self-confidence, self-awareness, socialization, and good morale.

As I begin a specific description of growth-oriented psychotherapy, I want to reiterate the importance of seeing it as representative of the coming of age of psychotherapy rather than a "method."

REFERENCES

1. ALEXANDER, F., "The Neurotic Character," *International J. of Psychoanalysis*, Vol. XI, 292-311, 1930.
2. FORD, F. and HERRICK, J., "Family rules," Presented at Southwest Regional Meeting, American Orthopsychiatric Assn., Galveston, Tex., Nov. 18, 1972.
3. JOURARD, S. M., *The Transparent Self*, New York, Van Nostrand Reinhold Co., 1971.
4. ARIETI, *Interpretation of Schizophrenia*, New York, Robert Brunner, 1955.
5. BOWERS, M. B., and ASTRACHAN, B. M., "Depression in acute schizophrenic psychosis," *Amer. J. Psychiat.*, 123 (8): 976-976, Feb. 1967.
6. RIESSMAN, F., COHEN, J. and PEARL, A. (Eds.), *Mental Health of the Poor*, New York, Free Press, 1964.
7. BLUM, R. H., Study on California Malpractice Suits, supplement, *Report to the National Malpractice Commission*, Washington, D. C., Department of Health, Education, and Welfare, 1974.

_____ **11**

Growth-promoting individual psychotherapy

In the following pages, I shall present a synthesis of material from earlier chapters directed toward a scientific, pluralistic, individual psychotherapy as a guide for growth-oriented therapists. Please note that this is *a* synthesis, not *the* synthesis. It is a blatantly subjective reality. I have no wish to add to the already too lengthy lists of treatment schools or cults. My hope is both more modest and more ambitious. With the emerging science of self, there will be generally accepted common ground, and, at the same time, individual therapists will be responsibly free to explore new approaches and new theory. I hope that future psychotherapists will know that it is more enjoyable and effective to be a first-class John Jones, Mary Smith, or Bob Beavers than an inhibited, second-class Sigmund Freud, Fritz Perls or Carl Rogers.

Other areas of medicine have evolved similarly. It does not make sense to ask a present-day internist if he is an Oslerian but many of his medical ancestors were ostracized if they questioned the wisdom of Galen. Transition from authoritarianism to individually responsible practice can only come as psychotherapeutic treatment schools fade and are replaced with humanistic, systems-conscious, data-oriented science.

One cannot give to others what he does not possess. Only when the psychotherapist is autonomous can he begin to emulate optimal families in providing a setting for competent self-development.

To emphasize the importance of the reader's own continuing evolution as an autonomous therapist, I recommend reading or rereading texts from several schools of psychotherapy; many are referenced in Chapters 7 and 8. Such reading will facilitate appreciation of similarities, differences, and possible syntheses, and increase acceptance of an open-system viewpoint.

From preceding chapters, it will be evident that I believe a growth-promoting therapist will have a systems orientation, know the scientific method and its limitations, and believe man's nature to be not destructive, but multipotentialed, dependent on past and present context. With such knowledge and tools, the therapist can integrate theory not yet evolved, and data not yet found, and he can treat aberrations society has not yet produced.

To refer to this kind of psychotherapy as scientific may sound presumptuous, or imply special claims. Such is not my intent. To label it as such came after long debate with myself. What single term would indicate a therapy that is egalitarian, undoctrinaire, that invites an experience in human intimacy, is systems-oriented, and depends on the patient as partner in a problem-solving, ego-building enterprise? *Scientific* is an honest effort at thumbnail description. I believe the scientific open system, with its uncertainty, lack of dogma, and respect for new input from others, is the most effective in promoting competence. (But I am not certain!)

INDICATIONS AND CONTRAINDICATIONS

Indications include the meeting between a therapist capable of the discipline required to be a genuine person involved in a contextually clear professional endeavor, and a person self-defined as emotionally ill, coming to treatment of his own choice, who is willing to share the responsibility of productive change.

Growth-oriented psychotherapy is not limited to any particular degree of illness; for example, acute schizophrenic patients are often better candidates than are some neurotics. It is not class-limited, and people from other cultures are often more comfortable with this approach than with controller means of treatment.

Contraindications include coercion into treatment. A therapist can manage a coerced person, or treat him in controller fashion, but inviting him into a treatment partnership produces a farce of contextual shifts. Prisoners and committed patients are candidates if the coercion does not extend to therapy. If there is no institutional reward for visiting the therapist, or punishment for not doing so, an equal-powered, trusting relationship can develop.

Acutely suicidal or homicidal patients must be in an environment where extra help with destructive impulses is available. Otherwise, the fear produced in a sensible therapist would preclude establishing necessary trust.

Classical manic-depressive illness in either the depressed or manic stages is a contraindication. Drug treatment, particularly the use of lithium salts, has improved the outlook for such patients tremendously; however, in an agitated manic state or in a deep depression, they are extremely difficult to reach by even the most skilled growth-oriented therapist.[1]

Finally, people whom the therapist, after evaluation, believes he does not and cannot like, should be referred to another therapist. A psychiatrist can treat people well by controller means even though he thoroughly dislikes them, but some degree of shared rapport is necessary for growth promotion.

This modest list of contraindications points up the usefulness of growth-oriented psychotherapy in a wide variety of clinical psychopathological states. Further, the demand for such treatment continually increases as our society, with its rapid changes and unclear lines of authority, develops individuals who wish to be autonomous rather than compliant.

BEGINNING

Patients come to treatment in one of two stances: acutely demoralized (my fantasy of this state is clutching the shrubbery on the edge of a cliff); or shaken but recovered from acute stress (I see these people as sitting on a park bench wondering why they were so recently cliff-hanging). It is important to determine in which state the patient is, because misdiagnosis here can lead to a quick rejection of possible help. A therapist will seem quite sadistic (and hence is, in a way) to a patient who is clinging to the edge of his symbolic world if he treats the patient as if he were safely benched ("Your next thought?"). Or he can be seen as ludicrous if he treats a relatively comfortable patient as an unexploded bomb ("Are you sure you can drive?" "Is there someone at home?"). Straightforward people can be separated easily, but there are histrionic, crisis-a-week patients, and stoics (untrustworthy types who cannot speak clearly and directly of their degree of difficulty). One must depend on a careful history, a thorough mental status, careful observation of body language, and close attention to one's own empathic responses to reduce errors so significant in the beginning relationship.

With the acutely demoralized, cliff-hanging group, there will be an immediate need for ego assistance, though directive, controlling activity is usually not required. The patient can be made aware that he is still in charge of his life, and the therapist will do everything in his power to help. Problem-solving proceeds as with park bench patients, but the problems are more immediate: "How can I live now that she has left me?" "My job was my life, and now I have nothing." "There is something wrong with my mind; I can't think, and I can't remember." Here is where a systems orientation is most helpful. The therapist will know at the end of a first interview what, if any, support system the patient has or has ever had (that is, friends, lovers, family, job), and he will work with the patient in a problem-solving fashion, described in this chapter, to assist in mobilizing available human resources and in reintegrating the self into a context meaningful to the patient.

The therapist rarely has to perform as a controller, even in the unusual situation where hospitalization is recommended. If he is scrupulously honest, shares his fears, and tells the patient clearly what is of concern and what is recommended, the new relationship seldom founders.

For example, if a new patient voices suicidal wishes and plans, he is clearly asking for help with overwhelming impulses. A direct response to his plea permits providing a protective environment without coercion and, even in such a desperate state, the patient can maintain personal dignity and choice. Psychotherapy of a growth-oriented nature can begin even with such handicaps, though requiring help from others.

Efforts to reduce the overt power differential are effective in these acute demoralized patients. Usually eight to fifteen sessions, once or twice a week, are adequate in eliminating acute symptomatology, bringing the suffering person to relative comfort. Whether this is more or less efficient than control-oriented approaches probably cannot be determined since there are so many variables. Therapist skill, technical differences, patient choice, and patient ability to solve problems all enter into the clinical equation. However, it is important to note that a problem-solving, equal-powered approach in the intense emotional state of acute demoralization is a powerful learning experience for a patient. If he has been on the edge of his symbolic world and returns to relative comfort without abdication of personal autonomy, he has a justified sense of having been battle-tested and found adequate. To use any or all of the controller methods (electroshock, directives, hypnosis, medication given in an authoritarian manner) unfortunately gives the sufferer a further lesson in the need for outside force foreign to himself in his apparent helplessness.

A pertinent analogy is the decision to deliver a woman by Caesarian section, which represents the taking over of a natural function by powerful outside intervention. Although it is necessary at times and can be life-saving, it usually means that further deliveries will also be by Caesarian section. Similarly, treatment that accents the power of the therapist and the impotence of the patient encourages a dependent life-style.

Using Drugs in Conjunction With Growth-Oriented Psychotherapy

As a pharmacologist/internist turned psychotherapist, I have been understandably intrigued with the relationship between psychopharmacology—treating emotional illness with medications, and psychotherapy—treating emotional illness with human encounter. My first impression is vivid and still powerful: There is an unfortunate tendency to dichotomize these treatment methods. Psychiatrists who are organically oriented treat by shock and drugs; psychotherapists of all disciplines tend to be ignorant of brain chemistry and psychoactive drugs and, in a near phobic way, avoid knowledge of them. I explain such a split in terms of the resistance to complicating one's life. The resistance to developing competence in both areas is similar to the early resistance to systems concepts: Complexity is not welcomed unless one is most dissatisfied with the results of a more simple world view.

The advances in chemical treatment of emotional illness in the last 20 years have been most impressive; antipsychotic drugs, pioneered by the use of reserpine, followed by the phenothiazines, and recently represented by phenothiazine-like drugs, have revolutionized the treatment of psychosis. Careful studies indicate that the use of phenothiazines promotes a better outcome of acute psychosis than any alternative treatment.[2] Psychotherapy of acute psychosis must, in good conscience, be an adjunct to, rather than a substitute for, effective drug treatment.

It is inhumane to treat an acute schizophrenic patient by relationship without providing antipsychotic medication; on the other hand, an exclusive reliance on drugs communicates to the patient that he must depend on resources outside himself for functioning and severely diminishes his already vulnerable self-esteem. Mosher and Menn[3] provide suggestive evidence that egalitarian relationship therapy, in addition to drugs, increases the social functioning of patients. In other words, it is sad to see a psychotic patient deprived of drug treatment, but equally sad to see him condemned to an exclusive reliance on such treatment. A combination approach, providing drugs to deal with the acute loss of functioning and psychotherapeutic encounter which offers new learning, has greater promise than either of them used alone.

In addition, antipsychotic drugs, such as the phenothiazines, can be offered to a patient in either a controller or a growth promoting fashion. In the controller mode, a diagnosis is made, and treatment is instituted with medication and dosage dictated by the therapist's cognitive structure, quite often independent of the patient's subjective reality. Though this conforms to the ancient doctor/patient relationship model, it is somewhat peculiar when one considers the nature of the disorder, which is as much a subjective difficulty as a behavioral one. An acutely psychotic person behaves strangely, but also feels strange; if his subjective reality is ignored, valuable information is cast aside.

A growth-promoting approach to providing drug treatment to the acutely psychotic person includes a careful evaluation of the problem and an explanation of its principal outlines to the patient. Further explanation is needed about the primary effects of the drug to be given and the enlistment of the patient's participation in determining both the proper drug and the proper dosage. Such a treatment contract can be the beginning of an equal-powered treatment alliance that continues long after the acute psychotic episode is passed. Since the results to be attained include subjective as well as objective improvement, such a partnership makes good sense initially as well as in the long run. The therapist provides his expertise, a technical contribution; the patient provides his perception of response, a personal, subjective contribution. The dangers of over- or under-medication are reduced with such a partnership.

Case example: A 24-year-old woman entered treatment with a previous diagnosis of paranoid schizophrenia. She had been treated in psychiatric hospitals on two prior occasions with electroshock. She was confused in her speech, had many ideas of reference, was quite suspicious, but was definite that she wanted to work on her problems while carrying on with her life, rather than return to a hospital.

She was offered a phenothiazine at the diagnostic interview in the manner described above. With drug and dosage manipulation over several weeks, she became comfortable and modestly functional on 500 mg. of thioridazine (Mellaril) a day. The dosage was gradually reduced as she improved in her relationship abilities. Four years later she could not tolerate 50 mg. of thioridazine without becoming somnolent and sluggish. Anxiety episodes were controlled by 10 mg. of chlordiazepoxide (Librium). During that four years, she had divorced, had dated widely, and at the time of re-evaluation was going with a man she subsequently married. The input from this patient was essential in providing useful medication during her many changes in character structure and diagnostic categories, as she moved from psychosis to neurosis and into a state her friends and family considered normal.

It is my opinion that the violent objections to the use of drug treatment by many groups concerned with the rights of psychiatric patients are related to their administration in a controller fashion, rather than to a rejection of the use of medicine.

The use of drugs for sane but limited patients can follow a similar pattern. Depressed patients can often benefit from modern antidepressant drugs,[4] but the exclusive reliance on medication allows for no new learning, no possibility of experiencing emotional growth that can reduce the chances of recurrence of the painful illness.

Contrarily, relying on psychotherapy alone in an acutely depressed patient deprives him of the clear benefits of drug treatment, and intensive psychotherapeutic intervention may fail or require many unnecessary months of work by patient and therapist while the patient grapples with despair and hopelessness. If the diagnosis of severe neurotic depression is made, a growth-oriented therapist can provide medication by spelling out the potential of drug treatment and rely on the patient for subjective reports that help determine dosage, response, and potentially dangerous side effects. The therapist needs to know, of course, the various alternative medications available, dosage limits, and particular effects of these drugs, and he needs to communicate much of this information to his patient to make him useful as a partner in the decision-making regarding these drugs.

Antianxiety medications, such as clordiazepoxide and diazepam (Valium) should never be used in psychotic patients and are of a limited value in the sane-but-anxious. Again, exclusive reliance on medication may assist a patient through an acute episode but deprives him of learning that can reduce recurrences. On the other hand, a disdain for chemical help in the treatment of acute anxiety can abort or prolong treatment efforts unnecessarily. It is relatively clear that people cannot learn when too anxious[5] even though, if anxiety is treated as an enemy to be constantly attacked with chemicals, the establishment of a problem-solving treatment relationship is subverted.

The key factor that differentiates modest anxiety, which can be a spur to relationships and new learning, and overwhelming anxiety, which prevents both, is the continuation of functioning in a social environment. Modest anxiety is somewhat painful but social functioning continues; overwhelming anxiety is intensely painful and social functioning is severely compromised. Educating the patient in such differences and inviting him to share the responsibility of determining the timing and amounts of medication are exercises in equal-powered negotiation; such procedures also prevent the otherwise frequent development of an oppositional relationship in which the lack of patient response (impotence) is a powerful force in defeating a therapist who wishes to fix things (omnipotence).

A therapist can give needed drug information along with drugs; his technical knowledge will determine whether the drugs should be given to combat psychosis, depression, or overwhelming anxiety. The patient's subjective reality will determine the specific

drug choice, dosage, and, as improvement occurs, the time for relying on relationship alone. Such a cooperative endeavor can allow
the inclusion of modern drug treatment without sacrificing patient
autonomy or the opportunity for increasing ego skills.

THE CONTRACT

During an evaluation period of one to three hours, it is important to explore the patient's view of his difficulty, find out the
length of time the acute problem has been present, and determine
the human support system enjoyed by the patient in the remote
and recent past and in the present circumstances. In addition, one
needs to evaluate the match between patient and therapist. Do we
seem to understand one another, at least at times? Does this person desire what I am offering; is he willing to try to remove acute
difficulties without turning his life over to another? (Some
therapists are "switch-hitters"; they are able to function in either
the controller or growth-oriented fashion. Others are not, and
these therapists need to feel comfortable in referring, in order that
patient choice and therapist style are matched.) If growth-
promoting treatment is elected, do I see qualities in the patient
that I think are admirable and likeable? Do I imagine this relationship could become enjoyable? (It is important to be "selfish"
here—early phases of treatment are often painful for therapist and
patient. I fully expect that later in my relationship with the patient
we both will enjoy the encounters. I would have a hard time with a
whole practice of new patients; there would be too much emotional
pressure.)

Further, there is an educational function in these early encounters. Koegler and Brill[6] found a much higher percentage of
psychotherapy contracts fulfilled to the satisfaction of patient and
doctor when there was a clear statement of what was expected of
the patient and what the patient could expect of the doctor. Such
contextual education increases the opportunity to mobilize conscious, responsible cooperation. It also provides a framework to

evaluate the degree of a patient's difficulty. It is meaningless to describe a patient's behavior and treatment as uncooperative, resistant, or inappropriate unless the expected is explicit. Sometimes, I have supervised psychotherapists who used such terms about a patient when the standard was inside the therapist's head rather than an open subject of discussion with his patient.

Mundane expectations such as appointment times, fees, and rights of cancellation must also be clear. I know of no data to support the often expressed idea that patients do better when they pay for their own therapy, but there is very good evidence that contextual confusion produces dysfunction and regression. If the patient is not told clearly what is expected of him, he is apt to do the unexpected; this behavior can be data for interpretations of various presumed ugly aspects of his personality, for example, underlying hostility, resistance, narcissism, sadism, and the like. The family studies make dramatically evident that mystification is the hallmark of severely disturbed human systems, and any psychotherapist who wishes to help his patients grow needs to keep in mind the importance of clarity. In trying to provide an atmosphere favorable to new learning, the therapist must avoid any qualities characteristic of disturbed families.

THE PURSUIT OF INTIMACY

Intimacy is inextricably intertwined with selfhood. Intimate (from the Latin word for *innermost*) relates to an inner character or essential nature. Webster quotes John Dewey in the definition, "It is in the purposes he entertains that an individual most completely realizes his *intimate* selfhood." Put simply, to be intimate is to be known, to have the innermost expressed and accepted. The family systems studies show that the most disturbed families, in offering little intimacy, hamstring the development of a capable self. In midrange families, intimacy, though scarce because of concern with control and pervasive power struggles, nevertheless appears, like flowers stubbornly peeking through cracks in city concrete. In the optimal families intimacy is most freely available, developed through their remarkable system qualities.

Symptoms of emotional illness are correlated with a subjective sense of being cut off, rejected, and excluded from others. Optimal treatment requires that a patient learn what intimacy is and how to obtain it. The data referred to in Chapter 6 suggest that psychotherapists who offer experiential learning in being known and accepted are most effective. Therapist potency is related to the capacity for offering a genuine intimate experience, and does not depend on the absolute cognitive input provided. Though a "non-playing coach" offering suggestions, technical advice, and helpful criticism, or listening and responding from anonymity may be helpful, such a therapist is less effective in promoting growth.

Growth-promoting therapy arose in response to the increasing awareness of the need to provide experiences in intimacy. Freud, the pioneer, advanced warily into the terra incognita of the human innermost with an understandably heavy armor of rigid compulsive defenses, and he advocated these defenses for therapists. When venturing alone into a strange and potentially dangerous territory, one uses every protection possible. There is safety in being a shadowy figure without unique values, feelings, and personal qualities that profoundly affect treatment results. If one develops a closed cognitive system that considers the relationship between therapist and patient only a result of the patient's inner drives and fantastic transference distortions, the fearsome other can be encountered with less anxiety.

Psychoanalytic revisionists, as Alexander, Horney, and especially Sullivan, were convinced of the importance of the treatment relationship, and they focused more intently on the nature of the patient/therapist interaction. But they stopped short of accepting the value of shared intimacy. It was left to Rogerians and classical existential therapists to describe vividly the usefulness of genuine human encounter in providing needed new learning for the emotionally disturbed person.

For a vulnerable, mistake-making mortal to become a thoroughly professional therapist, disciplined yet capable of providing intimate encounters, extensive experiential learning is necessary. All important schools of psychotherapy emphasize this fact and structure such learning. They recognize the essential problem that Freud encountered—how is one to expose himself to the innermost of another in a helpful way and not be damaged in the process? Training in technique, in ethics, and in the encouragement of a group identity as a member of a guild of honorable practitioners are methods to provide the individual therapist with the strength he needs to perform. There is implicit or explicit awareness that encountering the power of the innermost in another requires a secure personal identity only obtained by being a part of a group with shared values. Therapists, as well as patients, need a place to stand.

Seduction, by patient or therapist, is a real and continuing danger. Not just sexual seduction, which destroys the possibility of intimacy as assuredly as does incestuous sex, but a variety of manipulative uses of one person by another threaten the procedure. A patient can seduce a therapist to support his neurosis and inveigle him to side against a spouse. He may be capable of flattering the therapist into believing that the therapist is omniscient, able to provide absolute answers to eternally subjective questions. Conversely, a therapist may manipulate patients to "confirm" theory or act out the therapist's fantasies in a manner similar to parents in disturbed families.

All of these possible relationship perversions result in the betrayal of trust. This problem is addressed by all competent schools of psychotherapy as they attempt to develop integrity and trustworthiness in their members. There is no intimacy, no fruitful, healing encounter unless the therapist is trustable. I believe that the therapist's integrity and trustworthiness can only be developed and maintained by adhering to uncompromising honesty, a continual openness to patient questions as to motives and knowledge, a shared sense of community with others who perform as psychotherapists, and the development of an open system source of support, help, and criticism. Just as the severely disturbed centripetal families have the most closed system and the greatest isolation from the outside world, a therapist increases his potential for destructiveness by retreating to an insulated, isolated closed system of thought and relationships.

Though confidentiality is an important part of developing a trusting relationship, it is often used as a cover for running a "secret service" which supports closed-system thought. I have found it a boon always to have a trusted colleague available who is willing to receive my knotted-up feelings and thoughts about a patient. (I expect to respond in kind, though not necessarily in the same encounter.) The important point is that for patient and therapist alike, intimacy is furthered by having an open relationship system that eagerly includes others rather than shutting them out. People are more confident and trustable as they experience themselves a part of a valued social system, and can share with others the painful burden of decisions. Sharing is qualitatively different from unloading; one can share problems with others in an open system of relating. It is only by embracing a closed ideological system that decisions are abdicated. Here we encounter one of the myriad human paradoxes—intimacy is found in relationships open to the outside world; it is lost in walled-off twosomes. Further, a system of supportive relationships must itself be egalitarian to assist in the autonomy of a member, whether therapist or patient. To continue supervision with unequal power between supervisor and therapist years after training encourages an authoritarian, rigid, compulsive orientation rather than the development of intimacy. This is precisely analogous to parents who continue to relate to their own parents as authoritative, frightening, and intimidating; they therefore cannot be open and honest with their children. Somebody needs to present to the child or patient a model of a finite, limited but responsible person who does not evade responsibility by bowing to a superior, but models autonomy and personal responsibility in encounters.

In order to build trust and evolve intimacy, a therapist must be quite aware of the necessity for clarity in the contract. These expectations will need to be reiterated at intervals. In this way, the patient can see whether he is getting what he has bargained for. He may offer useful criticism that helps a therapist stay honest. I invite such feedback from patients, usually with a caveat, "I have an unconscious too." They can expect of me only conscious honesty, not god-like certainty.

This continual insistence on being received as an honest, uncertain, limited, but technically skilled person is important in reducing transference, an archenemy of intimacy (more about this later). It allows gradual education in adult trust which is *relative* trust, contrasted with the absolute trust desired by small children and disturbed adults.

As the experience of intimacy develops, the patient's self-esteem is raised, and his openness to risk is increased. Developing trust in himself acts as a powerful force to open up previously denied relationships and attitudes, and one result is the increase in the number of significant people in the patient's life. A systems analysis of relationships found in psychotic, neurotic, and normal people found that the meaningful people in the environment of the psychotic was five or six, ten to fifteen for the neurotic, and thirty to thirty-five for the healthy.[7] As the inner world of the self expands, the outer world similarly enlarges.

Disturbed individuals hunger for intimacy, but they are afraid that if they do not hide their inner being they will be worse off than they are presently. Rules of the family of origin are assumed to be the rules of the universe, and many hidden thoughts, fantasies, feelings, or behaviors are assumed to guarantee utter rejection if shared. Guilt is in direct proportion to the degree of hiddenness of the self; experience in shared intimacy is the only way to reduce this guilt. The psychotic individual has the greatest alienation and difficulty in sharing his hideous guilt. People suffering from severe depression and incapacitating obsessive compulsive neuroses rival the psychotic in guilt and the absence of intimate relationships. Individuals with mild and moderate neuroses have less incapacitating guilt and are able, in an accepting milieu, to show more of themselves without extensive therapy. With increasing experience in intimacy, a person increases his relationships, reduces his load of guilt, and raises his self-esteem. In short, he becomes healed.

Intimacy is to be sharply contrasted with regression. Intimacy is a healing force; regression is a fly in the ointment. Regression thrives on transference; intimacy is thwarted by it. Except for some unusual phenomena, for example, life-threatening psychosomatic illness,[8] the encouragement of regression by promoting transference has no place in psychotherapy. No data support the encouragement of transference or regression in psychotherapeutic endeavors to increase competence. When transference is encouraged rather than minimized, treatment time will lengthen and the results become more uncertain.

I will deal with transference and countertransference phenomena in a later section, but it is important to note here that transference is ubiquitous. It is not induced by the therapist but results from previous life experiences of the patient. If a therapist values the healing qualities of intimacy, he will resist at every turn the efforts of a patient to see him in a distorted way, rather than accepting or encouraging this unfortunate phenomenon.

POWER ISSUES

Because there is currently a hostile egalitarian thrust from some consumers and providers of psychotherapy that I believe to be misdirected and damaging to psychotherapist and patients alike, I wish to take pains to differentiate scientific, equal-powered psychotherapy from generalized attacks on society, authority, the "power structure," or any group of mental health professionals. Any demand for equal power in the treatment relationship that does not provide clearly defined role differences between therapist and patient is mischievous. Competent families illustrate that one can have equal-powered relationships without an oppositional set only if the roles are complementary. Any confusion of power issues and role definition produces a hopeless muddle.

A tennis coach can pursue professionalism while giving his pupil equal relationship power. An architect can be competent while respecting his client's subjective views, wishes and goals. Similarly, a psychotherapist may develop his complementary role definition while sharing overt power with the patient.

Technical words and concepts do not automatically make a power differential; diagnoses can be neutral, depending on what diagnoses are entertained and how they are used. There are certain concepts that *in themselves* are part of a superior power orientation and must be avoided by growth-oriented therapists; there are others which, when discussed with a patient, can be quite helpful in being more precise about the problems to be solved. Here are some problems in therapist behavior regarding diagnosis:

1) Communication with third parties. In *no way* can a therapist talk to family, to insurance companies, concerned employers, or any other outside person or group without the patient's knowledge and approval. Any comments, no matter how apparently benign, can reduce the social power of the patient. For example, one may be asked why the patient is in therapy. Responses such as "anxious," "upset," "lonely," can be as effective in torpedoing the patient's power position when spoken by an expert in human behavior as can obviously loaded descriptions such as "schizophrenic" or "sociopathic."

Yet people related in some way to the patient do call, and they are understandably put off if summarily rejected. My own way of dealing with this problem has both a practical and theoretical rationale. When family members call, I first try to determine whether the caller is aware that I see the person in question (some dishonest and indirect people engage in fishing expeditions). If my patient has informed the caller of his treatment contact with me I say that I want to be helpful, and if the patient wishes to invite the caller to share a visit, this will be agreeable to me, but such decisions belong to the patient. I further state that I will mention the call to my patient, and perhaps the two can have a discussion without using me as a go-between. This is important, since illicit bargains can be unwittingly made with family members by attempts to be discreet. Such misguided discretion can split therapist from patient and play into long-standing destructive family maneuvers.

Callers or writers who come as helpers in paying the bills (such as insurance companies) are increasingly important in psychotherapy; companies providing coverage for psychotherapy expect detailed information concerning the patient, particularly a diagnosis. Here the behavior of the therapist dramatically indicates the power aspects of the relationship. For an equal-powered relationship, any reports by the therapist must be read and approved by the patient, and negotiation occurs even in terms of the diagnosis itself.

For example, a 37-year-old, single, professional man began treatment because of continuing discomfort in relationships. He was perfectionistic, tedious, lonely, and mistrustful of others. As he engaged in therapy, his anxiety diminished, but he was still troubled by his inability to find friends or lovers. His insurance carrier asked for a diagnosis; I suggested that we use obsessive/compulsive neurosis since this was not only accurate, but would possibly allow him to receive more paid visits. He was mistrustful of how many people might have access to his records (I do not consider this paranoid but healthily suspicious) and, therefore, chose another diagnosis—anxiety neurosis—because he would rather gamble on his coverage than have what he considered a more severe diagnosis officially recorded. I was content with this, since either diagnosis (as a one-liner) described him, and the transaction increased his modest trust in me.

When patients realize the amount of personal information requested by insurance companies, they sometimes decide to pay for treatment themselves. This decision is not diagnostic of anything other than a high degree of awareness that computers are oblivious and so are many people who run them. I hope this discussion one day will be obsolete as we obtain adequate protection of privacy concerning illness, but it is sadly pertinent at present.

When a therapist works in a public clinic, the ethical and contextual problems are similar to those involving insurance companies. Any reports must be cleared with the patient. Related misunderstandings or disagreements are a part of the treatment process and facilitate growth-promoting therapy. Openness with the patient reduces a therapist's tendency to make power-oriented diagnoses and increases his effectiveness in being accountable to patients, to peers, and to courts.

There are some diagnoses that will be shunned by growth-oriented therapists and others that are descriptive and useful. One major criterion separates the two groups: "Does the diagnosis depend primarily on data available to patient and therapist?" Flagrant examples of diagnoses that rely on therapist power rather than the data for their significance include:

a) Latent conditions, e.g., latent homosexual, latent schizophrenia, latent behavior disturbance. These require no supporting data and represent a triumph of one person's fantasy life over another's.

b) Words and phrases that involve motivation, such as *masochistic* or *narcissistic*. If the person being labelled objects to these pejorative words, he has little recourse to data, since the material has been abstracted and filtered. An assumed expert opinion is stamped on the being of another. For example, "masochistic character" often means a person who fails repeatedly, which can be due to many reasons having nothing to do with any qualitative difference in responding to pain or pleasure. People who receive a diagnosis of narcissistic personality show less self-love than almost anyone. The label says little except that the labeller does not find the individual being labelled likeable.

c) Words and phrases that assume an objectified "real" world sharing the same attitudes and judgments as the labeller. These include such pejorative descriptions as "promiscuous," "acting-out" (when used in reference to presumably unwise, rather than illegal, behavior), "inappropriate," "paranoid" (when used to mean such things as, "He doesn't trust the insurance company, and I do.").

There are many diagnoses that rely on data and need to be a part of the professional's tool kit; for example, personality and character diagnoses that describe habitual behavior, such as compulsive, hysteric, passive/aggressive, and schizoid. When these words are used with patients, they can be defined clearly with examples of the behavior referred to. The interchange can assist in defining frequently used patterns that are mutually considered maladaptive.

In addition, there are many diagnoses related to symptoms, such as anxiety, depression, and psychosis. Most beginning treatment alliances will allow the use of such common words as anxious or depressed, but the powerful words related to a person's perception of the world such as psychotic, schizophrenic, and paranoid, though they may properly rely on data, can rupture a relationship if used insensitively. However, if there is too great an effort at diplomacy because of assumptions about the patient's feelings, the relationship can also suffer. As a resident, I was schooled in this problem of being overly diplomatic by an extraordinarily bright young nurse with paranoid schizophrenia. We were working in a hot basement room into which a buzzing fly had wandered. I picked up a newspaper while stating, "I've got to get that fly, he is driving me . . . . . , . " and I trailed off. She quickly began her supervision of me by asking how I could treat her, who was as crazy as a betsy bug, if I were frightened of using the word "crazy" in her presence. These words are a double-edged blade, and should be used carefully in discussing behavior or speech which seem out of social bounds, bizarre, and hence crazy. If these words are clearly defined as representing the therapist's subjective view of his patient's social functioning, they can further treatment. If institutional realities require giving a patient such a diagnosis, it is wise to take pains to define the label in a data-oriented fashion consistent with concepts of consensual validation.

The handling of overt power was a significant variable in the family system studies. In severely disturbed families, individual boundary confusion and mystification resulted in nebulous power which was likely to exist side by side with obvious impotence. Midrange families exert a constant effort to establish and maintain an overt power differential, and control is a major concern. Optimal families value intimacy in relating, and overt power is shared by all members. Sharing of overt power obviates the need for an illicit network, the backdoor power characteristic of disturbed human systems. If the aboveboard game can't be trusted, one tries to obtain gratification in a covert world of illicit games with others in and outside the family. In optimal families, the overt power differential decreased as a child moved toward adulthood. Competence was rewarded with increasing freedom of choice and autonomy. This system effectively abolishes the need for impotent/omnipotent relationships. Patients rarely, if ever, come from such a family.

The impotent/omnipotent pattern, always covert and illicit when extended beyond infancy, continues in the family of origin. Many years of training in the family setting have taught the patient that attempting competence is less effective than being helpless or rendering the other person helpless. These maneuvers, which may appear quite different at first blush, are twins. In an impotent/omnipotent interaction, it is impossible to determine who controls—whether hypnotized or hypnotist, tyrant or tyrannized, sadist or masochist, all-powerful therapist or submissive patient, or (the original template) mother/infant. The therapist of emotional illness really has two choices—to play the game of overt power differential and use coercion or persuasion, or to accomplish what the family of origin failed to do, provide an environment for self-development, increasing awareness of personal power, and greater interpersonal skills. If the therapist chooses the growth-oriented method, he must avoid relationship patterns that encourage or enforce overt power differential.

Here is another paradox. If the patient did not think his therapist was more powerful than he, he wouldn't come to see him. Training, degrees, experience, and kudos are necessary for a therapist's becoming accepted by peers and public, and these encourage a power differential. The growth-promoting therapist needs to possess as much power as possible and then throw it away, that is, share it generously with his patient. The pattern is similar to the role of parent who automatically has power with an infant and needs to relinquish it as the child becomes an adult. I have never been able to help anyone who saw himself as having more overt power than I; yet, I have never been able to help anyone grow who insists on seeing me as more powerful than he.

This conundrum may be what once caused psychiatrists to be known as *alienists*. I like the word; it calls attention to the social borderline so important in treating emotional illness. If a therapist has little social power, he is useless since he cannot give what he does not have. He must be comfortable with, and respected by, the larger community or he fails, but he must also be able to relate empathically to the wistful child in his patient. There is a displaced person residing in us all, a stranger in a strange land, who, if isolated, becomes a destructive force. Freud recognized this force and postulated a biologically destructive component in man. Growth-promoting therapists avoid the destructive potential of the impotent/omnipotent relationship. If a therapist opts for an omnipotent role, he must either be quick and skilled, raise the patient's morale and then disappear, to be remembered fondly from a distance; or he must be part of a powerful (e.g. hospital) system that is well-nigh omnipotent *in fact*, in comparison to a patient's meager personal power. If he elects to offer a patient an opportunity for ego development lacking in the original family, he must negotiate an equal-powered, open contract as soon as possible. His first sentence may be the beginning of a redefinition and a new experience in relating.

A depressed minister began his relationship with me by saying, "I want to put myself under your care." I immediately began to define our bargain, "I will help you as best I can with your pain and your problems, but I will not and cannot have you *under* me, and would be repulsed by it." I did not go into any other implications that the remark might have had at the time. Momentarily startled, the man pursued this, and treatment began.

All effective systems of growth-promoting therapy deal with the ominous threat of a therapist's being defeated by another's "weakness," his compliance, docility and impotence. Freudian orthodoxy warns the practitioner against concern about the patient's improvement. This can break the patient's hold, but raises the spectre of withdrawal, lack of investment in the encounter, and operational sadism. Gestaltists interpret all interaction as projection and use interpretations as judo to place the patient in the responsible "hot seat." Rogerians deal with this ominous possibility by avoiding responsibility for the patient's direction, and they try to care for the patient without being saddled with the blame of failure. Existential therapists may express despair, helplessness, and, occasionally, hopelessness to avoid the patient's control by relative impotence. Behavioral therapists accept the responsibility for cure but present themselves as technicians of an incomplete science, and patient failure is not defined as therapist failure but an illustration of the need for further research. All of these technical devices are efforts to mobilize the potential strengths of the patient, encourage his competence and render a therapeutic alliance possible.

This therapeutic alliance is necessarily based on evolving trust—trust in the patient's powers for healing and growth; trust in the therapist to avoid manipulating or being manipulated, and trust in the relationship.

A conscious effort to reduce the power differential will increase the therapist's effectiveness. One of the many ways a therapist communicates his expectation of shared power is through office props—the furniture and its placement. I have two identical chairs placed in an arrangement where the heads of occupants are about six feet from each other. I invite the patient to choose either of these chairs on his initial visit and any other time that he hesitates before being seated. (This concrete statement of expected equality is most easily grasped by the most disturbed patients.) The goal is to avoid the set of a "doctor's chair," a throne of privilege that negates other attempts at communicating the desire for equal power. A popular television show, *All in the Family*, has dramatized this power gambit: Archie Bunker defends *his* chair, which is a little more elegant and comfortable, putting others clearly in a less powerful place. The therapist who is aware of such manuevers can eliminate iatrogenic "transference" problems requiring months of "interpretation." A growth-promoting therapist carefully avoids behavior or communication that produces the illness he then attempts to treat.

As the encounter begins, with a context inviting equal power, the interaction must support this reality, emphasizing that the patient's subjective reality is an important as the therapist's—no more so, but decidedly not less.

For example, a patient comes to treatment with profound hopelessness; he feels trapped in a profession that gives him no pleasure and in a marriage with a chronically dissatisfied wife. After an evaluation, the therapist will have some idea of this person's strengths and weaknesses in relating. He would be insensitive and ineffective to suggest immediately solutions preferred from his own viewpoint—for example, stay with the job, get training for a new one, or court the wife. Such suggestions, though a common effort at helpfulness, express an implicit attempt at maintaining greater overt power. They implicitly state, "My reality is more significant, more correct, than yours." The person coming for help has been wrestling with his problems for some time; the therapist has struggled with them for only a little while. There is contempt in suggesting that a simple way out is to be found in the therapist's wisdom rather than in the patient's choice. Such suggestions invite immediate transference, either negative, or apparently positive, if the patient believes in the implication that the helper can direct him out of his wilderness.

A more honest alternative is to try to experience the patient's feelings and explore with him his previous efforts at solving the overwhelming problems. This is perhaps less dramatic, but consistent with respect between peers, the significance of the evolving relationship, and the reality that living problems are frequently difficult and knotty.

This insistence on defining the expert as knowledgeable about human problems rather than about proper decisions is a part of the overall effort to improve the patient's morale. By taking his dilemma seriously, the invitation to solve problems together is clear. The therapist senses the patient's feelings of helplessness produced by a sense of isolation; acknowledging this awareness diminishes the loneliness. People with serious emotional problems believe their feelings are too ridiculous or contemptible to share, or that others do not care. The attempt to shift a patient's perceptions to more effective and hopeful ones by offering solutions too quickly usually backfires. The patient can easily believe he has found another person who misunderstands, increasing his alienation and desire to withdraw.

I try to make understandable the concept that many problems not solvable either by patient or by therapist alone (no matter how knowledgeable) surrender to a joint effort. This notion communicates many important aspects of growth-oriented treatment: Being alone reduces one's power and capabilities; looking to others for solutions is futile; but working on a problem with an equal partner changes people in useful ways. I try to give a struggling person the necessary cognitive and experiential awareness of the role of fellow scientist. To receive help, he need not subject himself to an authority but instead is invited to dialogue about viable solutions to his problems. The expression of his choice is necessary for a good outcome.

Such dialogue is crucial to increase autonomy, self-esteem, and confidence in personal choice, yet no one who enters a patienthood is experienced in the practice. There has usually been a "right" way handed down by the family referee, or a constant contextual ambiguity that defeated efforts at clarifying personal wishes, choices, and goals. With statements and the actual experience, the therapist makes his patient aware of a new way of solving problems. Nothing magical or superhuman is expected of either partner, though the power resulting from a shared, equal relationship is often close to magic.

This is the primary technique of scientific growth-oriented psychotherapy—*problem-solving by two equal-powered humans who develop increasing respect for one another through struggling with a series of shared goals*.

Though equal in power, their roles are vastly different. Payment for the therapist's services becomes quite significant in defining these role differences. Whether such payment comes directly from a patient or from a third party (family members, insurance companies, or the institution that pays the therapist), it highlights the social contract that a disciplined and responsible therapist is to meet with a patient who also has a respected, powerful role.

The therapist is not there because of altruism, though he focuses on the needs of his patient rather than on his own needs. He tries to make only those decisions that are his, rather than those that are his patient's. In times of personal stress, I have immersed myself in this work with some relief and comfort in the clear and unmuddled role function. The hard work necessary to establish a clear relationship of shared responsibility has been helpful to my morale as well as to the patient's. There is comfort in the fact that I am not responsible *for*, but *to*, my patient. This allows closeness without exploitation of either person.

I have treated many patients referred by sensitive, concerned, non-professional therapists (for example, ministers) who do not have this protective barrier of payment. Because I see the problems resulting from such interaction, I believe it is too much to ask of any human that he focus over a prolonged period of time on the living problems of another without payment for this demanding task. The relationship must be relatively brief, or it will deteriorate into a mutual search for satisfaction that confuses and confounds the context. If meeting a suffering person's needs has no other reward than its own satisfactions, no human can keep from using that person in ways that frustrate growth. Equal power does not mean equal emotional rewards.

PROBLEM-SOLVING WITH ANOTHER: THE SCIENTIFIC METHOD

In Chapter 1, the description of a 20th-century scientific method was presented with the suggestion that this method is the most powerful tool of a growth-oriented psychotherapist. Popper has proposed that the basic structure of science is not its information but its methodology; science is not so much a body of knowledge, but a way of dialoguing with others.[9] This definition of science allows psychotherapists to take a position in the forefront of science, rather than settling for a modest back pew with a few research results clutched in outstretched hands, hoping for a legitimacy magnanimously given by practitioners of "hard" science. If we understand the scientific method well and practice it daily with our patients as competent technicians, the final results of growth-promoting encounters will be unique and new, tailored by shared experiences. We must acquaint ourselves with Freudian, Sullivanian, Gestaltist, existentialist, and behavior theory concepts and offer them to our suffering patients as we consider them useful. Never for one moment, however, can we assume that our power is due to quantitative knowledge. We must always be ready to learn something new, to discover along with our fellow scientists—the patients—their particular reality. In this way, we progress just as the leaders of psychotherapeutic schools progressed. In this way I can consider myself a Freudian, a Rogerian, and a Sullivanian. As these humanist scientists did, we do: risk the unknown with our patients, coming ever closer to truth that eternally eludes us.

A therapeutic alliance based on mutual respect and developing trust can have no preconceived answers for that patient. For example, a patient presents himself with a common problem: He has a painful marriage with great resentment of his spouse who is seen as uncooperative and unrewarding. To solve such a problem, the patient will either develop a better relationship with his wife, divorce and find another more gratifying partner, or continue the marriage and develop other satisfying relationships. These outside relationships, sexual or non-sexual, will be either with or without the knowledge of the spouse. (I know of no other possible solutions, but I wait for a patient who shows me another viable alternative.)

I do not define any of these solutions as the best, most mature, or healthy and, hence, the "proper" solution; I cannot. I have seen people who have tried every one of these and made a miserable mess of things; I have seen others who have been emotionally gratified by choosing any one of them. Nothing in my training or science can tell me what is mature or proper for a particular patient. As I struggle with the patient in his effort to solve his problem, I will offer all these possibilities, the widest spectrum that I know. I will then work with him to find the solution best fitted to his own unique situation. I will consider my therapeutic task completed when he is reasonably content, has good morale, and takes responsibility for his thoughts, feelings and actions.

The necessity for such a pragmatic, undoctrinaire therapeutic position is largely a product of our current social milieu. At this time in this country, all of the choices listed above have been found satisfactory to somebody and acceptable to the broader world. Citizens are radically, and often pathetically, free from socially reinforced, arbitrary definitions of proper performance. As a result, ego strength and the ability to make autonomous choices are needed more than ever before. An individual is not automatically rewarded for staying in any particular living situation. There is no social bulwark for absolute answers. This places the patient and therapist in a rather awkward position if "objective" answers are sought, but in an excellent position if the scientific method is used.

Functioning in this way eliminates many tedious and pointless arguments and resistance; as the therapist refuses to offer his biases as fact, therapist and patient are free to find workable solutions. Such work never challenges any deeply held religious beliefs of a patient; if they are meaningful to him, they are a part of his solution.

Carrying on such a dialogue with a peer is frequently exciting, sometimes frustrating, but always absorbing. I approach each session with a sense of anticipation much as I used to approach a research question when I had no fixed answers, but a method.

To reiterate Popper's description of the scientific method: We stumble on some problem; we try to solve it, for example, by proposing some theory. We try to learn from our mistakes, especially those brought home to us by the critical discussion of our tentative solutions. In these three words, "Problems . . . theories . . . criticism . . ." the whole procedure of natural science may be summed up.[9] This deceptively simple description is the bare bones of the growth-oriented psychotherapy method. Ego development is the extension of the method into human relationships. Satisfying, self-defining experiences occur as a patient works with an increasingly trusted and meaningful real person who does not fit into previously known slots of judgmental parent or manipulatable playmate. The driving force that brings most people into patienthood is pain—the severe emotional pain of living in isolation without direction, responsible choice, or satisfying decisions. An equal-powered relationship reduces this pain even before solutions are found.

Perhaps examples of treatment methods that fail to follow this approach may illustrate its value. Stein, writing of success and failure in psychoanalysis and psychotherapy,[10] gives two provocative case illustrations:

A young man with a schizoid personality came into treatment because of depressive symptoms and the inability to function. After some time in treatment he had improved, but was still unable to work. A wealthy uncle became interested and offered to help him in various ways including a job. The patient began to work, developed a close relationship to the uncle, who gave him many gifts, had him assigned to a well paying job and so on. Because the uncle was an unstable person and the help he offered was excessive and unrealistic, the therapist attempted to help the patient forego some of this and try to work out something for himself. The patient reacted with anger to these attempts and abruptly left treatment.

A young woman with two children came into treatment because of depressive symptoms related to her marriage. She was a dependent, narcissistic person with few resources of her own. The marriage was a pathological, sado-masochistic one, but the husband, although disturbed, was devoted to his wife. Her own family had been disrupted and, except for the husband, she had no one except a sick mother. The therapist tried to help her adjust to the difficulties in the marriage since she had nowhere else to turn. After some time in treatment, during which she had several depressive episodes in relation to her marital difficulty, she left her husband and left treatment.

Stein's comment in both of these instances was that the therapist had sought to help the patient in the direction the therapist defined as becoming independent and handling difficult situations better. The patients' goals were along different lines and, in order to achieve these, they left treatment. "Here therapeutic zeal was one of the major factors in the failure of the treatment."

Stein's conclusion was consistent with the Freudian method to combat patient helplessness; a therapist should be effective by remaining aloof, resisting the impulse to be involved.

This bland lack of involvement unnecessarily reduces therapist potency; emotional intensity is a necessary aspect of psychotherapeutic success. However, if a therapist is so blind to his biases and so deficient in his knowledge of the requirements for ego development as to assume that he knows what a patient should do, it is certainly better to reduce his "therapeutic zeal," since he will be, at least, less destructive.

With a knowledge of one's limits and respect for the subjective reality of patient and therapist, a therapeutic alliance can develop that is both more intense and less controlling. In the case of the young man, does the therapist actually perceive reality so much better than the patient? Can he diagnose instability in people he has never seen, and unilaterally decide what is healthy? I think not.

In the second case, the arrogance of closed-system thinking is apparent. Pigeonholing, pejorative labels pass for diagnosis, for example, "dependent," "narcissistic." This is omniscience in the guise of therapy. "The therapist tried to help her adjust to the difficulties of the marriage since she had nowhere else to turn." In her struggle to develop some autonomy, to choose and risk new patterns of behavior, the poor woman had to renounce not only her husband *but also her therapist,* who attempted psychotherapy via labelling and enforcing his own view of reality, rather than problem-solving with a partner.

In both of these cases, the essential respect for the other's point of view and right to choose goals was lacking. The errors had less to do with excessive zeal or over-concern for the patient's well-being than with closed-system thinking. The therapist who places his opinion above the patient's rules out the possibility of a therapeutic alliance unless the patient throws off one tyrant by accepting another. The scientific method obviates such treatment difficulties and is a growth-promoting way out of many problems, often ascribed to transference, built into the context of treatment. With the proper humility of a good workman who knows what he does not know, the therapist can express rather than inhibit his human desire to be helpful; for example, he can explore alternative solutions with the young man. Does he want to accept his uncle's help and avoid being trapped? Can he get on his feet financially, learn as much as he can about the business, and then, if he chooses, change jobs?

The uncle is a reality, regardless of whether the therapist wishes to include him in a cramped view of the realistic world. The therapist's efforts to increase "reality testing" parallel those of mid-range parents to help their children grow up by urging them to come to their senses and do what the parents believe is right. Many patients recognize this repetition of their own developmental history and leave treatment with a greater sense of aloneness. Theoretical systems with fixed definitions of health, unrelated to context or to individual choices, encourage this therapeutic arrogance; the therapist may be less capable of reality testing than his patient.

Let us use problem-solving with the first patient and see where it leads us. He comes into treatment with depression, poor self-esteem, and an inability to function. His morale is understandably low. The therapist explores his past and present relationships and finds that his family defined him as a rather inept and bumbling person in the shadow of an older brother and a controlling father. During this exploration, a therapeutic alliance develops and the patient feels better since he is no longer alone, but, alas, he is still not productive. When, from out of the blue his wealthy uncle bestows a job, personal interest, and gifts, he is functional, loved in some ways, and enjoys a previously denied place in the sun. He then explores his new surroundings and relationships and finds new problems. His autonomy, though significantly greater than that of an unemployed, depressed man, is only relative. Without real competence in his job, he will encounter new dissatisfactions and pain in work relationships, perhaps including others' resentment and envy over his unearned position. His success, if more form than substance, must be reinforced by developing skills. In his new position of relative power, what skills would the patient like to develop? If he hopes for heterosexual success, he will have an easier opportunity to approach women from his newfound power position. Therapeutic dialogue concerning problems, possible solutions, experimentations, review of success and failure, and required new behavior can develop satisfying, self-defining experiences in treatment and outside. Self-esteem can become less dependent on the largesse of an uncle and more dependent on personal capabilities.

This process of partnership could continue forever, but it does not. If life becomes rewarding, the paid relation to a therapist, with its many limitations, pales in comparison to evolving relationships with friends and lovers with whom a patient experiences the ability to help as well as to be helped. The patient can define himself as normal as he replaces the one-sided role of patient with the more complete possibilities of shared love and shared need.

Such treatment experiences are common for all effective psychotherapists who have transcended the limits of a particular system. This symbolic case may dramatize the opportunity for psychotherapists of any school to work as scientific humanists, with mutual discovery as the method. The use of problem-solving opens horizons for exploring, for shared learning, and for being useful to patients without indoctrination other than that which is unconscious, or inadvertent. By avoiding a dreary repetition of absolutes, the promotion of growth can rival that of optimal families.

INTERPRETATION VS. NEGOTIATION

This treatment method requires giving up interpretation in the conventional sense. To interpret, defined as to explain the meaning of, is an impossibility. Another definition of interpretation, however, is to explain a phenomenon as *it seems to me*; this is intensely and overtly subjective and the beginning of the problem-solving process. Adolph Meyer pioneered this concept of interpretation. From his abhorrence of dogmatism, one could consider treatment a process in which the patient comes to the doctor with one idea of what is wrong with him, the doctor has another, and psychotherapy consists of the two getting together.

I have found that I think of some patients as Freudian; most of the hypotheses that come to mind as we struggle with their dilemmas are classical analytic concepts. Other patients define themselves to me as Sullivanian, since most of their problems seem to be related to identity and personal boundaries. Some, troubled with difficulties or phobias, appear to me as candidates for behavioral modification. Still others initially (and all patients, at some point) struggle with existential problems, wishing to find purpose, goals, and meaning for themselves.

We make progress as we negotiate. We criticize each other's hypotheses and come to mutually acceptable conclusions. Patient and therapist alike experience competence, with both possessing only a glimpse of the awesome mystery of living.

Sharing and negotiating begin to be seen as not just a method of treatment but a way of relating in all other meaningful, potentially close relationships. These skills assist one in being successful in many relationship systems, since we are all finite beings in an infinitely complex world.

Self- or ego-development is the process of becoming, of becoming alive and related to others, relinquishing childhood's demand for absolutes—absolute trust, truth, or gratification. If we find people who are relatively satisfying, sensible, and trustable, we have moved from the child's desire for omnipotence (or impotence—the same mental set) to a satisfying, competent position, accepting a world of infinite possibilities and threats with limited skills, limited friends and loved ones. Interpretation, in the sense of providing meaning, thwarts this growth process by placing the patient in an untenable position: He must either deny his own subjective reality to maintain a treatment relationship or else claim his own perceptions and be defined as resistant, willful, or even bad. One always needs others, but in many human situations, affiliation is at the expense of denying a part of oneself. If significant others see one's subjective reality as bizarre or erroneous, one can either conform and lie or suffer the terror of aloneness. This dilemma is found not only in families that produce schizophrenics but also in those that produce sane but limited offspring, and is inadvertently present in therapeutic situations where absolute reality is presumed.

A patient came to a session five minutes late; the therapist interpreted this behavior as resistance to growth, treatment and the therapist. The patient responded that, as a matter of fact, he wasn't resistant. He had started at his usual time but encountered road repairs in front of the therapist's building that necessitated driving on a different street and parking at a distance from the office. So far, so good: One subjective reality faced a different one. His therapist, however, persisted in his own interpretation to the point of suggesting that the patient distorted the problem he had encountered. By this response, the therapist aborted an alliance; the possibility of negotiation was destroyed. The success of this sort of interpretation depends on a power differential which has no place in growth-oriented therapy.

The therapist might have said, "Well, you have been a bit late for three sessions, and I believe that your behavior is saying something that is out of your awareness. Let's see how it goes the next few visits." He would then have compromised neither his own reality nor his patient's. The appeal would have been to data rather than to a closed system that requires a power advantage. Interpretation of an absolute nature puts the patient in a need/fear dilemma; it repeats rather than alters the impact of previous disturbed family experience. A patient must become a compliant child to be defined as "good." The result is either a battle, with the patient using his impotent/omnipotent weapons, thus creating a never-ending job for the well meaning therapist or, alternatively, termination of the treatment effort.

The problem-solving approach requires explanations and methods of attaining goals defined as satisfactory *by the patient* and the therapist can always learn something new. (The aforementioned therapist might have had to detour when he left his office that afternoon!)

By relying on negotiation one avoids questions of how "deep" interpretation should be. Such a simple observation as, "You are angry," made because a patient sits tensely with whitened knuckles and an attacking phrase on his lips, may give way in negotiation to the remarkable discovery that the patient in his perception of reality feels scared to death and is unaware of any anger. The therapist's sensation of an angry patient, the patient's sensation of fear, may allow them both to learn of the intimate relationship between these two emotions and of the importance of being aware of two realities. Further exploration may assist the patient in learning that he characteristically covers his fear with hostile body language, and this in turn provokes others to counterattack, thus reinforcing his fear.

Exploration, negotiation, and mutual discovery are the processes that solve interpersonal problems. The spuriously objective interpretation of, "You're angry," can be received as one more dreary repetition of attack from a hostile world, even more painful when it comes from someone who is supposed to help.

A more abstract observation, such as, "You mistrust your mother, yet you are drawn to seductive, lonely women who remind you of her," can be received in the spirit of negotiation if the data for such a perception have been brought out in the mutual struggle. It is always better, however, even with the data available and dealt with, to approach such interpretations as the subjective reality that they are. It is useful to begin such an observation with, "It seems to me that . . ."

The "depth" of interpretative offering, then, is as acceptable as the data mutually available. It does not require great intuitive powers on the part of the therapist if he adheres to this respectful negotiation.

Frequent therapist input at a low level of inference fosters an equal-powered relationship. The data are fresh for discussion, the dependence on shared memory is lessened, and emotional intensity is encouraged. Frequent monologues on the part of the patient or therapist work against the capacity for intimacy, but a give-and-take discussion between equals increases this vital kind of learning.

THE PATIENT AS SUPERVISOR

If the therapist cannot rely on clearly defined truths of a particular treatment school for certainty, if he deliberately questions the infallibility of his theories, and if he respects a patient's subjective reality as much as his own, how can he be comfortable? What can he depend on for the reassurance he at times badly needs? It is important to realize that he has many advantages: His own position is quite secure and he has more power than he can use if he keeps it all for himself. It is surprising how well patients take to the idea that the therapist can be wrong and that he may need them to straighten him out from time to time. They do not need a positive transference to come back regularly and to think well of him.

The therapist can also develop supervision by peers, sharing problems in a small group which offers support, insights, and a sense of community.

In addition, he can learn to use his patient as supervisor. When disagreements between therapist and patient arise (one hopes from patient transference or projective distortions), he can invite the patient to criticize him, using shared data as the material.

The rules are simple: "I make an agreement with you that includes responsible efforts at problem-solving and respecting your subjective reality. I invite you to criticize me as any point that you believe I am not fulfilling my bargain, but you must also respect my own subjective view of reality. My views are no more important in the relationship but no less so."

For example, it is not uncommon for a patient to believe that the therapist is angry with him. This might be so. Everyone has an unconscious, and countertransference or real interactional phenomena can potentially compromise the alliance. Prior discussion reduces the patient's expectations of therapist omniscience and grooms him to be a supervisor.

If a patient suggests that I am angry with him, and I am not conscious of such feelings, I invite him to experiment with me just as he is learning to experiment in relations beyond the office. We will look at the data from which this perception is derived. Sometimes, none appears—good! We have discovered transference or projection resulting from living in the past rather than in the present.

Or there *are* data—I have cut off comments, pursued questioning more like a district attorney than a caring person. This is more serious. When the behavior is brought to my attention, do I experience the accuracy of the observation? If so, and we agree that the

anger expressed was a shabby and unfair intrusion into the relationship, I apologize and invite comment if the behavior recurs (usually I am then aware of some displacement, and will indicate it). I don't claim perfection, just an attempt at honesty within my limits.

However, If I become aware of the anger, and it seems to belong to the real transaction, my error is not in the feeling, but in having been unaware of it. Trust is a two-way street, and sometimes I become angry if a patient, to my perception, betrays the treatment bargain. Perhaps there is an underlying contemptuous tone to the patient's relationship to me that needs to be examined. It can be a clue to problems that the patient has with many people with whom he wishes intimacy. The leverage of an equal-powered alliance allows such confrontation and response, with better functioning of the patient and therapist as the goal.

But what if (heaven forbid!) I am accused of being angry, and the data presented lead me to no greater awareness of such feelings than I had before the confrontation? Such an impasse causes rifts in many relationships, and it can do so in therapy. Yet these are events that can bring about vital new learning necessary to heal the doctrinaire mistrust found in all patients who suffer from emotional illness.

I suggest that for the moment the supervisor/patient accept our disagreement and my own sovereignty as to my inner world. I depend on the many times that I have treated his inner feeling states as worthy of respect, never to be denied by anyone outside that subjective world. Respect for ego boundaries cuts both ways. We will follow our interaction together, and if the patient experiences a recurrence of the behavior that leads him to mistrust my feelings, perhaps we can both learn something. He may learn from me a different reason for my behavior, and I may learn from him unexpected ways that my behavior is interpreted. The acceptance of understood differences leads to an experimental appreciation of subjective truth that is always modifiable. Even highly mistrustful patients can thus be gratifying supervisors.

EGO-SYNTONIC AND EGO-DYSTONIC PARTS OF THE SELF

A regular requirement of psychotherapy with offspring of mid-range families is the alteration of fixed and rigid attitudes and behaviors (usually unconscious) derived from primary family experience. These beliefs and behavior patterns were once useful, even necessary, but they are now maladaptive and a prominent part of the current difficulty.

As the therapist explores a living problem with the patient partner, he recognizes these patterns as a source of pain before the patient does. A premature attack on these rigid, unexamined, but treasured (ego-syntonic) responses will be experienced by the patient as an attack on the self to be defended at all costs. As the patient's trust in the treatment alliance grows, and his dissatisfaction with present solutions increases, he will accept direct challenges with relative equanimity as the familiar responses have become ego-dystonic—identified as a source of pain and deprivation.

Spurious solutions to living problems that require, for example, submissiveness, helplessness and suffering can be challenged successfully only by focusing on the present rather than the past. The patient is no longer a helpless child whose survival depends on adapting to the family rule system. In the present, he has potentially greater power and is as much needed by others as he needs them. Gradual recognition of personal power, and differentiation of now from then, make stereotyped, childhood solutions to living problems ego-dystonic—ego alien—foreign to one's present self-image. Treatment can then proceed more comfortably for all concerned.

To identify these previously unexamined patterns as having been useful in a time of relative powerlessness in the primary family is an honest and face-saving approach to help the patient give them up. They are not wrong in any absolute sense; they are simply anachronisms in the present context.

For example, a 47-year-old married professional woman came to treatment because of chronic, severe depression. After many undepressed years in another state, her husband's precipitious decision to change careers required them and their three children to uproot and come to a (for her) strange environment. She became severely depressed and remained so for two years prior to seeking help. This woman had been raised in a rigid, low-midrange family where helplessness has been the only power method available to family members other than the father, who was tyrannically dominant. Though her mother and older brother had had extended periods of severe emotional problems, until this dislocation she had been relatively capable.

During treatment, it became clear that her continued depression served the purpose of punishing her husband for his unilateral decision which had radically disturbed her world. She reminded me of a displaced person, a political refugee, who cannot exert his energies to improve his lot without betraying a cherished self-image of suffering and being a living evidence of another's betrayal.

Her depression was a pattern of power-through-helplessness taught through her primary family system and revived by circumstances that produced impotent anger. I enthusiastically responded to any attempts she made to solve pressing problems in her new situation but was quite unsupportive and often hostile to her depressive attitudes and behavior. Our relationship was tenuous and volatile over a six-month period. I could not be an honest therapist who cared about her finding some pleasure in living and yet be silent about such a self-defeating maneuver. As long as she held the depression in an ego-syntonic fashion, she presented me with a dilemma: If I accepted her I was a party to perpetuating her pain, and if I attacked the depressive solution, I was attacking her. Finally she began to work as a more trusting partner in exploring methods of obtaining gratification from her husband, enjoying her children (with whom she had never had much pleasure) and finding outlets for her considerable talents. The turning point occurred as she identified her depressive pattern as ego-alien and saw me as an ally rather than an attacking, uncaring amalgam of both father and husband. Electing to operate in the here and now with the goal of personal satisfaction provided a new and more effective self-definition.

The most enduring aspect of a growth-oriented treatment experience is the development of a self that is aware of its own needs and can examine solutions on their merits rather than blindly following a dictated way of thinking and behaving. Personal choice then becomes an experiential reality. The effective therapist must avoid replacing one referee with another—himself. He must not claim power other than that of a competent technician. If he can maintain the legitimacy of his own and his patient's subjective views of the world, attend to the patient's definition of problems, and insist on using data to arrive at solutions, he assists the patient's expanded self-definition.

TRANSFERENCE AND COUNTERTRANSFERENCE

I shall begin a discussion of transference with an operational definition of a term often poorly defined. Greenson's, quite similar to Freud's, will be used: "The experiencing of impulses, feelings, fantasies, attitudes, and defenses with respect to a person in the present which do not appropriately fit that person, but are a repetition of responses originating in regard to significant persons of early childhood, unconsciously displaced onto persons in the present."[11] The two outstanding characteristics here are *non-selective repetition of the past* and the *ignoring or distorting of data in the present*. Sullivan's concept of parataxic distortion is similar. Behavior therapists approach the phenomenon in terms of conditioning. Gestaltists prefer to speak of "projection." Whatever the language, all growth-oriented therapists must deal with it.

I will speak in the language of transference and countertransference because of their general usage. However, I hope it is apparent from the family systems material that such concepts are cramped in explaining human reality in comparison to the subtle and complex realities of whole environments and relationships from the original family which are introjected and available for the interpretation of present reality. Speaking of "seductive mothers" or

"passive fathers" is a useful exercise but does an injustice to the human unconscious which carries within it whole systems.

The richness of relationships always includes an admixture of memory, fantasy, and present fact. To love is to see Cleopatra or Apollo in the loved one—the phenomenon is real, is fantasy, and is transference all at once. Such richness is no less true in the therapist/patient relationship. Friedman pointedly draws attention to this: "Two warnings for the therapist: Don't think that insistent troublesome strivings are the anerobic product of a sealed reality-proof id which he can sanitize with a little fresh air. They have grown up in the light of reality, these drives. Second, take heed that the reality with which you hope to reform the drives is half made by those drives—which is something to think about when next involved in an insistent erotic transference."[12]

Becoming aware that reality is made up of such a complex admixture of past and present, drives, fantasies and transference will intimidate the most stalwart of closed-system theorists. It requires an open system, a negotiative approach, to promote human growth.

Transference is ubiquitious and inevitable in human relationships. It is not damaging unless it interferes with adaptation to present reality, blotting out or distorting new data. As Anna Freud said, "With due respect for the necessary and strident handling and interpretation of the transference, I feel still that we should leave room somewhere for the realization that analyst and patient are also two real people of equal adult status and in a real personal relationship with each other."[13]

There is no place in growth-oriented psychotherapy for the fostering of transference—the deliberate effort to decrease genuine encounter by procedures calculated to distance; they will augment distorted perceptions. Self- or ego-development occurs in spite of transference, not because of it. Transference is accompanied by childlike regression and loss of overt power. When patients find that in the midst of overwhelming problems they have choice, personal adequacy, and relative autonomy in the relationship with the therapist, they can increase living skills without recourse to fantasies of god-like others. This is true regardless of patient diagnosis. Though lingering controversy exists on the point, it is centered not around severely disturbed people[1,5] or behavior disorders,[14] but on relatively healthy neurotics,[11] and even here the controversy revolves around theory rather than on conflicting data.[15]

All of the foregoing discussion of treatment can be seen as an effort to provide a powerful treatment alliance that does not augment transference and regression. Contextual clarity, the offering of equal power, the effective destruction of myths of certainty—all contribute. Searching for strengths already present, helping to make them effective, and expanding them in partnership with the sufferer discourage transference regression. In addition, the therapist must give himself permission to be an honest, genuine human who accepts full responsibility for his own intense feelings and occasional blind spots. I empathize with Bernstein when he says, "I am inclined to attribute many treatment failures to the prohibition against compassionate behavior on the part of psychoanalysts that misapplication of the fear of countertransference and the abstinence rule has led to. In the face of the patient's transference demand 'help me' an analyst must and should feel the countertransference demand of compassion."[16] And with Greenson who says, "Perhaps we should be more aware of the fact that persistent anonymity and prolonged affective atherosclerosis can also be seductive, but generally in the direction of inviting an irreversible and uninterpretable hostile transference and alienation.[11] Bernstein, however, defines transference and countertransference so broadly as to make it difficult to feel good about receiving or giving feelings in a treatment relationship. Such definitions are much like calling all sex by the name of rape and then trying to differentiate between appropriate and inappropriate rape.

To give feeling responses in patient or therapist a bad name is a distancing device and decreases therapist potency. Human feelings are never a source of mischief for patient or therapist—the problem lies in mistaking present situations for past ones. Transference does not consist of a person in pain calling "help me." Countertransference does not consist of feeling compassion. These terms, properly understood, relate to a distortion of the contracted relationship. An attempt by the therapist to reduce feeling responses is as ineffectual in solving problems as is the attempt of an obsessional husband to solve his relationship problems with a depressed spouse by retreating into distancing maneuvers and suppression of feelings. The effort to deny feelings or to define them as disturbed is the most devastating of all transference or countertransference maneuvers.

A competent, finite, and limited professional psychotherapist who uses the scientific method can problem-solve with his patients as a caring human who will reward and punish as his unique individuality and his role definition dictate. Accepting this fact (rather than retreating, apologizing, or denying it) enhances treatment effectiveness. It also allows for a synthesis of various therapeutic methods in a manner pioneered by Alexander and French,[17] defined by Marmor,[18] and currently wrestled with by many modern therapists.[19,20,21] Therapeutic effectiveness includes the comfortable use of one's own person to influence another in directions that the suffering person has requested. The therapist uses himself as a behavior-modifying tool. The discipline in avoiding dangerous countertransference resides in proper attention to patient choice, goals, and the treatment contract. not in obsessional defenses against feeling and caring.

RESISTANCE

Along with considerations of transference and countertransference, the issue of patient resistance is frequently discussed in the literature of psychoanalytic psychotherapy. Resistance is usually described as the patient's reluctance to deal with unpleasant, unconscious reality, and is often blamed for treatment failure. This is directly analogous to disturbed family assumptions of opposition in all human encounter, and to the previously discussed view of man's essentially antisocial drives. If these assumptions are true, any encounter, including psychotherapy, continues the war in the nursery with properly socialized people who have denied their essential nature struggling with similar frauds or willful children.

All of the attitudes and maneuvers of the scientific psychotherapist are attempts at minimizing resistance to growth and change. Any power differential encourages undesirable resistance, which is not a given but a contextual variable. Spurious certainty on the part of the therapist rekindles *in the present* the submerged fires of rebellion developed from the patient's experience of being pushed around. Contextual ambiguity leads to transference expectations with regression that is a resistance to competence. But even if all these pitfalls are avoided, it still takes quite a while for a patient to become autonomous and bid the therapist a cheerful good-by. Why? Why doesn't the patient eagerly and quickly learn from a wise, benign therapist who tends to his business and is respectful of his patient's subjective reality?

In the sane but limited patient, the overwhelming reason seems to be an understandable desire not to go crazy; he wishes to maintain a coherent inside and outside world and defends them with vigor even though both worlds are disappointing. When one becomes aware of the profound importance of a coherent self, such conservatism seems less resistance than plain good sense. It is easier to gird one's loins for battle with a known adversary than to face the unknown risks of new problems, even though they promise to provide opportunities for greater pleasure in living.

Though the 47-year-old depressed woman mentioned earlier began to see that she was defeating herself (and me, since I had thrown in with her as a partner) by holding on to her punitive depression, she was loath to take the next step required for increased living enjoyment. Giving up a distasteful past was threatening to her identity. I really could not blame her; she had learned to play skillfully the game of dominance/submission—being overtly submissive and covertly controlling. There was risk in seeing her husband as at times possessed of no more strength than she. Such a qualitative change in self and world definitions requires risk-taking comparable to the audacity of a displaced person's electing to go to any country that will accept him. What new demands, new difficulties, will be encountered? Can she cope with the new possibilities, or will she be worse off than before?

It is useful to consider resistance as the fear of the unknown. Viewing resistance as oppositional encourages a therapist to be pessimistic or excessively aggressive. If a patient is pushed, he may cease treatment or fall into a panic state from having too few landmarks to define a coherent self. If one has always been defined as a loser and subjugated to powerful others, it is not resistance to health nor masochism that causes him to hold on to that definition. It is the conservatism involved in maintaining an identity.

I have often thought of such emotionally deprived people as analogous to a starved infant. If the infant has been receiving just enough nourishment for life, sudden feeding does not produce blooming health, but vomiting and illness. Is the response a desire to be starved? Hardly. A shrunken stomach expands slowly. All people wish to enjoy life, but adaptation to new possibilities is a process that requires time.

In this way, resistance is no longer seen as inevitable opposition to a healer but a phenomenon a therapist can accept in an affiliative fashion. Therapists who misunderstand the conservatism of the self and describe themselves as encountering overwhelming resistance remind me of Twain's Connecticut Yankee in King Arthur's Court, who attempted to bring the presumed advantages of advanced technology to a populace that turned on him because of mutual misunderstanding. To receive new possibilities, one must re-evaluate everything in one's life. If a need for time to change is seen as an inevitable part of growth, we therapists will not feel beleaguered, or poorly treated, or pessimistic. The patient will move as fast as he is able; his wish for living satisfaction is as great as is the therapist's for him.

Implicit in this approach to patient resistance is the respect for subjective reality. Change that seems safe to the therapist may well be seen as a giant step over a wide chasm to the suffering patient who has a different past history, and both are right.

DREAMS

Freud described dreams as the royal road to the unconscious. They are a powerful tool in understanding the innermost in another, and present many of the previously described facets of self-definition and relationship in scientific psychotherapy, such as subjectivity, potential self-defined goals, excluded parts of the self, and resistance to change. However, dreams can be used to indoctrinate patients in a particular treatment system more easily than any other kind of data. This is because dreams, unlike conscious experiences, have no checkpoints outside the treatment relationship. If theory does not improve relationships with others, there is a built-in barrier to assuming certainty of the theorizing. But dream interpretation can operate in a relative vacuum, devoid of outside experience. As one result Freudian patients dream Freudian dreams, Jungian patients dream Jungian dreams, and Rogerian patients usually dream not at all.

Indoctrination into a system, rather than ego development, can easily start with a demoralized person's dream life. For this reason a therapist concerned with shared power will proceed cautiously in his discussions of dream material. As a rule of thumb, I would suggest that a therapist seeing a patient only once a week will confuse problem-solving efforts and lose track of the necessary attention to real-life difficulties by encouraging dream material. With only 45 or 50 minutes in a week's time for formal work on self-development, energetic delving into dreams is an expensive luxury unlikely to pay off in increasing patient competence. At intervals in such a treatment schedule, however, a patient who has been working diligently on problem solution will often have a profoundly meaningful dream and bring it in spontaneously, with the half-conscious knowledge that it represents the "aha!" experience that is at the core of all scientific discovery. Such an exciting experience should be met with the alert attention of any explorer encountering the unexpectedly meaningful. If, however, it appears that the patient desires to place more energy in dream life than in waking life, this observation can be shared with him, and the possibilities of avoiding living by investing in fantasy can be explored.

In patients safely "on the park bench," with good morale and attempting to expand capabilities and horizons, in intensive treatment of two or more sessions per week, dreams are often quite helpful. Just as psychoses can be approached as desperate efforts to jump track, to leap from the hopelessly rational to underlying, hitherto undeveloped and unconscious potential selfhood,[22] dreams can be encountered as safer attempts to explore new possibilities of hidden aspects of the self. Properly integrated, they may be quite helpful to an individual in broadening his definition of self and world.

Two useful approaches to dream life are the Freudian and the gestalt. Therapists with more intensive acquaintance with Jungian or other concepts may start from a different place, but if we adhere to an open-system approach we may find ourselves working with a patient in a similar fashion.

It is relatively easy to avoid the risk of potentially closed-system Freudian interpretation of dreams by using the method suggested for all interpretations. They will be offered tentatively, with the understanding that any interpretation is subjective. With an honest invitation for active participation by the dreamer, equal power is maintained and dreams can be treated similarly to waking material. The scientific approach (problem, theory, criticism) can include sleeping as well as waking subjective reality. Some patients bring many dreams, and others bring few. I know of no data that relate dream volume to treatment results. A growth-oriented therapist can remain a good scientist, respect the subjective in his patient and himself, and neither insist on dreams nor ignore them. He responds to patient material in the overall context of problem-solving.

Utilizing at least two methods of approaching dreams (as the Freudian and gestalt) offers greater openness for therapist and patient. Sometimes patient dreams seem insistently Freudian to me. For example, a young woman, who had long suffered under family and broader societal views that being a proper female meant being a second-class citizen, offered, "I dreamed I had a withered arm and was ashamed. Everybody around me thought it was not unusual and assured me that I would get along fine with it."

This patient had severe marital conflict and has made several suicide attempts. She alternated between submission and hostile domination with equally unsatisfying results. It became apparent that, as a female, she doubted she would ever become an effective person with good self-esteem. Presenting this possible meaning of the dream led to an open discussion of her problems in becoming a competent female adult.

A 35-year-old male from a poor family had felt isolated and different and, despite intellectual and job success, had no enjoyable personal relationships. "I've had a recurrent dream since childhood of a geometric nature. I'm crawling out on horizontal lines that reach toward a solid base and tip crazily toward an abyss as I move." He used his intellect to control the world, which made him feel powerful but lonely, and both sensations were frightening. We examined the dream in the context of the pitfalls in trying to see the world as an abstraction to be solved intellectually, and went on to explore his feelings which seemed to him a part of a frightening, uncontrollable void.

In the gestalt approach to dreams, the patient is considered the producer and director of dramas with all parts played by portions of himself. A therapist attempts to use dreams to help a patient claim rejected parts of his own being.

"I dreamed that my nephew had died and I was very upset. Everybody around me seemed to accept his death, but I was frantic with the loss, and thought it was such a waste since he had just received his Ph.D." This came from a woman who had had one unhappy marriage with a man she considered shiftless and incompetent; she was "a better man than he." After much anxiety, she had divorced him and married a gentle man prone to depression who was, however, capable in the business world and made a good living. I suggested that she be the dead nephew, ambitious and now gone. Her responses led to many memories of desiring to be a male, of being embarrassed by having breasts, pubic hair, and all the accouterments of womanliness. This limited self-definition had been promoted by her family experience with a tyrannical father and three older brothers who had more freedom and power than she. She explored the possibility that in her new marital relationship, she could be powerful and feminine if she gave up her fantasies that competence equalled maleness.

"I was alone in the wilderness, and a wolf was stalking me, trying to kill me. I finally quit running and broke its jaw, and it could do me no harm." This from a middle-aged survivor of a German concentration camp who presented himself as a benign and gentle person. Referred by his wife's therapist, he had no other conscious problems than a previous life-threatening heart attack, though his wife complained of being driven into a frenzy by his uninvolved behavior which she interpreted as hostile.

I asked him to be the wolf, the hostile destructive force that was attacking him. In subsequent work he accepted that there was considerable anger within him that threatened his own self-image. It was possible to use the dream imagery to find that he was already aware of some possible advantage in confronting this angry, destructive part of himself.

In discussing these dreams, I wish to make the point that it is not the particular system or concept a therapist offers that furthers treatment, but that he offers the best that he has. He relies on his partner/patient to accept or reject and to further negotiations. The precise interpretation is not so important as the negotiating itself. The examples above could probably have been reversed and gestalt methods used with the "Freudian" dreams, and vice versa, as long as the therapeutic alliance was not compromised by absolutism. Many times I am gratified to have a patient respond, "Yes, but that concept doesn't seem to fit here, it seems that I was struggling with this as well as that."

For example, the first patient said to my Freudian offering, "Perhaps so, perhaps I am ashamed of my femaleness, but I think it is important that everyone was trying to reassure me that the deformity was okay. Everybody in my family has tried to get me quiet and docile." And in the second, the 35-year-old male responded to my offering with, "Yes, I probably have tried to see my whole world in terms of the intellectual, but it was a strength that got me where I am today—important and significant rather than depressed and lost, as all my brothers and sisters seem to me." In the dream, the structure tips, but he is not lost in the abyss.

And the third patient said, "Perhaps this is a positive dream representing my pain at giving up the only hope of success that I have ever known (to be treated as a kind of male impersonator), but could I not also be the people who stand casually by and do not grieve the death of my own dream?" This led to both my grieving with her for the loss of a childhood dream and an offer to help in evolving a personality that includes both "female" and "male" characteristics.

The 45-year-old death camp survivor responded, "Perhaps I do have hostile feelings that I have kept hidden, but this kept me alive. Are you sure that if I admit my wolfness that I may not be destroyed, as the wolf was in the dream?"

And so it goes—problems, theories, criticisms, with each participant in the effort providing the best that he has in an ongoing process. Dreams are interwoven with waking data for a negotiated, shared comprehension satisfying to both parties. Such a mutual viewpoint will always be both a result and a cause of the essential equality of relationship power.

TRANSCENDENT VALUES

The attitude of a psychotherapist toward a patient's beliefs in some transcendent system is quite important in the quality and effectiveness of the therapeutic encounter. Without investing in some belief system, no human can exist without despair or energetic obliviousness to his own and other's feelings and needs.

The development of myths that touch each person and draw them together in a comprehensible whole is a task of every viable culture. The humanistic thrust of Freudian psychotherapy foundered on this problem, and its zeal to free people from the tyranny of religion created the potential tyranny of another closed system, a "nothing but" explanation of man's essence.

I have found similar difficulties in relating enjoyably and productively with some dedicated Freudians, proselytizing gestaltists, or zealots in behavior modification as I have with dedicated Communists or fundamentalist Christians concerned that I be "saved." In each of these there was an intense emotional conviction about a closed symbolic system that effectively blocked mutual discovery of a bit more about the never-solved mysteries of existence.

For this reason I devoted time and space in Chapter 1 to a modern view of science as limited, finite, and an unsuitable vehicle for transcendent belief. In this way, true believers in a secular religion can be separated from behavioral scientists engaged in the business of psychotherapy.

Freud pioneered a qualitatively different approach to emotional problems. Though biased by the residual of 19th-century absolutism, he opened the door to ego- or self-growth as a calculated enterprise. If we are aware of the powers and limits of scientific psychotherapy, we can assist individuals in defining for themselves what they believe is ultimately important, neither providing a second-rate religion nor ignoring this basic necessity for emotional health.

It should be humbling to remember that rationalists laughed at "primitive" American Indian beliefs in the community of man with animal life, with the land and waters, only to arrive at the science of ecology that tried to define explicitly what the Indian intuitively grasped. It is even more humbling for psychotherapists to learn that, by using reductionist scientific models, American psychiatrists turned away from the "moral treatment" of the late 18th century by which nearly three-quarters of emotionally ill people in institutions recovered. The dogged pursuit of an organic, allegedly scientific but definitely non-humanistic approach to mental illness reduced recovery rates to approximately 15 percent by 1920, and only recently have we achieved recovery rates approximating those found in New England psychiatric institutions, circa 1800.[23]

A therapist uses a scientific approach when he attempts the alleviation of suffering and has no need to challenge transcendent beliefs. A psychotherapist will probably have patients of many faiths—Catholic, Jew, Baptist, atheist, Buddhist, Methodist. He will never find it necessary to impugn the need for such beliefs as continuing evidence of poor reality testing or childlike faith in an illusion. On the contrary, if a patient works with a competent psychotherapist his transference and neurotic beliefs are lessened. As his private religion of emotional illness is dissipated, he develops the energy and consciousness to define for himself what is important and meaningful. His solutions will be both unique and shared with others. As he chooses a coherent belief system, he will find that it opens doors to relationships. I believe Frankl[24] is correct to see people as incurable searchers for meaning that transcends the body, and cooperating in this necessary task is a part of growth-promoting treatment. People I have appreciated as wise and profound always possess a faith that defines *for them* what is important, what is delightful, what is the point. I learn from these people, and not a few have been my patients.

It is true that some religious views are destructive of individual choice and autonomy. Many closed-systems approaches to treatment are similarly destructive. However, the family research showed that responsible adults can defang the harshness of authoritarian religion, deriving meaning but avoiding subjugation, just as sensitive therapists of many schools transcend the limits of their system.

When personal growth in a patient requires a definition of what is important to him, it is unfortunate if a therapist retreats and declares such exploration off limits. When he does so, it is usually because of his own muddle about transcendent values. Sometimes I encounter therapists who do not know where they stand on religious issues except they believe religion is bad, but it wouldn't be nice to say that to a believing patient.

Freud, the glorious rationalist atheist, was a powerful contributor to the evolution and maturing of religious thought. Defining neurosis a private religion, he assisted in the understanding of human emotional disturbance. Describing childlike patterns found in much religion, he provided a standard of measurement for religious thought. If one remains a child, he needs absolutes, but there is a high price for such certainty.

With patients who are victims of religious curses—who feel damned for divorce or extramarital affairs, for sexual or murderous thoughts, I first try to separate out the individual and family interpretation from the formal beliefs. I know of no widespread religious system that precludes emotionally mature adherents. Most of the destructive aspects of repressive religion come from family reinforcement. Often such identification of sources assists the patient in separating his needed beliefs from previously inescapable tyranny. He may shift membership from a less to a more humanistic congregation in the same religious tradition. At times, this is not sufficient, and I sometimes suggest that a patient discuss his religious concerns with a rabbi, priest, or clergyman who I know has a sympathetic understanding of human autonomy and personal growth. This does not compromise the treatment alliance; it strengthens it. It is a behavioral statement that my office is not a secular church.

If a psychotherapist knows his limits, he can happily view himself as a technician of relationships, providing a model for interaction. No one can tell a person why he should relate or what his purpose should be. This is the function of transcendent systems which, though hammered out individually, encourage a group identity.

Though I have used one definition of transcendent throughout this book—"something beyond the limits of experience or knowledge," there is another: "a person or thing that escapes classification in any accepted category." This is what intensive therapy, or raising children, or having a friend or lover is all about: Each self is respected, loved, and perceived as unique, an experience in transcendence, science, humanism, and religion.

TERMINATION

The end of equal-powered psychotherapy is the most delightful part of the experience. By the time termination is considered, demoralization is long gone, and considerable self-esteem has been developed by experience in intimacy and shared problem-solving.

If systems issues have been given their proper place, the patient has significant relationships outside treatment and is as capable of responding to others' needs as in communicating his own.

Patients choose when to stop. This is consistent with the thrust of growth-promoting work—the focus is always on the patient's desires and goals. Though the therapist is properly concerned that the treatment relationship remain intense and move in a coherent direction with a shared theme, the patient has never been asked to abdicate his responsibility for himself. Such an open-ended definition of treatment allows continuation or termination to remain in the patient's hands. If a psychotherapist insisted on keeping the unilateral power to dismiss a patient, there was never any real educative experience in growth-promoting choice. Recognizing the patient's choice to continue or stop throughout treatment helps him grow to authentic adulthood, as he might have done in an optimal family; neither held in a relationship by obligation and narrowly defined loyalties, or summarily kicked out, either as a reject or a finished product as defined by another. There is a continuing relationship of caring and expectation that continues after treatment ceases, just as adults from competent families know that separation does not mean banishment.

A patient leaves treatment because of satisfying living, the presence of unpaid for intimacy in his life, and hence the desire to invest elsewhere time and money previously involved in treatment. He is free without rejection. He has learned a method of problem-solving that can continue throughout his life.

Occasionally a patient calls years after treatment and wishes to share with me his current experiences. I consider this lagniappe for me. These are rarely regressive episodes, but represent a wish to touch base with a person who shares the battle scars in the campaign for adult competence.

REFERENCES

1. FROMM-REICHMANN, F., *Principles of Intensive Psychotherapy*, Chicago, U. of Chicago Press, 1950.

2. MAY, P. R. A., *Treatment of Schizophrenia, A Comparative Study of Five Treatment Methods*, New York, Science House, 1968.
3. MOSHER, L. R., and MENN, A. Z., "Community residential treatment of schizophrenia," (abstract) *Scientific Proceedings*, Washington, D. C., Am. Psychiatric Assn., 220, 1976.
4. GREENBLATT, M., GROSSER, G. H., WECHSLER, H., "A comparative study of selected antidepressant medications and EST," *Am. J. Psychiat.*, 119: 144-153, 1962.
5. SULLIVAN, H. S., *The Interpersonal Theory of Psychiatry*, New York, W. W. Norton, 1953.
6. KOEGLER, R. R., and BRILL, N. Q., *Treatment of Psychiatric Outpatients*, New York, Appleton-Century-Crofts, 1967.
7. PATTISON, E. M., "A psychosocial kinship model for family therapy," *Scientific Proceedings*, 128th Annual Meeting, American Psychiatric Assn., Anaheim, Ca., May, 1975.
8. MARGOLIN, S., "Symposium on psychotherapy in medical and surgical hospitals," *Bull. Am. Psychoanalyt. Assoc.*, 8: 170, 1952.
9. POPPER, K. R., "Science: problems, aims, responsibilities," *Proceedings of Meeting of the Federation of American Societies for Experimental Biology*, Atlanta City, N. J., April 17, 1963.
10. STEIN, A., "Causes of failure in psychoanalytic psychotherapy," in Wolman, B. B., (Ed.), *Success and Failure in Psychoanalysis and Psychotherapy*, New York, Macmillan, 1972.
11. GREENSON, R. R., *The Technique and Practice of Psychoanalysis*, Vol. I., New York, International Universities Press, 1967.
12. FRIEDMAN, L., "How real is the realistic ego in psychotherapy?" *Arch. Gen. Psychiat.*, 28: 377-383, March, 1973.
13. FREUD, A., "The widening scope of indications for psychoanalysis: discussion," *J. Amer. Psychoanalytic Assn.*, 2: 607-620, 1954.
14. GLASSER, W., *Reality Therapy, A New Approach to Psychiatry*, New York, Harper and Row, 1965.
15. MARMOR, J., "The nature of the psychotherapeutic process revisited," *Canadian Psychiat. Assoc. J.*, 20: 557-565, Dec., 1975.
16. BERNSTEIN, A., "The fear of compassion," in Wolman, B. B. (Ed.) *Success and Failure in Psychoanalysis and Psychotherapy*, New York, Macmillan, 1972.
17. ALEXANDER, F., and FRENCH, T. M., *Psychoanalytic Therapy, and Principles and Applications*, New York, Ronald Press, 1946.
18. MARMOR, J., "The future of psychoanalytic therapy," *Am. J. Psychiat.*, 130 (11): 1197-1202, Nov., 1973.
19. SLOANE, R. B., STAPLES, F. R., CRISTAL, A. H., YORKSTON, N. J. and WHIPPLE, Y., *Psychotherapy versus Behavior Therapy*, Cambridge, Harvard U. Press, 1975.
20. STEINZOR, B., *The Healing Partnership*, New York, Harper and Row, 1967.
21. BIRK, L., and BRINKLEY-BIRK, A. W., "Psychoanalysis and behavior therapy," *Am. J. Psychiat.*, 131 (8): 499-510, May 1974.
22. BEAVERS, W. R., "Schizophrenia and despair," *Comprehensive Psychiatry*, Vol. 13, No. 6, 561-572, 1972.
23. BOCHOVEN, J. S., *Moral Treatment in American Psychiatry*, New York, Springer, 1963.
24. FRANKL, V. E., *The Doctor and the Soul*, New York, Alfred A. Knopf, 1957.

_____ **12**

Group
therapy

A psychotherapy that purports to be scientific and egalitarian, using concepts from studies of family systems, should be significantly applicable to group therapy. Since its inception, this treatment modality has usually been democratic and clear in stressing that the whole is more than the sum of its parts. Many group therapists have observed that patients tend to repeat their family patterns, and successful group treatment requires experiential alteration of these patterns in ways that increase living skills and self-esteem. Often, the experience creates more love and concern for group members than is felt for members of the family of origin.

I will apply the eight significant factors found in optimal families to group therapy. Specific theories of group process and therapeutic intervention will be dealt with only slightly, since it seems clear that, as in individual therapy, the factors producing success do not include a particular ideology. As Yalom stated, "The nature of our data is so highly subjective that to a large degree it makes scientific methodology inapplicable. What we must do is to learn to live effectively with uncertainty, to consider the best available evidence from research, from intelligent clinical observation, and to evolve a reasoned therapy which offers the great flexibility needed to cope with an infinite range of human problems."[1] From the discussion in preceding chapters on science and scientific methodology, it will be apparent that Yalom's description of what must be done is a good definition of science at work, and his disclaimer of scientific respectability is unnecessary. Absence of dogma, an open-system focus on data, and a plea for flexibility are all indications that group therapy can be scientific and that Yalom is a sensitive scientist. His book, *The Theory and Practice of Group Psychotherapy*, along with Bion's *Experiences in Groups*,[2] Slavson's *A Textbook in Analytic Group Psychotherapy*,[3] and Berne's *Principles of Group Treatment*,[4] is a good beginning for anyone wishing to become a growth-oriented group therapist. Learning several theoretical approaches decreases the risk of falling prey to any closed system.

GENERAL CONCEPTS OF GROUP THERAPY

To reiterate the concept of emotional illness used throughout this book: It results from a deficiency of satisfying, coherent, self-defining experiences with significant others. Group treatment attempts to cure by providing these experiences in a setting more complex than the dyad. Of course, not all group therapy is growth-oriented, any more than is all individual psychotherapy. The grower/controller dichotomy holds here as well. There is an endless variety of group therapies, including supportive groups, didactic groups, groups to keep people taking their medicine and coming to clinics, etc. This chapter, similar to the preceding chapter, focuses on treatment which offers opportunities to increase competence in living.

The optimal number of patients is generally considered to be seven to ten. Below seven, the intensity of interaction may falter;

there is often a feeling of being at a family dinner when some anticipated relatives fail to show. Above ten, with the addition of a therapist or two, the group becomes unwieldy and demands a power differential to prevent it from disintegrating into subgroups. My fantasy as to the reason for this generally observed phenomenon is that this group size approximates that of a family with no birth-control methods before the oldest child was old enough to go off on his own. Fifty thousand years of evolutionary experience gives an upper limit to the human capacity for intimacy and closeness. If the group exceeds 10 to 12 persons, the rules necessarily change, and growth-promoting experiences of intimacy are sporadic rather than frequent, though didactic learning is possible.

Opinions differ as to whether a group should have one formal leader or two. I enjoy doing group alone or with a co-leader as long as that other person and I know each other well and have a deep caring and respect for one another. At the present time, I have two ongoing intensive groups as the single leader and one with a therapist friend of 15 years. It is well to avoid sharing leadership with a person you care little about. Such a group will teach patients to ignore reality (just as the families of origin did), or an inordinate amount of group time will be taken up as the leaders work through their own problems with each other in the necessary effort to develop an effective coalition. If such a coalition is present, it may be more effective in promoting patient growth than is any single-therapist group since it is so similar to the optimal family model.

The setting needs to be similar to those where group members have had opportunities to experience friendship. For example, an austere "medical" setting, or exotic trappings such as muted lights and incense are undesirable since few have previously experienced such situations as stimulants to intimacy. Comfortable furniture is needed in a room small enough to prevent physical withdrawal and large enough to provide some expression by body movements and maneuvers; a net space of about 11′ by 16′ is satisfactory. The quality of the furnishings should bear some relation to the clientele. If it is either too plush or too dreary, some members are unnecessarily made uncomfortable. As in individual work, there can be no "therapist's chair"; the leader is also a group member. Having a variety of furniture allows group members to become sensitive to physical cues as to feelings. For example, a large chair offers a refuge for a person who wishes to sink into it; a couch with room for three provides a center seat which is either lunged-for or avoided since it offers a combination of human closeness and relative impotence.

INDICATIONS AND CONTRAINDICATIONS

Likely candidates are roughly the same as for individual growth-oriented psychotherapy: those suffering from emotional illness who wish to increase living skills and are reasonably able to communicate verbally. In addition, the possibility of a patient's using intensive group therapy well increases if he has had individual treatment experience. Group experience can either encourage distancing and defensive maneuvers or the lowering of barriers and the expression of the innermost. A person needs to have had at least one relationship of relative trust prior to experience in intensive group therapy. Interpersonal learning is deterred by excessive fear and mistrust, and an intensive therapy group often does not develop effectively if *all* members are innocent of previous treatment. Once an open-ended (no planned termination time, new members expected as old ones leave) group has developed its own identity, history, pride, and cohesiveness, new members without previous therapy can be brought in without threatening the life of the group. However, the more preparation with didactic and experiential learning, the better. Patients invited into group with no prior psychotherapeutic experience require a longer time to obtain overt group power and to experience the work as enjoyable. They are quite apt to look for authority and become frustrated at the absence of certainty.

A reasonable way to avoid this is to develop some alliance with a patient prior to his being placed in a group, or to offer individual treatment for a period of time in tandem with the group experience. Some patients, either referred for group or specifically asking for this treatment, will benefit from this tandem approach. I believe that an ideal growth-oriented experience includes intensive individual work rounded out with group treatment. This closely follows the family model, with one-to-one intensity evolving into multiple interaction as self-development progresses. Developmental challenges of sharing a loved person with others are encountered naturally as living competence increases. Defining a person as ready for group is a "field promotion" recognized by therapist and patient. Occasionally, a patient expresses the wish to leave group and go back to individual work; this is usually an effort to handle current problems by regression, to go back to a time when a nurturing person was possessed exclusively. Such wishes can be met by tandem treatment, giving necessary support without sanctioning the regressive pull. The individual work can focus on the problem of using the strengths of others within the group. Every patient has a wish to be the favorite. It often takes much negotiation to experience the fact that a growth-promoting group atmosphere makes everyone special. If favorites exist, everyone suffers, both the preferred and the slighted, just as in dysfunctional families.

From every data source with which I am familiar, it appears that the attributes of a competent human (good morale, self-esteem, self-understanding, social skills, hope, purpose, and direction) are most effectively produced in a milieu similar to that found in optimal families, and are actively discouraged in surroundings with the characteristics of disturbed families. For example, Lieberman et al.[5] described group therapists' behavior related to high casualties among group members as being highly controlling, insensitive, unempathic, bizarrely confrontive, and productive of affect unaccompanied by understanding from either the individual, the group, or the leader. Such behavior is dramatically contrary to that of parents in optimal families. On the other hand, the most effective group leaders promote a group rule system quite like that found in optimal families.

USING THE FAMILY SYSTEMS VARIABLES IN GROUP THERAPY

A Systems Orientation

In its simplest form, this principle might be stated as John Donne did nearly 400 years ago, "No man is an island entire of itself; every man is a piece of the continent." An excessively intrapsychic theory is inadequate in understanding real people in a constantly changing interacting process as they define others and are defined by them, accepting and resisting these definitions in continuing negotiations. Also, no sociological group theory can apprehend the significance of individual subjective reality, of passions, hope, and despair that are the stuff of intimacy or alienation.

A systems viewpoint sees each stimulus as a response and viceversa. Each process has meaning at the group level and different, equally important meaning to every individual (hierarchies of structure being characteristic of systems). Such an awareness promotes growth without artificial and damaging dichotomies such as group or individual loyalties. It encourages giving up impotent/omnipotent behavior patterns and promotes competence.

If, for example, a group member is scapegoated, it is necessary to develop the awareness that this phenomenon is both an expression of group function and the active (though previously unconscious) choice of the individual. Neither group nor individual has the power to create the scapegoat. Either can prevent it or stop it. This realization opens up opportunities to eliminate maladaptive patterns dependent on fantasies of complete control or absolute helplessness.

Tom, a 30-year-old ex-hippie turned laundromat owner, had many problems with groups of people; he often thought they whispered about him and at times accused him of homosexuality. Initially, he was extremely polite and positive about his group experience, but after eight weeks he began to launch sharp attacks on group members and on the idea of treatment as being useful. At first he received support from other group members, but he systematically alienated everyone who reached toward him. After destroying every potentially warm relationship, he abruptly left the group. The other members were compelled to deal with their guilt over "driving him away," and they wrestled with their desire both to make him love the group and its members and also to destroy him. They finally decided that unless they could accept his power to reject them, they could never possess the power to run their own lives; autonomy means choice. They could then move on to other business.

Meanwhile, Tom, after three months of avoiding people and drinking heavily, decided to try group treatment again, but asked that he enter a different group since he believed he needed a fresh start. This sounded reasonable, so he came to a new group. He repeated his previous pattern except that this time he did not leave. He noted that he attacked one woman with particular viciousness and that some members were still supportive of him. He saw a similarity between the woman he was attacking and his mother, whom he had forbidden two years earlier ever to come near him again. He became aware of previously unconscious attitudes and behavior. For example, he believed women controlled everything, and he fought them by running. Other members agreed with him about some of the characteristics he saw in the woman he attacked, and the negotiating process continued. He wasn't crazy—many of his perceptions were verified, and even the attacked woman let him know that his perceptions of her, though painful, were also useful. As Allport once said in making a plea for open systems, "It is not only from sacred cows that we get good milk." Through a developing consciousness that cause and effect can be interchangeable, Tom, in his second trial, averted being scapegoated, and the other group members found value in his irritating part of their subjective reality. Appreciating the possibility of such reciprocal, mutually augmenting relationships between individuals and the group promotes a sense of community, essentially a systems view of one's interaction with the larger world. This realization is one of the basic curative factors of group. Corseni and Rosenberg[6] call it acceptance; Yalom refers to it as group cohesiveness. It brings a group alive with individual and shared identity, special caring about members, a sense of "us" as contrasted with "them" (a limiting boundary) and of belonging to a definite entity (a real rather than a theoretical system).

One way to foster this experience is to select patients who are homogeneous, i.e., relatively similar in social class, type of difficulty, interests, age, etc. Such selection will make the development of community relatively easy, as members have fewer difficulties in empathic sharing to obtain intimacy. However, excessive homogeneity reduces the potential for expanding self-definition and widening horizons. A therapist can stoke the group with as much human variety as possible; opportunities then abound for one class to learn how the other lives; homosexuals and heterosexuals can vicariously experience the others' preferences; hostile, acting-out individuals can learn the viewpoint of clinging vines; young people can experience the special problems of the aging. There are, however, significant tensions in such a group. Too much heterogeneity may result in too little empathic glue required to develop community experience, and the group can crumble. The therapist may well try to balance these attributes, relying on his judgment of what the group needs.

Another aspect of developing the sense of community is the manner in which the group leader responds to clashes between members. Developing a functioning system requires helping separate, lonely, and frightened individuals to see that their basic wishes are not opposed, but assisted by, the needs of others. The purpose of group for a person is the same as that of the primary family: to assist him in becoming an effective, competent adult. As this occurs, the group becomes outgrown just as the primary family becomes unnecessary. It is not rejected but superseded with membership in new groups.

There are phases that successful group patients move through. Initially tentative and uncommitted, they possess little overt power and are usually amazed and delighted that other people respond positively in what seems to be a totally unearned fashion. Group, as well as individual, treatment offers experience in understanding a concept usually considered religious—that of grace. This is a basic aspect of humanization without which no infant survives. In families, an infant arrives which members see as significant without *any performance demands*; crying, vomiting, soiling diapers are expected, and only in quite disturbed families is such behavior seen as willful or evil. Any viable group community has this sense of grace—whether family, therapist/patient dyad, or treatment group. The experience is required in order to develop basic trust in one's innermost, and in the potential benignness of the world outside. I am always amazed at the ease with which group members accept symptoms and behavior hitherto felt by the individual to be totally and incurably unacceptable. Such acceptance stems from empathically remembering one's own vulnerability. It is not godlike, but peculiarly human, and available from every person who is not himself feeling helpless and emotionally bankrupt.

As group membership continues, overt power, individual responsibility, and group expectations increase. Relative competence is rewarded and successes outside the group are met by rejoicing and shared excitement. Expectations are not arbitrary, but they are related to *where the person is*—a phenomenon not hard to develop in a useful treatment group, but one which has been beyond the capabilities of the primary families of these same group members.

During the later phases of group membership, an individual moves to the position of powerful senior group member who voices the prevailing group ethic and compassionately reaches out to others in pain. Finally, as separation nears, he becomes a near stranger in the group, investing more and more interest and energy in a valued and exciting outside world. Group commitment and the sense of community then drop below entry levels.

Movement of this sort in individual members is the rule if the milieu is growth-promoting, alive, and responsive to individual needs. In contrast to the beliefs and experiences of severely dysfunctional family members, no one stands still. People grow or regress, evolve or deteriorate, and an effective group promotes positive movement by being respectful of individual choice. System openness insures adequate attention to autonomy. The individual and society are not necessarily at war in these treatment groups or in larger social systems. They are much like the Taoist symbols of yin and yang, or the gestalt figure and ground—eternally related and dependent on each other.

Boundary Issues

The most important boundary issue is the one of "us" versus "them." Unless there is greater caring and investment in the community than in the outside world, there is no group. This is precisely analogous to the family; unless there is some distinction between inside and outside on the basis of qualities, history, sponsorship, beliefs, structure, and loyalties, no family exists.[7] Membership is both feared and desired by every member. There is comfort in shared identity and loyalty, but also a potential loss of freedom to group claims. A leader can minimize this tension by defining the minimum requirements necessary to become a full-fledged group member. As a group therapist, I always first explain role expectations, encourage all potential patients to focus on getting their needs met in the group, and then offer them two unbreakable rules: One pays one's bills and makes sure that no one is hurt by any gossip outside the group. This is usually reassuring; it states the minimal required responsibility to authority and to peers and offers more freedom in shared interaction than any patient has, at least at the beginning, imagined possible. It also promises that one may rely on at least the minimal expectation that he will not be attacked in ways he cannot respond to.

An open system is permeable to the outside, yet clearly defined as separate. The more group cohesiveness is developed and maintained by contempt of "them," the more impermeable is the system boundary. An extreme example was the Charles Manson "family": a group with strong cohesiveness developed by a charismatic leader who purposefully maximized the disparity between *us* and *them*, and hence reduced intragroup differences by external scapegoating. This is a common pattern among cultists. Strong, relatively impermeable group boundaries are forced by a charismatic leader accentuating the differences between the acquiescing, right-thinking group members and the hostile, unbelieving outer world.

Just as in family systems, the permeability of this external boundary affects the intrasystem boundary qualities. Entropic systems have either an extremely impermeable boundary, with a loss of intrasystem boundary integrity, forcing the choice of extrusion or amalgamation; or a tattered, unclear outer boundary, with little sense of shared community. A negentropic group accepts newcomers, defines them as special because of their choice in commitment to the group, and rejoices at individuals' activities outside the group boundary that will inexorably force separation and loss. Group competence and the possibilities for individual autonomy run parallel, and group members must deal with loss of loved ones and acceptance of newcomers with a regularity that promotes skill in these painful but self-defining experiences.

Jethro, a businessman, came from a severely dysfunctional family and had a chronically schizophrenic sister. He initially felt great anguish and hostility toward group members who reported relationship successes in the world outside the group. In addition, he expressed anger and frustration with new group members, expecting them to slow his progress by dragging the group down and forcing him to deal with childlike, simplistic issues. He resisted the opportunity to increase his social power in the group and attempted to maintain a role of intelligent helplessness, reciprocated by powerful others responding to his well-meaning bumbling. After much confrontation by other group members, he realized that he was seen by newer members as shrewd and offering valuable insights, and reluctantly he accepted the role of capable group member. As he did so, he found himself rejoicing for the first time with veteran members with their satisfactions outside the group. His self-esteem increased, and he made changes in his career and in his marriage that provided him with more licit power, not dependent on being needful and childlike. A tough group ethic that rewarded competence altered his lifetime pattern of experiencing power as evil and helplessness as virtue.

Contextual Clarity

I do not believe that any competent treatment group can exist with all of its members having another relationship definition to each other. Two examples: An attempt to have an intensive treatment group with staff members of a hospital team will produce double-binds as damaging to growth as generation boundary confusion in families; similarly, sensitivity or encounter groups with people who work together in industrial settings present group members with impossible conundrums of context.

A 37-year-old engineer had been required to be a member of a sensitivity group made up of fellow workers in his corporation, one of whom was his immediate supervisor. The group members were encouraged by an enthusiastic and committed leader to express previously hidden feelings. This man, egged on by the apparently sanctioned context, told of suspicions he had about his supervisor's homosexuality. After the sensitivity group was over, he felt, probably accurately, that the supervisor punished him; he became increasingly distraught and disintegrated, requiring emergency psychiatric hospitalization.

Realistic trust is relative and dependent on context; clarity of role provides contextual trust. Groups that invite intimacy, but which are made up of people who have significant relationships in work situations, present unsolvable choices to members. If they "let their hair down" to follow the group ethic, they can suffer damaging consequences; if they sensibly keep their innermost to themselves, they can be attacked for resistance and uncooperativeness. This is a real and frequent cause of emotional crises in groups whose members have more than one contextual definition.

The only outside relationship possible with group members is one of potentially similar intimacy—such as spouses or other family members in groups developed to explore particular family relationships. Contextual confusion that encourages regression rather than growth will result from inviting group members to deal simultaneously with different degrees of relationship integrity which have quite different rules for success.

The group leader has the same responsibility as an individual therapist in keeping role definitions clear. Any sexual involvements between therapist and group members destroy this clarity and are destructive to the development of a coherent, potentially trustworthy environment.

Sexual liaisons occur between group members, of course, and can be quite subversive to a developing sense of community unless the activity is brought into the group as licit. Group standards are not necessarily community standards, e.g., a separated or married member of the group may have a sexual relationship with another group member with acceptance rather than disapproval of group members, but the usefulness of the group is compromised if such a relationship is kept secret from the group, requiring the lovers to live in the confusing context of two or more realities. Such unfortunate occurrences are comparable to incestuous relationships in families with secrets that must be kept.

Power Issues

With co-therapists, power issues are immediately relevant. Having a therapist with an overtly defined assistant therapist clarifies context and prevents confusion of expectations, but is quite consistent with the limits of centripetal midrange families, the parents of which communicate behaviorally that equal-powered relationships are impossible or undesirable. Helping people to experience intimate, egalitarian relationships in such a setting is all but impossible. Good work can be accomplished, but will necessarily be limited in scope.

If there are two therapists, ideally they need to be aware of the importance of equal power in evolving intimacy and the necessity of complementary roles to provide such equal power without friction-filled competition. If the two know each other's strengths and character patterns, they can work out areas of competence that do not intrude continually on each other's activities, much as parents in optimal families negotiate complementary rather than symmetrical roles.

For example, in my group with a co-leader, I have a continuing fantasy of two space-walking astronauts who arrange that one of them goes out into zero atmosphere and gravity, dependent on the other for maintenance of life-sustaining necessities. Neither is subservient; both depend on the other, but their roles are dramatically different. The aggressive co-therapist may emulate Perls and vigorously approach a patient's conflicts, secure in the knowledge that his partner is maintaining an awareness of group needs. This may be the usual pattern for the two of them, or they may alternate aggressive and nurturant roles, but in either case they demonstrate power equality and shared respect through complementarity.

If there is a single therapist, power issues center around the sharing of therapist power with patients. Just as in individual treatment, technical competence does not necessarily mean a power differential; offering possibilities to patients can be an exercise in respect for individual boundaries and subjective reality. A group can dramatically illustrate this fact; it is rare that any interpretation of any event is the same for the whole group, and the therapist has many opportunities to demonstrate his respect for other perceptions of individual problems.

Although I have approached group therapy from essentially a psychoanalytic base, I have had the opportunity to treat many patients who were themselves group therapists with some other orientation, for example, gestalt, transactional analysis, psychodrama. Many times these patients have felt constrained in offering what they felt was useful because of my presumed disapproval. I have responded by suggesting that any group member can promote whatever he can get the whole group to go along with, and we may all learn something in the process. Approaching different subjective views of reality in this way reduces transference and provides patients with the experience of trying their wings at social power, attempting to influence others, with the attendant risks and satisfactions thereof. Transference belief in the disapproval of an authority figure such as a group leader perpetuates guilt and passivity, and therapist control, real or imagined, can encourage their continuation. I am sufficiently uncertain of my own techniques and sufficiently trusting of a group's good sense to allow it to respond to novel approaches suggested. The results have enriched the group experience. I do not hesitate to intervene if I feel that one member's experience in personal expression is at the expense of others' subjective reality—this is the function of a growth-promoting group leader—but new techniques and concepts arise if equaled-powered negotiation is the ethic.

Encouragement of equal power does not negate the group process realities of newcomers arriving with little overt power and successively achieving more. To the contrary, it allows for a flexible group structure that promotes advancement from neophyte, dependent on group grace, to "elder statesman" prior to separation.

Just as in individual treatment, equal power is behaviorally expressed in dialogue, not monologue. Complete silence or verbal domination reflects continuing impotent/omnipotent patterns and fantasies, and a most uncertain awareness of personal boundaries. Silent members and gabby members both are expressing mistrust of their own and others' innermost feelings and potential; interpersonal power maneuvers are used to avoid feared attacks on shaky self-esteem.

Nancy, an attractive 30-year-old dietician, was referred to treatment by a psychologist she engaged for career guidance. Socially capable, with many peripheral acquaintances, she had had a series of abortive relationships with men who saw her as the embodiment of their dreams, though she resisted any physical involvement. Her father, whom she adored, had died when she was eight; her mother was seen as an extremely intrusive and controlling person, using subtle and indirect methods that produced guilt. Silent in the group for many sessions, she interspersed this behavior with a few powerful and impressive dreams related to the group. The dream theme was consistently the group acting out sexual fantasies and insisting on her participation.

Sally, a vivacious 32-year-old woman with a troubled marriage and an infant daughter, entered group after lengthy intensive individual treatment. She had a talkative, histrionic mother who had divorced her father when the patient was seven and pursued an up-and-down business career since. Sally had been a shy and inhibited girl who hoped her father would rescue her from a lonely family life, and was painfully unaccepting of his two subsequent marriages that distanced him from her. She had learned in her mid-teens to become popular by imitating her mother's aggressive verbosity, being entertaining, and denying her loneliness. Sally initially attempted to control the group by telling involved stories and insisting that everyone must know her history before they could help.

The group members worked long and hard with both—reaching for Nancy and helping her see that her infrequent comments were significant and valued, and trying to cut through Sally's verbiage to find out her feelings hidden behind the barrage. Both Nancy and Sally became competent and powerful group members as they became aware that their behavior patterns effectively brought about self-fulfilling prophesies. Nancy, by her silence, invited intrusiveness, and Sally, by her verbosity, encouraged disinterest. They both had power potentially available to obtain gratification of their needs, but it was of negative value as long as they denied it and felt too vulnerable to expose their human hunger.

Encouragement of Autonomy

At the heart of any comprehension of autonomy are the twin factors of subjective reality and personal choice. Any effective system of growth-promoting group psychotherapy must attend these two factors; if this attention is part of the group ethic, encouraged and enforced by the leader, then operational evidences of autonomy will follow. By operational evidences, I refer to the system qualities discussed in the chapters on family systems—taking personal responsibility for thoughts, feelings, and actions, permeability to others' input, and an absence of invasiveness.

When people begin group treatment, they are lonely, frightened, and somewhat demoralized. Doctrinaire mistrust of self and others evokes obscuring, defensive maneuvers. The therapist's insistence that each person has a right and a responsibility to get something for himself from group may be the first approval he has experienced for personal expression and initiative. It can also begin to unwind a long-experienced delusion that individual satisfaction is gained only through others' loss. Comfortable autonomy is necessarily related to awareness that one's enjoyment augments the pleasure of caring others.

Appreciation of subjective reality and choice, however, is only possible for people who have a healthy respect for the ubiquitous ambivalence present in dreaming, finite, fumbling, and failing mortals. No one enters group without doubt, worry, and a haunting fear that it may be damaging rather than productive. Similarly, no one decides on individual treatment, marriage, divorce, or changing jobs without such frequently hidden "disloyal" thoughts. Autonomy—personal choice making—never occurs without ambivalence, but always in the awareness of it. Resolution, not elimination, of mixed feelings is necessary for capable decision making.

A schizophrenic patient profoundly wishes to have individual integrity and human intimacy; he cannot because he sees them as conflicting. Sane but limited people with emotional illness similarly possess such apparently irreconcilable needs which render autonomous decision-making impossible.

A common method used by emotionally disturbed people to handle this internal conflict is projection of one side of the ambivalence. This is a short-term advantage, but a long-term disadvantage: "I would express myself, but the group would destroy me." "I would divorce, but the therapist would define this as sick." "I would change jobs, but my wife would divorce me." "I am controlled; I cannot choose without the outside world attacking." Such is the thinking of people who enter patienthood; in their families such assumptions were realistic, now transference and projection keep the no-win position going.

If a patient enters a closed system of therapy, such assumptions continue to be accurate. In group therapy, however, he cannot continue to deny his power. Few, if any, expressions of wishes are not met by group members with varying positive and negative responses, some supportive, some challenging.

Julie, a 23-year-old divorced woman with a 26-month-old daughter, had been pleasant but guarded during her first few months of group. She announced one session that she had decided to give up custody of her daughter to her ex-husband, though she had previously described this man as irresponsible and untrustworthy. Several group members identified with her desire to be single and unencumbered and greeted her "decision" with joy. They responded to the part of her that desperately wanted to be free of responsibility. Others wondered if she would be content with this decision in years to come. Though she felt in a bad spot now, they had confidence in her ability to handle her personal needs as well as nurture a child and encouraged her to think through her decision. Martha, a new member of the group, was nonplussed, but intrigued with the whole process. No one, she noted, had suggested what Julie *should* do. Different aspects of a complex reality were expressed by group members, but the decision continued to rest with Julie. Subjective reality and choice were respected while various aspects of Julie's ambivalent feelings were explored in an atmosphere of concern without certainty.

Julie eventually decided to keep her child, partly because she felt she had a place to discuss her ambivalent feelings. Even though no one else in the group had a small child, she felt her various feelings were understood. Martha had joined the group after a painful divorce which was not yet worked through. After observing the response to Julie's conflict Martha was able to share her ambivalance about remaining divorced; she was continually encountering her ex-husband who asked her to return and insisted he would have no more extramarital affairs.

The therapist is responsible for developing a group ethic similar to that in optimal families—the relative absence of a referee system which provides inhuman, absolute answers to human uncertainty and a short-cut to self-definition by conformity or rebellion. Autonomous choice is not hostile toward evolving group intimacy, but necessary for such an evolution. If one person feels coerced and limited, every member is diminished.

Such an open system is possible if the therapist is certain only of his own subjective reality and is properly fearful of being the embodiment of previous family referees. Though every group member at times will invite him to provide the definitive word, he can continue to promote openness if he knows that he can never possess the answer for another. He can be aggressive, active, and confronting without augmenting destructive transference, if he remains aware that treatment consists of evolving personal choice rather than correct answers.

An affirmative stance toward subjective reality can be subverted by silence as effectively as by activity. If a therapist has a model of maturity defined by specific choices rather than personal responsibility, he will communicate this as effectively by emulating a silent Buddha as by being directive.

Affective Issues

People who become group members are unhappy; they have serious personal problems and oftentimes life-threatening despair. A group can become an agony clinic in which the member with the most pain is most powerful in demanding group time. An (often unrecognized) ethic that pain and helplessness are more powerful than enjoyment and hope results. This is comparable to individual treatment environments that invite patients to produce defects and symptoms in order to get the therapist's attention. Delight, excitement, hope, and enjoyment are at least as important as depression, pessimism, and pain, and it is up to the therapist to communicate this reality to the group. Otherwise, guilt accompanies growth, and virtue is attached to failure—much as midrange families hold onto chronologically adult offspring by a system that defines separate joy outside the group as disloyal and evil.

If the purpose of group and the group therapist is clear—the evolution of autonomous, successful human encounter—there will be room for joy as well as pain, for the sharing of competence as well as discussing failures. Patients who are edging toward graduation can see themselves as contributing to others by their successes rather than betraying others by losing their despair. The therapist's vital task is to respond to deeply felt hopes and satisfactions with the same facility that he responds to pain. In the same way, he can behaviorally express the idea that a competent group has no favorites. Everyone is special and unique, and the innermost can be accepted regardless of its content. There is more satisfaction in success than in failure unless a beloved family or group can only reward pain. This is a powerful source of so-called masochism—experiencing an environment that sees delight as foreign or even a betrayal; such lessons can occur in treatment settings just as they do in primary families.

This phenomenon is related to fundamental assumptions of therapists and group members about the oppositional or affiliative ground of human encounter. Most members come into group with some residual belief that individual pleasure comes out of others' pain; for example, a child's success will destroy a parent, the development of personal autonomy will deprive a spouse, the evolving power of an individual group member will diminish the power of others. It is the therapist's job to challenge this misunderstanding and assist group members in developing a milieu that experientially puts the lie to such closed-system assumptions.

The rejection of an open system is an intrinsic part of such either/or assumptions. If one member of a group sees another's growth and increasing living pleasure as a painful threat, he is still living as a prisoner, just as he did in his primary family—a "lifer" who will never escape into the larger world, but attains small satisfaction in not being as bad off as the next fellow, or in being so much in pain that he receives some caring.

Carl, a lawyer, entered group because of depression and marital strife. He came dutifully and tried to learn the right formula for group approval, though continually frustrated at his lack of success. Bridget entered the group somewhat after him and worked diligently on problems related to her marriage and her career. After about a year, Bridget announced that she was planning to leave, since both her marriage and her career had become valued and hopeful, and she felt that she had sufficient skills to continue on her own. Other group members responded warmly and shared their belief that she had used treatment and grown. Carl was perfunctory in his comments and finally expressed his anger with her. He believed her statement of improvement, but was envious and jealous, feeling cheated since he had been in group longer. Her success dramatized this poignant sense of inadequacy, and he wished that she were still demoralized.

Carl still expressed his need for a "critical parent" (a phrase obtained from a preceding experience in transactional analysis) and insisted on seeing the group as a controlling force to keep him from acting out his self-defined willful destructive impulses. The group struggled to help him see that he was defining the group as he had experienced his primary family (especially his mother) as a necessary controlling force to prevent him from being "himself." After much work, Carl lost his investment in a critical, controlling parent and, in retrospect, could rejoice with others that Bridget had lost her despair and her need to be defined as a patient. He began to experience satisfaction in his career and became aware that his expectations in marriage could only come about by possessing overt power, not helplessness.

The group therapist can be pivotal in promoting radically new self-defining experiences if he has a firm belief in the affiliative potential of human encounter and actively works against oppositional assumptions. Oppositional sets derive from distancing and intrusive family systems that express the pessimistic, cynical view of the nature of the innermost, and they are healed by experiences of sharing that promote hope as others succeed.

Negotiation and Task Performance

The most prominent characteristics of optimal families allowing them to succeed in assigned tasks include shared attentional focus, respect for individual subjective reality, equal power relationship matrix, and capacity to negotiate differences. Group goals are furthered by the expression of individual perceptions. The systems concept that individuals always exist in a group is played out, and group success is not at the expense of individual capitulation. Creative solutions arise as the needs of individual and group are seen as complementary rather than oppositional.

Similar processes occur in competent group therapy. One individual, trying to solve his problem, needs other members' honest input without which he will continue earlier maladaptive patterns and be deprived of new learning which can provide him with increasing interpersonal skills. For example, silence provides a haven, but oftentimes no new learning. Other group members usually reach out and challenge the defense.

Each statement in group is potentially a new learning experience, highly dependent on other group members' freedom of expression. A therapist can promote this by example and by frequent requests for feedback to any speaker—behavioral statements that personal freedom is positive and useful.

Intensive group experience is an exercise in becoming more effectively aware of others and being known. It is an experience in comprehending and accepting the environment. The group task needs every member to voice his own subjective reality as it becomes intense. The group can then be a microcosm of the world outside, offering varying responses that challenge maladaptive behavior.

Group efficiency depends on each individual's autonomy, his ability to express his here-and-now reality; groups succeed or fail as the individuals within them succeed or fail in this task. The successful group therapist performs much as a capable parent in bringing out others' viewpoints, expressing his own authentic, subjective perspective, and encouraging negotiation which promotes autonomy.

Interpretations are considered rather than swallowed. Identity evolves as an experience in consensual validation. Such an approach allows for behavioral modification through interaction.

Transcendent Values

One way of considering the family is as an experience in the development of a shared transcendent system of value to each member. The individual develops with a concept of himself going beyond his own skin—loyalties to family members, traditions, myths, and beliefs are as much a part of the person as his body, and provide direction, purpose, and meaning which can last as long as the individual lives. If these values do not reach beyond the boundaries of family, however, there is grave danger that individuation will be discouraged, the passage of time denied, and members will remain tied to specific persons—parents and children— with no possibility of emancipation and no ability to accept loss of others.

A successful group is also an example of the development of a transcendent system of great value to each member. Loyalties develop to the people, ideas, myths, and traditions of an intensive group which provide individual direction, meaning and purpose. Family and group are a micro-society, with shared beliefs related to shared relationships.

A treatment group has a powerful potential for being a midwife to a person unable to be autonomous because of family loyalties, delivering an adult free to make choices but invested in beliefs and loyalties that make him feel a part of a larger community, his value independent of specific, unchanging relationships.

Two curative group factors defined by Yalom are pertinent here: the installation of hope, and the experience of universality. Hope depends not only on personal confidence and interpersonal competence, but on a framework of meaning that allows relative trust in the world and its people. Experiencing the universality of one's individual innermost can assist in such trust development which spreads beyond the family, beyond the treatment group, extending to the larger society. Trust in people not yet met and situations not yet encountered is necessary for hope.

Yalom described an exercise in which the members of a non-patient population were asked to write down anonymously the things they thought were true about themselves that must be kept secret in order that they remain acceptable to others. When these bits of paper were gathered they could be sorted into three categories: feelings of inadequacy, a feeling of deficiency in the ability to love, and sexual secrets.[1] Such material makes up the shared interaction in intensive group therapy, and individuals have the healing experience of being accepted by others and of realizing the universality of hidden personal qualities previously thought evil or shameful. The not-me melts in the warmth of shared humanness. The capacity for loving others expands in proportion to the love for the self.

Losing a cherished person remains painful but not cataclysmic; with a loved self that is known to be acceptable to many and trust in the basic qualities of other people, loss can be accepted and new relationships anticipated. Coherence and optimism are maintained with the development of a transcendent value system that embraces the unknown and the larger world. Open-ended groups have members who come in, become loved, and leave. Loss of intimates occurs at an accelerated pace, when compared to families or naturally occurring friendships. Personal transcendent values must be developed to open one's self to care and to lose.

Formal religious systems are created to provide coherent community and to assist individuals in accepting losses. Group members usually develop not only tolerance, but some curiosity and respect for others' formal beliefs, and the group experience generally renders individually held formal beliefs more humane, more respectful of the grace necessary for trust and hope and less literal, referee oriented, and encouraging of alienation.

REFERENCES

1. YALOM, I. D., *The Theory and Practice of Group Psychotherapy*, New York, Basic Books, 1975.
2. BION, W. R., *Experiences in Groups*, New York, Basic Books, 1959.
3. SLAVSON, S. R., *A Textbook in Analytic Group Psychotherapy*, New York, International Universities Press, 1964.
4. BERNE, E., *Principles of Group Treatment*, New York, Oxford Press, 1966.
5. LIEBERMAN, M., YALOM, I., and MILES, M., *Encounter Groups: First Facts*, New York, Basic Books, 1973.
6. CORSENI, R., and ROSENBERG, B., "Mechanisms of group psychotherapy: processes and dynamics," *J. Abnormal Soc. Psychol.*, 51: 406-411, 1955.
7. BOSZORMENYI-NAGY, I., and SPARKS, G. M., *Invisible Loyalties: Reciprocity in Intergenerational Family Therapy*, Hagerstown, Md., Harper and Row, 1973.

Conclusion

The book could go on, of course. The application of the family variables to couple and family therapy is a rational extension. My treatment methods have changed considerably during the years of learning through doing family research. I hope that many readers will continue creating this book, changing and improving it with patients and colleagues. An open-system, scientific approach provides a never-ending process: a dialogue that develops, becomes more coherent and confident, only to perceive another mystery which moves the discussion in another direction.

I would like to provide a succinct list of some of the ideas I consider most important:

1) The development of a competent self is an interpersonal process which requires a rather special kind of growth-promoting milieu.

2) There is a relationship between ego development and the scientific method that, when clear, can help psychotherapists do their job well.

3) Any understanding of science as reductionist and certain is damaging to people.

4) Psychotherapy is potent, but may harm as well as help. Spurious certainty in closed psychotherapeutic systems promotes destructive tyranny.

5) Systems theory is an evolutionary step in science; it embraces concern with function, structure, and interrelationships.

6) Knowledge of the systems qualities of successful, adaptive families, as well as pained and inept ones, provides valuable information important in helping individuals achieve autonomy and emotional maturity.

7) Such family system information can provide a yardstick for evaluating therapeutic systems.

8) Combining a knowledge of the scientific method with family interactional concepts and facility with varied treatment systems can lead to an effective, scientific, and humanistic psychotherapy.

9) Emotional illness can be defined in a unitary fashion as a deficiency disease—a lack of satisfying, coherent, self-defining experiences with meaningful others.

10) Growth-promoting therapy requires equal overt power in the therapist/patient relationship; if this develops, intimacy, a healing experience greatly needed by emotionally ill people, can occur.

11) A belief in the innate evil or depravity of people diminishes growth-promoting relationships.

12) Scientific psychotherapy differs from the ancient shamanistic tradition by its effort to avoid transference power and by its open, straightforward and explicitly limited system approach.

13) These explicit limitations allow patients to get on with their responsibility for evolving a transcendent system of personal value.

14) To fellow humans who come in search of emotional health, we can offer respect, human dignity, and the possibility of increasing competence, experiencing community, and finding hope. We can never offer certainty or absolutes. Effective solutions are always dependent on the individual and his surroundings, his culture and his context.

Index